MCSE Database Design On SQL Server 7
The Cram Sheet

This Cram Sheet contains the distilled, key facts about Designing and Implementing Databases with SQL Server 7.0. Review this information last thing before you enter the test room, paying special attention to those areas where you feel you need the most review. You can transfer any of these facts onto a blank sheet of paper before beginning the exam.

RELATIONAL DATABASE DESIGN

1. Normal forms one, two, and three:
    - **First normal form** Eliminates repeating groups of attributes
    - **Second normal form** Eliminates redundant data and partial dependencies
    - **Third normal form** Eliminates attributes not dependent on the primary key

2. Redundant data is data that is stored multiple times in a database; or derived data, data generated by other columns.

3. A many-to-many relationship is resolved by creating a join table.

4. Recursive relationships are diagramed using a line connecting a table to itself.

5. A foreign key connects a dependant table with the primary key or a unique key from the parent table.

6. Referential integrity can be enforced with foreign keys, constraints, or triggers.

FILES AND DATABASES

7. SQL Server 7 uses file groups to allow for placing specific tables and indexes on a specific disk. Earlier versions of SQL Server use segments to accomplish this.

8. If a data file or a log file is not supplied on a **CREATE DATABASE** statement, SQL Server creates a default file for you.

9. When creating a database table or index, if you do not specify the file group to place them on, the table or index is placed on the primary file group.

10. If there are multiple files in a file group, SQL Server spreads tables and indexes across the files in the group.

11. The log files should be on a disk by themselves.

DATA DEFINITION

12. A column whose data type is uniqueidentifier (GUID) is unique across all SQL Servers.

13. An identity column does not guarantee that the column has a unique value.

14. When a value is manually inserted into an identity column, if the new value is larger than the current highest identity value, automatic identity values start at the new column.

15. A column cannot be dropped if it is replicated, used in an index, used in a constraint, has a default, or is bound to a rule.

16. Beware: The program defaults for nullable columns in programs like Query Analyzer and OSQL (columns are nullable) are different from the Server defaults (columns are not nullable).

SELECT STATEMENT

17. When using the substring function, the initial start position is one.

18. A function can be performed on the result of a function.

19. A **SELECT** statement without a **WHERE** or **HAVING** clause returns every row.

20. When using an aggregate function, all columns in the result set must either be an aggregate function or the columns must be used in the **GROUP BY** clause.

21. Aggregate functions cannot appear in a **WHERE** clause except as part of a subquery.

22. Every SQL statement sets the **@@error** value.

MODIFYING DATA

23. If an **UPDATE** statement does not modify any rows, no error is generated.

24. When using a **LIKE** clause, a **%** means any string, and an _ means any character.

INDEXES

25. A fill factor determines how much free space is available when creating an index or when using the DBCC DBREINDEX command. This blank space can improve insert performance.

26. If performance degrades, you might have to run update statistics.

VIEWS, DEFAULTS, RULES

27. With SQL Server 7, a view can contain a union.

28. A column can only have one rule and one default bound to it.

PROGRAMMING

29. Only execute the statement immediately following the **IF**. To execute multiple statements after an **IF**, you must use a statement block.

30. **IF** statements affect the **@@rowcount** global variable.

31. In SQL Server 7, object existence (like table existence) is not checked when stored procedures are created.

TRIGGERS

32. To automatically delete a child table when a parent table is deleted, you have to implement referential integrity with a **DELETE** trigger.

33. You can have multiple triggers of the same type for a single table.

LOADING DATA

34. **BCP** and **BULK INSERT** are used to load simple file data that does not need to be transformed.

35. DTS is used when you need to change the data that is being transferred.

FULL-TEXT SEARCH

36. A full-text search is used when you need to perform imprecise data searches.

37. When backing up or loading a database, the full-text index does not get backed up or restored with the data.

38. Full-text queries use the **CONTAINS** or **FREETEXT** predicates.

MONITORING

39. When using **dbcc showcontig**, if a low value for the actual count in the scan density is less than the best count, then the table is fragmented.

40. SQL Server writes errors to the SQL Server error log, NT Application log, or both, if the Server was started as a service.

41. SQL Server writes errors to the SQL Server error log only if the server was started at the command prompt.

42. The output from **sp_who** indicates whether a user's process is being blocked by another listing the blocking process's SPID in the BLK column.

43. The output from **sp_lock** indicates the type of locks being held by a process and on what objects.

Certification Insider Press

MCSE Database Design On SQL Server 7

Jeffrey Garbus
David Pascuzzi
Alvin Chang

The Coriolis Group, LLC
14455 N. Hayden Road, Suite 220
Scottsdale, Arizona 85260

480/483-0192
FAX 480/483-0193
http://www.coriolis.com

Library of Congress Cataloging-in-Publication Data
Garbus, Jeffrey
     MCSE database design on SQL Server 7 exam cram / by Jeffrey Garbus, David Pascuzzi, and Alvin Chang.
          p.   cm.
     Includes index.
     ISBN 1-57610-228-9
     1. Electronic data processing personnel--Certification.   2. Microsoft software--Examinations Study guides.   3. Database design--Examinations Study guides.   I. Pascuzzi, David.   II. Chang, Alvin   III. Title.
QA76.3.G38   1999
005.75'85--dc21   99-13166
                                                           CIP

Printed in the United States of America
10 9 8 7 6 5 4 3 2 1

Publisher
Keith Weiskamp

Acquisitions Editor
Shari Jo Hehr

Marketing Specialist
Cynthia Caldwell

Project Editor
Michelle Stroup

Technical Reviewer
David Anstey

Production Coordinator
Kim Eoff

Cover Design
Jesse Dunn

Layout Design
April Nielsen

CORIOLIS

14455 North Hayden Road, Suite 220 • Scottsdale, Arizona 85260

Coriolis: The Training And Certification Destination ™

Thank you for purchasing one of our innovative certification study guides, just one of the many members of the Coriolis family of certification products.

Certification Insider Press™ has long believed that achieving your IT certification is more of a road trip than anything else. This is why most of our readers consider us their *Training And Certification Destination*. By providing a one-stop shop for the most innovative and unique training materials, our readers know we are the first place to look when it comes to achieving their certification. As one reader put it, "I plan on using your books for all of the exams I take."

To help you reach your goals, we've listened to others like you, and we've designed our entire product line around you and the way you like to study, learn, and master challenging subjects. Our approach is *The Smartest Way To Get Certified*™.

In addition to our highly popular *Exam Cram* and *Exam Prep* guides, we have a number of new products. We recently launched Exam Cram Live!, two-day seminars based on *Exam Cram* material. We've also developed a new series of books and study aides—*Practice Test Exam Crams* and *Exam Cram Flash Cards*—designed to make your studying fun as well as productive.

Our commitment to being the *Training And Certification Destination* does not stop there. We just introduced *Exam Cram Insider*, a biweekly newsletter containing the latest in certification news, study tips, and announcements from Certification Insider Press. (To subscribe, send an email to **eci@coriolis.com** and type "subscribe" in the body of the email.) We also recently announced the launch of the Certified Crammer Society and the Coriolis Help Center—two new additions to the Certification Insider Press family.

We'd like to hear from you. Help us continue to provide the very best certification study materials possible. Write us or email us at **cipq@coriolis.com** and let us know how our books have helped you study, or tell us about new features that you'd like us to add. If you send us a story about how we've helped you, and we use it in one of our books, we'll send you an official Coriolis shirt for your efforts.

Good luck with your certification exam and your career. Thank you for allowing us to help you achieve your goals.

Keith Weiskamp
Publisher, Certification Insider Press

For Penny
—Jeff Garbus

I dedicate this book to the memory of my mother, Shirley Pascuzzi
—David Pascuzzi

For my parents
—Alvin Chang

಻

About The Authors

With a B.S. from Rensselaer Polytechnic Institute, **Jeff Garbus** has experience with PCs to mainframes, and back again. Jeff has many years of client/server and Sybase experience, with a special emphasis on assisting clients in migrating from existing systems to pilot and large-scale projects. Jeff has spoken at user conferences and user groups for many years, written articles and columns for national and international magazines, and has written over 10 books, among them *Sybase System 11 DBA Survival Guide*, *Sybase System 11 Unleashed*, *Optimizing SQL Server 7.0*, and the soon-to-be-published *MCSE Administering SQL Server 7 Exam Cram*, also published by the Coriolis Group.

Jeff is currently president of Tampa-based Soaring Eagle Consulting, an RDBMS consulting and training firm specializing in solving business problems. He can be reached at jeffg@soaringeagleltd.com.

David Pascuzzi is a technical trainer, author, and consultant in computer-related technologies specializing in database technologies for more than 10 years. He has written training courses for the government and private industries, and has written various articles on database technologies.

In his consulting work, David has performed tasks ranging from production database support to database performance tuning to database design. He currently is an MCP for SQL Server. Since attaining his MCP, David has concentrated on developing SQL Server courseware and SQL Server consulting. He can be reached at pascuzzi@concentric.net.

Alvin Chang is a technical trainer, author, and consultant working for Soaring Eagle Consulting, a Tampa-based consulting and training firm. An MCP for SQL Server, Alvin has taught SQL Server and consulted throughout the United States. Currently specializing in Microsoft and Sybase System Administration, Alvin started as a technical trainer for products like Microsoft Office, Lotus Smartsuite, and Lotus Notes before moving into RDBMSs. He can be reached at alvin@soaringeagleltd.com.

Acknowledgments

I'd like to thank all of the people whose time and support helped make this possible, from my agent who found Coriolis for us, to the editorial and production team at Coriolis who made this a better product.

Special thanks to Penny Garbus, for taking the time to format Appendix C.

Most of all, I'd like to thank my family, for giving me the time and space to get the work done.

Thank you all.

—*Jeff Garbus*

I would like to thank Jeff Garbus for including me in this book. Thanks to my parents, Frank and Shirley Pascuzzi, who instilled into me my thirst for knowledge and for teaching me how to analyze problems and get results. Special thanks to my wonderful wife Paula for letting me do this book in addition to my full-time job. And, thanks to my daughter Bailey and son Conner for letting daddy work on this book when they wanted to play.

—*David Pascuzzi*

I would like to thank Jeff Garbus for providing me the opportunity to contribute to this book. Thanks to Gary Tyrrell, who listened to me when I needed a break. Thanks to my brother Basil, whose late-night phone calls ran up my phone bill, but kept me sane. And a special thanks to my parents Yuling and Yuching Chang, who got me started on computers in the first place.

—*Alvin Chang*

Contents At A Glance

Chapter 1   Microsoft Certification Exams

Chapter 2   Data Models

Chapter 3   System Databases, Tables, And Stored Procedures

Chapter 4   Databases And Files

Chapter 5   Data Definition

Chapter 6   Retrieving Data

Chapter 7   Modifying Table Data

Chapter 8   Session Configuration

Chapter 9   Indexes

Chapter 10   Rules, Defaults, And Views

Chapter 11   Transact-SQL Programming

Chapter 12   Triggers

Chapter 13   Transactions

Chapter 14   Importing, Exporting, And Transforming Data

Chapter 15   Full-Text Search

Chapter 16   Monitoring

Chapter 17   Remote Data Access

Chapter 18   Sample Test

Chapter 19   Answer Key

Appendix A   Pubs Database

Appendix B   Functions

Appendix C   Transact-SQL Syntax

Table Of Contents

Introduction xvii

Self-Assessment xxxi

Chapter 1
Microsoft Certification Exams 1
    Assessing Exam-Readiness   2
    The Exam Situation   3
    Exam Layout And Design   4
    Microsoft's Testing Formats   5
    Strategies For Different Testing Formats   7
    Exam-Taking Basics   8
    Question-Handling Strategies   9
    Mastering The Inner Game   11
    Additional Resources   12

Chapter 2
Data Models 15
    Overview   16
    Logical Phase   17
    Physical Model   29
    Practice Questions   **33**
    Need To Know More?   36

Chapter 3
System Databases, Tables, And Stored Procedures 37
    System Databases   38
    File Locations   40
    System Tables   41
    System Stored Procedures   43
    Practice Questions   **46**
    Need To Know More?   48

Chapter 4
Databases And Files **49**

    Database Overview 50
    Creating Databases 52
    Altering Databases 54
    Configuring Databases 58
    Viewing Database Information 60
    Enterprise Manager 61
    Using Databases 61
    Practice Questions **62**
    Need To Know More? 65

Chapter 5
Data Definition **67**

    Creating Tables 68
    Unique Identifiers 70
    Constraints 72
    Computed Columns 76
    Altering Tables 76
    Temporary Tables 79
    Dropping Tables 80
    Practice Questions **81**
    Need To Know More? 84

Chapter 6
Retrieving Data **85**

    Parts Of The **SELECT** Statement 86
    The **Select** List 87
    The **FROM** Clause 89
    The **WHERE** Clause 92
    The **GROUP BY** Clause 96
    The **HAVING** Clause 101
    The **ORDER BY** Clause 102
    COMPUTE 102
    Functions 103
    Joining Tables 113
    UNION 118
    The **TOP** Clause 119

Retrieving Text And Image Data   120
Practice Questions   122
Need To Know More?   132

Chapter 7
Modifying Table Data 133
INSERT   134
SELECT INTO   140
BULK INSERT   141
UPDATE   145
Working With **TEXT** And **IMAGE** Data Types   147
Modifying Data With Views   150
Practice Questions   151
Need To Know More?   155

Chapter 8
Session Configuration 157
SET Statement   158
Viewing User-Configuration Options   174
Default User-Configuration Options   176
Practice Questions   177
Need To Know More?   181

Chapter 9
Indexes 183
Clustered And Nonclustered Indexes   184
Creating Indexes   187
Index Management   189
Practice Questions   191
Need To Know More?   194

Chapter 10
Rules, Defaults, And Views 195
Rules   196
Defaults   198
Views   201
Practice Questions   209
Need To Know More?   214

Chapter 11
Transact-SQL Programming **215**

Batches   216
Comments   217
Variables   217
T-SQL Statements   218
Cursors   227
Stored Procedures   235
Practice Questions   240
Need To Know More?   243

Chapter 12
Triggers **245**

Using Triggers   246
Firing Triggers   246
Creating Triggers   248
Removing Triggers   250
Modifying Triggers   250
Deleted And Inserted Tables   251
Triggers During Transactions   259
Nested Triggers   262
Examining Triggers   263
Practice Questions   265
Need To Know More?   269

Chapter 13
Transactions **271**

The Nature Of Transactions   272
Transaction Control Statements   273
Transaction Flow   275
Transaction Limitations   276
Distributed Transactions   277
Transaction Log   278
Locking In Transactions   279
Practice Questions   284
Need To Know More?   287

Chapter 14
Importing, Exporting, And Transforming Data 289
BCP   290
Data Transformation Service   294
Practice Questions   302
Need To Know More?   305

Chapter 15
Full-Text Search 307
Searching For Text   308
Preparing For A Full-Text Search   308
Creating A Full-Text Index   309
Full-Text Query   313
Practice Questions   317
Need To Know More?   320

Chapter 16
Monitoring 321
Showplan   322
Update Statistics   325
Detecting And Resolving Locking Problems   327
dbcc showcontig   330
SQL Server Profiler   331
Practice Questions   332
Need To Know More?   335

Chapter 17
Remote Data Access 337
Remote Procedure Call   338
Distributed Queries   340
Distributed Transactions   344
Practice Questions   348
Need To Know More?   352

Chapter 18
Sample Test **353**
    Questions, Questions, Questions 354
    Picking Proper Answers 354
    Decoding Ambiguity 355
    Working Within The Framework 356
    Deciding What To Memorize 357
    Preparing For The Test 358
    Taking The Test 358
    Sample Test 359

Chapter 19
Answer Key **383**

Appendix A
Pubs Database **393**

Appendix B
Functions **401**

Appendix C
Transact-SQL Syntax **413**

Glossary **433**

Index **451**

Introduction

Welcome to the *MCSE Database Design On SQL Server 7 Exam Cram*! This book aims to help you get ready to take—and pass—the Microsoft certification test numbered Exam 70-029, titled "Designing and Implementing a Database with Microsoft SQL Server 7.0." This Introduction explains Microsoft's certification programs in general and talks about how the Exam Cram series can help you prepare for Microsoft's certification exams.

Exam Cram books help you understand and appreciate the subjects and materials you need to pass Microsoft certification exams. Exam Cram books are aimed strictly at test preparation and review. They do not teach you everything you need to know about a topic (such as the ins and outs of designing or programming the SQL Server). Instead, we (the authors) present and dissect the questions and problems we've found that you're likely to encounter on a test. We've worked from Microsoft's own training materials, preparation guides, and tests, and from a battery of third-party test preparation tools. Our aim is to bring together as much information as possible about Microsoft certification exams.

Nevertheless, to completely prepare yourself for any Microsoft test, we recommend that you begin by taking the Self-Assessment included in this book immediately following this Introduction. This tool will help you evaluate your knowledge base against the requirements for an MCSE under both ideal and real circumstances.

Based on what you learn from that exercise, you might decide to begin your studies with some classroom training, or that you pick up and read one of the many study guides available from Microsoft or third-party vendors, including The Coriolis Group's Exam Prep series. We also strongly recommend that you install, configure, and play with the software or environment that you'll be tested on, because nothing beats hands-on experience and familiarity when it comes to understanding the questions you're likely to encounter on a certification test. Book learning is essential, but hands-on experience is the best teacher of all!

The Microsoft Certified Professional (MCP) Program

The MCP Program currently includes seven separate tracks, each of which boasts its own special acronym (as a would-be certificant, you need to have a high tolerance for alphabet soup of all kinds):

➤ **MCP (Microsoft Certified Professional)** This is the least prestigious of all the certification tracks from Microsoft. Attaining MCP status only requires an individual to pass one exam. Passing any of the major Microsoft exams (except the Networking Essentials Exam) qualifies an individual for MCP credentials. Individuals can demonstrate proficiency with additional Microsoft products by passing additional certification exams.

➤ **MCP+I (Microsoft Certified Professional + Internet)** This mid-level certification is attained by completing three core exams: "Implementing and Supporting Microsoft Windows NT Server 4.0," "Internetworking Microsoft TCP/IP on Microsoft Windows NT 4.0," and "Implementing and Supporting Internet Information Server 3.0 and Microsoft Index Server 1.1" or "Implementing and Supporting Microsoft Internet Information Server 4.0."

➤ **MCP+SB (Microsoft Certified Professional + Site Building)** This certification program is designed for individuals who are planning, building, managing, and maintaining Web sites. Individuals with the MCP+SB credential will have demonstrated the ability to develop Web sites that include multimedia and searchable content and Web sites that connect to and communicate with a back-end database. It requires one MCP exam, plus two of these three exams: "Designing and Implementing Commerce Solutions with Microsoft Site Server, 3.0, Commerce Edition," "Designing and Implementing Web Sites with Microsoft FrontPage 98," and "Designing and Implementing Web Solutions with Microsoft Visual InterDev 6.0."

➤ **MCSD (Microsoft Certified Solution Developer)** The new MCSD credential reflects the new skills required to create multitier, distributed, and COM-based solutions, in addition to desktop and Internet applications, using new technologies. To obtain an MCSD, an individual must demonstrate the ability to analyze and interpret user requirements; select and integrate products, platforms, tools, and technologies; design and implement code and customize applications; and perform necessary software tests and quality assurance operations.

To become an MCSD, you must pass a total of four exams: three core exams and one elective exam. The required exam is Analyzing Requirements and Defining Solution Architectures (Exam 70-100). Each candidate must also choose one of these two desktop application exams—Designing and Implementing Desktop Applications with Microsoft Visual C++ 6.0 (Exam 70-016) or Visual Basic 6.0 (Exam 70-176)—*plus* one of these two distributed application exams—Designing and Implementing Distributed Applications with Visual C++ 6.0 (Exam 70-015) or Visual Basic 6.0 (Exam 70-175).

Elective exams cover specific Microsoft applications and languages, including Visual Basic, C++, the Microsoft Foundation Classes, Access, SQL Server, Excel, and more. If you are on your way to becoming an MCSD and have already taken some exams, visit microsoft.com/train_cert for information about how to proceed with your MCSD certification under this new track.

➤ **MCSE (Microsoft Certified Systems Engineer)** Anyone who has a current MCSE is warranted to possess a high level of expertise with Windows NT (either version 3.51 or 4) and other Microsoft operating systems and products. This credential is designed to prepare individuals to plan, implement, maintain, and support information systems and networks built around Microsoft Windows NT and its BackOffice family of products.

To obtain an MCSE, an individual must pass four core operating system exams, plus two elective exams. The operating system exams require individuals to demonstrate competence with desktop and server operating systems and with networking components.

You must pass at least two Windows NT-related exams to obtain an MCSE: one on Implementing and Supporting Windows NT Server (version 3.51 or 4) and the other on Implementing and Supporting Windows NT Server in the Enterprise (version 3.51 or 4). These tests are intended to indicate an individual's knowledge of Windows NT in smaller, simpler networks and in larger, more complex, and heterogeneous networks, respectively.

Note: The NT 3.51 version is scheduled to be retired by Microsoft sometime in 1999.

You must pass two additional tests as well. These tests are networking and desktop operating system related. At present, the networking requirement can only be satisfied by passing the Networking Essentials test. The desktop operating system test can be satisfied by passing a Windows 95, Windows NT Workstation (the version must match whichever core curriculum is pursued), or Windows 98 test.

The two remaining exams are elective exams. An elective exam may fall in any number of subject or product areas, primarily BackOffice components. These include tests on Internet Explorer 4, SQL Server, IIS, Proxy Server, SNA Server, Exchange Server, Systems Management Server, and the like. However, it is also possible to test out on electives by taking advanced networking topics like "Internetworking with Microsoft TCP/IP on Microsoft Windows NT 4.0" (but here again, the version of Windows NT involved must match the version for the core requirements taken). If you are on your way to becoming an MCSE and have already taken some exams, visit www.microsoft.com/mcp/certstep/mcse.htm for information about how to proceed with your MCSE certification.

Whatever mix of tests is completed toward MCSE certification, individuals must pass six tests to meet the MCSE requirements. It's not uncommon for the entire process to take a year or so, and many individuals find that they must take a test more than once to pass. Our primary goal with the Exam Cram series is to make it possible, given proper study and preparation, to pass all of the MCSE tests on the first try. Table 1 shows the required and elective exams for the MCSE certification.

➤ **MCSE + Internet (Microsoft Certified Systems Engineer + Internet)** This is a newer Microsoft certification and focuses not just on Microsoft operating systems, but also on Microsoft's Internet servers and TCP/IP.

To obtain this certification, an individual must pass seven core exams, plus two elective exams. The core exams include not only the server operating systems (NT Server and Server in the Enterprise) and a desktop OS (Windows 95, Windows 98, or Windows NT Workstation), but also include Networking Essentials, TCP/IP, Internet Information Server (IIS), and the Internet Explorer Administration Kit (IEAK).

The two remaining exams are elective exams. These elective exams can be in any of four product areas: SQL Server, SNA Server, Exchange Server, or Proxy Server. Table 2 shows the required and elective exams for the MCSE + I certification.

➤ **MCDBA (Microsoft Certified Database Administrator)** The MCDBA credential reflects the skills required to implement and administer Microsoft SQL Server databases. To obtain an MCDBA, an individual must demonstrate the ability to derive physical database

Table 1   MCSE Requirements*

Core

All 3 of these are required	
Exam 70-067	Implementing and Supporting Microsoft Windows NT Server 4.0
Exam 70-068	Implementing and Supporting Microsoft Windows NT Server 4.0 in the Enterprise
Exam 70-058	Networking Essentials
Choose 1 from this group	
Exam 70-064	Implementing and Supporting Microsoft Windows 95
Exam 70-073	Implementing and Supporting Microsoft Windows NT Workstation 4.0
Exam 70-098	Implementing and Supporting Microsoft Windows 98

Elective

Choose 2 from this group	
Exam 70-088	Implementing and Supporting Microsoft Proxy Server 2.0
Exam 70-079	Implementing and Supporting Microsoft Internet Explorer 4.0 by Using the Internet Explorer Administration Kit
Exam 70-087	Implementing and Supporting Microsoft Internet Information Server 4.0
Exam 70-081	Implementing and Supporting Microsoft Exchange Server 5.5
Exam 70-059	Internetworking with Microsoft TCP/IP on Microsoft Windows NT 4.0
Exam 70-028	Administering Microsoft SQL Server 7.0
Exam 70-029	Designing and Implementing Databases on Microsoft SQL Server 7.0
Exam 70-056	Implementing and Supporting Web Sites Using Microsoft Site Server 3.0
Exam 70-086	Implementing and Supporting Microsoft Systems Management Server 2.0
Exam 70-085	Implementing and Supporting Microsoft SNA Server 4.0

* This is not a complete listing—you can still be tested on some earlier versions of these products. However, we have included mainly the most recent versions so that you may test on these versions and thus be certified longer. We have not included any tests that are scheduled to be retired.

designs, develop logical data models, create physical databases, create data services by using Transact-SQL, manage and maintain databases, configure and manage security, monitor and optimize databases, and install and configure Microsoft SQL Server.

To become an MCDBA, you must pass a total of five exams: four core exams and one elective exam. The required core exams are "Administering Microsoft SQL Server 7.0," "Designing and Implementing Databases with Microsoft SQL Server 7.0," "Implementing and Supporting Microsoft Windows NT Server 4.0," and "Implementing and Supporting Microsoft Windows NT Server 4.0 in the Enterprise."

The elective exams that you can choose from cover specific uses of SQL Server and include "Designing and Implementing Distributed Applications with Visual Basic 6.0," "Designing and Implementing Distributed

Table 2   MCSE+Internet Requirements*

Core

All 6 of these are required	
Exam 70-067	Implementing and Supporting Microsoft Windows NT Server 4.0
Exam 70-068	Implementing and Supporting Microsoft Windows NT Server 4.0 in the Enterprise
Exam 70-058	Networking Essentials
Exam 70-059	Internetworking with Microsoft TCP/IP on Microsoft Windows NT 4.0
Exam 70-087	Implementing and Supporting Microsoft Internet Information Server 4.0
Exam 70-079	Implementing and Supporting Microsoft Internet Explorer 4.0 by Using the Internet Explorer Administration Kit
Choose 1 from this group	
Exam 70-064	Implementing and Supporting Microsoft Windows 95
Exam 70-073	Implementing and Supporting Microsoft Windows NT Workstation 4.0
Exam 70-098	Implementing and Supporting Microsoft Windows 98

Elective

Choose 2 from this group	
Exam 70-088	Implementing and Supporting Microsoft Proxy Server 2.0
Exam 70-081	Implementing and Supporting Microsoft Exchange Server 5.5
Exam 70-028	System Administration for Microsoft SQL Server 7.0
Exam 70-029	Designing and Implementing Databases on Microsoft SQL Server 7.0
Exam 70-056	Implementing and Supporting Web Sites Using Microsoft Site Server 3.0
Exam 70-085	Implementing and Supporting Microsoft SNA Server 4.0

* This is not a complete listing—you can still be tested on some earlier versions of these products. However, we have included mainly the most recent versions so that you may test on these versions and thus be certified longer. We have not included any tests that are scheduled to be retired.

Applications with Visual C++ 6.0," "Designing and Implementing Data Warehouses with Microsoft SQL Server 7.0 and Microsoft Decision Support Services 1.0," and two exams that relate to NT: "Internetworking with Microsoft TCP/IP on Microsoft Windows NT 4.0" and "Implementing and Supporting Microsoft Internet Information Server 4.0."

Note that the exam covered by this book can be used as the elective for the MCDBA certification. Table 3 shows the requirements for the MCDBA certification.

➤ **MCT (Microsoft Certified Trainer)** Microsoft Certified Trainers are individuals who are deemed capable of delivering elements of the official Microsoft training curriculum, based on technical knowledge and instructional ability. Thus, it is necessary for an individual seeking MCT credentials (which are granted on a course-by-course basis) to pass the related certification exam for a course and successfully complete the

Table 3   MCDBA Requirements

Core

All 4 of these are required	
Exam 70-028	Administering Microsoft SQL Server 7.0
Exam 70-029	Designing and Implementing Databases with Microsoft SQL Server 7.0
Exam 70-067	Implementing and Supporting Microsoft Windows NT Server 4.0
Exam 70-068	Implementing and Supporting Microsoft Windows NT Server 4.0 in the Enterprise

Elective

Choose 1 from this group	
Exam 70-015	Designing and Implementing Distributed Applications with Microsoft Visual C++ 6.0
Exam 70-019	Designing and Implementing Data Warehouses with Microsoft SQL Server 7.0 and Microsoft Decision Support Services 1.0
Exam 70-059	Internetworking with Microsoft TCP/IP on Microsoft Windows NT 4.0
Exam 70-087	Implementing and Supporting Microsoft Internet Information Server 4.0
Exam 70-175	Designing and Implementing Distributed Applications with Microsoft Visual Basic 6.0

official Microsoft training in the subject area, as well as demonstrate an ability to teach.

This latter criterion may be satisfied by proving that one has already attained training certification from Novell, Banyan, Lotus, the Santa Cruz Operation, or Cisco, or by taking a Microsoft-sanctioned workshop on instruction. Microsoft makes it clear that MCTs are important cogs in the Microsoft training channels. Instructors must be MCTs before Microsoft will allow them to teach in any of its official training channels, including Microsoft's Affiliated Certified Technical Education Centers (CTECs), and the Microsoft Online Institute (MOLI).

Certification is an ongoing activity. Once a Microsoft product becomes obsolete, MCSEs (and other MCPs) typically have 12 to 18 months in which they may recertify on current product versions. (If individuals do not recertify within the specified time period, their certification becomes invalid.) Because technology keeps changing and new products continually supplant old ones, this should come as no surprise.

The best place to keep tabs on the MCP Program and its various certifications is on the Microsoft Web site. The current root URL for the MCP program is titled "Microsoft Certified Professional Web site" at www.microsoft.com/mcp. But Microsoft's Web site changes often, so if this URL doesn't work, try using the Search tool on Microsoft's site with either "MCP" or the quoted phrase

"Microsoft Certified Professional Program" as a search string. This will help you find the latest and most accurate information about Microsoft's certification programs.

You can also obtain a special CD from Microsoft that contains a copy of the Microsoft Education And Certification Roadmap. The Roadmap covers much of the same information as the Web site, and it is updated quarterly. To obtain your copy of the CD, call Microsoft at 1 (800) 636-7544, Monday through Friday, 6:30 A.M. through 7:30 P.M. Pacific Time.

Taking A Certification Exam

Alas, testing is not free. Each computer-based exam costs between $50 and $100, and if you do not pass, you may retest for an additional $50 or more each time. In the U.S. and Canada, tests are administered by Sylvan Prometric. Sylvan Prometric can be reached at 1 (800) 755-3926 or 1 (800) 755-EXAM, any time from 7:00 A.M. to 6:00 P.M., Central Time, Monday through Friday. If this number doesn't work, please try (612) 896-7000 or (612) 820-5707.

To schedule an exam, call at least one day in advance. To cancel or reschedule an exam, you must call at least 12 hours before the scheduled test time (or you may be charged regardless). When calling Sylvan Prometric, please have the following information ready for the telesales staffer who handles your call:

➤ Your name, organization, and mailing address.

➤ Your Microsoft Test ID. (For most U.S. citizens, this will be your social security number. Citizens of other nations can use their taxpayer IDs or make other arrangements with the order taker.)

➤ The name and number of the exam you wish to take. (For this book, the exam number is 70-029, and the exam name is "Designing and Implementing a Database with Microsoft SQL Server 7.0.")

➤ A method of payment must be arranged. (The most convenient approach is to supply a valid credit card number with sufficient available credit. Otherwise, payments by check, money order, or purchase order must be received before a test can be scheduled. If the latter methods are required, ask your order taker for more details.)

When you show up to take a test, try to arrive at least 15 minutes before the scheduled time slot. You must bring and supply two forms of identification, one of which must be a photo ID.

All exams are completely closed-book. In fact, you will not be permitted to take anything with you into the testing area, but you will be furnished with a blank sheet of paper and a pen. We suggest that you immediately write down on that sheet of paper all the information you've memorized for the test.

In Exam Cram books, this information appears on a tear-out sheet inside the front cover of each book. You will have some time to compose yourself, to record this information, and even to take a sample orientation exam before you must begin the real thing. We suggest you take the orientation test before taking your first exam, but because they're all more or less identical in layout, behavior, and controls, you probably won't need to do this more than once.

When you complete a Microsoft certification exam, the software will tell you whether you've passed or failed. All tests are scored on a basis of 1,000 points, and results are broken into several topic areas. Even if you fail, we suggest you ask for—and keep—the detailed report that the test administrator should print for you. You can use this report to help you prepare for another go-round, if needed.

If you need to retake an exam, you'll have to call Sylvan Prometric, schedule a new test date, and pay another $50 or $100 to take it again. Microsoft has recently implemented a new policy regarding failed tests. The first time you fail a test, you are able to retake the test the next day. However, if you fail a second time, you must wait 14 days before retaking that test. The 14-day waiting period is in effect for all tests after the first failure.

Tracking MCP Status

As soon as you pass any Microsoft exam other than Networking Essentials, you'll attain Microsoft Certified Professional (MCP) status. Microsoft also generates transcripts that indicate which exams you have passed and your corresponding test scores. You can order a transcript by email at any time by sending an email addressed to mcp@msprograms.com. You can also obtain a copy of your transcript by downloading the latest version of the MCT Guide from the Web site and consulting the section titled "Key Contacts" for a list of telephone numbers and related contacts.

Once you pass the necessary set of exams (six for MCSE or nine for MCSE + Internet), you'll be certified. Official certification normally takes anywhere from four to six weeks, so don't expect to get your credentials overnight. When the package arrives, it will include a Welcome Kit that contains a number of elements, including:

➤ An MCSE or MCSE + I certificate, suitable for framing, along with a Professional Program Membership card and lapel pin.

➤ A license to use the MCP logo, thereby allowing you to use the logo in advertisements, promotions, and documents, and on letterhead, business cards, and so on. Along with the license comes an MCP logo sheet, which includes camera-ready artwork. (Note: Before using any of the artwork, individuals must sign and return a licensing agreement that indicates they'll abide by its terms and conditions.)

➤ A one-year subscription to TechNet, a collection of CDs that includes software, documentation, service packs, databases, and more technical information than you can possibly ever read. In our opinion, this is the best and most tangible benefit of attaining MCSE or MCSE + I status.

➤ A subscription to *Microsoft Certified Professional Magazine*, which provides ongoing data about testing and certification activities, requirements, and changes to the program.

➤ A free Priority Comprehensive 10-pack with Microsoft Product Support, and a 25 percent discount on additional Priority Comprehensive 10-packs. This lets you place up to 10 free calls to Microsoft's technical support operation at a higher-than-normal priority level.

➤ A one-year subscription to the Microsoft Beta Evaluation program. This subscription will get you all beta products from Microsoft for the next year. (This does not include developer products. You must join the MSDN program or become an MCSD to qualify for developer beta products.)

Many people believe that the benefits of MCP certification go well beyond the perks that Microsoft provides to newly anointed members of this elite group. We're starting to see more job listings that request or require applicants to have an MCSE, MCSE + I, MCSD, etc., and many individuals who complete the program can qualify for increases in pay or responsibility. As an official recognition of hard work and broad knowledge, one of the MCP credentials is a badge of honor in many IT organizations.

How To Prepare For An Exam

Preparing for any Windows NT Server-related test requires that you obtain and study materials designed to provide comprehensive information about NT Server and the specific exam for which you are preparing. The following list of materials will help you study and prepare:

➤ The Microsoft Windows NT Server 4 manuals (or online documentation and help files, which ship on the CD with the product and also appear on the TechNet CDs).

➤ *The Microsoft Windows NT Server 4 Resource Kit*, published by Microsoft Press, Redmond, WA, 1996. ISBN: 1-57231-343-9. Even though it costs a whopping $149.95 (list price), it's worth every penny—not just for the documentation, but also for the utilities and other software included (which add considerably to the base functionality of Windows NT Server 4).

➤ The exam prep materials, practice tests, and self-assessment exams on the Microsoft Training And Certification Download page (www.microsoft.com/Train_Cert/download/downld.htm). Find the materials, download them, and use them!

In addition, you'll probably find any or all of the following materials useful in your quest for Windows NT Server expertise:

➤ **Study Guides** Publishers like Certification Insider and Sybex offer MCSE study guides of one kind or another. We've reviewed them and found the Certification Insider Press and Sybex titles to be informative and helpful for learning the materials necessary to pass the tests. The Certification Insider Press series includes:

   ➤ **The Exam Cram series** These books give you information about the material you need to know to pass the tests.

   ➤ **The Exam Prep series** These books provide a greater level of detail than the Exam Crams.

   Together, the two series make a perfect pair.

➤ **Classroom Training** CTECs, MOLI, and unlicensed third-party training companies (like Wave Technologies, American Research Group, Learning Tree, Data-Tech, and others) all offer or will soon be offering classroom training on Exchange Server 5.5. These companies aim to help prepare network administrators to run Windows NT-based networks and pass the MCSE tests. While such training runs upwards of $350 per day in class, most of the individuals lucky enough to partake (including your humble authors, who've even taught such courses) find them to be quite worthwhile.

➤ **Other Publications** You'll find direct references to other publications and resources in this text, but there's are other materials available about SQL Server 7. To help you sift through some of the publications out there, we end each chapter with a "Need To Know More?" section that provides pointers to more complete and exhaustive resources covering the chapter's information. This should give you an idea of where we think you should look for further discussion.

➤ **The TechNet CD** TechNet is a monthly CD subscription available from Microsoft. TechNet includes all the Windows NT BackOffice Resource Kits and their product documentation. In addition, TechNet provides the contents of the Microsoft Knowledge Base and many kinds of software, white papers, training materials, and other good stuff. TechNet also contains all service packs, interim release patches, and supplemental driver software released since the last major version for most Microsoft programs and all Microsoft operating systems. A one-year subscription costs $299—worth every penny, even if only for the download time it saves.

By far, this set of required and recommended materials represents a nonpareil collection of sources and resources that should give you everything you need. We anticipate that you'll find that this book belongs in this company. In the section that follows, we explain how this book works, and we give you some good reasons why this book counts as a member of the required and recommended materials list.

About This Book

Each topical Exam Cram chapter follows a regular structure, along with graphical cues about important or useful information. Here's the structure of a typical chapter:

➤ **Opening Hotlists** Each chapter begins with a list of the terms, tools, and techniques that you must learn and understand before you can be fully conversant with that chapter's subject matter. We follow the hotlists with one or two introductory paragraphs to set the stage for the rest of the chapter.

➤ **Topical Coverage** After the opening hotlists, each chapter covers a series of at least four topics related to the chapter's subject title. Throughout this section, we highlight topics or concepts likely to appear on a test using a special Study Alert layout, like this:

This is what a Study Alert looks like. Normally, a Study Alert stresses concepts, terms, software, or activities that are likely to relate to one or more certification test questions. For that reason, we think any information found offset in Study Alert format is worthy of unusual attentiveness on your part. Indeed, most of the information that appears on the Cram Sheet appears as Study Alerts within the text.

Occasionally, you'll see tables that we call Vital Statistics tables. They are formatted as normal tables, but have a special shaded background. The contents of Vital Statistics tables are worthy of an extra once-over. These tables usually contain informational tidbits that might show up in a test question, but they're not quite as important as Study Alerts.

Pay close attention to material flagged as a Study Alert; although all the information in this book pertains to what you need to know to pass the exam, we flag certain items that are really important. You'll find what appears in the meat of each chapter to be worth knowing, too, when preparing for the test. Because this book's material is very condensed, we recommend that you use this book along with other resources to achieve the maximum benefit.

In addition to the Study Alerts and Vital Statistics tables, we have provided tips that will help build a better foundation for SQL Server knowledge. Although the information may not be on the exam, it is certainly related and will help you become a better test taker.

This is how tips are formatted. Keep your eyes open for these, and you'll become an SQL Server guru in no time!

➤ **Practice Questions** Although we talk about test questions and topics throughout each chapter, this section at the end of each chapter presents a series of mock test questions and explanations of both correct and incorrect answers. We also try to point out especially tricky questions by using a special icon, like this:

Ordinarily, this icon flags the presence of a particularly devious inquiry, if not an outright trick question. Trick questions are calculated to be answered incorrectly if not read more than once, and carefully, at that. Although they're not ubiquitous, such questions make regular appearances on the Microsoft exams. That's why we say exam questions are as much about reading comprehension as they are about knowing your material inside out and backwards.

➤ **Details And Resources** Every chapter ends with a section titled "Need To Know More?", which provides direct pointers to Microsoft and third-party resources offering more details on the chapter's subject. In addition, this section tries to rank or at least rate the quality and thoroughness of the topic's coverage by each resource. If you find a resource you like in this collection, use it, but don't feel compelled to use all the resources. On the other hand, we only recommend resources we use on a regular basis, so none of our recommendations will be a waste of your time or money (but purchasing them all at once probably represents an expense that many network administrators and would-be MCSEs might find hard to justify).

Finally, the tear-out Cram Sheet attached inside the front cover of this Exam Cram book represents a condensed and compiled collection of facts, figures, and tips that we think you should memorize before taking the test. Because you can dump this information out of your head onto a piece of paper before answering any exam questions, you can master this information by brute force— you only need to remember it long enough to write it down when you walk into the test room. You might even want to look at it in the car or in the lobby of the testing center just before you walk in to take the test.

How To Use This Book

If you're prepping for a first-time test, we've structured the topics in this book to build on one another. Therefore, some topics in later chapters make more sense after you've read earlier chapters. That's why we suggest you read this book from front to back for your initial test preparation. If you need to brush up on a topic or you have to bone up for a second try, use the index or table of contents to go straight to the topics and questions that you need to study. Beyond the tests, we think you'll find this book useful as a tightly focused reference to some of the most important aspects of SQL Server 7.

Given all the book's elements and its specialized focus, we've tried to create a tool that will help you prepare for—and pass—Microsoft Certification Exam 70-029, "Designing and Implementing a Database with Microsoft SQL Server 7.0." Please share your feedback on the book with us, especially if you have ideas about how we can improve it for future test-takers. We'll consider everything you say carefully, and we'll respond to all suggestions.

Thanks, and enjoy the book!

Self-Assessment

Based on recent statistics from Microsoft, as many as 250,000 individuals are at some stage of the certification process but haven't yet received an MCP or other Microsoft certification. We also know that three or four times that number may be considering whether or not to obtain a Microsoft certification of some kind. That's a huge audience!

The reason we included a self-assessment in this *Exam Cram* book is to help you evaluate your readiness to tackle MCSE (and MCSE+I) certification. It should also help you understand what you need to master the topic of this book—namely, Exam 70-029, "Designing and Implementing Databases with Microsoft SQL Server 7.0." But before you tackle this self-assessment, let's talk about concerns you may face when pursuing an MCSE, and what an ideal MCSE candidate might look like.

MCSEs In The Real World

In the next section, we describe an ideal MCSE candidate, knowing full well that only a few real candidates will meet this ideal. In fact, our description of that ideal candidate might seem downright scary. But take heart: Although the requirements to obtain an MCSE may seem pretty formidable, they are by no means impossible to meet. However, you should be keenly aware that it does take time, requires some expense, and consumes substantial effort to get through the process.

More than 90,000 MCSEs are already certified, so it's obviously an attainable goal. You can get all the real-world motivation you need from knowing that many others have gone before, so you will be able to follow in their footsteps. If you're willing to tackle the process seriously and do what it takes to obtain the necessary experience and knowledge, you can take—and pass—all the certification tests involved in obtaining an MCSE. In fact, we've designed these *Exam Crams*, and the companion *Exam Preps*, to make it as easy on you as possible to prepare for these exams. But prepare you must!

The same, of course, is true for other Microsoft certifications, including:

➤ MCSE+I, which is like the MCSE certification but requires seven core exams, and two electives drawn from a specific pool of Internet-related topics, for a total of nine exams.

➤ MCSD, which is aimed at software developers and requires one specific exam, two more exams on client and distributed topics, plus a fourth elective exam drawn from a different, but limited, pool of options.

➤ Other Microsoft certifications, whose requirements range from one test (MCP or MCT) to many tests (MCP+I, MCP+SB, MCDBA).

The Ideal MCSE Candidate

Just to give you some idea of what an ideal MCSE candidate is like, here are some relevant statistics about the background and experience such an individual might have. Don't worry if you don't meet these qualifications, or don't come that close—this is a far from ideal world, and where you fall short is simply where you'll have more work to do.

➤ Academic or professional training in network theory, concepts, and operations. This includes everything from networking media and transmission techniques through network operating systems, services, and applications.

➤ Three-plus years of professional networking experience, including experience with Ethernet, token ring, modems, and other networking media. This must include installation, configuration, upgrade, and troubleshooting experience.

➤ Two-plus years in a networked environment that includes hands-on experience with Windows NT Server, Windows NT Workstation, and Windows 95 or Windows 98. A solid understanding of each system's architecture, installation, configuration, maintenance, and troubleshooting is also essential.

➤ A thorough understanding of key networking protocols, addressing, and name resolution, including TCP/IP, IPX/SPX, and NetBEUI.

➤ A thorough understanding of NetBIOS naming, browsing services, and file and print services.

➤ Familiarity with key Windows NT-based TCP/IP-based services, including HTTP (Web servers), DHCP, WINS, DNS, plus familiarity with one or more of the following: Internet Information Server (IIS), Index Server, and Proxy Server.

➤ Working knowledge of NetWare 3.x and 4.x, including IPX/SPX frame formats, NetWare file, print, and directory services, and both Novell and Microsoft client software. Working knowledge of Microsoft's Client Services for NetWare (CSNW), Gateway Services for NetWare (GSNW), the NetWare Migration Tool (NWCONV), and the NetWare Client for Windows (NT, 95, and 98) is essential.

Fundamentally, this boils down to a bachelor's degree in computer science, plus three years of work experience in a technical position involving network design, installation, configuration, and maintenance. We believe that well under half of all certification candidates meet these requirements, and that, in fact, most meet less than half of these requirements—at least, when they begin the certification process. But because all 90,000 people who already have been certified have survived this ordeal, you can survive it too—especially if you heed what our self-assessment can tell you about what you already know and what you need to learn.

Put Yourself To The Test

The following series of questions and observations is designed to help you figure out how much work you must do to pursue Microsoft certification and what kinds of resources you may consult on your quest. Be absolutely honest in your answers, or you'll end up wasting money on exams you're not yet ready to take. There are no right or wrong answers, only steps along the path to certification. Only you can decide where you really belong in the broad spectrum of aspiring candidates.

Two things should be clear from the outset, however:

➤ Even a modest background in computer science will be helpful.

➤ Hands-on experience with Microsoft products and technologies is an essential ingredient to certification success.

Educational Background

1. Have you ever taken any computer-related classes? [Yes or No]

   If Yes, proceed to question 2; if No, proceed to question 4.

2. Have you taken any classes on computer operating systems? [Yes or No]

   If Yes, you will probably be able to handle Microsoft's architecture and system component discussions. If you're rusty, brush up on basic operating system concepts, especially virtual memory, multitasking regimes, user mode versus kernel mode operation, and general computer security topics.

If No, consider some basic reading in this area. We strongly recommend a good general operating systems book, such as *Operating System Concepts*, by Abraham Silberschatz and Peter Baer Galvin (Addison-Wesley, 1997, ISBN 0-201-59113-8). If this title doesn't appeal to you, check out reviews for other, similar titles at your favorite online bookstore.

3. Have you taken any networking concepts or technologies classes? [Yes or No]

If Yes, you will probably be able to handle Microsoft's networking terminology, concepts, and technologies (brace yourself for frequent departures from normal usage). If you're rusty, brush up on basic networking concepts and terminology, especially networking media, transmission types, the OSI Reference model, and networking technologies such as Ethernet, token ring, FDDI, and WAN links.

If No, you might want to read one or two books in this topic area. The two best books that we know of are *Computer Networks*, *3rd Edition*, by Andrew S. Tanenbaum (Prentice-Hall, 1996, ISBN 0-13-349945-6) and *Computer Networks and Internets*, by Douglas E. Comer (Prentice-Hall, 1997, ISBN 0-13-239070-1).

Skip to the next section, "Hands-On Experience."

4. Have you done any reading on operating systems or networks? [Yes or No]

If Yes, review the requirements stated in the first paragraphs after questions 2 and 3. If you meet those requirements, move on to the next section. If No, consult the recommended reading for both topics. A strong background will help you prepare for the Microsoft exams better than just about anything else.

Hands-On Experience

The most important key to success on all of the Microsoft tests is hands-on experience, especially with Windows NT Server and Workstation, plus the many add-on services and BackOffice components around which so many of the Microsoft certification exams revolve. If we leave you with only one realization after taking this self-assessment, it should be that there's no substitute for time spent installing, configuring, and using the various Microsoft products upon which you'll be tested repeatedly and in depth.

5. Have you installed, configured, and worked with:

➤ Windows NT Server? [Yes or No]

If Yes, make sure you understand basic concepts as covered in Exam 70-067 and advanced concepts as covered in Exam 70-068. You should also study the TCP/IP interfaces, utilities, and services for this test, Exam 70-059, plus Internet Information Server capabilities for Exam 70-087.

 You can download objectives, practice exams, and other information about Microsoft exams from the company's Training and Certification page on the Web at www.microsoft.com/train_cert/. Use the "Find an Exam" link to get specific exam info.

If you haven't worked with Windows NT Server, TCP/IP, and IIS (or whatever product you choose for your final elective), you must obtain one or two machines and a copy of Windows NT Server. Then, learn the operating system, and do the same for TCP/IP and whatever other software components on which you'll also be tested.

In fact, we recommend that you obtain two computers, each with a network interface, and set up a two-node network on which to practice. With decent Windows NT-capable computers selling for about $500 to $600 apiece these days, this shouldn't be too much of a financial hardship. You can order a BackOffice Trial Kit from Microsoft, which includes evaluation copies of both Workstation and Server, for under $50 from www.backoffice.microsoft.com/downtrial/.

➤ Windows NT Workstation? [Yes or No]

If Yes, make sure you understand the concepts covered in Exam 70-073.

If No, you will want to obtain a copy of Windows NT Workstation and learn how to install, configure, and maintain it. You can use *MCSE NT Workstation 4 Exam Cram* to guide your activities and studies, or work straight from Microsoft's test objectives if you prefer.

 For any and all of these Microsoft exams, the Resource Kits for the topics involved are a good study resource. You can purchase softcover Resource Kits from Microsoft Press (search for them at http://mspress.microsoft.com/), but they're also included on the TechNet CD subscription (www.microsoft.com/technet). We believe that Resource Kits are among the best preparation tools available, along with the *Exam Crams* and *Exam Preps*, that you can use to get ready for Microsoft exams.

You have the option of taking the Window 95 (70-064) exam or the Windows 98 (70-098) exam, instead of Exam 70-073, to fulfill your desktop operating system requirement for the MCSE. Although we don't recommend these others (because studying for Workstation helps you prepare for the Server exams), we do recommend that you obtain Resource Kits and other tools to help you prepare for those exams if you decide to take one or both of them for your own reasons.

6. For any specific Microsoft product that is not itself an operating system (for example, FrontPage 98, SQL Server, and so on), have you installed, configured, used, and upgraded this software? [Yes or No]

If the answer is Yes, skip to the next section. If it's No, you must get some experience. Read on for suggestions on how to do this.

Experience is a must with any Microsoft product exam, be it something as simple as FrontPage 98 or as challenging as Exchange 5.5 or SQL Server 7.0. You can grab a download of BackOffice at www.backoffice.microsoft.com/downtrial/; for trial copies of other software, search Microsoft's Web site using the name of the product as your search term.

 If you have the funds, or your employer will pay your way, consider taking a class at a Certified Training and Education Center (CTEC) or at an Authorized Academic Training Partner (AATP). In addition to classroom exposure to the topic of your choice, you get a copy of the software that is the focus of your course, along with a trial version of whatever operating system it needs (usually, NT Server), with the training materials for that class.

Before you even think about taking any Microsoft exam, make sure you've spent enough time with the related software to understand how it may be installed and configured, how to maintain such an installation, and how to troubleshoot that software when things go wrong. This will help you in the exam, and in real life!

Testing Your Exam-Readiness

Whether you attend a formal class on a specific topic to get ready for an exam or use written materials to study on your own, some preparation for the Microsoft certification exams is essential. At $100 a try, pass or fail, you want to do everything you can to pass on your first try. That's where studying comes in.

If you still don't hit a score of at least 70 percent on this book's practice exam, you'll want to investigate the other practice test resources we mention in this section.

For any given subject, consider taking a class if you've tackled self-study materials, taken the test, and failed anyway. The opportunity to interact with an instructor and fellow students can make all the difference in the world, if you can afford that privilege. For information about Microsoft classes, visit the Training and Certification page at www.microsoft.com/train_cert/ (use the "Find a Course" link).

If you can't afford to take a class, visit the Training and Certification page anyway, because it also includes pointers to free practice exams and to Microsoft Certified Professional Approved Study Guides and other self-study tools. And even if you can't afford to spend much at all, you should still invest in some low-cost practice exams from commercial vendors, because they can help you assess your readiness to pass a test better than any other tool. All of the following Web sites offer practice exams online for less than $100 apiece (some for significantly less than that):

➤ Beachfront Quizzer at www.bfq.com/

➤ CramSession at www.cramsession.com/

➤ Hardcore MCSE at www.hardcoremcse.com/

➤ LANWrights at www.lanw.com/books/examcram/order.htm/

➤ MeasureUp at www.measureup.com/

7. Have you taken a practice exam on your chosen test subject? [Yes or No]

   If Yes, and you scored 70 percent or better, you're probably ready to tackle the real thing. If your score isn't above that crucial threshold, keep at it until you break that barrier.

   If No, obtain all the free and low-budget practice tests you can find (see the list above) and get to work. Keep at it until you can break the passing threshold comfortably.

 When it comes to assessing your test readiness, there is no better way than to take a good-quality practice exam and pass with a score of 70 percent or better. When we're preparing ourselves, we shoot for 80-plus percent, just to leave room for the "weirdness factor" that sometimes shows up on Microsoft exams.

Assessing Readiness For Exam 70-029

In addition to the general exam-readiness information in the previous section, there are several things you can do to prepare for the Designing and Implementing a Database With Microsoft SQL Server 7.0 exam. As you're getting ready for Exam 70-029, visit the MCSE mailing list. Sign up at www.sunbelt-software.com (look for the "Subscribe to…" button). You will also find a great source of questions and related information at the CramSession site at www.cramsession.com. This is a great place to ask questions and get good answers, or simply to watch the questions that others ask (along with the answers, of course).

You should also cruise the Web looking for "braindumps" (recollections of test topics and experiences recorded by others) to help you anticipate topics you're likely to encounter on the test. The MCSE mailing list is a good place to ask where the useful braindumps are, or you can check Shawn Gamble's list at www.commandcentral.com (he's also got some peachy—and free—practice tests on this subject) or Herb Martin's Braindump Heaven at http://209.207.167.177/.

When using any braindump, it's OK to pay attention to information about questions. But you can't always be sure that a braindump's author will also be able to provide correct answers. Thus, use the questions to guide your studies, but don't rely on the answers in a braindump to lead you to the truth. Double-check everything you find in any braindump.

Microsoft exam mavens also recommend checking the Microsoft Knowledge Base (available on its own CD as part of the TechNet collection, or on the Microsoft Web site at http://support.microsoft.com/support/) for "meaningful technical support issues" that relate to your exam's topics. Although we're not sure exactly what the quoted phrase means, we have also noticed some overlap between technical support questions on particular products and troubleshooting questions on the exams for those products.

One last note: It might seem counterintuitive to talk about hands-on experience in the context of the Designing and Implementing a Database With Microsoft SQL Server 7.0 exam. But as you review the material for that exam, you'll realize that hands-on experience with SQL Server 7 will be invaluable. Surprisingly, you'll also benefit from hands-on experience with Windows NT Server, particularly when it comes to configuring files and file groups.

Onward, Through The Fog!

Once you've assessed your readiness, undertaken the right background studies, obtained the hands-on experience that will help you understand the products and technologies at work, and reviewed the many sources of information to help you prepare for a test, you'll be ready to take a round of practice tests. When your scores come back positive enough to get you through the exam, you're ready to go after the real thing. If you follow our assessment regime, you'll not only know what you need to study, but when you're ready to make a test date at Sylvan or VUE. Good luck!

Microsoft Certification Exams

Terms you'll need to understand:

- √ Radio button
- √ Checkbox
- √ Exhibit
- √ Multiple-choice question formats
- √ Careful reading
- √ Process of elimination
- √ Short-form tests
- √ Combination tests
- √ Adaptive tests
- √ Fixed-length tests
- √ Simulations

Techniques you'll need to master:

- √ Assessing your exam-readiness
- √ Preparing to take a certification exam
- √ Practicing (to make perfect)
- √ Making the best use of the testing software
- √ Budgeting your time
- √ Guessing (as a last resort)

Exam taking is not something that most people anticipate eagerly, no matter how well prepared they may be. In most cases, familiarity helps ameliorate test anxiety. In plain English, this means you probably won't be as nervous when you take your fourth or fifth Microsoft certification exam as you'll be when you take your first one.

Whether it's your first exam or your tenth, understanding the details of exam taking (how much time to spend on questions, the environment you'll be in, and so on) and the exam software will help you concentrate on the material rather than on the setting. Likewise, mastering a few basic exam-taking skills should help you recognize—and perhaps even outfox—some of the tricks and gotchas you're bound to find in some of the exam questions.

This chapter, besides explaining the exam environment and software, describes some proven exam-taking strategies that you should be able to use to your advantage.

Assessing Exam-Readiness

Before you take any more Microsoft exams, we strongly recommend that you read through and take the Self-Assessment included with this book (it appears just before this chapter, in fact). This will help you compare your knowledge base to the requirements for obtaining an MCSE, and it will also help you identify parts of your background or experience that may be in need of improvement, enhancement, or further learning. If you get the right set of basics under your belt, obtaining Microsoft certification will be that much easier.

Once you've gone through the Self-Assessment, you can remedy those topical areas where your background or experience may not measure up to an ideal certification candidate. But you can also tackle subject matter for individual tests at the same time, so you can continue making progress while you're catching up in some areas.

Once you've worked through an *Exam Cram*, have read the supplementary materials, and have taken the practice test, you'll have a pretty clear idea of when you should be ready to take the real exam. We strongly recommend that you keep practicing until your scores top the 70 percent mark; 75 percent would be a good goal to give yourself some margin for error in a real exam situation (where stress will play more of a role than when you practice). Once you hit that point, you should be ready to go. But if you get through the practice exam in this book without attaining that score, you should keep taking practice tests and studying the materials until you get there. You'll find more information about other practice test vendors in the Self-Assessment, along with even more pointers on how to study and prepare. But now, on to the exam itself!

The Exam Situation

When you arrive at the testing center where you scheduled your exam, you'll need to sign in with an exam coordinator. He or she will ask you to show two forms of identification, one of which must be a photo ID. After you've signed in and your time slot arrives, you'll be asked to deposit any books, bags, or other items you brought with you. Then, you'll be escorted into a closed room. Typically, the room will be furnished with anywhere from one to half a dozen computers, and each workstation will be separated from the others by dividers designed to keep you from seeing what's happening on someone else's computer.

You'll be furnished with a pen or pencil and a blank sheet of paper, or, in some cases, an erasable plastic sheet and an erasable felt-tip pen. You're allowed to write down any information you want on both sides of this sheet. Before the exam, you should memorize as much of the material that appears on The Cram Sheet (inside the front cover of this book) as you can, so you can write that information on the blank sheet as soon as you are seated in front of the computer. You can refer to your rendition of The Cram Sheet anytime you like during the test, but you'll have to surrender the sheet when you leave the room.

Most test rooms feature a wall with a large picture window. This permits the exam coordinator standing on the other side to monitor the room, to prevent exam takers from talking to one another, and to observe anything out of the ordinary that might go on. The exam coordinator will have preloaded the appropriate Microsoft certification exam—for this book, that's Exam 70-029—and you'll be permitted to start as soon as you're seated in front of the computer.

All Microsoft certification exams allow a certain maximum amount of time in which to complete your work (this time is indicated on the exam by an onscreen counter/clock, so you can check the time remaining whenever you like).

All Microsoft certification exams are computer generated and most use a multiple-choice format. Although this may sound quite simple, the questions are constructed not only to check your mastery of basic facts and figures about SQL Server 7, but they also require you to evaluate one or more sets of circumstances or requirements. Often, you'll be asked to give more than one answer to a question. Likewise, you might be asked to select the best or most effective solution to a problem from a range of choices, all of which technically are correct. Taking the exam is quite an adventure, and it involves real thinking. This book shows you what to expect and how to deal with the potential problems, puzzles, and predicaments.

Exam Layout And Design

Some exam questions require you to select a single answer, whereas others ask you to select one or more correct answers. The following multiple-choice question requires you to select a single correct answer. Following the question is a brief summary of each potential answer and why it is either right or wrong.

Question 1

When is a trigger fired?

○ a. When the trigger fire statement is executed

○ b. Before data modification

○ c. Before constraint validation

○ d. After the transaction completes

○ e. After constraint validation but before the transaction commits

The correct answer to this question is e. A trigger is an integral part of the transaction which fires it, and it needs access to the before and after image of the data to do its work.

This sample question format corresponds closely to the Microsoft certification exam format—the only difference on the exam is that questions are not followed by answer keys. To select an answer, position the cursor over the radio button next to the answer. Then, click the mouse button to select the answer.

Let's examine a question where one or more answers are possible. This type of question provides checkboxes rather than radio buttons for marking all appropriate selections.

Question 2

How long does a trigger persist in a database? [Check all correct answers]

❑ a. Until the session is terminated

❑ b. Until it is dropped

❑ c. Until a new trigger is created without the append option

❑ d. Until another trigger replaces it

❑ e. None of the above

The correct answers to this question are b, c, and d. Triggers are permanent objects in a database, so answer a is not true.

For this type of question, more than one answer is required. As far as the authors can tell (and Microsoft won't comment), such questions are scored as wrong unless all the required selections are chosen. In other words, a partially correct answer does not result in partial credit when the test is scored. For Question 2, you have to check the boxes next to items b, c, and d to obtain credit for a correct answer. Notice that picking the right answers also means knowing why the other answers are wrong!

Although these two basic types of questions can appear in many forms, they constitute the foundation on which all the Microsoft certification exam questions rest. More complex questions include so-called exhibits, which are usually screenshots of SQL Server Enterprise Manager. For some of these questions, you'll be asked to make a selection by clicking on a checkbox or radio button on the screenshot itself. For others, you'll be expected to use the information displayed therein to guide your answer to the question. Familiarity with the underlying utility is your key to choosing the correct answer(s).

Other questions involving exhibits use charts or network diagrams to help document a workplace scenario that you'll be asked to troubleshoot or configure. Careful attention to such exhibits is the key to success. Be prepared to toggle frequently between the exhibit and the question as you work.

Microsoft's Testing Formats

Currently, Microsoft uses four different testing formats:

➤ Fixed-length

➤ Adaptive

➤ Short-form

➤ Combination

Some Microsoft exams employ more advanced testing capabilities than might immediately meet the eye. Although the questions that appear are still multiple choice, the logic that drives them is more complex than older Microsoft tests, which use a fixed sequence of questions, called a *fixed-length test*. Other exams employ a sophisticated user interface, which Microsoft calls a *simulation*, to test your knowledge of the software and systems under consideration in a more or less "live" environment that behaves just like the original.

For many upcoming exams, Microsoft is turning to a well-known technique, called *adaptive testing*, to establish a test-taker's level of knowledge and product competence. Adaptive exams look the same as fixed-length exams, but they discover the level of difficulty at which an individual test-taker can correctly answer questions. At the same time, Microsoft is in the process of converting some of its older fixed-length exams into adaptive exams as well. Test-takers with differing levels of knowledge or ability therefore see different sets of questions; individuals with high levels of knowledge or ability are presented with a smaller set of more difficult questions, whereas individuals with lower levels of knowledge are presented with a larger set of easier questions. Two individuals may answer the same percentage of questions correctly, but the test-taker with a higher knowledge or ability level will score higher, because his or her questions are worth more.

Also, the lower-level test-taker will probably answer more questions than his or her more-knowledgeable colleague. This explains why adaptive tests use ranges of values to define the number of questions and the amount of time it takes to complete the test.

Adaptive tests work by evaluating the test-taker's most recent answer. A correct answer leads to a more difficult question (and the test software's estimate of the test-taker's knowledge and ability level is raised). An incorrect answer leads to a less difficult question (and the test software's estimate of the test-taker's knowledge and ability level is lowered). This process continues until the test targets the test-taker's true ability level. The exam ends when the test-taker's level of accuracy meets a statistically acceptable value (in other words, when his or her performance demonstrates an acceptable level of knowledge and ability) or when the maximum number of items has been presented (in which case, the test-taker is almost certain to fail).

Microsoft has recently introduced the short-form test for its most popular tests (as of this writing, only Networking Essentials [70-058] and TCP/IP [70-059] adhere to this format). This test delivers exactly 30 questions to its takers, giving them exactly 60 minutes to complete the exam. This type of exam is similar to a fixed-length test, in that it allows readers to jump ahead or return to earlier questions, and to cycle through the questions until the test is done. Microsoft does not use adaptive logic in this test, but claims that statistical analysis of the question pool is such that the 30 questions delivered during a short-form exam will conclusively measure a test-taker's knowledge of the subject matter in much the same way as an adaptive test will. You can think of the short-form test as a kind of "greatest hits" (that is, most important questions) version of the adaptive exam on the same topic.

A fourth kind of test you could encounter is what we've dubbed the combination exam. Several test-takers have reported that some of the Microsoft exams, including Windows NT Server (70-067), NT Server in the Enterprise (70-068), and Windows NT Workstation (70-073), can appear as combination exams. Such exams begin with a set of 15 to 25 adaptive questions, followed by 10 fixed-length questions. In fact, many test-takers have reported that although some combination tests claim that they will present both adaptive and fixed-length portions, when the test-taker has finished the adaptive portion (usually in exactly 15 questions), the test ends there. Because such users have all attained passing scores, it may be that a high enough passing score on the adaptive portion of a combination test obviates the fixed-length portion, but we're not completely sure about this, and Microsoft won't comment. Most combination exams allow a maximum of 60 minutes for the testing period.

Microsoft tests can come in any one of these forms. Whatever you encounter, you must take the test in whichever form it appears; you can't choose one form over another. Currently, exam 70-029 consists of about 70 randomly selected questions. You may take up to 90 minutes to complete the exam. If anything, it pays off even more to prepare thoroughly for an adaptive or combination exam than for a fixed-length or a short-form exam: The penalties for answering incorrectly are built into the test itself on an adaptive exam or the first part of a combination exam, whereas the layout remains the same for a fixed-length or a short-form test, no matter how many questions you answer incorrectly.

 The biggest difference between an adaptive test and a fixed-length or short-form test is that on a fixed-length or short-form test, you can revisit questions after you've read them over one or more times. On an adaptive test, you must answer the question when it's presented and will have no opportunities to revisit that question thereafter.

In the next section, you'll learn more about how Microsoft test questions look and how they must be answered.

Strategies For Different Testing Formats

Before you can choose a test-taking strategy, you need to know if your test is fixed-length, short-form, adaptive, or combination. When you begin your exam, the software will tell you the test is adaptive, if in fact the version you're taking is presented as an adaptive test. If your introductory materials fail to mention this, you're probably taking a fixed-length test. If the total number of questions involved is exactly 30, then you're taking a short-form test. Combination tests announce themselves by indicating that they will start with a set of adaptive questions, followed by fixed-length questions, but don't actually call themselves "combination tests" or "combination exams"—we've adopted this nomenclature for descriptive reasons.

You'll be able to tell for sure whether you are taking an adaptive, short-form, fixed-length, or combination test by the first question. If it includes a checkbox that lets you mark the question for later review, you're taking a fixed-length or short-form test. If the total number of questions is 30, it's a short-form test; if it's more than 30, it's a fixed-length test. Adaptive test questions (and the first set of questions on a combination test) can be visited (and answered) only once, and they include no such checkbox.

Exam-Taking Basics

The most important advice about taking any exam is this: Read each question carefully. Some questions are deliberately ambiguous, some use double negatives, and others use terminology in incredibly precise ways. The authors have taken numerous exams—both practice and live—and in nearly every one have missed at least one question because they didn't read it closely or carefully enough.

Here are some suggestions on how to deal with the tendency to jump to an answer too quickly:

➤ Make sure you read every word in the question. If you find yourself jumping ahead impatiently, go back and start over.

➤ As you read, try to restate the question in your own terms. If you can do this, you should be able to pick the correct answer(s) much more easily.

➤ When returning to a question after your initial read-through, read every word again—otherwise, your mind can fall quickly into a rut. Sometimes, revisiting a question after turning your attention elsewhere lets you see something you missed, but the strong tendency is to see what you've seen before. Try to avoid that tendency at all costs.

➤ If you return to a question more than twice, try to articulate to yourself what you don't understand about the question, why the answers don't appear to make sense, or what appears to be missing. If you chew on the subject for a while, your subconscious might provide the details that are lacking or you might notice a "trick" that will point to the right answer.

Above all, try to deal with each question by thinking through what you know about SQL Server 7—the characteristics, behaviors, facts, and figures involved. By reviewing what you know (and what you've written down on your information sheet), you'll often recall or understand things sufficiently to determine the answer to the question.

Question-Handling Strategies

Based on exams the authors have taken, some interesting trends have become apparent. For those questions that take only a single answer, usually two or three of the answers will be obviously incorrect, and two of the answers will be plausible—of course, only one can be correct. Unless the answer leaps out at you (if it does, reread the question to look for a trick; sometimes those are the ones you're most likely to get wrong), begin the process of answering by eliminating those answers that are most obviously wrong.

Things to look for in obviously wrong answers include spurious menu choices or utility names, nonexistent software options, and terminology you've never seen. If you've done your homework for an exam, no valid information should be completely new to you. In that case, unfamiliar or bizarre terminology probably indicates a totally bogus answer.

Numerous questions assume that the default behavior of a particular utility is in effect. If you know the defaults and understand what they mean, this knowledge will help you cut through many Gordian knots.

As you work your way through the exam, another counter that Microsoft thankfully provides will come in handy—the number of questions completed and questions outstanding. For fixed-length tests, it's wise to budget your time by making sure that you've completed one-quarter of the questions one-quarter of the way through the exam period (or the first 17 or 18 questions in the first 22 or 23 minutes) and three-quarters of them three-quarters of the way through (52 or 53 questions in the first 66 to 69 minutes).

If you're not finished when most of the minutes have elapsed, use the last five minutes to guess your way through the remaining questions. Remember, guessing is potentially more valuable than not answering, because blank answers are always wrong, but a guess may turn out to be right. If you don't have a clue about any of the remaining questions, pick answers at random, or choose all a's, b's, and so on. The important thing is to submit an exam for scoring that has an answer for every question.

The Fixed-Length And Short-Form Exam Strategy

A well-known principle when taking fixed-length or short form exams is to first read over the entire exam from start to finish while answering only those questions you feel absolutely sure of. On subsequent passes, you can dive into more complex questions more deeply, knowing how many such questions you have left.

Fortunately, the Microsoft exam software for fixed-length or short-form tests makes the multiple-visit approach easy to implement. At the top-left corner of each question is a checkbox that permits you to mark that question for a later visit.

> *Note: Marking questions makes review easier, but you can return to any question by clicking on the Forward or Back button repeatedly.*

As you read each question, if you answer only those you're sure of and mark for review those that you're not sure of, you can keep working through a decreasing list of questions as you answer the trickier ones in order.

There's at least one potential benefit to reading the exam over completely before answering the trickier questions: Sometimes, information in later questions sheds more light on earlier questions. Other times, information you read in later questions might jog your memory about SQL Server 7 facts, figures, or behavior that also will help with earlier questions. Either way, you'll come out ahead if you defer those questions about which you're not absolutely sure.

Keep working on the questions until you're certain of all your answers or until you know you'll run out of time. If questions remain unanswered, you'll want to zip through them and guess. Not answering a question guarantees you won't receive credit for it, and a guess has at least a chance of being correct.

At the very end of your exam period, you're better off guessing than leaving questions unanswered.

The Adaptive Exam Strategy

If there's one principle that applies to taking an adaptive test, it could be summed up as "Get it right the first time." You cannot elect to skip a question and move on to the next one when taking an adaptive test, because the testing software uses your answer to the current question to select whatever question it plans to present next. Nor can you return to a question once you've moved on, because the software gives you only one chance to answer the question. You can, however, take notes, because sometimes information supplied in earlier questions will shed light on later questions.

Also, when you answer a question correctly, you are presented with a more difficult question next, to help the software gauge your level of skill and ability. When you answer a question incorrectly, you are presented with a less difficult question, and the software lowers its current estimate of your skill and ability. This continues until the program settles into a reasonably accurate estimate of what you know and can do, and takes you on average through somewhere between 15 and 25 questions as you complete the test.

The good news is that if you know your stuff, you'll probably finish most adaptive tests in a significantly shorter amount of time than it would take to run through an entire fixed-length test. The bad news is that you must really, really know your stuff to do your best on an adaptive test. That's because some questions are so convoluted, complex, or hard to follow that you're bound to miss one or two, at a minimum, even if you do know your stuff. So the more you know, the better you'll do on an adaptive test, even accounting for the occasionally weird or unfathomable questions that appear on these exams.

Because you can't tell in advance whether a test is fixed-length, short-form, adaptive or combination you will be best served by preparing for the exam as if it were adaptive. That way, you should be prepared to pass no matter what kind of test you take. But if you do take a fixed-length or short-form test, remember our tips from the preceding section. They should help you improve on what you could do on an adaptive test.

If you encounter a question on an adaptive test that you can't answer, you must guess an answer immediately. Because of the way the software works, you may have to suffer for your guess on the next question if you guess right, because you'll get a more difficult question next!

Mastering The Inner Game

In the final analysis, knowledge breeds confidence, and confidence breeds success. If you study the materials in this book carefully and review all the practice questions at the end of each chapter, you should become aware of those areas where additional learning and study are required.

Next, follow up by reading some or all of the materials recommended in the "Need To Know More?" section at the end of each chapter. The idea is to become familiar enough with the concepts and situations you find in the sample questions that you can reason your way through similar situations on a real exam. If you know the material, you have every right to be confident that you can pass the exam.

After you've worked your way through the book, take the practice exam in Chapter 18. This will provide a reality check and help you identify areas you need to study further. Make sure you follow up and review materials related to the questions you miss on the practice exam before scheduling a real exam. Only when you've covered all the ground and feel comfortable with the whole scope of the practice exam should you take a real one.

If you take the practice exam and don't score at least 75 percent correct, you'll want to practice further. Though one is not available for the SQL Server Database Design yet, Microsoft usually provides free Personal Exam Prep (PEP) exams and the self-assessment exams from the Microsoft Certified Professional Web site's download page (its location appears in the next section). If you're more ambitious or better funded, you might want to purchase a practice exam from a third-party vendor.

Armed with the information in this book and with the determination to augment your knowledge, you should be able to pass the certification exam. However, you need to work at it, or you'll spend the exam fee more than once before you finally pass. If you prepare seriously, you should do well. Good luck!

Additional Resources

A good source of information about Microsoft certification exams comes from Microsoft itself. Because its products and technologies—and the exams that go with them—change frequently, the best place to go for exam-related information is online.

If you haven't already visited the Microsoft Certified Professional site, do so right now. The MCP home page resides at www.microsoft.com/mcp (see Figure 1.1).

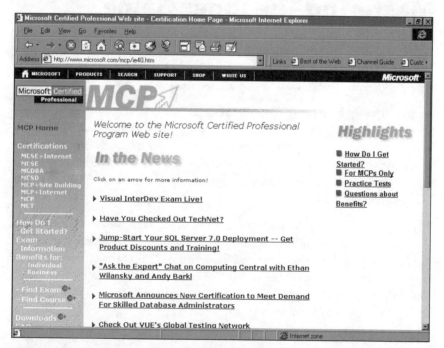

Figure 1.1 The Microsoft Certified Professional home page.

Note: This page might not be there by the time you read this, or it might have been replaced by something new and different, because things change regularly on the Microsoft site. Should this happen, please read the sidebar titled "Coping With Change On The Web."

The menu options in the left column of the home page point to the most important sources of information in the MCP pages. Here's what to check out:

➤ **Certification Choices** Use this menu entry to read about the various certification programs that Microsoft offers.

➤ **Search/Find An Exam** Use this menu entry to pull up a search tool that lets you list all Microsoft exams and locate all exams relevant to any Microsoft certification (MCPS, MCSE, MCT, and so on) or those exams that cover a particular product. This tool is quite useful not only to examine the options, but also to obtain specific exam preparation information, because each exam has its own associated preparation guide. This is Exam 70-029.

➤ **Downloads** Use this menu entry to find a list of the files and practice exams that Microsoft makes available to the public. These include several items worth downloading, especially the Certification Update, the Personal Exam Prep (PEP) exams, various assessment exams, and a general exam study guide. Try to make time to peruse these materials before taking your first exam.

These are just the high points of what's available in the Microsoft Certified Professional pages. As you browse through them—and we strongly recommend that you do—you'll probably find other informational tidbits that are every bit as interesting and compelling.

Coping With Change On The Web

Sooner or later, all the information we've shared with you about the Microsoft Certified Professional pages and the other Web-based resources mentioned throughout the rest of this book will go stale or be replaced by newer information. In some cases, the URLs you find here might lead you to their replacements; in other cases, the URLs will go nowhere, leaving you with the dreaded "404 File not found" error message. When that happens, don't give up.

There's always a way to find what you want on the Web if you're willing to invest some time and energy. Most large or complex Web sites—and Microsoft's qualifies on both counts—offer a search engine. Looking back at Figure 1.1, you can see that a Search button appears along the top edge of the page. As long as you can get to Microsoft's site (it should stay at www.microsoft.com for a long while yet), you can use this tool to help you find what you need.

The more focused you can make a search request, the more likely the results will include information you can use. For example, you can search for the string "training and certification" to produce a lot of data about the subject in general, but if you're looking for the preparation guide for Exam 70-029, "Designing and Implementing a Database with Microsoft SQL Server 7.0," you'll be more likely to get there quickly if you use a search string similar to the following:

```
"Exam 70-029" AND "preparation guide"
```

Likewise, if you want to find the Training and Certification downloads, try a search string such as this:

```
"training and certification" AND "download page"
```

Finally, feel free to use general search tools—such as www.search.com, www.altavista.com, and www.excite.com—to search for related information. Although Microsoft offers the best information about its certification exams online, there are plenty of third-party sources of information, training, and assistance in this area that need not follow Microsoft's party line. The bottom line is this: If you can't find something where the book says it lives, start looking around. If worse comes to worst, you can always email us jeffg@soaringeagle.ltd.com. We just might have a clue.

Data Models

Terms you'll need to understand:

- √ Relational database
- √ Entities
- √ Attributes
- √ Relationships
- √ Primary keys
- √ Foreign keys
- √ Referential integrity
- √ Data integrity
- √ No nulls, no duplicates, and no changes
- √ Normalization
- √ Business rules
- √ Cardinality
- √ Optionality

Techniques you'll need to master:

- √ Converting from a logical to a physical model
- √ Being able to read a physical model
- √ Modeling steps
- √ Normalizing databases
- √ Denormalizing databases
- √ Designing for performance, maintainability, extensibility, availability, and security

Overview

Relational means based on relations. A relational database consists of *entities* ("tables") that are related to each other, and *tuples* ("rows"), or instances of data, and *attributes* ("columns") of data.

Databases can be designed many different ways. It is important that you remember how Microsoft wants you to design databases.

Database design includes two main phases: the logical modeling phase and the physical modeling phase. During the logical modeling phase, the designer gathers requirements and develops an RDBMS (Relational Database Management System) independent model. (An RDBMS allows you to store information in entities, perform mathematical intersections and deferences, and create unions among the entities.) Normalization is performed during the logical modeling phase.

During the physical modeling phase, the designer creates a model tuned for the application and the RDBMS being used; this is the model that is implemented.

> *Note: If you are familiar with a three-phase design methodology, you should be aware that Microsoft considers there to be only a logical and physical model. The conceptual phase is merged in with the logical modeling phase.*

All database design should follow these basic steps:

1. Gathering information

2. Identifying the objects

3. Modeling the objects

4. Identifying the types of information for each object

5. Identifying the relationships

6. Normalization

7. Conversion to physical model

8. Database creation

Steps 1 through 6 are part of the logical modeling phase. Step 7 is the physical modeling phase. And the final step, the implementation phase, is covered in the rest of this book.

Transaction Processing Databases

The two basic types of databases are the Online Transaction Processing (OLTP) database, the most common database type, and the decision support database

(DSS). An OLTP database processes day-to-day transactions. Normally, many users run a lot of well-defined transactions that both read and write data.

Decision Support Databases

A decision support database, also called a Decision Support System (DSS), is the other of the two basic types of databases. It analyzes data after the day-to-day processing has been done. One special type of DSS is a data warehouse. Normally, a few users run a few ad-hoc long-running queries against the data.

This database can be a copy of an OLTP database, or many OLTP databases merged into one database. They are also called *reporting databases*.

Logical Phase

The logical phase of database creation includes five basic steps: gathering requirements, identifying the entities, modeling the entities, identifying the types of information (attributes) for each entity, and identifying the relationships.

Gathering Requirements

The first step in designing a database is to figure out exactly how the database will be used and what data the database will hold. If the new system will replace an existing one, the existing system will provide most of the information you'll need. You should interview anyone who has anything to do with the current system to find out his or her function, workflow, and what information he or she needs to track. You also need to identify what has been changed from the existing system and identify any existing problems, limitations, and bottlenecks. Gather as much information as you can on what the system does and does not need to do. Basically, you should simply follow good requirement-gathering practices.

Modeling The Objects

Once the objects are identified, you should store the information about them. The best way to do this is with a visual model. This model should also track all of the basic information that you have gathered. You can use your database model as a reference when you implement the database.

You can use any of hundreds of different modeling tools, ranging from pencils and scratch paper, to word processing or spreadsheet programs, to software programs specifically dedicated to the job of data modeling for database designs. These models are called *entity relationship models*, or E/R diagrams for short. There are multiple different sets of symbols you can use. The tool you select will dictate your exact methodology and the symbols you use.

SQL Server Enterprise Manager includes visual design tools, such as the database design tool, that you can use to design and create objects in the database. The database design tool is mainly for physical design. You should use some other tool for the logical design phase.

Entities

An entity is a noun—a person, place, or thing. An entity is the subject or object of an action, and may be related to other entities. These entities consist of rows, or instances of data, and attributes, commonly thought of as "columns" in the row.

An entity can be a tangible thing, such as a person, place, or animal, or it can be something intangible, such as a banking transaction, a division in a company, or a payroll period. Most databases include a few main entities, with a lot of related child entities. The main entities are called *independent* entities, and they can exist without relying on any other entities. The related child entities are called *dependent* entities, and they must have a related parent table to exist.

An entity is normally represented as a rectangular box in an Entity Relationship model, with the entity name listed outside of the rectangle. Most modeling tools use a slightly different shape for dependent and independent entities. Usually a dependent entity has a slightly different look on the database diagram. Figure 2.1 shows an example of what an entity can look like on an E/R diagram.

Attributes

An attribute is a noun or property that describes an entity or a relationship. Attributes are often values, adjectives, or dates. All data stored in an attribute must be the same type and have the same properties.

After you've identified the main entities, the next step is to identify the attributes, the types of information that must be stored for each entity. In the logical modeling phase, a relationship can also have attributes.

An attribute is usually listed inside the entity rectangle. With most tools, you have to convert a relationship to an entity to track attributes on a relationship. Figure 2.2 shows an entity with attributes.

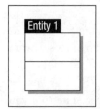

Figure 2.1 An independent entity called Entity 1.

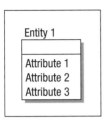

Figure 2.2   An entity with three attributes.

An attribute domain tracks the base information about the attribute. An attribute database independent data type and length are tracked, as are a list of valid values and any business rules that apply to the attribute. Some of the business rules that are tracked are *attribute optionality*, *changeable*, and *uniqueness*.

Attribute optionality tracks whether an attribute is a required part of the entity. It also tracks whether an attribute is an optional part and not a part of each tuple. If an attribute is not optional, it does not allow null values. This is also called *no nulls*.

You need to track whether the attribute is changeable. Some attributes cannot be changed after the row has been created.

The uniqueness of each attribute also needs to be tracked. An attribute can be unique, have a set number of duplicates, or have an unlimited number of duplicate entries. A unique attribute allows no duplicate values.

Entities And Data

When retrieving data, you get the data and a header back from SQL Server. The header states the name of each attribute. The publishers entity, in Table 2.1, has five attributes and three tuples (rows).

Keys

A *key* is a set of columns that define a table. There are five types of keys: candidate keys, primary keys, alternate keys, common keys, and foreign keys. Along with the five types of keys, there are two basic key classes: composite and singleton.

Table 2.1	Publisher table and data.			
pub_id	**pub_name**	**city**	**state**	**country**
0736	New Moon Books	Boston	MA	USA
0877	Binnet & Hardley	Washington	DC	USA
1389	Algodata Infosystems	Berkeley	CA	USA

A composite key is a key composed of more than one attribute. Composite keys force joins to be more complex. A singleton key, on the other hand, is any key made up of only one attribute.

Candidate Keys

A candidate key is any possible unique identifier for a row within a database table. A candidate, or surrogate, key can be either a singleton key or a composite key. Every entity must have at least one candidate key, but it is possible for a table to have more than one candidate key. Any candidate key that is not the primary key is called an *alternate* key. None of the attributes in a candidate key can allow nulls.

> Note: *Microsoft calls a candidate key a surrogate key. In most modeling paradigms, a surrogate key is an artificially generated key used in the physical design.*

Primary Keys

A primary key is one or more attributes that uniquely identify a row in an entity. One candidate key will become the primary key of the entity. Primary keys are often depicted as either being above a line in the list of attributes or they may have a special symbol in front of the attribute name. Figure 2.3 shows an entity with both key and non-key attributes.

Alternate Keys

Alternate keys are the candidate keys that do not become the primary key. There can be many candidate keys in an entity. Most modeling tools do not display alternate key groups.

Common Keys

A common key is any attribute used to join two entities. Normally, a common key is a foreign key. If you have common keys that are not foreign keys, you probably have not normalized the database.

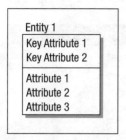

Figure 2.3   Key attributes.

Foreign Keys

A foreign key exists when one or more attributes in an entity refer to a primary key or an alternate key in an entity. A foreign key can only contain null values when it does not relate to the primary entity. In that case, if it is a composite key, all of the foreign key attributes must be null. Foreign keys will either have a special symbol to indicate which columns contain the foreign keys, or "FK" will appear before or after the key columns. Figure 2.4 shows two related entities and the foreign keys that result.

In Figure 2.4, Entity 1 has a composite key consisting of Key Attribute 1 and Key Attribute 2. Entity 2 has a foreign key from Entity 1. This foreign key says that the key columns from Entity 1 are part of Entity 2.

Keys are logical constructs, not physical items. In a relational database, some mechanism, like integrity constraints, needs to be implemented to maintain the keys.

Relationships

A relational database has the ability to relate or associate information about different entities in the database. You identify relationships in the design process by looking at the different tables and determining how they are logically related, then adding relational columns that establish a link from one table to another. If two entities are not related on candidate keys from one entity, then the database is not normalized. A relationship can exist between one or more entities.

A relationship is normally a verb, an action, or an ongoing interaction between entities. Relationships stand between entities and describe their interaction. In the logical design, a relationship may have attributes. Three basic items are tracked about every relationship: the relationship's name, cardinality, and optionality.

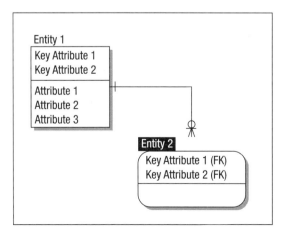

Figure 2.4   Foreign keys.

The relationship's name or action being performed is tracked. This action can be tracked in both directions, but most tools will only display the name in one direction. That is, if entity A is related to entity B, there is some named action. But there also is a named action from entity B to entity A. Figure 2.5 shows two entities with a named relationship between them.

The *relationship cardinality* tracks the number of rows in one entity to the number of rows in the other entity. There are three basic types of cardinality:

➤ **One to one** For each row in the first entity, there can be only one row in the second entity. And for each row in the second entity, there can be only one row in the first entity. An example would be an author who has only one current title. This relationship is often drawn as a single line across the relation near each entity.

➤ **One to many** For each row in the first entity, there can be multiple rows in the second entity. And for each row in the second entity, there can be only one row in the first. An example would be a publisher who has published many titles. A one-to-many relationship is often drawn as a single line near the "one" side and crow's feet near the other entity, the "many" side.

➤ **Many to many** For each row in the first entity, there can be multiple rows in the second entity. And for each row in the second entity, there can be multiple rows in the first entity. For example, an author can write many books, and a book can be written by more than one author. A many-to-many relationship is drawn with crow's feet near both entities.

With some special types of cardinality, you know what the exact number is for the many. But they are all treated the same.

The relationship optionality tracks whether the relationship must exist. This is tracked against all entities in the relationship. Two types of optionality are tracked: mandatory or optional.

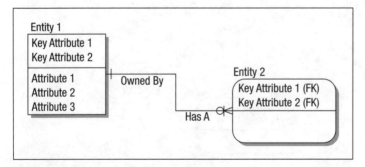

Figure 2.5 A named relationship.

➤ *Mandatory* specifies that the entity must have rows or the related entity cannot exist. A mandatory optionality can be represented with an extra single line near the mandatory side of the relationship.

➤ *Optional* specifies that the related entity does not have to have a related row. This is also called an *independent* relationship. An optional relationship can have an open circle near the optional side of the relationship.

The optionality is tracked for each entity in the relationship. All entities can have the same optionality in the relationship. Or, the entities can have different optionality. That is, one entity can be mandatory and the other entity can be optional.

Two special types of relationships are commonly used:

➤ A *dependent* relationship is a mandatory relationship in which the first entity's key columns are part of the second entity's primary key. This relationship is also called a parent-child relationship.

➤ A *self-recursive* relationship is an entity related to itself. You may also hear this type of relationship referred to as an "elephant ear" relationship. A self-recursive relationship cannot be a mandatory relationship; at some point in the chain, you cannot have a parent or a child. Figure 2.6 shows a self-recursive relationship.

Most tools do not allow you to directly draw relationships between more than two entities. If you need to draw relationships between more than two entities, you must use an *associative entity* as a focal point of the relationship. An associative entity is another name for a relationship. It is an entity whose primary key is made up of the key attributes of two or more entities. Figure 2.7 shows a three-way relationship with an associative entity between the three related entities.

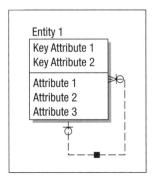

Figure 2.6   A self-recursive relationship.

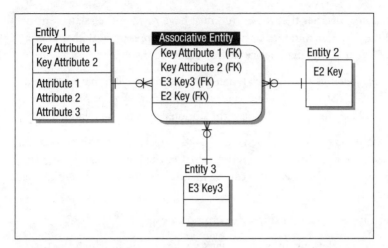

Figure 2.7   An associative entity.

Normalization

Normalization describes the act of removing redundant data. A data element should be stored once and only once within a database. There are five common forms of normalization based upon mathematical relation theory. You may have heard of forms beyond five, but they have only theoretical implications. Most of the time, you strive to get a database in third normal form. The forms are as follows:

➤ **First normal form**   Eliminates repeating groups.

➤ **Second normal form**   Eliminates redundant data.

➤ **Third normal form**   Eliminates attributes not dependent on the primary key.

➤ **Fourth normal form**   Isolates independent multiple relationships.

➤ **Fifth normal form**   Isolates semantically related multiple relationships.

Most databases are normalized to third normal form.

Normalization involves following a set of methods to remove redundant data. A normalized entity should contain a set of attributes that are all related to the entity's primary key. This usually results in creating more entities with fewer data attributes in each entity.

Following these steps can improve performance and allow for faster sorting and index creation, more clustered indexes, narrower and more compact indexes, fewer indexes per entity, improving inserts and updates, and fewer nulls.

A normalized database tends to be more flexible. As the queries change or the data you need to store changes, you will usually make fewer changes to the database if it is normalized—and any changes you make have less impact. For example, if you have repeating groups and you need to add another instance of the group to a non-normalized database, you would have to change the entity and the queries accessing the entities. If the database was normalized, you would not have to change the database or your queries to accommodate this.

First Normal Form

To place an entity first normal form, you eliminate repeating groups and make each attribute contain only one value. That is, each attribute should be stored only once in an entity. The following entity, Home, is not in first normal form because there are multiple attributes in which to track the owners. Figure 2.8 shows an entity that has not been normalized.

In Figure 2.8, Owner1 to Owner N attributes are repeating attributes. You resolve this by making a separate entity for each set of related attributes; you will be left with two entities. Figure 2.9 shows the Home entity normalized into first normal form.

Second Normal Form

In second normal form, you eliminate redundant data. This rule also implies that every entity should have a unique identifier, or primary key. A redundant attribute is one that is not dependent on the primary key. If it is a multipart key, the attribute should be dependent on all parts of the key. To be in second normal form, you must already have been in first normal form.

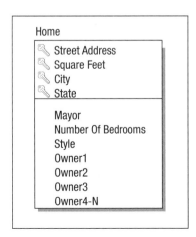

Figure 2.8   An unnormalized entity.

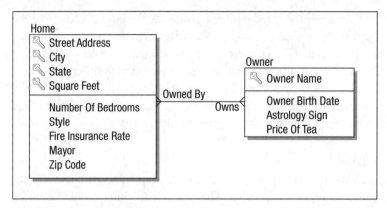

Figure 2.9 The first normal form.

Continuing with our homeowner example, we see that the previous model is not in second normal form, because the Price Of Tea attribute has nothing to do with the homeowner. Because the Mayor attribute is not dependent on the whole primary key, the Home entity is not in second normal form.

You fix the data model by removing Price Of Tea (which we decide not to track anymore) and by putting Mayor in its own entity. Figure 2.10 shows the home-owner database in second normal form.

Third Normal Form

The third normal form states that you need to eliminate attributes not dependent on the whole key. Any entity in third normal form must also be in second

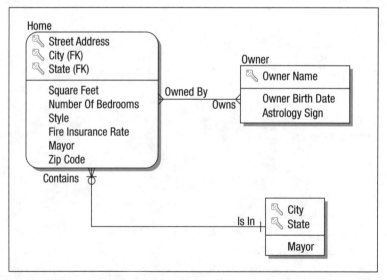

Figure 2.10 The second normal form.

normal form. This is the most common form for databases. Think of it like this: Each attribute must be dependent on the key, the whole key, and nothing but the key. Any entity that is in second normal form and does not have a multipart primary key is automatically in third normal form.

For example, even though each person has an astrology sign, the astrology sign is dependent on the birthdate. It should not be in the same entity as the rest of the owner information. Figure 2.11 shows the homeowner database in third normal form.

BCNF

A normal form exists between third and fourth called Boyce Codd Normal Form (BCNF). This form says that if there is more than one set of primary keys, the entity should be split into one entity for each candidate key. To be in BCNF, the entity must begin from third normal form. Any entity with only one candidate key that is in third normal form is automatically in BCNF.

Fourth Normal Form

Fourth normal form deals with isolating multivalued dependencies. A multivalued dependency exists when two completely independent attributes are brought together by a third attribute, typically a key attribute. To be in fourth normal form, the entity must begin from third normal form or BCNF.

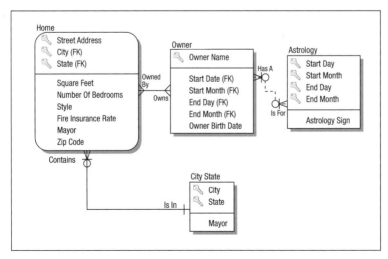

Figure 2.11   The third normal form.

Figure 2.12   A movie entity.

The entity in Figure 2.12 is in BCNF normal form, with all columns being keys. It is not in fourth normal form, because Director is dependent on Movie Name, and Actor is dependent on Movie Name, but there is no relationship between Director and Actor.

A movie can have many directors and many actors independent of each other. A director can direct multiple movies and an actor can be in multiple movies. The movie entity should be split into two entities for it to be in fourth normal form. Figure 2.13 shows the movie entity in fourth normal form.

Fifth Normal Form

Fifth normal form isolates semantically related multiple relationships. This mainly deals with three-way or greater relationships. It is used to make sure that the three-way relationships will generate the correct data. The entities must first be in fourth normal form. An entity is in fifth normal form if decomposing the table into smaller tables does not result in any lost information. That is, after an entity is decomposed into three or more smaller entities, the entities must then be able to be joined together to reform the original entity.

Data Integrity

Data integrity is the set of rules that ensure the validity of the data within a relational database. The four types of data integrity rules are:

➤ **Entity integrity**   Enforces that each row in an entity has a unique identifier and must contain data.

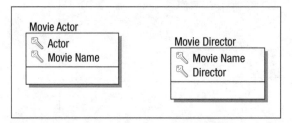

Figure 2.13   Normalized movie entities.

➤ **Domain integrity**   Enforces the set of valid values stored in an attribute.

➤ **Referential integrity**   Refers to the rules that ensure that primary and foreign keys remain consistent whenever rows are inserted, updated, and deleted. Referential integrity (RI) is the quality, within a relational database, of all foreign keys having corresponding primary keys. You should enforce RI when you're performing actions that modify rows in an entity. You need to evaluate every action to determine whether it will remove or modify primary keys where related foreign keys exist. Also, whether it will create or modify a foreign key for a primary key that does not exist.

➤ **User-defined integrity**   Used to define integrity rules that do not fit into one of the other types of integrity rules.

Business Rules

Business rules define the restrictions imposed on the data by the business. They govern the more complex and specific rules relating to your organization. Business rules may include data integrity. They are different from other rules in that their purpose is to make sure that the business operates correctly.

Physical Model

After creating your logical model, you need to make the physical model. This model represents the database as you are going to implement it. It defines the physical objects that you are going to implement.

Converting A Logical Model To A Physical Model

When you're converting a logical model to a physical model, you convert entities to tables, and attributes to columns. Relationships between entities can be converted to a table or left as foreign keys.

You should follow these general rules when designing the physical database:

➤ Each table should have a unique identifier (primary key).

➤ All data in a table should be for one entity.

➤ A table should avoid nullable attributes.

➤ A table should not have repeating columns.

Keys

Primary keys should be converted to primary key constraints—you can also convert them to unique constraints. It is also alright, but not recommended, to convert primary keys to unique indexes.

Candidate keys should be converted to unique constraints. Alternately, you can convert canidate keys to unique indexes.

Foreign keys should be converted to foreign key constraints. You can also enforce them with triggers. You should create an index on the foreign key columns, if you are enforcing the foreign keys.

Enforcing Integrity

When you're converting your logical model to a physical model, you should enforce your integrity. You can use several different options with the different integrity types. Table 2.2 lists the integrity type, Microsoft's recommended enforcement option, and other options to enforce integrity.

If possible, you should not use triggers to enforce referential integrity or user-defined integrity. However, triggers are more flexible than constraints.

Denormalization

It is possible to over-normalize a database causing every data retrieval to have to join multiple tables. A query should normally access four or fewer tables. If you are using more than four entities, the database is probably over-normalized.

In most databases, third normal form is as far as you should go. If you go further, you will probably end up having to denormalize the database.

Denormalization is the process of adding redundant data back into the database. Common denormalization techniques are: combining multiple tables into one table, storing the same columns in multiple tables, or storing summary or calculated information in a table.

Table 2.2 Integrity enforcement.		
Integrity Type	**Recommended Options**	**Other Options**
Entity	PRIMARY KEY, UNIQUE KEY, IDENTITY	Unique indexes
Domain	FOREIGN KEY, CHECK, DEFAULT, NULL/NOT NULL	Data types, defaults, rules
Referential	FOREIGN KEY, CHECK	triggers
User-Defined	ALL	Constraints, triggers, stored procedures

Performance

You need to take performance into consideration when creating your physical database. The physical database should take advantage of SQL Server features.

A database application needs to perform all of its functions within a given time frame. But certain functions tend to be more important and must be performed faster. You should be certain that your design supports the performance for these functions.

Large tables and complex functions often cause bottlenecks in a database. You will need to take extra care when designing the tables used in these areas. You need to make sure that you have the correct indexes and table design.

Another item to consider is what happens to your database design as the number of users increase. A design will often work fine for just a few users, but as more users are added to the system, the performance can drastically decrease.

When implementing the database, you normally get better performance as you add faster or more hardware components to the server machine. If you add more memory, SQL Server can cache more data. The more and faster disk drives, the better SQL Server can spread I/O out to perform multiple tasks concurrently. If you have multiple CPUs, then SQL Server can handle more concurrent user requests.

You need to look into creating indexes that correspond with your queries. If you access a table by lots of different columns, you need to consider creating many indexes to speed up that access. But remember, too many indexes will slow down inserts and updates.

Maintainability

SQL Server requires several maintenance tasks, such as database consistency checking and database backups. You should consider these tasks when you're designing the physical database. You will need to make sure you minimize the impact on users and the amount of maintenance that will need to be done.

By keeping the database size as small as possible, you will reduce the time needed to perform many maintenance tasks. If the database is normalized, that will help reduce its size. This will speed up the backup and restore tasks.

Implement a design that will keep the number of rows in the active tables to a minimum. You can do this by partitioning the table, or by archiving out old data. This will speed up index creation time.

Security

When implementing a database, you need to set up your security plan. You will need to determine which users can access which table.

SQL Enterprise Manager Database Drawing Tool

SQL Server Enterprise Manager provides a database diagramming tool that you can use to maintain SQL Server databases. It can only maintain the database you are directly connected to, which is the database in which those database objects are stored.

This tool can perform most of the standard database implementation functions. It can view tables and their relationships. You can make changes and analyze the new diagram without changing the underlying database. If you decide that you do not like the changes, you can discard the changes you don't like. If you like the changes, you can save the diagram and have the changes take effect immediately, or you can build a change script to apply later.

Practice Questions

Question 1

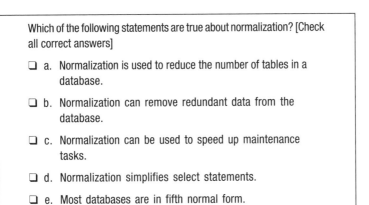

Which of the following statements are true about normalization? [Check all correct answers]

❑ a. Normalization is used to reduce the number of tables in a database.

❑ b. Normalization can remove redundant data from the database.

❑ c. Normalization can be used to speed up maintenance tasks.

❑ d. Normalization simplifies select statements.

❑ e. Most databases are in fifth normal form.

Answers b and c are correct. Normalization is used to remove redundant data and it can speed up maintenance tasks by keeping table sizes smaller. The normalization process normally creates more tables, which makes answer a incorrect. With more tables, select statements tend to have more joins. This makes the select statements more complex and answer d incorrect. Answer e is incorrect—most databases are in third normal form.

Question 2

Which of the following are integrity types? [Check all correct answers]

❑ a. Domain integrity

❑ b. Attribute integrity

❑ c. Entity integrity

❑ d. Referential integrity

❑ e. Table integrity

Answers a, c, and d are all valid integrity types. Answers b and e are not integrity types.

Question 3

> Entity integrity should be enforced using which of the following? [Check all correct answers]
>
> ❑ a. Primary keys
>
> ❑ b. Foreign keys
>
> ❑ c. Unique indexes
>
> ❑ d. Unique constraints
>
> ❑ e. Identity

Answers a, d, and e are correct. Answer c is incorrect because although unique indexes can enforce entity integrity, Microsoft does not recommend it. And answer b is incorrect because foreign keys are used to enforce referential integrity, not entity integrity.

Question 4

> What should be done to convert the entity US Tax Payer into first normal form?
>
> US Tax Payer contains the following attributes:
>
> Social Security Number, First Name, Last Name, Street Address, City, State, Phone Number 1, Phone Number 2, Phone Number 3, Phone Number 4.
>
> ○ a. Combine the phone numbers into one field
>
> ○ b. Make an entity to contain the phone numbers
>
> ○ c. Move City and State to another entity
>
> ○ d. All of the above
>
> ○ e. None of the above

Answer b is correct; an entity in first normal form will not have any repeating groups. Answer a is incorrect; it would get rid of repeating groups, but the new column would contain more than one data element. Answer c is incorrect because even after moving City and State to another entity, US Tax Payer will still have repeating groups.

Question 5

For the entity US Tax Payer, what attributes should be used as the primary key attributes for it to be in third normal form?

After normalizing US Tax Payer into first normal form, it contains the following attributes:

Social Security Number, First Name, Last Name, Street Address, City, State.

- ○ a. Social Security Number, Last Name
- ○ b. First Name, Last Name
- ○ c. First Name, Last Name, City
- ○ d. First Name, Last Name, Street Address, City, State
- ○ e. None of the above

Answer e is correct. An entity in third normal form has all attributes dependent on the complete set of primary key attributes. The attribute Social Security Number is the primary key attribute for this entity. Answer a is incorrect; the data in the table is dependent on Social Security Number, a person's last name does not help in identifying the record. Answers b, c, and d are wrong, because the data in the table does not depend on the columns listed.

Need To Know More?

 Coffman, Gayle. *SQL Server 7: The Complete Reference*, Osborne/ McGraw-Hill, Berkley, CA, 1999. ISBN 0-07-882494-X. Chapter 19 provides an overview of database design.

 Date, Chris J. *An Introduction to Database Systems*, Addison-Wesley, Reading, MA, 1994. ISBN 0-201-54329-X. The complete book provides a detailed description of the theory behind relational database systems.

 Fleming, Candace C. and Barbara Vonhalle. *Handbook of Relational Database Design*, Addison-Wesley, Reading, MA, 1988. ISBN 0-201-11434-8. The book provides a good step-by-step approach to designing a database. Even though it is older, it is a real good reference book on the subject.

 MS SQL Server Books Online has a section on database design in the Optimizing Database Performance section.

 Search the TechNet CD or its online version at **www.microsoft.com**.

 www.microsoft.com/sql
Find up-to-date information about using SQL Server here.

System Databases, Tables, And Stored Procedures

3

Terms you'll need to understand:

√ Metadata

√ Data dictionary

√ System database

√ System table

√ **master** database

√ **tempdb** database

√ **model** database

√ **msdb** database

√ System stored procedure

Technique you'll need to master:

√ How to examine system tables and databases to discern information

When you use SQL Server, you must store information about how the database's data is stored. Information about data storage is called *metadata*. Metadata is stored in a *data dictionary* (a set of system tables), which is populated by **CREATE** and **ALTER** statements. SQL Server's data dictionary is organized into tables, like all other SQL Server data.

To give a metadata example, when you create a table, you add a row to the **SYSOBJECTS** table, which contains a row for every database object; you add a row to the **SYSINDEXES** table, which contains a row for every table and index; and you add many rows to the **SYSCOLUMNS** table, one per column of data.

In addition to system tables, many of which are in every database, there are also several *system databases*, which contain system-specific information and aid in tasks, such as replication. SQL has four system databases: **MASTER** (which contains high-level server information), **TEMPDB** (which contains temporary tables specific to individual processes or queries), **MODEL** (the template for new databases to be created), and **MSDB** (information for SQL Server Agent scheduling).

There are two types of system tables, those that are in every database (containing information or metadata about each database), and those only in the system databases (those that contain server-specific, vs. database-specific information).

Finally, there are a variety of system stored procedures that you can use to work with system tables. You can use stored procedures to assist you in tasks such as populating system tables and querying them (for example, an **SP_WHO** will give you information about all server processes that are currently running). System procedures are important for two reasons: first, because they're shortcuts you will use to get information out of the system tables, and second, because you'll use them to populate the system tables.

System Databases

System databases exist to seperate server-specific data from your user data. Think of it as a high-level form of normalization.

Microsoft SQL Server systems have four system databases: master, tempdb, model, and msdb. The following sections describe SQL Server's four system databases in detail.

master

The *master* database records the server-level information for a SQL Server system. This includes logins (access to the server), server configuration settings, and databases and their extensions to the physical devices (that is, when you write to a database, the page is actually going out to a file on a disk). All of this information goes into system tables.

Because the **MASTER** database contains SQL Server-specific information for your system, as well as certain OS-level information (some memory parameters, physical file names, and so on), you should ensure that you *always* have a backup copy of the **MASTER** database.

tempdb

The *tempdb* database holds SQL Server's temporary tables and temporary stored procedures. This means that tempdb contains temporary tables that are intentionally created by developers, as well as temporary tables and intermediary result sets required by SQL Server to resolve queries. Furthermore, the **TEMPDB** database also fills any other temporary storage needs, such as during the resolution of **GROUP BY** clauses or unions.

Keep in mind that **TEMPDB** is a global resource. In other words, **TEMPDB** stores the temporary tables and stored procedures for all users connected to the system. Because temporary tables and stored procedures are automatically dropped if a user disconnects, and no connections are active when the system is shut down, **TEMPDB** never contains data that needs to be saved from one session of SQL Server to the next. The **TEMPDB** database is re-created from the definition in **SYSDATABASES** and the contents of the **MODEL** database every time SQL Server starts. This guarantees a fresh, clean database (one that is empty of any data not in the model database).

The **TEMPDB** database *autogrows* (that is, it expands the disk file space dynamically) as needed (autogrow is a new feature introduced in SQL Server 7). Each time the system is started, tempdb is reset to its default size, which is the size of the model database. You can avoid the overhead of having **TEMPDB** autogrow by using **ALTER TABLE** to increase the size of tempdb.

 In prior versions of SQL Server, tempdb could be kept in RAM— this is no longer an option.

model

The *model* database is the template from which other databases are created. When a **CREATE DATABASE** statement is issued, the **MODEL** is copied into the new database, and then the rest of the new database is filled with empty pages, ready to be allocated to tables for insertion of additional data. As mentioned earlier, **TEMPDB** is created every time SQL Server is started; therefore, **TEMPDB** needs to use the **MODEL** database each time SQL Server is started. This means that the **MODEL** database must always exist on a SQL Server system.

msdb

The *msdb* database is used by the SQL Server Agent for scheduling alerts and jobs, and recording operators. Each database in a SQL Server contains system tables that are used to record the data needed by the SQL Server components (the metadata).

File Locations

In SQL Server version 7, every database has its own set of system files. By default, the files are stored in C:\Mssql7\Data. Table 3.1 shows the system file's names and default size for a typical setup.

 Data and logs are kept in separate files. With version 7, there is no attempt to make the transaction log look like a real table, as there was in previous versions (the syslogs table).

In earlier versions of SQL Server, the **MASTER** and **MODEL** system databases were stored in a single file, known as the *master device*. The first 2MB allocation of **TEMPDB** also resided on the master device. Having these databases residing in a single file could sometimes cause space problems in the **MASTER** and **MODEL** databases. Now, because each database has its own set of files, each database can grow without affecting other databases.

Table 3.1   Default system files.

Database File	Physical File Name	Default Size (Typical Setup)
master primary data	Master.mdf	7.5MB
master log	Mastlog.ldf	1MB
tempdb primary data	Tempdb.mdf	8MB
tempdb log	Templog.ldf	0.5MB
model primary data	Model.mdf	0.75MB
model log	Modellog.ldf	0.75MB
msdb primary data	Msdbdata.mdf	3.5MB
msdb log	Msdblog.ldf	0.75MB

System Tables

System tables are tables in the database like any other, except that they contain information about the database's contents or about the server, rather than user information. They are automatically populated when you issue **CREATE** statements or issue specific system store procedures. You *should not* directly update system tables. Furthermore, you cannot place triggers on the system tables; doing so might alter the operation of the system.

Basically, system tables store two types of information: server-wide information and database-specific information. As you might guess, server information is located in the master database only. The database-specific information is located in each individual database. Tables 3.2 through 3.5 show the list of system tables by database. Table 3.2 presents the tables that store server-level system information in the master database. Table 3.3 presents the tables that store information used by SQL Server Agent. Table 3.4 presents the tables that store information used by database backup and restore operations, and

Table 3.2 Server-specific tables (located in the master database).	
Table Name	**Contents**
sysallocations	One row per allocation unit.
sysaltfiles	One row per database file.
syscharsets	One row per installed character set and sort order.
sysconfigures	Defined system configuration, which will take effect when the server reboots.
syscurconfigs	System configuration as running.
sysdatabases	One row per database.
sysdevices	One row per device.
syslanguages	One row per installed language.
syslockinfo	One row for each placed lock.
syslogins	One row for each server account.
sysmessages	One row for each server-defined message.
sysoledbusers	Contains one row for each user and password mapping for the specified linked server.
sysperfinfo	Internal performance counters for the Performance Monitor.
sysprocesses	One row per connected process.
sysremotelogins	One row per remote account.
sysservers	One row per accessible server, including the current one.

Table 3.5 presents the tables that store database-level system information for each database.

You do not need to memorize all of the system tables or the contents of each, but it is useful to know the type of information that is stored in each system table. The table contents are not listed in Tables 3.3 and 3.4 because the information is not necessary to know for the test.

Table 3.3 Server-specific tables for system agent (located in the msdb database).
Table Name
sysalerts
syscategories
sysdownloadlist
sysjobhistory
sysjobs
sysjobschedules
sysjobservers
sysjobsteps
sysnotifications
sysoperators
systargetservergroupmembers
systargetservergroups
systargetservers
systaskids

Table 3.4 Tables in the msdb database.
Table Name
backupfile
backupmediafamily
backupmediaset
backupset
restorefile
restorefilegroup
restorehistory

Table 3.5	Database-specific tables (located in all databases).
Table Name	**Contents**
syscolumns	One row for each column in each table.
syscomments	Creation text of all user objects.
sysconstraints	One row per defined constraint.
sysdepends	One row for each object dependency.
sysfilegroups	One row for each file group.
sysfiles	One row for each file.
sysforeignkeys	One row per foreign key.
sysfulltextcatalogs	Set of full-text catalogs.
sysindexes	One row per index and table.
sysindexkeys	Information on each column in an index.
sysmembers	One row for each member of a database role.
sysobjects	One row for each database object.
syspermissions	User permissions granted and revoked.
sysprotects	Security role permissions granted or denied.
sysreferences	Mapping of foreign key constraints.
systypes	User-defined data types.
sysusers	One for each user and group.

System Stored Procedures

You should only modify system tables through the existing system stored procedures. System stored procedures are categorized by their use, as shown in Table 3.6.

 Unless specifically documented as being otherwise, all system stored procedures return a value of zero, which indicates success. This sometimes frustrates folks who are new to SQL Server, because many front ends do not report a zero return code, and correspondingly, there is no "All done!" positive feedback to the user.

After using the system-defined stored procedures for a while, you may find that you'd like to customize them or use your own.

Table 3.6 System stored procedure categories.

Category	Description
Catalog Procedures	Implement ODBC data dictionary functions and isolate ODBC applications from changes to underlying system tables.
Cursor Procedures	Implement cursor variable functionality.
Distributed Queries Procedures	Implement and manage Distributed Queries.
SQL Server Agent Procedures	Enable SQL Server Agent to manage scheduled and event-driven activities.
Replication Procedures	Manage, enable, or disable replication tasks.
Security Procedures	Enable security.
System Procedures	Assist in general maintenance of the SQL Server.
Web Assistant Procedures	Assist the Web Assistant.
General Extended Procedures	Provide an interface from SQL Server to external programs for various mainte-nance activities.
SQL Mail Extended Procedures	Perform email operations from within SQL Server.
SQL Server Profiler Extended Procedures	Provide SQL Server Profiler capabilities. When using the shared memory network library, SQL Server does not support impersonation unless connected by using Windows NT Authentication. To execute a SQL Server Profiler Extended Procedure against a local server through SQL Server Query Analyzer, use Windows NT Authentication.
OLE Automation Procedures	Allow standard OLE automation objects to be used within a standard Transact-SQL batch.
Data Transformation Services Procedures	Manage data transformation services persistence methods and the namespace.

Administrator-Defined System Stored Procedures

You, as an administrator, may choose to create your own system-stored procedures. This has many benefits, not the least of which is that system stored procedures automatically change database context to the database in which you are current. (By default, stored procedures execute within the context of the database in which they are created; if you create a stored procedure in the pubs database, it will always look for objects in the pubs database, even if it is executed from another database.)

To create your own system procedures, use the master database, prefix your stored procedure name with *sp_*, and grant execute permission to those to whom you'd like to be able to run it. For example:

```
create proc sp_listtables as select name from
sysobjects where type = 'U'
```

Practice Questions

Question 1

Which database(s) contains system tables? [Check all correct answers]

❑ a. master

❑ b. model

❑ c. tempdb

❑ d. msdb

❑ e. All of the above

Answer e is correct. All databases contain system tables.

Question 2

Which database(s) contains server-specific system tables? [Check all correct answers]

❑ a. master

❑ b. model

❑ c. tempdb

❑ d. msdb

❑ e. All of the above

Answers a (it contains server-specific information on configuration) and d (it contains information for System Agent) are correct. Answers b and c are incorrect, because they contain only database-specific system tables.

Question 3

Which system table contains information pertaining to who may access a server?

- ○ a. syslogins
- ○ b. sysusers
- ○ c. sysaccesses
- ○ d. sysdatabaseaccess
- ○ e. None of the above

Answer a is correct. Answer b is database-specific; options c and d don't exist.

Question 4

Which system table contains information pertaining to who may access a database?

- ○ a. syslogins
- ○ b. sysusers
- ○ c. sysaccesses
- ○ d. sysdatabaseaccess
- ○ e. None of the above

Answer b is correct. Answer a is database-specific; options c and d don't exist.

Need To Know More?

 Coffman, Gayle. *SQL Server 7: The Complete Reference*, Osborne/McGraw-Hill, Berkley, CA, 1999. ISBN 0-07-882494-X. Chapter 22 describes system tables.

 McGehee, Brad and Matthew Shepker. *Using Microsoft SQL Server 7.0*, QUE, Indianapolis, Indiana, 1998. ISBN 0-7897-1628-3. Chapter 2 describes system databases.

 MS SQL Server Books Online provides a complete list of the system tables look in the index under "system tables" and system databases look in the index under "system databases".

 Search the TechNet CD or its online version at **www.microsoft.com**.

 www.microsoft.com/sql
Find up-to-date information about using SQL Server here.

Databases
And Files

. . . .

Terms you'll need to understand:

√ Database

√ File

√ File group

Techniques you'll need to master:

√ Creating and using databases

√ Altering databases

√ Creating file groups

√ Altering file groups

√ Configuring databases

One of the basic structures in SQL Server is the database. It provides the context in which data is stored and controlled.

Database Overview

Besides the four system databases, SQL Server can handle up to 32,734 user-defined databases. All SQL Server database objects revolve around the use, access, and integrity of tables.

A database is:

➤ A collection of tables that relate to one another.

➤ A linked set of page allocations in SQL Server storage.

➤ The unit of data for backup.

➤ Two or more files.

➤ An important unit of data for security and control.

Database Files

A database consists of two or more database files, each of which may be used by only one database. A file has two names: a logical name and a physical name. The logical name follows standard SQL Server object naming limitations. A physical file name can be the fully qualified name of any local or networked file. Unlike previous versions of SQL Server, database files can automatically grow larger. At most, a database can consist of 32,768 files. The three types of files are:

➤ **Primary file** Used to store database startup information and data. There is only one primary file in a database. Its standard file extension is .mdf.

➤ **Secondary files** One or more optional areas in which to store data. They can be used to spread database reads and writes across multiple disks. Their standard file extension is .ndf.

➤ **Log files** Used to store the database transaction log. There must be at least one log file per database. Their standard file extension is .ldf. The log keeps track of changes made to the data before it is actually written to the data files.

Note: Every database must have at least one primary file and one log file.

SQL Server does not enforce file name extensions, but we recommend that you follow Microsoft's convention. Each database file can belong to only one database.

Database File Groups

File groups are a way of linking together a set of files. A file can belong to at most one group. Log files, however, cannot belong to any group. A file group is used to spread disk reads and writes out across multiple disks. If a file group has more than one file, writes to that group are spread out across the files in the group. At most, a database can have 32,768 file groups.

Every database has a primary file group. This group contains the primary data file and all data files that are not specifically assigned to another file group. Its name is PRIMARY.

Tables and indexes can be specifically assigned to any file group. If they are not assigned to a group, they are placed in a default file group. Only one file group can be configured as the default file group at any given time.

File And File Group Issues

A file or file group can only be used by one database. A file, in turn, can be a member of only one file group. You must also have a separate file for data and log information. Log files are never part of any file groups.

Most of the time, your database will meet your performance requirements with a single data file and a single log file. If you plan to use multiple files, use the primary file only for system tables and objects. Then create at least one secondary file to store user data and objects. You should create files or file groups on as many different local physical disks as are available, and you should place objects that compete heavily for space in different file groups. For performance reasons, you should not use network drives for your database.

Place different tables that are used in the same queries into different file groups. This will improve performance due to parallel disk I/O searching for joined data. Also, place heavily accessed tables and the nonclustered indexes belonging to those tables on different file groups. This will improve performance due to parallel I/O if the files are located on different physical disks. For better performance, log files should not be on the same devices as data files. If at all possible, you should put no operating system files on any disk that contains a SQL Server data or log file.

Devices

It is still possible in SQL Server to create devices, or predefined data files, before you create the database, using the **DISK INIT** command. However, Microsoft recommends that you do not use the **DISK INIT** command. This command is included in version 7.0 only for backward compatibility. The syntax of the **DISK INIT** command is as follows:

```
DISK INIT
    NAME = 'logical_name',
    PHYSNAME = 'physical_name',
    VDEVNO = virtual_device_number,
    SIZE = number_of_2K_blocks
    [, VSTART = virtual_address]
```

The device will then show up in the **SYSDEVICES** table in the **MASTER** database. This table will also contain any dump devices and the devices for the **MASTER** database, the **MODEL** database, and for the **TEMPDB** database.

Creating Databases

Databases are created with the **CREATE DATABASE** command. Any user with the system administrator role, or anyone to whom the system administrator has specifically given permissions (may create a database). The syntax for the **CREATE DATABASE** command is as follows:

```
CREATE DATABASE db_name
  [ ON [PRIMARY] ([ NAME = logical_file_name, ]
          FILENAME = 'os_file_name'
          [, SIZE = size]
          [, MAXSIZE = { max_size | UNLIMITED } ]
          [, FILEGROWTH = growth_increment] )
          | {FILEGROUP filegroup_name FILEDEFINITIONS}
          [,...n] ]
  [LOG ON {[ NAME = logical_file_name, ]
          FILENAME = 'os_file_name'
          [, SIZE = size]
          [, MAXSIZE = { max_size | UNLIMITED } ]
          [, FILEGROWTH = growth_increment] } [,...n]
      [FOR LOAD | FOR ATTACH]
```

You can use the **CREATE DATABASE** command to assign devices created with the **DISK INIT** command to a database. We recommend that you use the **CREATE DATABASE** command to create the database files and assign them to the database. When you're creating a database, if you do not specify both a primary and a log file, whichever one (or both) that is missing will be created for you with a default name. The physical file will be located in the default data file location with the name *database_name*.mdf for the primary file and *database_name*_log.ldf for the log file.

If you do not specify a file size, the database files will be the same as the **MODEL** database's primary data device for the primary file and 1MB for the log file and any secondary data files. The size can be larger if your model database primary file is larger than 1MB. Although it is optional to specify files and sizes, in practice you should always specify them. SQL Server creates a database in two steps—the first step is to copy the **MODEL** database into the new database, and the second step is to initialize all unused space.

The parameters for the **CREATE DATABASE** command are as follows:

➤ **PRIMARY** specifies the file as a primary device.

➤ **NAME** is the logical file name; it defaults to the file name.

➤ **FILENAME** is the fully qualified disk file name.

➤ **SIZE** is the initial size of the file. The minimum size for a log file is 512K.

➤ **MAXSIZE** is the largest size the file can grow to.

➤ **UNLIMITED** specifies that the file can grow to an unlimited size.

➤ **FILEGROWTH** is the increment of growth in megabytes (MB), kilobytes (KB), or a percentage (%). The default is 10 percent.

➤ **FOR LOAD** is for backward compatibility with SQL Scripts written for previous versions of SQL Server.

➤ **FOR ATTACH** specifies that the database files already exist.

The user that created the database owns the database. All database configuration options are copied from the **MODEL** database, unless the database is created with the **FOR ATTACH** options. In that case, the database configuration options are read in from the existing database files. Here are some examples of the **CREATE DATABASE** command:

```
/* database with default size on default files */
CREATE DATABASE test1

/* database size is 2 megabytes for data and default size for log*/
CREATE DATABASE test2
    ON (FILENAME ='c:\d1.mdf', SIZE = 2 , NAME = 'd1')

/* database is 20 MB, with a 10 MB primary and one Filegroup
** and log 10 MB */
CREATE DATABASE test3
ON PRIMARY (FILENAME ='c:\test3.mdf',
            SIZE = 10 , NAME = 'd1'),
FILEGROUP g1 (FILENAME ='c:\g1.mdf',
            SIZE = 10 , NAME = 'g1')
LOG ON (FILENAME ='c:\test3.ldf',
            SIZE = 10 , NAME = 'log1')
```

Altering Databases

With SQL Server 7.0, you usually won't need to alter a database. You may still want to add files and file groups, shrink a database size, change a database owner, change a database name, or reconfigure an existing file or file group. You can do everything except rename a database when the database is in multiuser mode.

Removing A Database

You can remove databases with the **DROP DATABASE** command. The syntax for the **DROP DATABASE** command is:

```
DROP DATABASE database_name[, n]
```

You can drop one or more databases. When you remove a database, the files it uses are deleted. If the database is currently in use, you cannot drop the database. After you've dropped a database, the database and its files cannot be used.

Changing A Database Owner

You can change the database owner with the **sp_changedbowner** stored procedure. You can change the database owner to any login that is not currently a user of the database. If there are existing aliases to the current dbo, you can specify whether you want them to be assigned to the new dbo. The syntax of the change database owner stored procedure is as follows:

```
sp_changedbowner [@loginame =] 'login' [,[@map =] drop_alias_flag]
```

Only users with system administration permissions can change a database owner.

 You cannot change the owner of system databases.

When you change a database's owner, you must first be in the database you want to change. The following example shows the use of the **sp_changedbowner** procedure:

```
USE MyDb
go
sp_changedbowner @loginame='NewDBO'
go
```

Renaming Databases

If you want to change the name of a database, SQL Server provides the **sp_renamedb** stored procedure. The following listing shows the syntax of the procedure used to change a database name:

```
sp_renamedb "old_name","new_name"
```

Only the system administrator can change a database name. To change a name, the database must first be put into single user mode (see "Configuring Databases," later in this chapter). Remember to put the database back into multiple user mode when you are done. Here's how to use the **sp_renamedb** procedure:

```
use master
go
sp_dboption MyDB,'single','true'
go
sp_renamedb MyDB,'MyNewDB'
go
sp_dboption MyNewDB,'single','false'
go
```

ALTER Databases

The **ALTER DATABASE** command allows you to change both the definition and the size of a database. Here's the syntax of the **ALTER DATABASE** command:

```
ALTER DATABASE database
  { ADD FILE <filespec> [,...n] [TO FILEGROUP filegroup_name]
  | ADD LOG FILE <filespec> [,...n]
  | REMOVE FILE logical_file_name
  | ADD FILEGROUP filegroup_name
  | REMOVE FILEGROUP filegroup_name
  | MODIFY FILE <filespec>
  | MODIFY FILEGROUP filegroup_name filegroup_property
  }

<filespec> ::=
  (NAME = 'logical_file_name'
  [, FILENAME = 'os_file_name' ]
  [, SIZE = size]
  [, MAXSIZE = { max_size | UNLIMITED } ]
  [, FILEGROWTH = growth_increment] )
```

The **ALTER DATABASE** command allows you to add a file to an existing file group or add a new log file to a database. If you are adding a new data file and do not specify a file group, the file will be added to the primary file group. The **ALTER DATABASE** command can also be used to perform the following functions:

➤ **Remove empty files** There must always be at least one file in the primary file group and one log file in the database. When you remove a file, the physical file is deleted.

➤ **Add new file groups** When you add a new file group, no file is automatically added to it.

➤ **Remove a file group** If there are any files in the file group, they must be empty or you cannot remove the file group. You cannot remove the primary file group.

When you're using **ALTER DATABASE** to modify files, you must specify the logical name of the file you are modifying. You can change the rest of the options in the file specification, but in a single **ALTER DATABASE** command, you can change only one option. If you change the size of a file, it must be at least as large as the current file size.

When you're modifying a file group, you can set the following properties: **READONLY**, **READWRITE**, and **DEFAULT**.

The **READONLY** property specifies that the file group is read-only. This prevents objects in the file group from being modified. The primary file group cannot be made read-only. Only users who have exclusive access to the database can mark a file group **READONLY**.

The **READWRITE** property reverses the **READONLY** property. Updates are allowed to the objects in the file group. Only users who have exclusive access to the database can mark a file group **READWRITE**.

The **DEFAULT** property specifies that the file group is the default file group for the database. When you set the default property for a file group, the default property is removed from the previous file group that had been the default. When a database is created, the primary file group is set as the default file group. New tables and indexes are created in the default file group if no file group is specified in the **CREATE TABLE, ALTER TABLE,** or **CREATE INDEX** statements.

It is not possible to move a file from one file group to another file group. If you need to do this, you must first remove the file, then add it to the new file group. Here are some examples of the **ALTER DATABASE** command:

```
/* the following example will add a new data file,
pubs_data2.ndf  size = 50m to a new group grp2 */

ALTER DATABASE pubs ADD FILEGROUP grp2

ALTER DATABASE pubs ADD FILE ( NAME = 'PubsFile2',
    FILENAME = 'c:\temp\pubsdata2.ndf',
    SIZE = 50 ) TO FILEGROUP grp2

/* the following example will remove the group grp2
that was added in the last example from the pubs database*/
ALTER DATABASE pubs REMOVE FILE PubsFile2

ALTER DATABASE pubs REMOVE FILEGROUP grp2
```

Manually Shrinking Databases

To reduce a database's size, you run the **DBCC SHRINKDATABASE** command. The syntax of the **SHRINKDATABASE** command is as follows:

```
DBCC SHRINKDATABASE
( database_name [, target_percent]
[, {NOTRUNCATE | TRUNCATEONLY}]
)
```

When you're shrinking a database, you can specify an optional percentage, which is the amount of free space you would like to leave in the database. The **NONTRUNCATE** option overrides the default behavior and leaves the free space in the operating system files after shrinking the file. The **TRUNCATEONLY** option causes any unused space in the data files to be released to the operating system and reduces the file to the last allocated extent. No attempt is made to relocate rows to unallocated pages. The *target_percent* is ignored when the **TRUNCATEONLY** option is used. The **NOTRUNCATE** option will not shrink a file smaller than the minimum file size. **DBCC SHRINKFILE** will not shrink a file past the minimum size needed to store the data in the file. If you use the **NOTRUNCATE** option with the *target_percent*, the only effect is that used pages will move to the front of the file. A database cannot be made smaller than the **MODEL** database.

To shrink a database file, you run the **DBCC SHRINKFILE** command in the database containing the file you want to reduce. The syntax of the **SHRINKFILE** command is as follows:

```
DBCC SHRINKFILE
( {file_name | file_id }
{ [, target_size]
```

```
| [, {EMPTYFILE | NOTRUNCATE | TRUNCATEONLY}]
}
)
```

You can shrink a file using either its file name or its file id. When you're shrinking a file, data is normally moved to the pages at the front of the file.

The *target size* is an integer specifying how big you want the file to be. If you do not specify a size, the file will be shrunk until it reaches the smallest possible size required to store the data.

The **EMPTYFILE** option moves all the data from the file to other files in the file group. After you've used the **EMPTYFILE** option, SQL Server no longer allows data to be placed on the file. This prepares the file for being removed with the **ALTER DATABASE** command.

The **NOTRUNCATE** option releases unused space, but it does not relocate data rows. The target size is ignored with this option.

Configuring Databases

Multiple options within SQL Server can be configured at a database level. You use the **sp_dboption** stored procedure to set the options. The syntax of the **sp_dboption** procedure is as follows:

```
sp_dboption ['database'] [, 'option_name'] [, 'value']
```

If you do not specify a database, **sp_configure** will list all of the configurable options. The valid options are shown in Table 4.1.

Table 4.1 Database configuration options.	
Option	**Description**
AUTOCLOSE	When TRUE, the database is shut down cleanly and its resources are freed after the last user exits.
AUTOSHRINK	When TRUE, the database files are candidates for automatic periodic shrinking.
ANSI NULL DEFAULT	When TRUE, if you do not specify NOT NULL for a column when you're creating or altering a table, the column will use the SQL-92 rules to determine whether a column allows NULL values.
ANSI NULLS	When TRUE, all comparisons to a NULL value evaluate to UNKNOWN. When FALSE and not using UNICODE values, NULL = NULL will evaluate to TRUE.

(continued)

Table 4.1   Database configuration options *(continued)*.

Option	Description
ANSI WARNINGS	When TRUE, errors or warnings are issued when conditions such as "divide by zero" occur.
CONCAT NULL YIELDS NULL	When TRUE, if either operand in a concatenation operation is NULL, the result is NULL.
CURSOR CLOSE ON COMMIT	When TRUE, any cursors that are open when a transaction is committed or rolled back are closed. When FALSE, such cursors remain open when a transaction is committed. When FALSE, rolling back a transaction closes any cursors except those defined as INSENSITIVE or STATIC.
DBO USE ONLY	When TRUE, only the database owner can use the database.
DEFAULT TO LOCAL CURSOR	When TRUE, cursor declarations default to LOCAL.
MERGE PUBLISH	When TRUE, the database can be published for a merge replication.
OFFLINE	When TRUE, the database is offline and cannot be used by anyone.
PUBLISHER	When TRUE, the database can be published for replication.
QUOTED IDENTIFIER	When TRUE, double quotation mark (") characters can be used to surround delimited identifiers.
READ ONLY	When TRUE, users can only read data in the database, not modify it.
RECURSIVE TRIGGERS	When TRUE, enables triggers to be able to cause the same trigger to fire as a result of its data modifications.
SELECT INTO/BULKCOPY	When TRUE, the **SELECT INTO** statement, unlogged WRITETEXT, unlogged UPDATETEXT, and fast bulk copies are allowed.
SINGLE USER	When TRUE, only one user at a time can access the database.
SUBSCRIBED	When TRUE, the database can be subscribed for publication.
TORN PAGE DETECTION	When TRUE, incomplete pages can be detected.
TRUNC. LOG ON CHKPT.	When TRUE, the database is truncated every time the log becomes 70 percent full and the log is automatically checkpointed.

The only option you can set for the **MASTER** database is **TRUNC. LOG ON CHKPT**. When you're creating a new database, the options that are currently set in the model are the options that will be turned on in the new database.

 When you're setting a configuration value, the value does not take effect until the database is checkpointed. But SQL Server 7 will automatically checkpoint the database for you after you use the **sp_configure** procedure.

Viewing Database Information

SQL Server provides three standard catalog procedures for viewing information about databases, files, and file groups: **sp_helpdb**, **sp_helpfile**, and **sp_helpfilegroup**.

The catalog procedure **sp_helpdb** displays information about databases and how the database is configured. The syntax of the **sp_helpdb** stored procedure is as follows:

```
sp_helpdb [database_name]
```

If you do not provide the name of the specific database, SQL Server returns a one-line report about every database. If you run **sp_helpdb** from inside the database you are trying to get information about, the procedure will produce a more detailed report containing the same information as **sp_helpfile**.

The **sp_helpfile** stored procedure lists information about files attached to the current database. The syntax of **sp_helpfile** is as follows:

```
sp_helpfile [[@filename = ] 'name']
```

If you do not specify a file name, SQL Server returns information about all files in the database.

The **sp_helpfilegroup** stored procedure lists information about file groups in the current database. The syntax of **sp_helpfilegroup** is as follows:

```
sp_helpfilegroup [[@filegroupname = ] 'name']
```

If you do not supply the name, the program returns information about every file group. If you set the file group name parameter, **sp_helpfilegroup** will also run **sp_helpfile** on every file in the group.

If you want to find out information about the primary file group, you must use quotes, because it is a reserved word. For example:

```
sp_helpfilegroup @filegroupname = 'primary'
```

Enterprise Manager

You can manage databases with the Enterprise Manager tool. This tool allows you to use wizards for most of the database creation and modifications.

Using Databases

All user sessions have a *current* database; Microsoft calls that "using" a database. The system administrator defines your default database when you are given access to the server. Your default database is *master* if one is not provided at login creation, but can be changed at any time by the system administrator. To find out what database you are in, use this SQL Server built-in function:

```
/* display current database */
SELECT db_name()
```

The **USE** command allows you to change your current database. When using the **USE** command, any SQL syntax following the **USE** command will be executed in the new database. The syntax is as follows:

```
/* change current database to "student07" */
USE student07
```

Practice Questions

Question 1

> If you want to remove a file from a database, which of the following statements are true? [Check all correct answers]
>
> ❏ a. You must be in the database from which you want to remove the file.
>
> ❏ b. You must run the **DBCC SHRINKFILE** command to make sure that the file is empty.
>
> ❏ c. You cannot remove the file if its file group has data in it.
>
> ❏ d. You run the **DBCC REMOVEFILE** command to remove the file from the database.
>
> ❏ e. The OS file will still have the data in it after it is removed from the database.
>
> ❏ f. The database must be in single user mode.
>
> ❏ g. None of the above.

Answer g is correct. Answer a is wrong—you do not have to be in the database to run the **ALTER DATABASE** command. Although the file must not have any data in it, you do not have to shrink a file before removing it, making answer b wrong. Answer c is wrong—you can remove a file if other files in its file group still have data in them. There is no **DBCC REMOVEFILE** command, so answer d is wrong. After removing a database file, the operating system file will be deleted, making answer e wrong.

Question 2

> Which of the following will create a database called MyDB with an
> initial size of 50MB for the database files?
>
> O a.
> ```
> create database MyDB datasize=40 ,
> logsize = 10
> ```
>
> O b.
> ```
> create database MyDB on File1 =40 log on
> file2=10
> ```
>
> O c.
> ```
> create database MyDB on NAME='File1', size
> = 40 log on name=file2, size = 10
> ```
>
> O d.
> ```
> create database MyDB on( NAME='File1',
> size = 40) log on( name=file2, size = 10)
> ```
>
> O e.
> ```
> create database MyDB on (NAME='File1',
> size = 40 log on name=file2, size = 10)
> ```

The only answer that is syntactically correct is d. Answer a is missing the **on**
and **log on** keywords. Answer b follows the pre SQL Server 7.0 syntax. Answer
c is missing parentheses. Answer e has the parentheses in the wrong place.

Question 3

> To find out information about all files used in the current data-
> base, you would use which of the following SQL statements?
>
> O a. sp_helpgroup
> O b. sp_helpdb
> O c. sp_helpfile
> O d. sp_listfiles

Answer c is correct. Answer a, **sp_helpgroup** without a file name, will only list
groups. Answer b, **sp_helpdb**, will only list the one-line database report without supplying a name. The stored procedure **sp_listfiles** does not exist.

Question 4

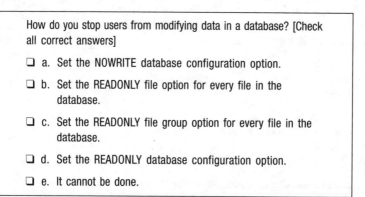

How do you stop users from modifying data in a database? [Check all correct answers]

❑ a. Set the NOWRITE database configuration option.

❑ b. Set the READONLY file option for every file in the database.

❑ c. Set the READONLY file group option for every file in the database.

❑ d. Set the READONLY database configuration option.

❑ e. It cannot be done.

Answers c and d are correct. There is no NOWRITE database configuration option, so answer a is incorrect. There is no READONLY file option, so answer b is incorrect.

Need To Know More?

 Amo, William C. *Transact-SQL*, IDG Books Worldwide, Foster City, CA, 1998. ISBN 0-7645-8048-5. Chapter 5 describes Data Manipulation Language (DML).

 Coffman, Gayle. *SQL Server 7: The Complete Reference*, Osborne/McGraw-Hill, Berkley, CA, 1999. ISBN 0-07-882494-X. Chapter 21 provides a complete T-SQL reference for the commands used to manipulate databases.

 McGehee, Brad and Matthew Shepker. *Using Microsoft SQL Server 7.0*, QUE, Indianapolis, Indiana, 1998. ISBN 0-7897-1628-3. Chapter 8 describes databases and files in detail.

 MS SQL Server Books Online contains a complete DDL reference, look in the table of contents under Creating and Maintaining Databases or you can look in the index for specific DDL statements.

 Search the TechNet CD or its online version at **www.microsoft.com**.

 www.microsoft.com/sql
Find up-to-date information about using SQL Server here.

Data Definition

. . . .

Terms you'll need to understand:

√ Table

√ Constraint

√ Primary key

√ Foreign key

√ Datatype

√ Identity

Techniques you'll need to master:

√ Creating tables

√ Altering tables

√ Temporary tables

√ Dropping tables

One definition of a relational database is "a collection of tables that relate to one another." Tables are most easily described as lists. To make the entries in the table as identifiable as possible, tables are broken down into columns, which hold the specific items you're listing in the table. A database is a collection of lists, and lists are collections of details. Or, to be more accurate, the database is a collection of tables and the tables are collections of columns.

The first step in developing a database is to decide what tables need to be created and what columns should appear in them. (This is discussed at length as part of physical design in Chapter 2.) When planning the columns, the designer needs to consider the type of data that is being stored, whether or not it allows nulls—that is, whether a value is required or optional. Allowing nulls means that you are going to allow a column to be optional.

Creating Tables

You create tables with the CREATE TABLE command. Any user that has been granted authority (by the SA or database owner) to use the CREATE TABLE command or has the SA_ROLE can create tables. Listing 5.1 displays the syntax for the CREATE TABLE command.

Listing 5.1   CREATE TABLE syntax.

```
CREATE TABLE table_name
( { ColumnName DataType
[ NULL | NOT NULL ] [ IDENTITY [(seed, increment )
[NOT FOR REPLICATION] ] ]
[ ROWGUIDCOL ]
[CONSTRAINT ConstraintName]
{ { PRIMARY KEY | UNIQUE } [CLUSTERED | NONCLUSTERED]
[WITH [FILLFACTOR = fillfactor_value]
[ON {filegroup | DEFAULT} ]
| [FOREIGN KEY] REFERENCES RefTable [ ( RefColumn ) ]
[NOT FOR REPLICATION]
| DEFAULT Constant_Expression
| CHECK [NOT FOR REPLICATION]
(LogicalExpression)
}] [ ...n]
| ColumnName AS computed_column_expression
| <table_constraint>
} [, ...n]
)
[ON {filegroup | DEFAULT} ]
[TEXTIMAGE_ON {filegroup | DEFAULT} ]
<column_definition> ::= { ColumnName DataType }
[ NULL | NOT NULL ]
[ IDENTITY [(seed, increment )
```

```
[NOT FOR REPLICATION] ] ]
[ ROWGUIDCOL ]
[ <column_constraint> ::=
[CONSTRAINT ConstraintName]
{ { PRIMARY KEY | UNIQUE }
[CLUSTERED | NONCLUSTERED]
[WITH [FILLFACTOR = fillfactor]
]
[ON {filegroup | DEFAULT} ]
| [FOREIGN KEY]
REFERENCES ref_table
[ ( ref_column ) ]
[NOT FOR REPLICATION]
| DEFAULT constant_expression
| CHECK [NOT FOR REPLICATION]
(logical_expression)
}
] [ ...n]

Example
CREATE TABLE authors_short
(author_id int not null,
 lastname varchar(40) not null,
 firstname varchar(20) null)
```

In this listing, the table is named authors_short. It will hold a list of authors. The details of the list are the author's last name, first name, and an ID number. Table 5.1 shows the contents of the authors table.

Table Names

A table name can be up to 128 characters in length and must be unique to its owner—that is, you cannot own two tables of the same name, but you and another user can both own tables of the same name.

Columns

Tables are allowed a maximum of 1,024 columns. Columns must have at least a name and a datatype. A column name can be up to 128 characters in length

Table 5.1 The authors table.		
author_id	**lastname**	**firstname**
1	Bennet	Abraham
2	Blotchet-Halls	Reginald
3	DeFrance	Cheryl

and must be unique to the table. Naming conventions must conform to normal identifier naming, which includes letters, symbols (_, @, or #), and numbers.

Datatypes

SQL Server supports the following base datatypes for the creation of table columns (see Table 5.2).

Be careful when you're deciding on a datatype for a column. For instance, it takes more space to store an int datatype than a tinyint. So when you're creating a column that will store integer type values, you should consider how high the values are going to get. If the values will never be higher than 10, then choosing the tinyint datatype makes more sense and is a more efficient use of storage space.

Null Or Not Null

If a column is created with a null, then the database will allow the column to be left blank when data is entered. If the column will contain mandatory data, it should be made not null. Columns are created Not Null (ODBC alters this setting; the server's default is Not Null) by default.

Unique Identifiers

The theory behind relational databases requires that you have a unique way of identifying a row for retrieval. Sometimes it's easy to uniquely identify a row, but when there is no convenient way, you must use an incremental key or other contrived mechanism for uniqueness. SQL Server provides identity columns as one way to achieve unique values in rows automatically.

Identity Columns

An identity column is an automated column that generates its own unique, incremental values. They are often used to help define uniqueness for the rows in a table. Identity columns are not nullable and must be of a numeric datatype, such as int, smallint, tinyint, numeric(p,0), or decimal(p,0). Unless declared with a seed (beginning)and increment value, the column will act as a counter starting at 1 and incrementing by 1 with each insert.

Note that identity columns may occasionally have skips in them due to incomplete transactions or unexpected server crashes.

Table 5.2	Base datatypes.
Datatype	**Description**
Bit	Integer value of 0 or 1.
Int	Integer value, whole numbers only. Range: -2,147,483,648 to 2,147,483,648.
Smallint	Integer value, whole numbers only. Range: -32,768 to 32,768.
Tinyint	Integer value, whole numbers only. Range: 0 to 255.
Decimal(p,s)	Numeric data, fixed precision(p) and scale(s). Range: $-10^{38}-1$ to $10^{38}-1$.
Numeric(p,s)	Synonym for decimal.
Float	Floating precision number. Range: -1.79 E+308 to 1.79 E+308.
Real	Floating precision number. Range -3.40E+38 to 3.40E+38.
Char(n)	Fixed-length (n) character string. Maximum length: 8,000 characters.
Varchar(n)	Variable-length (n) character string. Maximum length: 8,000 characters.
Text	Variable-length character data. Maximum length: 2,147,483,647 characters.
Money	Monetary values. Range: -922,337,203,685,477.5808 to 922,337,203,685.5807.
Smallmoney	Monetary values. Range: -214,748.3648 to 214,748.3647.
Datetime	Date and time data. Range is Jan 1, 1753 to Dec 31, 9999. Note that the time is stored in 3-millisecond intervals, so you are only accurate to within 3 milliseconds.
Smalldatetime	Date and time data. Range: Jan 1, 1900 to Jun 6, 2079. Accurate to 1 minute.
Timestamp	Machine-assigned value used for change management.
Uniqueidentifier	A Globally Unique Identifier (GUID).
Binary(n)	Fixed-length (n) binary string data. Maximum length: 8,000 bytes.
Varbinary	Variable-length binary string data. Maximum length: 8,000 bytes.
Image	Binary data. Maximum length: 2GB.
Nchar	Multibyte (Unicode) fixed-length character string. Maximum length of 4,000 characters.
Ntext	Variable-length multibyte (Unicode) text data. Maximum length: 1,073,741,823 characters.
Nvarchar	Multibyte (Unicode) variable-length character string. Maximum length of 4,000 characters.
Sysname	Synonym for nvarchar(128).

Be careful in the selection of a datatype for an identity column. As illustrated in the following example, it is possible to create problems for yourself if the identity column is too small.

```
CREATE TABLE too_short
(id_num tinyint IDENTITY,
 name varchar(25) NOT NULL)
```

In this example, the identity column is declared as a tinyint, which has a maximum value of 255. When the maximum value of 255 is reached, the table will reject all further inserts.

Note: An identity column does not guarantee uniqueness.

ROWGUIDCOL

The ROWGUIDCOL column property, used in conjunction with the UNIQUEIDENTIFIER datatype, is designed to produce globally unique values across all computers in the network. This is useful when you're dealing with multiple database systems that need to be merged together.

Constraints

Constraints place conditions on data that is being entered into a table. These conditions may require that the entries be unique, lie within a certain range of values, or that a foreign key has a corresponding primary key (referential integrity constraints).

SQL Server supports four types of constraints (primary key, foreign key, check, and unique). All four may be declared with the column definition or appended to the end of the table definition.

Primary Key

Primary key constraints require that the entries in the constrained columns be unique. Declaring a primary key guarantees that the rows in a table are uniquely identifiable. (A primary key or unique constraint is a requirement for maintaining referential integrity via reference or foreign key constraints. In other words, when you start defining foreign keys that refer back to this table, the foreign key will need to have the primary key defined.)

The following code declares a primary key constraint by use of a column declaration. Note that the constraint is included with the declaration of the author_id column. This method is adequate for single-column primary keys, but should you need to declare a multicolumn primary key, the table-level declaration is required. Listings 5.2 and 5.3 shows an example of a CREATE TABLE statement with a primary key declaration.

Listing 5.2   Creating a table with column-level primary key declarations.

```
CREATE TABLE authors_short
(author_id int NOT NULL
 CONSTRAINT author_pk PRIMARY KEY,
 lastname varchar(40) NOT NULL,
 firstname varchar(20) NULL)
```

Listing 5.3 has the same function as Listing 5.2. The only difference is that the constraint is defined after the last column (firstname) has been declared. Note that in a table declaration, the PRIMARY KEY keywords are followed by a list of constrained columns. This allows the creation of multicolumn primary keys.

Listing 5.3   Creating a table with table-level primary key declarations.

```
CREATE TABLE authors_short
(author_id int not null,
 lastname varchar(40) not null,
 firstname varchar(20) null,
 CONSTRAINT author_pk PRIMARY KEY (author_id))
```

The keyword CONSTRAINT followed by the constraint name is optional. However, if a constraint name is not supplied, SQL Server will name the constraint for you. A primary key will also generate a clustered index by default. (We will explain indexes further in Chapter 9.) There is also an alternative to the primary key constraint called *unique*. The difference is that a unique constraint will allow the entry of a null value and will generate a non-clustered index.

Foreign Key

As we mentioned before, a database is a collection of tables that relate to one another. The foreign key constraint is one method of expressing the relationships that exist between the tables. The foreign key constraint will reference the primary key column in the related table to verify that the data in their shared columns match. This will become a requirement when maintaining referential integrity. In Listing 5.4, you can see a reference constraint.

Listing 5.4 CREATE TABLE with column-level reference constraint.

```
CREATE TABLE book_author
(book_name varchar(30) NOT NULL,
Author_id int NOT NULL
CONSTRAINT author_fk REFERENCES authors_short ( author_id))
```

Listing 5.5 generates a table containing book names with their respective authors. The column-level REFERENCE constraint requires that the author_id already exist in the authors_short table.

Listing 5.5 CREATE TABLE with table-level foreign key reference constraint.

```
CREATE TABLE book_author
(book_name varchar(30) NOT NULL,
author_id int NOT NULL,
CONSTRAINT author_fk FOREIGN KEY (author_id)
REFERENCES authors_short ( author_id))
```

Listing 5.5 performs the same function as the previous one. The key differences are syntax and functionality. The second example is a table-level constraint and, unlike the previous one, actually uses the term FOREIGN KEY followed by the column(s) in the book_author table that need to be checked. The REFERENCES constraint specifies the authors_short table and the author_id columns that are going to need existing, corresponding data.

Foreign key constraints can be multicolumn constraints if they are declared at the table level. Their columns should reference columns that are declared as primary keys or have unique indexes. Like the primary key constraints, the CONSTRAINT *ConstraintName* part of the declaration can be omitted; however, SQL Server will name the constraint for you.

Creating a foreign key constraint does not index the column used in the constraint.

Check Constraints

In some situations, the data needs to be checked not for existence (as in a foreign key), but for correctness. A business rule may demand certain requirements on data being entered. This can be maintained via a check constraint. Check constraints can also compare data from different columns, provided the columns exist in the same table and the constraint is declared at the table level. Listing 5.6 creates a table called a_authors that holds a list of authors whose last names begin with the letter "A."

Listing 5.6   CREATE TABLE with a column-level check constraint.

```
CREATE TABLE a_authors
( author_id int NOT NULL,
 lastname varchar(40) NOT NULL
CONSTRAINT lastname_ck CHECK (lastname LIKE "A%" ),
firstname varchar(20) NULL)
```

The lastname column is maintained by the column-level check constraint that examines the first letter of any last name entered into the table (see Listing 5.7).

Listing 5.7   CREATE TABLE with a table-level check constraint.

```
CREATE TABLE a_authors
( author_id int NOT NULL,
 lastname varchar(40) NOT NULL,
 firstname varchar(20) NULL,
CONSTRAINT lastname_ck CHECK (lastname LIKE "A%" ))
```

Listing 5.7 is functionally identical to Listing 5.6, except that it declares the constraint at the table level. The advantage to this declaration is that the check could compare its column to another column in the same table.

Default Definitions

When you're entering data into the database, columns are either populated or left null. In some cases, leaving a null value is not permissible because of business rules or a not null option. What you need is a fallback value. Default definitions can provide that fallback value. Listing 5.8 shows a default definition.

Listing 5.8   Examples of default definitions.

```
/* Column Level Declaration*/
CREATE TABLE book_sales
(book_id int NOT NULL,
 Volume int NOT NULL CONSTRAINT vol_def DEFAULT 0)

/* Table Level Declaration */
CREATE TABLE book_sales
(book_id int NOT NULL,
```

```
Volume int NOT NULL,
CONSTRAINT vol_def DEFAULT 0 FOR Volume)
```

Note that in the table-level declaration, the DEFAULT must be declared FOR a specific column in the table.

Default information, as well as other constraints, can be accessed via the **sp_help** or **sp_helpconstraint** stored procedures.

Computed Columns

SQL Server 7 supports the creation of computed virtual columns that are based on data from functions, constants, or other columns in the table. These columns are defined by a computed column expression, which is a T-SQL formula for computing the values that will be presented. Listing 5.9 shows a table with a computed column.

Listing 5.9 CREATE TABLE with a computed column.

```
CREATE TABLE book_price
(book_id int NOT NULL,
whsl_price smallmoney NOT NULL,
markup_pct numeric (5,2) NOT NULL,
msrp AS whsl_price *(1+(markup_pct/100)))
```

Listing 5.9 stores a three-column table containing the columns book_id, whsl_price, and markup_pct. The msrp column is calculated and does not need to be stored. The code results in a four-column table stored as a three-column table.

Altering Tables

After a table is created in the database, you can apply changes to it. These changes can include, but are not limited to adding columns, changing the datatypes in existing columns, or declaring primary keys. Note that you cannot delete a primary key constraint if it has a corresponding foreign key constraint pointing to it. Listing 5.10 contains full syntax for the ALTER TABLE statement.

Listing 5.10 ALTER TABLE syntax.

```
ALTER TABLE Table_name
{
[WITH CHECK | WITH NOCHECK]
  { [ALTER COLUMN ColumnName
      { [ NewDataType [ (precision[, scale] ) ]
          [ NULL | NOT NULL ] ]
```

```
        | [ {ADD | DROP} ROWGUIDCOL ]
    }
]
| ADD
    { [{ ColumnName DataType }
        [ NULL | NOT NULL ]
        [ IDENTITY [(seed[, increment] )
        [NOT FOR REPLICATION] ] ]
        [ ROWGUIDCOL ]
    ]
    | ColumnName AS computed_column_expression
    | [[CONSTRAINT ConstraintName]
        { [ { PRIMARY KEY | UNIQUE }
            [ CLUSTERED | NONCLUSTERED]
            { ( column[,...n] ) }
                [ WITH [FILLFACTOR = fillfactor]
                ]
        [ON {filegroup | DEFAULT} ]]
        | FOREIGN KEY [(column[,...n])]
        REFERENCES ref_table [(ref_column[,...n])]
        [NOT FOR REPLICATION]
        | DEFAULT constant_expression [FOR column]
        | CHECK [NOT FOR REPLICATION]
        (logical_expression)
        }]
    }[,...n]
    | DROP
    { [CONSTRAINT] constraint
    | COLUMN column
    }[,...n]
    | {CHECK | NOCHECK} CONSTRAINT {ALL | constraint[,...n]}}
}
}
```

Adding To The Table

You can add columns, constraints, and defaults to a table after creating it. You add columns after defining a table using the ALTER TABLE command, as shown in Listing 5.11.

Listing 5.11   The ALTER TABLE command with added columns and constraints.

```
ALTER TABLE authors_short ADD
MI char(1) NULL CONSTRAINT MI_ck
CHECK (MI like "[A-Z]")
```

```
ALTER TABLE authors_short ADD
MI char(1) NULL,
CONSTRAINT MI_ck CHECK (MI LIKE "[A-Z]")
```

The two ALTER TABLE commands in Listing 5.11 are functionally identical. The first uses a column-level declaration for the check constraint. The second uses a table-level constraint.

Modifying Tables With *ALTER TABLE ADD*

SQL Server assumes that the column will be null unless otherwise specified. If the new column is not null, a default must be provided. New columns, which may be a computed column expression, can be declared with column-level constraints.

Dropping From The Table

After you create a table, you can alter it by removing columns or constraints. When dropping constraints, be aware that certain dependencies may prevent the command from executing. For instance, if a column is the primary key, SQL Server will not allow it to be dropped until the constraint is removed. Likewise, if a column is referenced by another table, SQL Server will not allow the column to be dropped until the constraint is removed. Drop syntax is presented in Listing 5.12.

Listing 5.12   Examples of ALTER TABLE DROP.

```
ALTER TABLE authors_short
DROP CONSTRAINT MI_ck

ALTER TABLE authors_short
DROP COLUMN MI
```

Altering Columns

Sometimes people underestimate or overestimate the type of data they are going to store. This may affect the database, because it might waste storage space, or the data might become too large for the table to handle. In these cases, you can modify the table columns from their original form by using the ALTER TABLE command. Here is an example of the ALTER TABLE command with column alteration.

```
ALTER TABLE authors_short
ALTER COLUMN firstname varchar(40)
```

This example illustrates how a column can be enlarged with the ALTER TABLE command. Originally, the authors_short table had a firstname column declared as varchar(25). The ALTER TABLE command extends that range to 40 characters.

> *Note: The OldDataType must be implicitly convertible to the NewDataType; the NewDataType may not be a timestamp. If the altered column is an identity, the NewDataType must be valid for identity columns.*

Temporary Tables

Temporary tables are similar to regular tables, except they are not meant to be permanent structures. They are often used to temporarily store data that will be modified or used later. They can be created, dropped, and used just like normal tables. The differences lie in that temporary tables:

➤ Must be preceded by the # or ## symbols.

➤ Have names that are limited to 116 characters in length.

➤ Are dropped once the owner disconnects from the database.

➤ Function like part of the current database, but the data is actually stored in tempdb.

SQL Server supports two forms of temporary tables: local and global.

Local Temporary Tables

Local temporary tables are accessible only by their owner. All local temporary table names must be preceded by a #. This code creates a local temporary table:

```
CREATE TABLE #temp1
( a int NULL,
 b varchar(25) NULL)
```

This example generates a temporary table called #temp1. The only difference in the syntax is that the name must be preceded with the # symbol.

Global Temporary Tables

Global temporary tables are just like local tables, except they are accessible to other users and their names must start with ##. The following code creates a global temporary table:

```
CREATE TABLE ##temp2
( a int NULL,
  b varchar(25) NULL)
```

When temporary tables are no longer necessary, they may be dropped like any other table.

Dropping Tables

When a table becomes obsolete, it may be removed via the DROP command. Dropping a table removes it permanently from the database. The action cannot be undone. Here is an example of DROP TABLE syntax:

```
DROP TABLE table_name
```

```
DROP TABLE authors_short
```

 You can only drop user tables, not SQL server system tables.

A table cannot be dropped if it is referenced by any other constraints. Furthermore, all referencing constraints must be disabled or dropped before a table can be removed. A table can only be removed by its owner. Once a table is dropped, it cannot be recovered—and there is no "un-drop." It must be re-created.

 It is an excellent idea to keep the text of all of your object creation statements in a file someplace separate from the rest of your server, so that in an emergency (database corruption, database migration), you can rebuild. This also simplifies migration across environments.

Practice Questions

Question 1

> What is the maximum length of a table name for SQL Server?
>
> ○ a. 128
>
> ○ b. 116
>
> ○ c. 90
>
> ○ d. 30
>
> ○ e. None of the above

Answer a is correct. However, in earlier versions of SQL Server, the maximum length was 30.

Question 2

> What is the maximum character length for a char or varchar datatype?
>
> ○ a. 255
>
> ○ b. 128
>
> ○ c. 8,000
>
> ○ d. 2,000
>
> ○ e. None of the above

Answer c is correct. Earlier versions of SQL Server only permitted 255 characters for these datatypes.

Question 3

Which of the following are true about local temporary tables? [Check all correct answers]

❑ a. Their names are preceded by #.

❑ b. They are stored in tempdb.

❑ c. They are accessible to other users.

❑ d. Their names are preceded by ##.

❑ e. They can be dropped like normal tables.

Answers a, b, and e are correct. Answers c and d are true for global temporary tables.

Question 4

What datatypes are valid for an identity column? [Check all correct answers]

❑ a. numeric (5,1)

❑ b. decimal (4,0)

❑ c. int

❑ d. bit

❑ e. tinyint

Answers b, c, and e are correct. Answer a is incorrect, because an identity column must be a whole number. Answer d is simply too small and not permitted.

Question 5

> A foreign key constraint can be created provided that:
>
> ○ a. The referenced table already exists.
>
> ○ b. Its referenced column(s) have a primary key or unique constraint.
>
> ○ c. The constraint name is unique within the database.
>
> ○ d. All of the above.
>
> ○ e. None of the above.

Answer d is correct. The other answers are incomplete.

Question 6

> Which of the following correctly completes the phrase "A table may be dropped _____"
>
> ○ a. by using the ALTER TABLE table_name DROP command.
>
> ○ b. by any user with access to the table.
>
> ○ c. if there are no constraints referencing it.
>
> ○ d. All of the above.
>
> ○ e. None of the above.

Answer c is correct. Answer a is incorrect, because the ALTER TABLE DROP command removes columns, not data or tables. Answer b is incorrect, because a table may only be dropped by its owner (whoever created it).

Need To Know More?

 Amo, William C. *Transact-SQL*, IDG Books Worldwide, Foster City, CA, 1998. ISBN 0-7645-8048-5. Chapter 5 describes Data Manipulation Language (DML).

 Coffman, Gayle. *SQL Server 7: The Complete Reference*, Osborne/McGraw-Hill, Berkley, CA, 1999. ISBN 0-07-882494-X. Chapter 21 provides a complete T-SQL reference for the commands used to define database objects.

 MS SQL Server Books Online contains a complete DDL reference you can find information either in the table of contents under Accessing and Change Data or you can look in the index for specific SQL statements.

 Search the TechNet CD or its online version at **www.microsoft.com**.

 www.microsoft.com/sql
Find up-to-date information about using SQL Server here.

6

Retrieving Data

. . . .

Terms you'll need to understand:

√ **SELECT** statement

√ Subquery

√ Aggregate

√ Union

√ SQL

√ Joining tables

√ Using subqueries

√ Qualifying object names

√ Retrieving text and images

Techniques you'll need to master:

√ Specifying rows

√ Using functions

√ Using the **like** keyword

√ Formatting and sorting data

√ Grouping results

√ Outer join

√ Inner join

√ Cross join

√ Result set

√ Derived table

Storing data in a database does you no good unless there is some way to retrieve the data. Not surprisingly, Microsoft SQL Server uses Structured Query Language (SQL) to access data stored in databases. The SQL **SELECT** statement is used to retrieve data.

 SQL is an ANSI standard database access layer. One of its main purposes is to hide the underlying data structures from users, thereby making it simpler for users to manipulate the data. SQL Server has extensions to ANSI SQL called *Transact-SQL* (TSQL).

Parts Of The SELECT Statement

A **SELECT** statement consists of seven basic parts:

➤ select list

➤ FROM

➤ WHERE

➤ GROUP BY

➤ HAVING

➤ ORDER BY

➤ COMPUTE

All of the **SELECT** statement clauses, except the select list, are optional. The order in which the clauses appear is mandatory. Listing 6.1 shows the **SELECT** statement's syntax.

Listing 6.1   The SELECT statement's syntax.

```
SELECT [ ALL | DISTINCT ] [ TOP n [PERCENT] [ WITH TIES] ] select_list
[ INTO table_name ]
[FROM {table_name | view_name}
    [ , {table_name | view_name} ... ]
[ WHERE search_conditions ]
[ GROUP BY aggregate_free_expression
    [ , aggregate_free_expression ... ]
    [WITH CUBE|ROLLUP] ]
[ HAVING search_conditions ]
[ ORDER BY { column_name | select_list_no } [ ASC | DESC ]
    [ , { column_name | select_list_no } [ ASC | DESC ] ... ] ]
[ COMPUTE row_aggregate(column_name)
    [ , row_aggregate(column_name) ] ...
    [ BY column_name [ , column_name ] ... ] ] ]
```

When performing a **SELECT**, you receive a *result set*, a table of results, from the SQL Server. A result set consists of three parts—columns, column headings, and rows. A result set can have one or more columns. In addition, it can have column headings that are blank and it can contain zero or more rows of data.

> *Note: Table and column names can be configured to be either case sensitive or case insensitive. SQL keywords are always case insensitive. With SQL Server 7, the names can have a bracket around them, such as '[object_name]'. The following code example shows a SELECT statement written both with and without brackets around column and table names.*

```
SELECT [d].[discounttype] FROM [dbo].[discount] d
-- Performs the same select as
SELECT d.discounttype FROM dbo.discount d
```

In the upcoming sections, we'll take a closer look at the **SELECT** statement's seven clauses. To keep our presentation orderly, we'll look at each clause in the order in which the clause should appear in a **SELECT** statement. Therefore, the first clause we'll look at is the select list.

The Select List

The select list portion of a **SELECT** statement appears as follows:

```
SELECT [ ALL | DISTINCT ] [ TOP n [PERCENT] [ WITH TIES] ] select_list
```

The clause provides a way to specify which columns should be included in the **SELECT** statement's result set. Columns are returned in the order in which they appear in the select list clause.

When you use a **SELECT** statement, the select list returns a virtual table of results (a result set). This table can contain constants, columns, functions, and derived columns. For example, the following code snippet returns a constant value ('**constant value**'), a database column (**Column1**), a function (**@@SERVERNAME**), and a derived column (**Column2+Column2**):

```
SELECT 'constant value', Column1, @@SERVERNAME, Column2+Column2
    FROM MyTable
```

To specify all columns in a table, you can either list each column or use an asterisk (*) in the select list. When you use an asterisk, all of the columns in the table will be returned. You can specify an * along with constraints, columns, and derived columns in the result set. The following example shows how to use an * in **SELECT** statements:

```
SELECT * FROM MyTable
SELECT *, Column1+Column2 FROM MyTable
```

By default, **SELECT** statements return all rows, including duplicate rows. To explicitly ask for all rows, include the **ALL** keyword before the select list. The **ALL** keyword does not ever have to be used, it is provided to make TSQL ANSI-compliant. To have a **SELECT** statement return only the unique rows, precede the select list with the **DISTINCT** keyword. If used, the **DISTINCT** or **ALL** keywords must immediately follow the **SELECT** keyword, as shown here:

```
SELECT DISTINCT 'constraint value', Column1,
                @@SERVERNAME, Column2+Column2
    FROM MyTable
```

You can assign values to variables or retrieve a result set with a **SELECT** statement. You cannot do both in the same **SELECT** statement. For example, if **@a** is an integer variable, this is a valid **SELECT**:

```
SELECT @a = 5
```

If **@a** is an integer variable, this is an invalid **SELECT**:

```
SELECT @a=5, au_id  FROM authors
```

When you perform a **SELECT**, the result set includes a default column heading for each column returned. Constant values, functions, and other derived columns have blank column headings. The default column heading is the column name. The headings for the previous example would be a blank value for the constant, **Column1** for Column1, a blank value for **@@SERVERNAME**, and a blank value for **Column2+Column2**.

You can change column headings by assigning aliases to them in the select list. SQL Server provides three ways to assign column headings to a result set:

```
Column_Heading = column
Column Column_Heading
Column AS Column_Heading
```

If the column heading has any special characters, such as spaces, you must enclose the column heading in quotes.

MS SQL Server allows you to use either single quotes (') or double quotes (") in SQL statements. The ANSI standard uses double quotes for object names and column headings with special characters, and single quotes for everything else. We recommend that you follow this practice.

In conjunction with the select list, you use the **FROM** clause to specify the tables that contain the data you are looking for.

The FROM Clause

The **FROM** clause specifies which data source(s) you are accessing. You can access data from tables, views, or derived tables. Listing 6.2 shows the **FROM** syntax.

Listing 6.2   The FROM syntax.

```
FROM
{ <table_or_view>| (select_statement)
    [AS] table_alias (column_alias ,. . .]
| <table_or_view> CROSS JOIN <table_or_view>
{ { INNER | { FULL | LEFT | RIGHT } [OUTER]  JOIN } <table_or_view>
    ON <join_condition>}
}[, ...n]
```

Without a **FROM** clause, a **SELECT** statement can only assign variables, return variables, and run functions. There can be up to 256 tables, views, or derived tables in a **SELECT** statement. Here's a multiple table example:

```
SELECT * FROM MyTable, MyOtherTable
```

This statement indicates that you want to select all columns from the tables named MyTable and MyOtherTable. To simplify SQL statements, you can use *table aliases*.

Table Aliases

When you use a table alias, you assign a shorter or more easily remembered name to a table that has a long or hard-to-remember name. If you specify a table alias, you can no longer reference the table by its name in the **SELECT** statements unless you list the table multiple times in the **FROM** clause, like this:

```
SELECT M.Column1, MyTable.Column2 FROM MyTable M, MyTable
```

In this example, the alias name for the first instance of MyTable is M. The **FROM** clause also has MyTable without an alias. The column Column1 comes from the aliased instance of MyTable (M). And the column Column2 is from the unaliased MyTable. The following example shows the use of an alias to shorten a long table name:

```
SELECT M.Column1 FROM MyVeryVeryVeryVeryVeryVeryVeryLongTableName
AS M
```

In this example, the alias name is **M** and the table name is **MyVeryVeryVery-VeryVeryVeryVeryLongTableName**. Because the table has an alias name, you cannot refer to the table in a **SELECT** statement without also referencing the alias name.

Another time you use table aliases is when you create *derived tables*. A derived table occurs when a **FROM** clause contains a **SELECT** statement instead of a table name. In this case, the derived table's data consists of the data returned from the **SELECT** statement that is embedded within the **FROM** clause. When you use a derived table, you must assign the table an alias, like this:

```
SELECT * FROM (SELECT * FROM master..sysprocesses) B
```

In this example, **SELECT * FROM master..sysprocesses** is a derived table. This derived table has a table alias B.

To simplify your SQL, you can also assign aliases to columns in the **FROM** clause, as shown here:

```
SELECT AA FROM (SELECT LongColumnName FROM
  MyTable WHERE b != 123)  AS t1 (AA)
```

This example creates a table alias called t1 that consists of the column LongColumnName from MyTable. This column is aliased to AA.

 When using a derived table, you must provide an alias for all derived columns.

Table and column aliases are used to simplify and clarify the objects being used in the query. Often, if you have to qualify an object name, it becomes cumbersome to create your SQL.

Qualifying Object Names

A fully qualified table name consists of ServerName.DatabaseName.Owner-Name.TableName.

➤ **ServerName**   Defaults to the current SQL Server.

➤ **DatabaseName**   Defaults to the current database.

➤ **OwnerName**   Defaults to first check to see if the current user owns the table; if that fails, OwnerName defaults to dbo.

➤ **TableName**   Specifies the table's name. The TableName must be specified.

When specifying ServerName, you must either specify the DatabaseName and OwnerName or use a placeholder (a ".." is a placeholder). When specifying the DatabaseName, you must either specify the OwnerName components to the left or use a placeholder, as follows:

```
pubs.dbo.titles
pubs..titles
otherserver.yourdb.user2.TheTable
```

In the first example, pubs is the database name, dbo is the table owner, and titles is the table. The second example also has pubs as the database name, the table owner is either the current user or dbo, and the table is titles. The third example accesses another server called otherserver, the database name is yourdb, the table owner is user2, and the table is TheTable.

When using a table alias, the fully qualified column name is TableAlias.Column-Name. If you do not use a table alias, a fully qualified column name consists of ServerName.DatabaseName.OwnerName.TableName.ColumnName.

➤ **ServerName**   Defaults to the current SQL Server.

➤ **DatabaseName**   Defaults to the current database.

➤ **OwnerName**   Defaults to first check to see if the current user owns the table; if that fails, OwnerName defaults to dbo.

➤ **TableName**   Is the name of the table containing the column.

➤ **ColumnName**   Is the name of the column.

If you do not qualify the ColumnName, the ColumnName must be unique in all the tables used in the **FROM** clause, otherwise SQL Server has no way of knowing what table the column is from. If you qualify the column, the column qualifier must exactly match the way you qualified the table name.

If you do not qualify the table in the **FROM** clause, you cannot qualify the column with the table owner, database name, or server name.

If you use a table alias, a fully qualified column name is TableAlias.ColumnName. Again, if the TableAlias is not specified, the ColumnName must be unique. The following code snippet shows examples of qualified column names.

```
Column1
titles.title
pubs.dbo.titles.title
```

The first example refers to the column called Column1. The second example refers to the column title from titles. The third example refers to the column title, from the table titles, owned by the database owner, in the database pubs.

Whereas the **FROM** clause specifies where to obtain data to fulfill a **SELECT** statement, the **WHERE** clause specifies which rows of the data to return as part of the result set.

The WHERE Clause

The **WHERE** clause is used to specify which rows to return in the result set. Only rows that match the conditions in the **WHERE** clause are returned. Listing 6.3 shows the syntax for the **WHERE** clause.

Listing 6.3   The WHERE clause's syntax.

```
WHERE [ NOT ] <predicate> [ { AND | OR } [ NOT ] <predicate> ]
} [, ...n]

<predicate> ::=
{ expression { = | <> | != | > | >= | !> | < | <= | !< } expression
| string_expression [NOT] LIKE
                    string_expression[ESCAPE 'escape_character']
| expression [NOT] BETWEEN expression AND expression
| expression IS [NOT] NULL
| expression [NOT] IN (subquery | expression [,...n])
| expression { = | <> | != | > | >= | !> | < | <= | !< }
{ALL | SOME | ANY} (subquery)

| EXISTS (subquery)
}
```

Using the **WHERE** clause, you can compare columns, variables, constants, functions, and any other expressions. The items being compared do not have to be in the select list. You can join together multiple predicates, called search conditions or search arguments, with **AND** and **OR**. In addition, you can use **NOT** to cause the opposite of a condition to come true. Predicates can be grouped with parentheses to control the order of the comparisons. There is no limit to the number of predicates that can be in a **WHERE** clause.

Comparison operators are used to compare two expressions. Table 6.1 shows common comparison operators and their meanings.

The following examples show SQL statements using comparison operators with different expressions:

```
SELECT title, price FROM titles WHERE price = 19.99

SELECT title, price FROM titles WHERE SQRT(price) !< 19.99

SELECT title, price FROM titles
            WHERE NOT ( (price >21.00) AND (price <30.00) )
```

The first **SELECT** statement will only return rows in which the price is equal to 19.99. In the second example's **WHERE** clause, the SQRT function is performed on price, and then rows with this result not less than 19.99 are returned. In the final example, price is checked to be greater than 21.00 and less than 30.00; only rows in which price is not in this range are returned. One special part of the **WHERE** clause is the **IN** clause.

Table 6.1 Comparison operators.	
Operator	**Meaning**
=	Equal
<>	Not equal
!=	Not equal
>	Greater than
>=	Greater than or equal to
!>	Not greater than
<	Less than
<=	Less than or equal to
!<	Not less than

The IN Clause

The **IN** clause determines whether a column is in a set (list) of values. It is used when you want to check a column to see if it is any one of a list of possible values. An **IN** statement can always be rewritten as a group of **OR** conditions. Following are two examples of using **IN** clauses:

```
SELECT title, price FROM titles
    WHERE price IN( 19.99, 21.00, 25.00, 29.99)

SELECT title, price FROM titles
    WHERE price NOT IN( 19.99, 21.00, 25.00, 29.99)
```

The first example returns rows where the price is either 19.99, 21.00, 25.00, or 29.99. In the second example, only rows in which the price is not 19.99, 21.00, 25.00, or 29.00 are returned.

The next commonly used part of the **WHERE** clause is the **LIKE** clause.

The LIKE Clause

The **LIKE** clause performs pattern matching on character strings. You use a **LIKE** clause when you do not want to do an exact comparison—for instance, when you do not know which way "smith" is spelled in a column. The patterns can contain regular characters and wildcard characters. The **LIKE** clause syntax is as follows:

```
string_expression1 [NOT] LIKE string_pattern
            [ESCAPE 'escape_character']
```

The **LIKE** clause checks to see if the string expression contains the string pattern. The second string expression can contain both regular characters and wildcard characters. Table 6.2 shows the pattern matching characters and their meanings.

You can combine wildcard characters in the pattern. If you want to match any of the wildcard characters, you have to use an **escape** character, which is identified with the **ESCAPE** keyword. There is no default **escape** character.

The following examples show **LIKE** clauses in use:

```
-- match all Column1 containing with two or more characters
Column1 LIKE '_%_'
-- return all Column1 containing a open bracket
Column1 LIKE '%\[%' ESCAPE '\'
-- match the different forms of the name smith
Column1 LIKE '[Ss]m[iy]th'
```

Table 6.2	Pattern matching characters.
Wildcard	**Description**
%	Matches zero or more characters in the string expression.
_ (underscore)	Matches exactly one character in the string expression.
[characters]	Matches one character in the string expression with the characters between the brackets. The brackets can contain either a range of characters to match ([L-Z]) or it can contain a specific set of characters to match against ([AbK12M]).
[^characters]	Similar to [characters], but it searches for strings that do not contain the character set or range.

The first example checks for any string that is at least two characters long. In the second example, the backslash is set to be the escape character. It is then used to escape the open bracket. This **LIKE** clause finds all values for Column1 that contains an open bracket. The final example looks for smith, with either a capital or lowercase "s," and either an "i" or a "y."

The BETWEEN Clause

The **BETWEEN** clause is used to specify the lower and upper boundaries of a range. You use the **BETWEEN** clause when you know the minimum and maximum values that you are looking for. A **BETWEEN** clause is inclusive of the end points. If the lower boundary is greater than the upper boundary, then no rows will be returned. All expressions must be of data types that can implicitly convert to each other or must be explicitly converted in your **SELECT** statement. (Data type conversions will be covered later.) The following code example shows how to use the **BETWEEN** clause:

```
SELECT title, price FROM titles
    WHERE price BETWEEN 10 AND 20
```

This example finds all rows in which the price is greater than or equal to 10 and less than or equal to 20.

The NOT Keyword

The **NOT** keyword can be included with any of the comparisons in the **WHERE** clause. It causes the opposite of the comparison to be checked. The following example uses the **NOT** keyword:

```
SELECT title, price FROM titles
    WHERE price NOT BETWEEN 10 AND 20
```

The example with the **NOT** keyword returns all rows in which the price is less than 10 and all the rows in which the price is greater than 20.

The NULL Options

To test for a SQL Server **NULL**, you must either use the **IS NULL** option or the Transaction SQL extension =**NULL**. You can use the **IS NULL** function in the select list to return a different value if the column is null. The following example shows how to check for nulls, and how to retrieve rows that are not **NULL**.

```
SELECT * FROM titles WHERE notes IS NULL
SELECT * FROM titles WHERE notes = NULL
SELECT * from titles WHERE notes IS NOT NULL
SELECT * from titles WHERE notes != NULL
```

Both of the first two examples are retrieving the rows from titles in which the notes column does not have a value. The last two examples are retrieving rows in which the notes column does have a value.

 The character string "NULL" is not the same as a null column. Also, the empty character string " " is not the same as a database null.

The GROUP BY Clause

The **GROUP BY** clause is used to display subtotals as part of the result set. It is used in conjunction with aggregate functions (aggregate functions are discussed in more detail later in this chapter) to provide summary results. In short, an aggregate function is a summary function that calculates the summary result that is returned as part of the select list. When using **GROUP BY**, all the columns in the result set must either be an aggregate function or used in the **GROUP BY** clause. The **GROUP BY** syntax is:

```
GROUP BY [ALL] group_by_list [WITH CUBE|ROLLUP]
```

The **ALL** keyword instructs SQL Server to produce a row for columns that normally would have not produced rows based upon the **WHERE** clause. The group_by_list can be any column from the select list. Any time the value for the columns in the group_by_list changes, another result value is calculated. Optionally, you can specify either a **CUBE** or a **ROLLUP** grouping to be performed.

CUBE And ROLLUP

The **CUBE** and **ROLLUP** keywords enable you to perform multidimensional analysis of data in one SQL statement. You cannot use both a **CUBE** and a **ROLLUP** in the same **SELECT** statement. **CUBE** and **ROLLUP** produce result sets that are typically used in reports. Summary values are returned as separate result sets intermixed with the result sets for each group, or appended after the main result set.

➤ If you are using **CUBE** or **ROLLUP**, the **GROUP BY** clause can only have 10 columns or expressions, and the returned data must be 8,060 bytes or less.

➤ Furthermore, the **GROUP BY** clause must contain at least one column or expression.

➤ You cannot use the **DISTINCT** keyword with aggregate functions when you are using **CUBE** or **ROLLUP** keywords.

➤ The **GROUP BY ALL** keyword cannot be used with the **CUBE** or **ROLLUP** keywords.

➤ **CUBE** and **ROLLUP** can be used with any aggregate function.

The following section covers the use of the **CUBE** keyword.

CUBE

The **CUBE** statement specifies that, in addition to the usual aggregate values that are provided by the **GROUP BY** clause, summary rows, or cumulative aggregates, are included in the result set. These rows are generated by grouping a subset of the columns in the **GROUP BY** clause.

Every combination of column values in the columns included in the **GROUP BY** clause produces a superset of groups. For every different value in a column in the group_by list, an extra **CUBE** row is produced with a **NULL** value assigned to that column for all the values of the other columns. This **NULL** value represents all the values for a particular column. The aggregate function(s) in the select list are applied to these groups to produce summary values generating the additional rows.

The **CUBE** operator can be used to generate cross-referenced information without having to write additional procedures. The **CUBE** operator creates all combinations of groupings from the list of columns in a **GROUP BY** clause. Listing 6.4 shows an example of using the **CUBE** keyword.

Listing 6.4   CUBE example.

```
SELECT stor_id, pub_name, title,  AVG(qty)
  FROM sales, titles, publishers
  WHERE sales.title_id = titles.title_id
  AND publishers.pub_id = titles.pub_id
  GROUP BY pub_name, title, stor_id
  WITH CUBE
```

This example will produce extra aggregate rows, calculating the **CUBE** for the AVG(qty).

ROLLUP

The **ROLLUP** keyword is used to specify a cumulative aggregate that is computed along with the usual aggregate rows for elements within a **GROUP BY** clause. This is useful when you have sets within sets, such as column sums or averages. The main difference between **ROLLUP** and **CUBE** is that **ROLLUP** is sensitive to the position of the column in the **GROUP BY** clause. **ROLLUP** groupings are made up of columns to the right of the current column value. And changes in the operator are applied from the right to the left across the columns in the **GROUP BY** clause. Listing 6.5 shows an example of a **ROLLUP**.

Listing 6.5   ROLLUP example.

```
SELECT stor_id, pub_name, title,  AVG(qty)
  FROM sales, titles, publishers
  WHERE sales.title_id = titles.title_id
  AND publishers.pub_id = titles.pub_id
  GROUP BY pub_name, title, stor_id
  WITH ROLLUP
```

This example will produce extra aggregate rows, calculating the **ROLLUP** for the AVG(qty).

CUBE Vs. ROLLUP

Tables 6.3 and 6.4 illustrate the differences between the results of a **CUBE** statement and a **ROLLUP** statement. Listing 6.6 creates a sample table and fills it with data for the **CUBE** versus **ROLLUP** example. Listing 6.7 shows the **SELECT** statements that will be run against the table created in Listing 6.6. The results of the **SELECT** statements can be found in Table 6.3 for the **CUBE** example and in Table 6.4 for the **ROLLUP** example. As you can see, the **CUBE** keyword returns more rows than the **ROLLUP** keyword. The columns with a **NULL** are the generated aggregate totals.

Table 6.3   CUBE result.

a	b	c	SUM
1	abc	2	1
1	abc	NULL	1
1	def	3	2
1	def	NULL	2
1	NULL	NULL	3
2	abc	2	3
2	abc	NULL	3
2	def	2	4
2	def	NULL	4
2	NULL	NULL	7
3	abc	2	5
3	abc	NULL	5
3	def	2	6
3	def	NULL	6
3	NULL	NULL	11
4	abc	2	7
4	abc	NULL	7
4	NULL	NULL	7
5	def	2	8
5	def	NULL	8
5	NULL	NULL	8
NULL	NULL	NULL	36
NULL	abc	2	16
NULL	abc	NULL	16
NULL	def	2	18
NULL	def	3	2
NULL	def	NULL	20
1	NULL	2	1
2	NULL	2	7
3	NULL	2	11

(continued)

Table 6.3   CUBE result (continued).

a	b	c	SUM
4	NULL	2	7
5	NULL	2	8
NULL	NULL	2	34
1	NULL	3	2
NULL	NULL	3	2

Table 6.4   ROLLUP result.

a	b	c	SUM
1	abc	2	1
1	abc	NULL	1
1	def	3	2
1	def	NULL	2
1	NULL	NULL	3
2	abc	2	3
2	abc	NULL	3
2	def	2	4
2	def	NULL	4
2	NULL	NULL	7
3	abc	2	5
3	abc	NULL	5
3	def	2	6
3	def	NULL	6
3	NULL	NULL	11
4	abc	2	7
4	abc	NULL	7
4	NULL	NULL	7
5	def	2	8
5	def	NULL	8
5	NULL	NULL	8
NULL	NULL	NULL	36

Listing 6.6   Sample table and data.

```
CREATE table t1 ( a int, b char(10), c int, d int)
go
INSERT t1 VALUES (1,'abc',2,1)
INSERT t1 VALUES (1,'def',3,2)
INSERT t1 VALUES (2,'abc',2,3)
INSERT t1 VALUES (2,'def',2,4)
INSERT t1 VALUES (3,'abc',2,5)
INSERT t1 VALUES (3,'def',2,6)
INSERT t1 VALUES (4,'abc',2,7)
INSERT t1 VALUES (5,'def',2,8)
go
```

Listing 6.7   SELECT statements.

```
SELECT a,b,c, SUM(d)
    FROM t1
    GROUP BY a,b,c
    WITH CUBE

SELECT a,b,c, SUM(d)
    FROM t1
    GROUP BY a,b,c
    WITH ROLLUP
```

The HAVING Clause

A **HAVING** clause behaves similarly to a **WHERE** clause, except it can only be used with **GROUP BY** clauses. A **HAVING** clause can only use columns that are in the select list. You can use aggregate functions, and they can be different functions than were in the select list. The following example illustrates the use of a **HAVING** clause:

```
SELECT stor_id, pub_name, title,  AVG(qty)
  FROM sales, titles, publishers
  WHERE sales.title_id = titles.title_id
  AND publishers.pub_id = titles.pub_id
  GROUP BY pub_name, title, stor_id
  HAVING AVG(qty) > 10
```

This example will compute the average of the qty column for the pub_name, title, and stor_id. Only rows with an average greater than 10 will be returned.

The main difference between a **HAVING** and a **WHERE** clause is illustrated by when they are executed. A **WHERE** clause is performed as the results are being generated. The **HAVING** clause is executed after an intermediate result is generated. This is why you can have aggregate functions in a **HAVING** clause, and not in a **WHERE** clause.

The ORDER BY Clause

When you retrieve data, it is returned in the order in which SQL Server finds it. The **ORDER BY** keyword allows you to override this behavior and specify the order in which you want the rows returned. The exact order depends on the system sort order. You can sort the result by multiple columns; the limitations are that the total data length of all columns being sorted must be less than 8.060 bytes. If you exceed this limit, the query won't run.

When specifying columns to use in ordering the results, you can use column headers, actual column names (even if they are not specified in the select list), or an integer representing the columns order in the select list.

You can use the **ASC** and **DESC** keywords to specify whether you want the data to be sorted in ascending or descending order. The default behavior is to sort in ascending order. The **ASC** and **DESC** keywords apply to one column at a time. Here's an example of a **SELECT** statement with an **ORDER BY** clause:

```
SELECT au_lname FROM authors  ORDER BY au_fname ASC
```

The previous example returns all au_lname from the table authors. The results are sorted by au_fname (which is not in the select list) in ascending order.

COMPUTE

The **COMPUTE** and **COMPUTE BY** TSQL extensions allow you to include both detail and summary information from a single SQL query in a result set. **COMPUTE** and **COMPUTE BY** run aggregate functions (aggregate functions are discussed in more detail in the next section) to calculate totals and subtotals, as shown here:

```
COMPUTE aggregate_function(expression)
    [,aggregate_function(expression) ...]

COMPUTE aggregate_function(expression)
    [,aggregate_function(expression) ...]
  BY column_list
```

When using **COMPUTE BY**, all columns in the column list must appear in the **ORDER BY** clause and in the same order. You cannot skip any columns, but you do not have to use all the columns in the **ORDER BY** clause. For example, if the **ORDER BY** column list is LastName, FirstName, Zip, you can do a **COMPUTE BY** on LastName or LastName, FirstName or LastName, FirstName, Zip.

The *expression* in the **COMPUTE** and **COMPUTE BY** must match an expression in the select list. For example, if you use **price*2** in a **COMPUTE**, you must also use **price*2** in the **SELECT** expression. This is the one time it might look like you are using an aggregate function on an aggregate function, which is normally not allowed. The following code snippet illustrates using a **COMPUTE** clause.

```
SELECT type, SUM(price) FROM titles
    GROUP BY type
    COMPUTE AVG(SUM(price))
```

The code will return the type and the SUM(price) for value of type in the titles table. It will provide a final row that performs the **COMPUTE** clause; this row will contain the average of all of the summary prices.

 You cannot use column aliases in the **COMPUTE** clause. If you try, SQL Server will return a syntax error.

Functions

Functions provide SQL Server with the ability to perform calculations upon the data to generate results. These functions are similar to functions in any other programming language. SQL server has three function types:

➤ **Scalar** Operates on a single value, or no value, and returns a single value.

➤ **Aggregate** Operates on a set of values.

➤ **Rowset** Replaces a table name.

The upcoming sections describe the function types in greater detail.

Scalar Functions

As noted earlier, scalar functions operate on a zero or one value and return a single value. Scalar functions that take parameters can be nested so that a function can be called on by another function. There are seven basic types of scalar functions, as shown in Table 6.5.

Table 6.5   SQL Server function types.

Function Type	Function Use
String Function	Performs string manipulation.
Math Function	Performs basic mathematical operations.
Date Function	Performs data manipulation.
System Function	Returns system information.
Security	Returns security information.
Metadata	Checks information about database objects.
Text and Image	Performs data retrieval and modification of text and image columns.

 If you are familiar with previous versions of SQL Server, you should be aware that global variables are now called scalar functions.

These functions can be used in most **SELECT** statement clauses. However, they cannot be used in a **HAVING** clause, unless they are also used in the select list. Table 6.6 shows some of the most commonly used scalar functions.

 Any of the scalar functions listed in this book's Appendix B may appear on the test. Table 6.6 shows the most important functions for our purposes.

Table 6.6   Commonly used scalar functions.

Function	Description
@@CURSOR_ROWS	Returns the number of rows in the last cursor opened.
@@ERROR	Returns the error number for the last TSQL statement.
@@FETCH_STATUS	Returns the status of the last cursor **FETCH** statement.
@@IDENTITY	Returns the last inserted identity value.
@@NESTLEVEL	Returns the stored procedure nesting level.
@@ROWCOUNT	Returns the number of rows affected by the last SQL statement.

(continued)

Table 6.6 Commonly used scalar functions *(continued)*.	
Function	**Description**
@@SERVERNAME	Returns the name of the local server.
@@SPID	Returns the server process ID.
@@VERSION	Returns the date, exact release of SQL Server being used, and processor type.
ABS(*numeric_expr*)	Returns the absolute value of a specified value.
ASCII(*char_expr*)	Returns the ASCII value of the first character in a *char_expr*.
CASE	Evaluates a list of conditions, and returns a result.
CAST	Converts between data types.
CHAR(*int_expr*)	Converts an integer to an ASCII character.
CONVERT(*datatype, expression[,style]*)	Converts columns, variables, and constants from one SQL Server data type to another data type.
DATALENGTH(*char_expr*)	Returns an integer number of characters in *char_expr*, ignoring trailing spaces.
DATEADD(*datepart, number, date_expr*)	Returns the date produced by adding specified *number* of date parts to *date_expr*. To subtract, add a negative number.
DATEDIFF(*datepart, date_expr1, date_expr2*)	Returns *date_expr2 - date_expr1*, as measured by specified *datepart*.
DATENAME(*datepart, date_expr*)	Returns a specified part of *date_expr* value as a string, converted to a name (such as June) if appropriate.
DATEPART(*datepart, date_expr*)	Returns a specified part of *date_expr* value as an integer.
DB_NAME([*db_id*])	Specifies the database name.
GETDATE()	Returns the current system date and time.
ISDATE(*expression*)	Returns **1** if the expression is a valid date; 0 if it is invalid.
ISNULL(*expression, constant_value*)	Replace **NULL** values with a specified constant.

(continued)

Table 6.6   Commonly used scalar functions *(continued)*.

Function	Description
ISNUMERIC(*expression*)	Returns **1** if the expression is a valid numeric; 0 if it is not a valid numeric expression.
LEFT(*char_expr, int_expr*)	Returns *int_expr* characters from left of *char_expr*.
LEN(*char_expr*)	Returns the integer number of characters in *char_expr*, ignoring trailing spaces.
LOWER(*char_expr*)	Converts *char_expr* to lowercase.
LTRIM(*char_expr*)	Removes leading spaces.
MONTH(date)	Returns the integer for the month.
NULLIF(*expression1, expression2*)	Returns a **NULL** value if expression1 equals expression2.
RIGHT(*char_expr, int_expr*)	Returns *int_expr* characters from the right of *char_expr*.
RTRIM(*char_expr*)	Removes trailing spaces.
STR(*float_expr* [, *length* [, *decimal*]])	Results in a numeric to character conversion.
STUFF(*char_expr1, start, length, char_expr2*)	Replace *length* characters from *expr1* at *start* with *expr2*.
SUBSTRING(*expression, start, length*)	Returns a part of a string.
SUSER_SID([*'login_name'*])	Returns a user's SQL Server ID number.
SUSER_SNAME([*server_uses_sid*])	Returns a user's SQL Server login name.
UPPER(*char_expr*)	Converts *char_expr* to uppercase.
USER_NAME([*user_id*]) or **SESSION_USER**	Returns the user's name in a database.
YEAR(*'date expression'*)	Returns the four-digit integer for the year.

Most of the scalar functions are simple and do not need a detailed explanation. The **CASE**, date functions, and conversion functions are not only more complex, but will also be covered in greater detail on the test.

CASE Clause

Unlike the other scalar functions, the **CASE** function is really a clause—it evaluates conditions to return a single result. In the simple format, it compares an expression to a set of simple expressions. The more complex format, the search **CASE** format, evaluates a set of Boolean expressions. Listing 6.8 shows the syntax for the **CASE** function.

Listing 6.8   **CASE** syntax.

```
CASE input_expression
WHEN when_expression THEN result_expression
[,...n]
[ELSE else_result_expression]
END

-- or --
CASE
WHEN boolean_expression THEN result_expression
[,...n]
[ELSE else_result_expression]
END
```

CASE returns the result for the first statement that is true. If no statements are true, it returns the **ELSE** statement. If there is no **ELSE**, then **NULL** is returned. Listing 6.9 shows a simple **CASE** statement, and Listing 6.10 shows a search **CASE** statement.

Listing 6.9   A simple **CASE** statement.

```
SELECT    Category = CASE type
              WHEN 'popular_comp' THEN 'Popular Computing'
              WHEN 'mod_cook' THEN 'Cooking'
              WHEN 'business' THEN 'Business'
              WHEN 'psychology' THEN 'Psychology'
              WHEN 'trad_cook' THEN 'Cooking'
              ELSE 'unknown'
        END,
    title  AS 'Book Title', price
FROM titles
ORDER BY Category
```

Listing 6.10   A search **CASE** statement.

```
SELECT    Category = CASE
              WHEN type = 'popular_comp' THEN 'Popular Computing'
              WHEN type like '%cook' THEN 'Cooking'
              WHEN type = 'business' THEN 'Business'
              WHEN type = 'psychology' THEN 'Psychology'
              WHEN type = 'trad_cook' THEN 'Cooking'
              ELSE 'unknown'
        END,
```

```
        title  AS 'Book Title', price
FROM titles
ORDER BY Category
```

A CASE can search on different columns in each of the **WHEN** clauses. This allows you to generate the result column on widely different conditions. In the real world, you will not normally have a need to perform this sort of calculation. The following code example shows a **CASE** clause using a **WHEN** on different columns.

```
SELECT   Category =  CASE
        WHEN price IS NULL THEN '!!Unpriced book!!'
        WHEN type = 'popular_comp' THEN 'Popular Computing'
        WHEN type like '%cook%' THEN 'Cooking'
        ELSE 'No Category'
     END,
     title  AS 'Book Title', price
FROM titles
ORDER BY Category
```

Date Functions

SQL Server provides many date functions for working with dates. Many of these functions use date parts as a parameter. Table 6.7 shows the date parts.

 Know the valid date parts that are listed in Table 6.7.

Table 6.7   Date parts.

Part Name	Abbreviation	Valid Values
Year	Yy	1753-9999
Quarter	Qq	1-4
Month	Mm	1-12
Dayofyear	Dy	1-366
Day	Dd	1-31
Week	Wk	1-54
Weekday	Dw	1-7 (1=Sunday)
Hour	Hh	0-23
Minute	Mi	0-59
Second	Ss	0-59
Millisecond	Ms	0-999

When using date parts in a date function, you can either use the part's name or abbreviation. The most common date functions are **DATEADD**, **DATEDIFF**, **DATENAME**, and **DATEPART**. The following code example illustrates the use of date functions and date parts.

```
SELECT DATENAME(DW,GETDATE())

SELECT title, "Days Since Published" =
    DATEDIFF(dd, pubdate, GETDATE())
  FROM titles
```

The first example retrieves the day of the week for the current day. The second example calculates the number of days since the book was published.

Data Type Conversion

SQL Server implicitly converts between many data types. When it performs implicit conversions, the data type precedence rules specify which of the data types get converted. Data types with a lower precedence get converted to data types with a higher precedence. The data conversion precedence, from highest to lowest, is as follows:

➤ DATETIME

➤ SMALLDATETIME

➤ FLOAT

➤ REAL

➤ DECIMAL

➤ MONEY

➤ SMALLMONEY

➤ INT

➤ SMALLINT

➤ TINYINT

➤ BIT

➤ NTEXT

➤ IMAGE

➤ TIMESTAMP

➤ NVARCHAR

➤ VARCHAR

➤ CHAR

➤ VARBINARY

➤ BINARY

➤ UNIQUEIDENTIFIER

When performing implicit data conversions, user-defined datatypes take the precedence of their base datatype. If one of the expressions is an aggregate function (as described in the next section), then the aggregate function's datatype will be used as the datatype for the expression. If one of the functions is a column and the other expression is not a column or aggregate function, then the column's datatype is used as the datatype for the expression.

You can perform explicit conversions when the implicit conversions do not meet your needs. There are two functions you can use—**CAST** and **CONVERT**. The **CAST** function is an ANSI standard function used to convert between data types. The **CONVERT** function, shown in the following code snippet, is a TSQL extension that can convert between datatypes:

```
CONVERT (datatype [(length)], expression [,style])
CAST(expression AS data_type)
```

The **CONVERT** function has the added capability of choosing a style, picking a format, when converting into character data. This allows you to reformat the data in SQL. Styles can be used with date and numeric conversions. Tables 6.8, 6.9, and 6.10 show the style values and the converted values.

Table 6.8   Date conversion styles.

No Century	With Century	Format Of The Converted String
N/A	0 or 100	mon dd yyyy hh:miAM (or PM)
1	101	mm/dd/yy
2	102	yy.mm.dd
3	103	dd/mm/yy
4	104	dd.mm.yy
5	105	dd-mm-yy
6	106	dd mon yy
7	107	mon dd, yy
8	108	hh:mm:ss
N/A	9 or 109	mon dd, yyyy hh:mi:ss:mmmAM (or PM)

(continued)

Table 6.8	Date conversion styles *(continued)*.	
No Century	With Century	Format Of The Converted String
10	110	mm-dd-yy
11	111	yy/mm/dd
12	112	Yymmdd
13	113	dd mon yyyy hh:mi:ss:mmm (24 hr clock)
14	114	hh:mi:ss:mmm (24 hr clock)
20	120	Yyyy-mm-dd hh:mi:ss(24h)
21	121	yyyy-mm-dd hh:mi:ss:mmm(24h)

Table 6.9	Float and real conversion styles.	
Value	Description	Example
0	Default conversion, 6 digits, scientific notation when appropriate	1.23457e+006
1	Always 8-digit scientific notation	1.2345671e+006
2	Always 16-digit scientific notation	1.234567125000000e+006

Table 6.10	Money data types conversion style.	
Value	Description	Example
0	Default conversion: no commas, two digits to the right of the decimal	123456.12
1	Commas every three digits to the left of the decimal, two digits after	123,234.12
2	No commas, four digits to the right of decimal point	1234.1234

Not all data types can be converted, even with explicit conversion functions. Figure 6.1 shows the allowed conversions.

Aggregate Functions

Aggregate functions perform summary information on an expression and return one value. They are used in conjunction with **GROUP BY** and **HAVING** clauses. Table 6.11 lists the aggregate functions and their definitions.

Aggregate functions perform on the non-**NULL** values in the expression. Unlike scalar functions, aggregate functions cannot be performed on aggregate functions. Also, aggregate functions cannot be in a **WHERE** clause, unless the functions are in a subquery. In contrast, aggregate functions can be in a **HAVING** clause.

From \ To	BINARY	BIT	CHAR	DATETIME	DECIMAL	FLOAT	IMAGE	INT	MONEY	NCHAR	NVARCHAR	NTEXT	NUMERIC	REAL	SMALLDATETIME	SMALLINT	SMALLMONEY	TEXT	TIMESTAMP	TINYINT	UNIQUEIDENTIFIER	VARBINARY	VARCHAR
BINARY	-	I	I	I	X	I	I	I	I	I	X	I	X	I	I	I	X	I	I	I	I	I	I
BIT	I	-	I	I	I	I	I	I	I	I	I	X	I	I	I	I	I	X	I	I	X	I	I
CHAR	E	I	-	I	I	I	I	E	I	I	I	I	I	I	I	I	E	I	E	I	I	I	I
DATETIME	E	E	I	-	E	E	X	E	E	I	I	I	X	E	E	X	E	I	E	I	I	I	I
DECIMAL	I	I	I	I	C	I	X	I	I	I	I	I	C	I	I	I	I	I	X	I	I	X	I
FLOAT	I	I	I	I	I	-	X	I	I	I	I	I	X	I	I	I	I	I	X	I	I	X	I
IMAGE	I	X	X	X	X	X	-	X	X	X	X	X	X	X	X	X	X	X	I	X	X	I	X
INT	I	I	I	I	I	I	X	-	I	I	I	I	X	I	I	I	I	I	X	I	I	X	I
MONEY	I	I	E	I	I	I	I	X	-	I	I	I	X	I	I	I	I	I	X	I	I	X	I
NCHAR	E	I	I	I	I	I	I	I	I	-	I	I	I	I	I	I	I	E	I	E	I	I	I
NVARCHAR	E	I	I	I	I	I	I	I	I	E	-	I	I	I	I	I	I	E	I	E	I	I	I
NTEXT	X	X	E	X	X	X	X	X	X	I	I	-	X	X	X	X	X	X	X	X	X	X	E
NUMERIC	I	I	I	I	C	I	X	I	I	I	I	I	C	I	I	I	I	I	X	I	I	X	I
REAL	I	I	I	I	I	I	X	I	I	I	I	I	X	-	I	I	I	I	X	I	I	X	I
SMALLDATETIME	E	E	I	I	E	E	X	E	E	I	I	I	X	E	-	E	E	I	E	I	I	X	I
SMALLINT	I	I	I	I	I	I	X	I	I	I	I	I	X	I	I	-	I	I	X	I	I	X	I
SMALLMONEY	I	I	E	I	I	I	X	I	I	E	E	X	I	I	I	I	-	I	I	X	I	I	E
TEXT	X	X	I	X	X	X	X	X	X	E	E	X	X	X	X	X	X	-	X	X	X	X	I
TIMESTAMP	I	I	I	I	I	X	X	I	I	I	I	I	X	I	I	I	I	I	-	I	I	X	I
TINYINT	I	I	I	I	I	X	X	I	I	X	X	X	I	X	I	I	I	X	I	-	I	I	I
UNIQUEIDENTIFIER	I	X	I	X	X	X	X	X	X	X	X	X	X	X	X	X	X	X	X	X	-	X	I
VARBINARY	I	I	I	I	I	X	I	I	I	I	I	X	I	X	I	I	I	I	X	I	I	-	I
VARCHAR	E	I	I	I	I	I	I	I	I	E	I	I	I	I	I	I	I	E	I	E	I	I	-

X   stands for no conversion allowed
I   stands for implicit conversion
E   stands for explicit conversion
C   stands for use convert function if precision changes

Figure 6.1   Data conversions.

Table 6.11   Aggregate functions.

Function	Definition
sum([all | distinct] expression)	Specifies the total of the (distinct) values in the numeric column.
avg([all | distinct]) expression)	Specifies the average of the (distinct) values in the numeric column.
count([all | distinct] expression)	Specifies the number of (distinct) non-null values in the column.
count(*)	Specifies the number of selected rows. This is the only aggregate function that includes nulls.
max(expression)	Specifies the highest value in the expression.
min(expression)	Specifies the lowest value in the expression.
STDEV(expression)	Returns the standard deviation.
STDEVP(expression)	Returns the standard deviation for the population.
VAR(expression)	Returns the statistical variance.
VARP(expression)	Returns the statistical variance for the population.

If you are using an aggregate function in a select list, all noncolumns that are not aggregate functions must be in the **GROUP BY** clause.

Rowset Functions

Rowset functions can be used in place of table names in a **SELECT** statement. There are four rowset functions:

➤ **CONTAINSTABLE** Returns a table that matches the free text selection performing "fuzzy" or not precise matching (covered in Chapter 15).

➤ **FREETEXTTABLE** Returns a table that matches the free text selection matching the meaning, but not exact wording, of the free text criteria (covered in Chapter 15).

➤ **OPENQUERY** Accesses a linked remote server to return data.

➤ **OPENROWSET** Opens a one-time connection to a remote server to access data.

The first two functions are used with free text searches, and the second two are used when connecting with remote data sources through OLE-DB. The difference between OPENQUERY and OPENROWSET is that with OPENQUERY, you must first set up the linked server.

```
SELECT *
   FROM OPENQUERY(MyServer,
      'SELECT au_fname, au_lname FROM pubs..titles')
```

This example uses an existing link called MyServer to access data from the table titles in the pubs database. Many queries use just one table. But a lot of the more complex things your application needs to do requires data from more than one table. The SQL **JOIN** clause allows you to retrieve data from more than one table in a **SELECT** statement.

Joining Tables

Often when you need to retrieve data, it is not in one table. A *join* clause allows you to select data from two to 256 tables or views or derived tables.

➤ You cannot join directly on **NTEXT**, **TEXT**, and **IMAGE** columns.

➤ When you join a table to itself, you need to provide a table alias.

➤ A special way of joining data from multiple tables into a **SELECT** statement is the subquery.

There are three join types: cross, inner, and outer.

Cross Joins

A cross join, also called a Cartesian Product, returns all the rows from all tables being joined together. The total number of rows returned is each table's number of rows multiplied by the other tables' number of rows. For example, let's say you have three tables involved in a join. The first table returns 30,000 rows, and the other two tables each return 1,000 rows. The total number of rows returned by a cross join is 30,000 * 1,000 * 1,000, or 30,000,000,000 rows. Obviously, you have to be very careful when using cross joins. The following examples show a cross join:

```
SELECT * FROM titles CROSS JOIN titleauthor

SELECT * FROM titles, titleauthor
```

The first example performs an ANSI standard **CROSS JOIN** between titles and titleauthor. The second example does the same join, using TSQL extensions.

Inner Join

An inner join is the most common join. It uses a comparison operator to limit the rows returned. In inner joins, you specify common columns (called *common keys*) to use in relating the tables together. This is the most common type of join. The following example illustrates an inner join:

```
SELECT* FROM titles, titleauthor
  WHERE titles.title_id = titleauthor.title_id
```

Outer Join

Outer joins are used to join tables, but they also return results from the tables when they do not match the join conditions. There are three types of outer joins: left outer joins, right outer joins, and full outer joins.

Left Outer Join

A left outer join returns all rows from the left table in the join even if the rows in the right table do not exist. Null values are returned for columns in the right table when the join condition does not evaluate true. The following example shows a left outer join:

```
SELECT * FROM titles, titleauthor
   WHERE titles.title_id *= titleauthor.title_id
```

This example will return all rows in the left table, titles, even when the corresponding rows in the right table, titleauthor, does not exist.

Right Outer Join

The right outer join returns all rows from the right table in the join even if the rows in the left table do not exist. Null values are returned for columns in the left table when the join condition does not evaluate true. The following example shows a right outer join:

```
SELECT * FROM titles, titleauthor
   WHERE titleauthor.title_id =* titles.title_id
```

The example will return all rows in the right table, titles, even when the corresponding rows in the left table, titleauthor, does not exist.

Full Outer Join

A full outer join returns all rows for the left and the right table, even when the join conditions are not true. When there's a match between the tables, all columns from the tables are set to their appropriate values. When there isn't a match, rows from one table are returned and nulls are returned for the other table.

SQL Server provides two ways of doing joins. You have the TSQL join extensions and ANSI standard joins. You can mix the two joins in a **SELECT** statement, but it is not recommended.

TSQL Join Extensions

TSQL joins appear in the **WHERE** clause. In a TSQL join, you use a comparison operator between columns, or expressions containing columns, from the tables being joined, like this:

```
SELECT * FROM titles, titleauthor
   WHERE titles.title_id = titleauthor.titles_id
```

If you have no comparison operators between tables, you perform a CROSS join. INNER joins are performed by using the standard comparison operators between columns. SQL Server provides special comparison operators to perform OUTER joins. An asterisk followed by an equal sign, *=, is used for TSQL left OUTER joins. An equal sign followed by an asterisk, =*, is used for right OUTER joins.

There is no way to do a full OUTER join with the TSQL join extensions. Using *=* will generate an error.

The TSQL join extensions have some limitations on a join. For example, if a table is used as the outer table in an OUTER join, it can be an inner table of either an OUTER join or an INNER join.

The following examples show TSQL join extensions. The first example shows a CROSS join:

```
SELECT * FROM titles t, titleauthor ta
```

All of the rows from the title and titleauthor tables are returned. The total number of rows returned is the number of rows in titles * the number of rows in titleauthor. The next example shows an INNER join:

```
SELECT * FROM titles t, titleauthor ta
    WHERE t.title_id = ta.title_id
```

This example only returns rows where the title_id matches in both the titles table and titleauthor table. This final example shows an OUTER join:

```
SELECT * FROM titles t, titleauthor ta
    WHERE t.title_id *= ta.title_id --  a outer join
```

This example returns all of the rows in titles even when the title_id does not have a corresponding title_id in titleauthor. TSQL joins are the historical way of joining tables; it is recommend that you write all new SQL with the ANSI join syntax.

ANSI Joins

SQL Server supports ANSI joins. With an ANSI join, you specify the join type and the join conditions in the **FROM** clause. ANSI joins support inner joins, outer joins, and cross joins. Unlike TSQL join extensions, ANSI joins can use a table as both an inner table and an outer table in a join.

Cross joins are identified by the **CROSS JOIN** keywords between the tables in the **FROM** clause. If you are doing a cross join, you cannot have any join conditions. An inner join is identified by the keywords **INNER JOIN** between the tables. An outer join is identified by the join type **LEFT**, **RIGHT**, or **FULL** followed by the optional keyword **OUTER** and then the **JOIN** keyword (for example, **LEFT OUTER JOIN**).

Inner and outer joins must have a *join condition*. A join condition is used to reduce what rows are returned. You can have multiple join conditions in each join clause using the **AND** and **OR** keywords. A join condition looks similar to other clauses in a **WHERE** statement, as demonstrated in Listing 6.11.

Listing 6.11   Join examples.

```
FROM title t INNER JOIN titleauthor ta ON t.title_id = ta.title_id
    AND ta.au_id > 10

FROM author a LEFT OUTER JOIN titleauthor ON a.au_id = ta.au_id
    INNER JOIN title t ON t.title_id = ta.title_id
            AND t.ytd_sales > 4000
```

The previous examples all show how to use multiple join conditions in the ANSI JOIN syntax. The following examples show ANSI join types. The first example shows a CROSS join:

```
SELECT * FROM titles t CROSS JOIN titleauthor ta
```

All of the rows from the title and titleauthor tables are returned. The total number of rows returned is the number of rows in titles * the number of rows in titleauthor. The next example shows an INNER join:

```
SELECT * FROM titles t INNER JOIN titleauthor ta
    ON  t.title_id = ta.title_id
```

This example only returns rows where the title_id matches in both the titles table and titleauthor table. This final example shows an OUTER join:

```
SELECT * FROM titles t LEFT OUTER JOIN titleauthor ta
        on t.title_id = ta.title_id --  a left outer join
```

This example returns all of the rows in titles even when the title_id does not have a corresponding title_id:

```
SELECT * FROM titles t FULL OUTER JOIN titleauthor ta
        on t.title_id = ta.title_id --  a  full outer join
```

This example shows a **FULL OUTER JOIN**; all of the rows in titles and titleauthor are returned even when the join condition is false. The ANSI JOIN syntax is much easier to read than the TSQL syntax. You can see what tables are being joined and the conditions on which the tables are joined. The TSQL join extensions may not be supported in future releases of SQL Server.

Subqueries

A *subquery* is a way to nest a **SELECT** statement inside another query. If a table is in a subquery, but not the outer query, columns from the table can only be used in the subquery. Subqueries cannot contain **ORDER BY, COMPUTE,** or **FOR BROWSE** clauses. They can appear anywhere that a single value can be returned, in a **FROM** clause as a derived table, or in **WHERE** and **HAVING** clauses.

If a subquery is in a **WHERE** or **HAVING** clause, it can be used with the **EXIST, ANY, SOME, ALL,** and **IN** keywords.

 A special type of subquery, called a *correlated subquery,* can be passed columns from the main query to be used to limit the rows returned from the subquery. The following example shows a correlated subquery:

```
SELECT title_id, ( SELECT SUM(royaltyper) FROM
titles_authors ta
    WHERE ta.title_id = t.title_id)
    FROM titles t
```

This example illustrates the use of a correlated subquery as part of the select list.

Similar to a join, a **UNION** allows you to get data from multiple tables back in one result set.

UNION

A **UNION** allows you to join data from two or more result sets into one result set. Unlike a join, which adds more columns to a result, a **UNION** merges columns from multiple **SELECT** statements together. The following is the syntax of the UNION statement:

```
Select_statement
UNION [ALL]
Select_statement
[ . . .]
```

Each select list in the **UNION** must have the same number of columns or the SQL Server will generate an error. Corresponding columns must be of the same data type or must be converted implicitly or explicitly using the convert functions. Implicit data type conversions follow the rules of data type precedence. The first **SELECT** statement in the **UNION** determines the column headers for the results.

It is possible to use **GROUP BY** and **HAVING** statements with each **SELECT** statement. The **GROUP BY** and **HAVING** apply only to the individual **SELECT** statement. You cannot apply them to the **UNION** statement as a whole.

If you are using an **ORDER BY** or **COMPUTE** statement, it can only be specified with the last **SELECT** statement in the **UNION**. The **ORDER BY** and **COMPUTE** will apply to the whole **UNION** statement.

By default, a **UNION** will only return distinct rows. The **ALL** keyword specifies to return every row. You can mix **UNION** and **UNION ALL** in the same statement.

 If both **UNION** and **UNION ALL** are included in a statement, parentheses can be used to specify what duplicate rows are removed.

The TOP Clause

In a select list, SQL Server allows you to specify that you only want a part of the returned result set. This is done using the **TOP** clause. The **TOP** clause must come before the select list. The following is the syntax of the **TOP** clause:

```
[ TOP n [PERCENT] [ WITH TIES] ]
```

And if you are using the **TOP** clause with either **ALL** or **DISTINCT**, it must come after the **ALL** or **DISTINCT** keywords.

The **TOP** clause specifies that, after the first *n* rows that satisfy the query are generated, the query should stop processing. If there is not an **ORDER BY** clause, the rows will be in whatever order SQL Server finds them. In the basic form, the **TOP** clause performs the same as setting **ROWCOUNT**. The value of *n* is a non-negative integer. If *n* is zero, no rows will be returned. If *n* is greater than the number of rows in the table, all rows in the table will be returned.

The **PERCENT** option changes the value of *n* from a number of rows to a percent of rows. When using the **PERCENT** option, any value greater than or equal to 100 will cause all the rows in the table to be returned. If the percent causes only part of a row to be returned, the whole row will be returned.

The **WITH TIES** option causes the **TOP** clause to extend to any rows with the same values in the columns as what have been the last result row to be returned. You can only use this option if you are using the **ORDER BY** clause.

The **ALL** keyword has no effect on the rows returned when using **TOP**. The **DISTINCT** keyword has its normal behavior—only one copy of each unique result in the select list will be returned. The following code snippet illustrates the use of the **TOP** command:

```
SELECT TOP 6 * FROM authors ORDER BY qty DESC
```

This example returns the top size rows from the authors table, ordered by the qty column in ascending order. The top percentage option is as follows:

```
SELECT TOP 6 PERCENT * FROM authors ORDER BY qty DESC
```

This example returns the top six percent of rows from the author table, ordered by qty descending. The next example shows the use of **TOP** with the **TIES** option:

```
SELECT TOP 6 WITH TIES * FROM authors ORDER BY qty DESC
```

This example will return the top six rows from the authors table, ordered by the qty column in descending order. If any rows after the sixth row have the same value for qty as the top six rows, these other rows will also be returned.

Retrieving Text And Image Data

When retrieving data from a **TEXT**, **NTEXT**, or **IMAGE** column, SQL Server will retrieve **@@TEXTSIZE** worth of data. To control the retrieval of **TEXT**, **NTEXT**, or **IMAGE** columns, SQL Server has the **READTEXT** command, which uses the following syntax:

```
READTEXT {databse.owner.}table.column
        {text_ptr offset size} [HOLDLOCK]
```

You can only retrieve data with a **READTEXT** if the column has a valid text pointer. Inserting or updating a **TEXT**, **NTEXT**, or **IMAGE** to a non-null value creates a valid text pointer. *Offset* is the number of bytes to skip before starting to retrieve data from the column. *Size* is the number of bytes to read. If size is 0, 4K is read. If size is larger than **@@TEXTSIZE**, the read is limited to **@@TEXTSIZE**.

To read data with the **READTEXT**, you must first retrieve the text pointer, which is **BINARY** or **VARBINARY**, at least 16 bytes long, and uses a **SE-LECT** with the **TEXTPTR** function. If multiple rows are retrieved with the **SELECT**, the text pointer is set to the last row retrieved. Here is an example of reading a text column:

```
DECLARE @Tpoint BINARY(16)
SELECT  @Tpoint = TEXTPTR(MyTextColumn)
    FROM MyTextTable
READTEXT MyTextTable.MyTextColumn @Tpoint  200 2024
```

In this code snippet, a local variable @Tpoint is declared; local variables will be covered later. A **SELECT** is used to initialize the text pointer. Then the text pointer is used to retrieve bytes 200 through 2024 from the column MyTextColumn.

 Remember, there are no commas between the options in a **READTEXT** statement.

Practice Questions

Question 1

Which of the following SQL statements retrieves the unique list of cities from the publisher table with a column heading of Publisher City? [Check all correct answers]

❏ a. select distinct Publisher City = city from publishers

❏ b. select unique city as "Publisher City" from publishers

❏ c. select distinct "Publisher City" = city from publisher

❏ d. select "Publisher City" = distinct city from publisher

❏ e. select distinct city as "Publisher City" from publisher

Answers c and e are correct. They use a different form of the column alias. Answers a, b, and d are all invalid SQL statements.

Question 2

Which of the following SQL statements returns all authors whose last name has l as the second-to-last character and a zip code greater than 50000? [Check all correct answers]

❏ a. select * from authors where au_lname like '_l%' and zip > 50000

❏ b. select * from authors where au_lname like '%l_' and zip !< 50001

❏ c. select * from authors where au_lname = '%l_' and zip > 50000

❏ d. select * from authors where au_lname like '%l%' and zip > 50000

❏ e. select * from authors where au_lname like '%l_ ' escape 'l' and zip >50000

❏ f. You cannot return the request data.

Answer b is correct—it returns all authors whose last name has an 'l' as the second-to-last character and a zip code greater than 50000. Answer a is incorrect, because it will check for last names that have an *l* in the second position from the front. Answer c in incorrect, because it has an equal sign instead of the **LIKE** clause. Answer d is incorrect, because it looks for any last name containing an *l* in any position. Answer e is incorrect, because its **ESCAPE** clause specifies to look for any last name with at least one character.

Question 3

Which of the following SQL statements returns the job ID, job description, and the employee's full name from the job and employee table, even if there are no employees with the job?

○ a.
```
select j.job_id, job_desc, fname, lname from
    jobs j
left outer join employee e on j.job_id *=
    e.job_id
```

○ b.
```
select j.job_id, job_desc, fname, lnameb from
    jobs j
left outer join employee e on j.job_id =
    e.job_id
```

○ c.
```
select job_id, job_desc, fname, lname from
    jobs j,
employee e where j.job_id *= e.job_id
```

○ d.
```
select j.job_id, job_desc, fname, lname from
    jobs j
left outer join employee e where j.job_id =
    e.job_id
```

○ e.
```
select j.job_id, job_desc, fname, lname from
    jobs j
hright outer join employee e on j.job_id =
    e.job_id
```

Answer b is correct, because it returns the job ID, job description, and the employee's full name from the job and employee table, doing an outer join between job and employee. Answer a is incorrect, because it uses the *= in an ANSI join, making it an invalid statement. Answer c is incorrect, because it does not qualify job_id in the select list, so SQL Server does not know what table to return the job_id column from. Answer d is incorrect, because it doesn't have an ON clause to go with its ANSI join. Answer e is incorrect, because it will return all the employees, even if they have no job.

Question 4

Review the following query:

```
select title, count(*)
from titles t left outer join sales s on
      t.title_id = s.title_id
where stor_id > 4000
order by 1
group by all title
```

Which of the following statements are true in relation to the preceding query? [Check all correct answers]

○ a. No rows will be returned.

○ b. It will return the number of a count of sales for each title.

○ c. Data will be sorted by title.

○ d. Data will be sorted by the number of sales.

○ e. It will return zero for the second column when stor_id
      <=4000.

Answer a is correct, because the sample SQL statement's clauses are out of order; therefore, it will not return any rows and all of the other answers are incorrect.

Question 5

> Which of the following queries returns all titles that contain the word
> *IS without concern for the case*? [Check all correct answers]
>
> ❑ a.
> ```
> select title from titles where UPPER(title) =
>     '%IS%'
> ```
> ❑ b.
> ```
> select title from titles where upper(title)
>     like 'IS%'
>     or lower (title) like '%is%' or title like
>     '%[Ii][Ss]%'
> ```
> ❑ c.
> ```
> select title from titles where upper(title)
>     like'%IS'
> ```
> ❑ d.
> ```
> select title from titles where title in ['IS
>     %','% IS %','% IS']
> ```

Answer b is correct, because the first condition returns rows that start with IS,
and the second and third conditions return rows that contains is—no matter
what the case is. Answer a is incorrect, because it requires an exact match on
'%IS'. Answer c is incorrect, because it will find any title that ends in 'IS', not
just titles that contain the word *IS*. Answer d is incorrect, because it returns
titles that match 'IS %', '% IS %', or '% IS'.

Question 6

> Which **SELECT** statements return all authors' first and last names as
> well as all employees' first and last names? [Check all correct an-
> swers]
>
> ❑ a.
> ```
> select au_lname, au_fname, fname,
>     employee.lname
>       from employee e cross join authors a
> ```
> ❑ b.
> ```
> select au_lname, au_fname from authors
>     union
>     select lname, fname from employee
> ```
> ❑ c.
> ```
> select au_lname, au_fname from authors
>     union all
>     select lname, fname from employee
> ```
> ❑ d. None of the above

Answers b and c are correct, because they both return the desired results. Answer b returns a distinct set, while answer c returns the results with duplicate
rows. Answer a is incorrect, because it is an invalid statement. If you use a table
alias, you cannot refer to the table by its real name without also referencing the
table alias.

Question 7

Which **SELECT** statement returns the five characters immediately following the first occurrence of *the* from a string (if *the* is not found, the
statement must return *N/A*)?

○ a.
```
select ISNULL( substring(title,CHARINDEX
     ('the',LOWER(title)),3),'NA')
from titles
```

○ b.
```
select case
   when title like ' %the%'  then
     next('the',5)
   else 'M/A'
<Q    end
     from titles
```

○ c.
```
select ISNULL(substring (title,charindex
     ('the',lower(title))+3 ,
   charindex ('the',lower(title))+5) ,
           'N/A')from titles
```

○ d.
```
select case
     when charindex ('the',lower(title)) = 0
     then 'N/A'
     else substring (title,
     charindex('the',lower(title))+3,5)
     end
     from titles
```

○ e. None of the above

Answer d is correct because it returns the five characters immediately following the first occurrence of *the* from a string; if *the* is not found, the statement
must return *N/A*. Answer a is incorrect, because it will return the word *the* if it
is found in the title, not the five characters following the word *the*. Answer b is
incorrect, because **INEXT** is not a function. Answer c is incorrect, because it
does not return *N/A* for the rows that do not have *the* in the title.

Question 8

Which of the following queries return publisher names and the maximum last name of their employees, even if they have no employees, for publishers that have not published cooking books? [Check all correct answers]

❑ a.

```
select pub_name, max(lname)
     from publishers p left join employee e on
     p.pub_id = e.pub_id
     inner join titles t on t.pub_id = p.pub_id
            and t.type not like '%cooking'
     group by pub_name
```

❑ b.

```
select pub_name , max(lname)from ( select
     pub_name,
     p.pub_id from publishers p
       inner join titles t on t.pub_id =
     p.pub_id
        where t.type not like '%cooking')
            AS t1
    left outer join employee e on
            t1.pub_id = e.pub_id
    group by pub_name
```

❑ c.

```
select distinct pub_name ,(select
        max(lname)from employee e
          where e.pub_id = t1.pub_id)
    from ( select pub_name, p.pub_id from
            publishers p
         inner join titles t on t.pub_id =
            p.pub_id
       where t.type not like '%cooking') AS t1
```

❑ d. None of the above

Answers a, b, and c are correct. They all return publisher names and the maximum last name of their employees, even if they have no employees, for publishers that have not published cooking books.

Question 9

> Which of the following **SELECT** statements return the titles and the
> total order number for titles that have at least 5,000 books ordered?
> [Check all correct answers]
>
> ❑ a.
> ```
> select title, sum(qty) from titles t inner join
>       sales s
>    on t.title_id = s.title_id having
>    count(qty) > 5000
> ```
> ❑ b.
> ```
> select title , total(qty) from titles t inner
>       sales s
>         on t.titleiId = s.title_id
>    group by title
>    having count(qty) > 5000
> ```
> ❑ c.
> ```
> select title, sum(qty) from titles t inner join
>       sales s
>         on t.title_id = s.title_id
>    where sum(qty) > 5000
>    group by title
> ```
> ❑ d.
> ```
> select title, sum(qty) from titles t inner join
>       sales s
>         on t.title_id = s.title_id
>    group by title_id
>    having sum(qty) > 5000
> ```
> ❑ e. None of the above

Answer e is correct, because none of the statements fulfill the criteria. Answer
a is incorrect, because there are columns in the select list that are not aggregate
functions and are not in **GROUP BY**. Answer b is incorrect, because **total** is
not an aggregate function. Answer c is incorrect, because you cannot use aggregate functions in the **WHERE** clause. Answer d is incorrect, because **title_id**
in the **GROUP BY** clause could be from either table, and because ambiguous
columns must have a table reference.

Question 10

Which of the following **SELECT** clauses can you use to limit the rows returned in a **SELECT** statement? [Check all correct answers]

❑ a. **WHERE**

❑ b. **HAVING**

❑ c. **FROM** using ANSI joins

❑ d. **FROM** using TSQL joins

❑ e. None of the above

Answers a, b, and c are correct. You can limit rows returned from a **SELECT** statement by using the **WHERE** and **HAVING** clauses, as well as using a **FROM** clause that uses ANSI joins. Answer d is incorrect because TSQL joins can limit the number of rows returned, but in the **WHERE** clause, not in the join clause.

Question 11

For the following table,

```
CREATE TABLE MyTable ( a int, b text)
```

what happens when the following SQL statements are executed?

```
DECLARE @TP BINARY(15)
SELECT @TP =TEXTPTR(b) FROM MyTable ORDER BY a
     DESC
READTEXT MyTable.b @TP 10 20
```

○ a. The 10 through 30 characters are retrieved for every row.

○ b. The 10 through 30 characters are retrieved for the row with the lowest value for a.

○ c. The 10 through 30 characters are retrieved for the row with the highest value for a.

○ d. The 10 through 20 characters will be retrieved for the row with the lowest value for a.

○ e. An error will be generated.

Answer e is correct. An error will be generated, because the **TEXTPOINTER**, @TP, is not at least 16 bytes long. This would make the other answers incorrect.

Need To Know More?

 Amo, William C. *Transact-SQL*, IDG Books Worldwide, Foster City, CA, 1998. ISBN 0-7645-8048-5. Chapter 6 describes the basic **SELECT** statement, and Chapter 7 contains details on functions. Chapters 8 and 12 contain information on grouping, cubes, and rollups. Finally, Chapter 11 describes joins, unions, and subqueries.

 Celko, Joe. *Joe Celko's SQL Puzzles & Answers*, Morgan Kaufman, San Francisco, CA. ISBN 1-55860-453-7. The book provides complex SQL problems and their answers.

 Coffman, Gayle. *SQL Server 7: The Complete Reference*, Osborne/McGraw-Hill, Berkley, CA, 1999. ISBN 0-07-882494-X. Chapter 21 provides a complete T-SQL reference.

 MS SQL Server Books Online contains a complete DML reference you can find information either in the table of contents under Accessing and Change Data or you can look in the index for specific SQL statements.

 Search the TechNet CD or its online version at **www.microsoft.com**.

 www.microsoft.com/sql
Find up-to-date information about using SQL Server here.

Modifying Table Data

Terms you'll need to understand:

√ **INSERT**

√ **BULK INSERT**

√ **SELECT INTO**

√ **UPDATE**

√ **WRITETEXT**

√ **UPDATETEXT**

√ **TEXT** and **IMAGE** data types

Techniques you'll need to master:

√ Inserting data

√ Updating data

√ Using **SELECT INTO**

√ Using **BULK INSERT**s

√ Working with **TEXT** and **IMAGE** data types

Most databases do not have static data; normally, you'll have to add and update data. If you cannot insert data into a database, there will never be any data to retrieve. Microsoft SQL Server provides several ways to modify table data. You can use the following statements:

➤ INSERT

➤ SELECT INTO

➤ BULK INSERT

➤ UPDATE

➤ WRITETEXT

➤ UPDATETEXT

INSERT

There are four basic syntax forms of the **INSERT** statement. In the first two forms, you specify the values for a single row. In the other two forms, you can add multiple rows based on a **SELECT** statement or a stored procedure. The **INSERT** syntax for all forms is as follows:

```
INSERT [INTO] {table|view} {column_list}
VALUES ({DEFAULT | constant_expression }[,...n])

INSERT [INTO] {table|view} {column_list}DEFAULT VALUES

INSERT [INTO] {table|view} {column_list} select_statement

INSERT [INTO] {table|view} {column_list} execute_statement
```

INSERT Statement Basics

Keep in mind that the **INSERT** statement appends rows to a table—it doesn't modify existing rows. The only time an **INSERT** can modify existing data is when there's a trigger that will modify existing rows (triggers will be covered in more detail in Chapter 12), as a result of the **INSERT**. There are a few across-the-board **INSERT** basics that you need to be aware of, which involve column lists, identity columns, **UNIQUEIDENTIFIER**, **character and binary column padding**, and @@ROWCOUNT.

Column List

A *column list* is a comma-separated list of column names enclosed in parentheses, as in the following code example:

```
INSERT PhoneList ( PersonName, PhoneNumber)
    VALUES (John Doe,200-567-1234)
```

In this example, PersonName and PhoneNumber are the column list. The column list doesn't have to list the column names in the same order as the table columns. However, all non-null columns that don't have a default value, or a value provided with a trigger, must be supplied in the **INSERT** statement column list. Furthermore, derived columns can't be inserted or specified in a column list.

If you perform an **INSERT** without specifying a column list, the **INSERT** is processed as if all columns were in the list in the same order as the columns are in the table, except any derived columns (which are automatically skipped). This implies that if you don't specify a column list, the values must be in the same order as the table columns.

Identity Column

Normally, you can't insert data into an *identity column* (see Chapter 5 for a description of an identity column). To insert data into an identity column, you must turn on the table's **IDENTITY_INSERT** property for the table, as shown here:

```
SET IDENTITY_INSERT [database.[owner.]]{table} {ON | OFF}
```

When a table's **IDENTITY_INSERT** option is turned on, you can insert data into the identity column. If you do not specify a table's identity column in the **INSERT** statement, the identity column will get the next identity value. If you explicitly assign a value to a table's identity column, the value will be assigned to the column. If an assigned value is greater than the current identity value, the identity column will start counting at the new value. Remember, as we covered in Chapter 5, the identity property does not guarantee uniqueness.

UNIQUEIDENTIFIER

When inserting into a column with the **UNIQUEIDENTIFIER** data type, you have to be aware of the special behavior of these columns. Unless the columns have a default value, columns with the **UNIQUEIDENTIFIER** do not get values assigned to them automatically. The value inserted into a column with the **UNIQUEIDENTIFIER** property is a 36-digit hexadecimal value in the format xxxxxxxx-xxxx-xxxx-xxxx-xxxxxxxxxxxx. The dashes are mandatory. You can use the **NEWID()** function to get a unique global ID to assign to the column. The following example illustrates how to insert data into a table with a column that has a **UNIQUEIDENTIFIER** data type:

```
INSERT MyPhoneList
    (PhoneId, PersonName, PhoneNumber)
    VALUES
        (NEWID(), "John Doe","200-000-0000")
```

Character And Binary Column Padding

When using an **INSERT** statement to modify **CHAR, VARCHAR,** or **VARBINARY** data types, the actual value inserted depends on the **ANSI_PADDING** option at table-creation time (see Chapter 5 for information on creating tables and Chapter 8 for information on setting configuration options). If **ANSI_PADDING** is set to **OFF**:

➤ **CHAR** values are padded with spaces to the column width.

➤ **VARCHAR** values remove trailing spaces, and strings containing only spaces are set to a single space.

➤ **VARBINARY** values have trailing zeros removed.

If **ANSI_PADDING** is turned **ON**:

➤ **CHAR** columns are padded with spaces to the column width.

➤ **VARCHAR** and **VARBINARY** columns are not truncated, but are not padded.

The default value for **ANSI_PADDING** is **OFF**. But the MS SQL Server ODBC driver and the MS SQL Server OLE DB provider both turn it on when connecting. MS recommends that you always turn on this parameter.

@@ROWCOUNT

After an **INSERT**, the @@ROWCOUNT function returns the number of rows inserted. This number will be a nonnegative number that is equal to the number of inserted rows. Zero rows inserted for a multirow **INSERT** doesn't necessarily mean that there is an error. For example, it could mean that the **SELECT** statement or stored procedure used to generate the rows being inserted didn't return any rows.

These basic functions behave the same no matter which **INSERT** syntax you use. The following section will cover the syntax of single row inserts.

Inserting Single Rows

The most common use of the **INSERT** statement is to add a single row to a table. Normally, to specify a single row **INSERT**, you use the **VALUES** keyword, optionally followed by the value list. The value list contains the value to assign to the corresponding column in the column list. The following examples show various ways in which you can insert a single row into a table called MyTable with two columns (a and b)

```
INSERT MyTable VALUES ('a',1234)
```

This example inserts a row into MyTable. Here's how to add a row with column a set to "a" and column b to 1234.

```
INSERT INTO MyTable (a) VALUES ('ccc')
```

This example uses the optional keyword **INTO**, which has no effect on the behavior of the INSERT statement. The column list is specified to contain just the column a.

```
INSERT MyTable DEFAULT VALUES
```

This example uses the **DEFAULT VALUES** option. No column list is allowed. Every column in MyTable will get its default value assigned.

```
INSERT MyTable VALUES (DEFAULT,5)
```

This example does not supply a column list. Column a will have its default value assigned, and column b will be set to five.

```
INSERT MyTable (b,a) VALUES (@@ROWCOUNT, user_name())
```

In this example, the column list specifies that column b is the first column and column a is the second column. Column b will get the value returned from the function **@@ROWCOUNT** assigned to it, and column a will get the value returned from the function **USER_NAME()** assigned to it.

When performing an **INSERT**, every column in the column list must have a scalar expression (an expression that returns one value) specified in the value list to generate its value. This expression can be a constant, any scalar function, or any expression containing constants and scalar functions or the **DEFAULT** keyword. You cannot specify a subquery, columns, or an aggregate function in the value clause. The value inserted into a column must either implicitly convert to the column's data type or you have to perform an explicit conversion.

When inserting data into a table, you may want to have SQL Server assign the column's default value to a column. This is done with the **DEFAULT** keyword. There are two ways the **DEFAULT** keyword can be used in an **INSERT** statement. If **DEFAULT** is used in the values list, it applies to the corresponding column in the column list. If you use **DEFAULT** before the values list, it applies to every non-derived column in the table, and you cannot have a column list.

The **DEFAULT** keyword causes the following behavior:

➤ If the column has a default assigned to it, the default will be used.

➤ If you have not assigned a default value to the column, a null value will be inserted.

➤ If the column does not allow nulls, SQL Server will generate an error.

➤ If the column has a **TIMESTAMP** datatype, the next timestamp value will be assigned to it.

➤ SQL Server does not allow you to use **DEFAULT** in a value list with an identity column, but you can use **DEFAULT VALUES** keywords with an identity column.

The following example shows the use of the **DEFAULT** keyword with an identity column:

```
-- table as follows
CREATE TABLE Test ( Col1 NUMERIC(10) IDENTITY,
    Col2 VARCHAR(32) DEFAULT 'Test' NOT NULL)

-- this insert is valid
INSERT Test DEFAULT VALUES

-- this insert is invalid
INSERT Test VALUES ( DEFAULT,DEFAULT)
```

The first **INSERT** will add a row with the next value for the **Col1** and 'Test' for **Col2**. The second **INSERT** will fail, even if the table is configured to allow **INSERT**s into identity columns.

Inserting Multiple Rows

You can insert multiple rows into a table by using an **INSERT** statement with either a **SELECT** statement or a stored procedure instead of the value clause.

Using A *SELECT* Statement

You can use **INSERT** with most valid **SELECT** statements to add multiple rows to a table. When using a **SELECT** statement as part of an **INSERT** statement, the **SELECT** statement cannot use the **COMPUTE** or **COMPUTE BY** clause. You can insert data with a **SELECT** from the table you want to insert into, but you have to make sure that you do not violate any unique indexes or the insert will fail.

➤ If the session's **ROWCOUNT** (see Chapter 8 on how to set user configuration options) is set to anything other than zero, the **INSERT** will stop when the **ROWCOUNT** number of rows is reached.

➤ It is possible that a **SELECT** statement will not return any rows. When this happens as part of an **INSERT,** this is not an error.

➤ If any inserted row violates a constraint on the table, the entire **INSERT** will fail.

Here's an example of an **INSERT** with a **SELECT** statement:

```
INSERT MyTable ( a, b )   SELECT c,SUM(d) FROM MyTable2 GROUP BY c
```

This example will insert a row into the table MyTable for every row returned from the **SELECT** statement.

Using A Stored Procedure

You can execute a stored procedure to generate multiple rows to add to a table. Any stored procedure that returns data with a **SELECT** or a **readtext** can be used. SQL Server places very few limitations on the stored procedure used with an **INSERT** statement. The following rules apply when using a stored procedure as part of an **INSERT** statement:

➤ If the procedure uses **readtext** to retrieve data, the text column is limited to 1,024K in each **readtext**.

➤ When you use a stored procedure to generate multiple rows, the procedure can also be used to perform updates and inserts into other tables.

➤ The procedure can be on a local server or remote server, or it can be an extended stored procedure.

➤ It can retrieve multiple results, by performing more than one **SELECT** statement.

➤ The data retrieved must match the data type and number of columns from the column list.

➤ If the sessions **ROWCOUNT** is set to anything other than zero, the **INSERT** will stop when the **ROWCOUNT** number of rows is reached.

In some instances, it is possible that the stored procedure will not return any rows. This might not be an error. If any inserted row violates a constraint on the table, the entire **INSERT** will fail. Here's an example of inserting with a stored procedure:

```
INSERT MyTable ( a, b ) EXECUTE SomeValidProcedure
```

In this example, **SomeValidProcedure** must return one or more result sets. Each result set contains two values. These values will be inserted into MyTable column a and b.

SELECT INTO

The **INTO** option in the **SELECT** statement can create a table and insert data in one step. To use this means of populating a table, the database option **SELECT INTO** must be turned on; otherwise, you can't create tables in the database. Normally, a **SELECT INTO** is not run in production databases.

> *Note: If a SELECT INTO is used in a production database, it tends to be used to create a temporary table.*

The syntax of a **SELECT** statement using **SELECT INTO** is:

```
SELECT select_list INTO table_name FROM TableList
       [where_clauses] [groupby_clause] [having_clause]
       [orderby_clause]
```

The *select_list* is the list of values to retrieve. It can be any valid select list. The *table_name* is any valid table name that does not currently exist. (See Chapter 5 for information about tables names. Chapter 6 contains a full explanation of all of the clauses in a **SELECT** statement.)

Using a **SELECT** with the **INTO** clause creates a new table matching the **SELECT** results. The new table will have columns matching the columns in the select list. You can use all the **SELECT** clauses except the **COMPUTE** and **COMPUTE BY** clauses, and you must use the **FROM** clause, as shown earlier. All columns in the select list must have a unique non-null name. If two columns have the same column name, you must give one of them a column alias. Any expressions or functions must be given a column alias. And you cannot perform **SELECT INTO** inside of a transaction.

 The table being created with a **SELECT INTO** must not exist before you execute the **SELECT INTO** statement.

To limit the number of rows inserted, you can use the **WHERE** and **HAVING** clauses. If the **SELECT** statement returns no rows, then a blank table is created. Often, you will see a table created with a **SELECT INTO** using **1=2** in the **WHERE** clause to create a blank table that can then be populated later.

When using the **SELECT INTO** statement, identity properties are inherited unless the **SELECT** contains a join, an aggregate function, a **GROUP BY** clause, a **UNION**, multiple identity columns in the select list, or a column used as an expression. Compute columns will become regular noncomputed columns in the new table. Constraints and indexes are not created on the new table.

To perform a **SELECT INTO**, you must have **CREATE TABLE** privileges in the database you are selecting into, and data retrieval privileges on the tables you are selecting from, or the process will fail. The database you are creating the table in must have the database option **SELECT INTO/BULKCOPY** turned on, or the **SELECT INTO** statement will fail. Here's an example of a **SELECT** with the **INTO** clause:

```
SELECT * INTO TestTable FROM authors
```

This **SELECT** statement will copy all rows and columns from the **authors** table into a new table, **TestTable**.

 When using a **SELECT INTO** statement, the table being selected into does not have to be in the current database. You can use any fully qualified table name that does not exist. It can also be a temporary table.

BULK INSERT

SQL Server 7 provides a new way to load data into a table. You can use the **BULK INSERT** statement, as shown in Listing 7.1. This statement behaves similarly to the command-line BCP program, both being used to insert batches of data into an existing table. For every parameter to the **BULK INSERT** statement, there is an equivalent parameter to the BCP program.

 One difference between a **BULK INSERT** and the command-line BCP program is that the **BULK INSERT** statement can only load data—it can't export data from SQL Server to a data file. The command-line BCP program can import and export data.

Listing 7.1 BULK INSERT syntax.

```
BULK INSERT [['database_name'.]['owner'].]
    {'table_name' FROM data_file}
```

```
[WITH (
  [ BATCHSIZE  = batch_size]
  [[,] CHECK_CONSTRAINTS]
  [[,] CODEPAGE  = ACP | OEM | RAW | code_page]
  [[,] DATAFILETYPE  =
       {'char' | 'native'| 'widechar' | 'widenative'}]
  [[,] FIELDTERMINATOR  = 'field_terminator']
  [[,] FIRSTROW  = first_row]
  [[,] FORMATFILE  = 'format_file_path']
  [[,] KEEPIDENTITY]
  [[,] KEEPNULLS]
  [[,] LASTROW  = last_row]
  [[,] MAXERRORS  = max_errors]
  [[,] ORDER ({column [ASC | DESC]} [, …n])]
  [[,] ROWTERMINATOR  = 'row_terminator']
  [[,] TABLOCK]
)
]
```

 Any parameters in the **BULK INSERT** statement can show up in the test. Fortunately, most of the parameters are fairly simple in what they can do. If you have multiple parameters, remember to separate them with a comma. Furthermore, remember that there are parentheses around everything after the **WITH** keyword.

The only required parts of the **BULK INSERT** statement are the name of the table in which the data will be inserted and the *data file*. All other parts are optional and use the following defaults:

➤ If you do not specify a database name, the default is the current database.

➤ If you do not specify an owner, the default is the current user.

➤ If you do not own the table, the default is to try to insert into a table owned by the dbo. But this will fail, because you have to be the dbo to insert into a table owned by someone else.

In the **BULK INSERT** statement shown earlier, **data_file** represents the full path name of the file to load. The path is based on the machine running SQL Server—not your local machine. To load a data file from your local machine, you must specify the fully qualified name of the file, including the network name of your local machine. After the initial **BULK INSERT** statement, the parameters are inserted within the **WITH** clause. The following list briefly describes each **BULK INSERT** parameter:

➤ **BATCHSIZE** Specifies the number of rows to send to the server in a batch. By default, all rows are sent in a single transaction. If the **BULK**

INSERT aborts, the current batch will be rolled back. Any previous batches will be rolled forward. This number can have a significant impact on load performance.

➤ **CHECK_CONSTRAINTS** Tells the SQL Server to check all constraints on the table. Without this parameter, you can load data with a **BULK INSERT** that you cannot normally insert, because the rows would violate table constraints.

➤ **CODEPAGE** Specifies what character code page to use for data in the data file. This parameter only affects character columns. It only has an effect if there are characters that have an ASCII value less than 32 or greater than 127. **ACP** specifies that the file contains the ANSI/Microsoft Windows code page ISO 1252. **OEM** specifies that the file contains the OEM code page. **RAW** specifies that there isn't any character conversion—this option will load data the fastest. Any other value specifies a specific code page to use.

➤ **DATEFILETYPE** Specifies what the data file looks like.

➤ **CHAR** Specifies that files have all the data stored in character format, with a tab character between fields and a newline character at the end of each row. This is the default type.

➤ **NATIVE** Specifies that the file contains SQL Server data types. It is used for files that were exported from SQL Server with the BCP utility.

➤ **WIDECHAR** Specifies that the file contains UNICODE characters. Otherwise, it behaves the same as CHAR.

➤ **WIDENATIVE** Specifies that the file contains SQL Server data types, but it has any character fields stored as UNICODE characters.

For data files that are **CHAR** and **WIDECHAR,** you can change the field and row terminators.

➤ **FIELDTERMINATOR** Allows you to change the field terminator from the default, tab, to any character string.

➤ **FIRSTROW** Enables you to load part of a file. If **FIRSTROW** is greater than the number of rows in the file, no rows are inserted, and no errors are generated. **FIRSTROW** should be less than or equal to **LASTROW**. If it is not, **LASTROW** is ignored.

➤ **FORMATFILE** Allows you to have a wider variety of datafiles. You can have fixed-length fields, use different terminators for each field, and skip over columns, to name a few of the options.

➤ **KEEPIDENTITY** Loads the value for an identity column from the data in the file.

➤ **KEEPNULLS** Causes defaults to be ignored for columns that are not loaded. A null value will be put in any of the columns that are not loaded.

➤ **LASTROW** Enables you to load part of a file. If **LASTROW** is greater than the number of rows in the file, the **BULK INSERT** stops at the end of the file and no errors are generated. **FIRSTROW** should be less than or equal to **LASTROW**. If it is not, **LASTROW** is ignored.

➤ **MAXERRORS** Allows you to specify how many errors can occur before a **BULK INSERT** will stop. Normally, the **BULK INSERT** will stop after 10 errors occur.

➤ **ORDER** Enables you to sort the datafile in a clustered index in order to help speed up the insert. If the data turns out not to be sorted, the **ORDER** option is ignored. If you sort the data, but SQL Server sort order would sort it differently, it is consider to be unsorted.

➤ **ROWTERMINATOR** Allows you to pick a different row terminator. You can use any string that is one or more characters long as a terminator.

➤ **TABLOCK** Directs SQL Server to use a table lock instead of its default page lock.

Following is an example of a **BULK INSERT**:

```
BULK INSERT pubs.dbo.authors FROM 'c:\data\authors.blk'
WITH FIELDTERMINATOR ='||', LASTROW = 300
```

Assuming you have the correct permissions, this **BULK INSERT** statement will insert up to the first 300 rows from the datafile. The file will have data in character format. Each field will use two pipes '||' as a separator, and each record will have the default record terminator, new line, at the end of the row.

SQL Server can perform a fast, unlogged form of **BULK INSERT** under the following conditions:

➤ The database option **SELECT INTO/BULKCOPY** is set to **TRUE**.

➤ The table has no indexes.

➤ The table has no triggers.

➤ The table is not being replicated.

Any bulk copy into SQL Server that does not meet these conditions is logged in the transaction log. This logged bulk copy will run slower than a non-logged bulk copy, but should be done in production databases. See Chapter 13 on transactions for more information about logging.

UPDATE

UPDATE modifies existing rows in an existing table. An **UPDATE** statement can modify zero or more rows. If it does not update any rows, an error is not generated. If you are going to use the table name of the table being updated in the **WHERE** clause or in a subquery, it is usually easier to give the table an alias. The **UPDATE** syntax is as follows:

```
UPDATE {<table_or_view>}
  SET
    {column_name = {expression | DEFAULT}
       | @variable = expression } [,... n]
  [FROM
      from_clause ]
  [WHERE
      <search_conditions>
      | CURRENT OF
          { { [GLOBAL] cursor_name } | cursor_variable_name} }
  ]
```

In the **UPDATE** statement, you can update one or more column(s) from the table after the **UPDATE** keyword. With MS SQL Server 7, it is possible to modify data and set a variable in the same statement. Each column and variable must be separated with a comma. The following rules apply when performing an update:

➤ A column can be assigned to an expression.

➤ Columns that are in the tables in the **FROM** clause can be used in the expression.

➤ A column cannot directly be assigned to an aggregate function. But it can be assigned to a subquery that returns an aggregate function.

➤ If the column is set to the **DEFAULT** keyword, the column will be assigned its default value.

The **FROM** clause in the **UPDATE** statement can be any valid **FROM** clause (as shown in Chapter 6), as a **SELECT** statement clause. It can include ANSI joins and table aliases.

Note: If you want to join to the table being updated, you have to either list the table again in the FROM clause, or use TSQL join extensions.

```
UPDATE titles SET ytd_sales  = 123
    FROM titleauthor ta
    WHERE ta.au_ord = 1
    AND titles.title_id = ta.title_id
```

This first example illustrates using a TSQL join extension to join the table being updated to another table.

```
UPDATE titles SET ytd_sales  = 123
    FROM titleauthor ta join titles t
        ON  t.title_id = ta.title_id
    WHERE ta.au_ord = 1
```

This example performs the exact same update as the first example, but it uses the ANSI join instead of the TSQL join extensions.

Continuing through the **UPDATE** syntax, the **WHERE** clause can be any valid **WHERE** clause, as shown in the **SELECT** statement. It can include columns from the table being updated and any tables listed in the **FROM** clause. Without a **WHERE** clause that references a column from the table being updated, all rows in the table will be changed. If you are setting a variable in the statement and the **WHERE** clauses cause no rows to be changed, the variable value does not change.

The **CURRENT OF** option is used with cursors and will be covered with cursors in Chapter 11.

When performing an **UPDATE**, you cannot change an identity column. If any of the rows being changed violate a rule or constraint on the table, the entire **UPDATE** is aborted. You cannot change the clustered index for multiple rows and modify a **TEXT, IMAGE,** or **UNICODE** column for multiple rows in the same statement. The following examples illustrates the use of the **UPDATE** statement's features:

```
UPDATE authors  SET au_fname  = 'hi ' + au_fname
```

The following **UPDATE** statement illustrates setting a variable and modifying a column in the same **UPDATE** statement. If no rows in the authors table have an au_id of '172-32-1176,' the variable @a will not be set.

```
DECLARE @a int
UPDATE authors SET au_lname = 'Smith' , @a = -99
    WHERE au_id = "172-32-1176"
```

In this example, the **WHERE** uses a subquery to decide which rows in the titles table will be updated.

```
UPDATE titles
SET advance = advance * 1.5
WHERE pub_id in
      (SELECT pub_id FROM publishers
      WHERE state = "CA")
```

The following example illustrates that you can list the table being updated as a table in the **FROM** clause.

```
UPDATE titles
SET advance = advance * 1.5
FROM publishers p, titles t
WHERE p.pub_id = t.pub_id
AND state = "CA"
```

Working With TEXT And IMAGE Data Types

With MS SQL Server 7, you can use the normal **INSERT** and **UPDATE** statements to modify text and image fields without limitations. SQL Server also provides two statements—**WRITETEXT** and **UPDATETEXT**—that provide better performance and more options when you are working with text data types. The **WRITETEXT** and **UPDATETEXT** syntax are as follows:

```
WRITETEXT {table.column text_ptr}
[WITH LOG] {data}
```

```
UPDATETEXT {table_name.dest_column_name dest_text_ptr}
{ NULL | insert_offset}
{ NULL | delete_length}
[WITH LOG]
[ inserted_data | [{table_name.src_column_name src_text_ptr}]
```

Before you can use the text statements to read and modify text and image data types, you must first initialize the text pointers. You create a valid text pointer by inserting or updating the field to a non-null value. This creates a text pointer as well as allocates the first 8K page for the field. A text pointer is then retrieved into a binary variable that is at least 16 bytes long.

By default, **WRITETEXT** and **UPDATETEXT** operations are not logged. To run these statements in this unlogged mode, you must set the 'select into/ bulkcopy' option to **TRUE** to configure the database to allow non-logged operations. Otherwise, you can only run these commands using the **WITH LOG** option. This option causes data changes to be written to the transaction log.

With **UPDATETEXT**, you can specify where in the text field to delete the existing data and insert the new data. The **insert_offset** tells where to start to insert the data. A value of zero specifies the beginning of the field, and a null specifies to append the data to the end of the field. **Delete_length** is the number of bytes, starting at the offset, to remove. If **delete_length** is zero, no data will be removed. A null value for the **delete_length** will overwrite from the **insert_offset** to the end of the field. The **UPDATETEXT** statement inserts the new data starting at the **insert_offset**; it will delete the old data starting at the **insert_offset** for the **delete_length** number of bytes. For example, if the **insert_offset** is 10 and the **delete length** is 20, the existing data starting at byte 10 and continuing for the next 20 bytes will be removed. The next data will then be inserted into the column at the byte 10 position.

UPDATETEXT also allows you the option of taking data from one text or image column and copying it into another text or image column. This is useful if you want to replicate a text or image column, or if you want to make the same changes to multiple text or image columns.

With SQL Server 7, if you want to set a text column to null without logging the data changes, you use the **WRITETEXT** command with a null value for the data. A **WRITETEXT** with null data will set the text field to an empty string.

To use a **WRITETEXT** or **UPDATETEXT**, you must have created a text pointer, which is an internal SQL Server pointer to the spot where it stores the text or image column. To create a valid text pointer, you have to either set the text or image column to a non-null value with the **INSERT** statement or use the **UPDATE** statement to set the column to any value (including null). Listing 7.2 illustrates how to set text pointers:

Listing 7.2   Initializing text pointers.

```
CREATE TABLE MyBook (
    ChapterNumber    INT    NOT NULL,
    Chapter          TEXT      NULL )


-- setting a text pointer with an insert
INSERT MyBook (ChapterNumber, Chapter)
     VALUES (7,"")


-- setting a text pointer with an insert followed by an update
INSERT MyBook (ChapterNumber)
     VALUES (7)
UPDATE MyBook SET Chapter = NULL
     WHERE ChapterNumber = 7
```

This example creates a table, MyBook, which contains two columns. It then illustrates the two ways of initializing a text pointer. The first example, using an **INSERT** statement, sets Chapter to an empty string. The second example inserts into MyBook, but does not supply a value for the Chapter column. The Chapter column will be set to its default value, **NULL**. Remember, inserting a **NULL** into a text column does not initialize the text pointer. The second example updates MyBook, setting the Chapter to **NULL**. Using the **UPDATE** statement to set a text column to a **NULL** value will create a valid text pointer in the column.

The next step is to retrieve the text pointer into a local variable. The variable you store the text pointer in must be either a **BINARY** or **VARBIARY** data type with a length of at least 16. You retrieve the text pointer with the **TEXTPTR** function. The following example shows how to retrieve a text pointer:

```
DECLARE @MyPtr BINARY(16)

SELECT @MyPtr = TEXTPTR(Chapter)
     FROM MyBook
     WHERE ChapterNumber = 7
```

In this example, @MyPtr is set up as a local variable of data type **BINARY** with a length of 16. The **SELECT** statement retrieves the text pointer for the column Chapter and assigns it to @MyPtr.

After retrieving a valid text pointer, you can proceed with using the **WRITETEXT** and **UPDATETEXT** commands.

```
WRITETEXT MyBook.Chapter @MyPtr WITH LOG "Chapter 7
Terms you'll need to Understand ..."

UPDATETEXT MyBook.Chapter @MyPtr
      33 1 WITH LOG "u"
```

In this example, the **WRITETEXT** will overwrite the Chapter column for the text pointer @MyPtr. Then the **UPDATETEXT**, using the same text pointer, will replace the thirty-third character, "U," with a lower case "u."

> *Note: Once it has been initialized, the text pointer does not change when the data in a column changes.*

Modifying Data With Views

Modifying data with views is similar to modifying data directly in tables. You can both insert and update data through views. Chapter 10 covers modifying data with views.

Practice Questions

Question 1

Using the Pubs database in Appendix A, which answers are true about the following **INSERT** statement? [Check all correct answers]

```
insert    discounts ( stor_id, lowqty, discount,
    discounttype )
    values    (6380, 10, 20,'MyDiscount')
```

☐ a. The statement will insert one row into the **discount** table if the **stor_id 6380** exists in the **stores** table.

☐ b. The **INSERT** will fail, because **stor_id** is a character column and you are trying to insert an integer into it.

☐ c. The column highqty will be set to **NULL**.

☐ d. If a **discounttype 'MyDiscount'** already exists, the row will not be added.

☐ e. None of the above.

Answers a and c are correct. Answer a is correct, because there are referential integrity rules enforcing the stor_id to be in the stores table before it can be in the discount table. Answer c is correct, because there is no default on highqty, but it allows nulls; SQL Server will set it to NULL. Answer b is incorrect, because SQL Server will automatically convert an integer to a character. Answer d is incorrect, because there are no unique indexes or constraints or triggers enforcing uniqueness.

Question 2

Using the Pubs database in Appendix A, which SQL statement will update the **employee** table by setting the hire date to the publish date of the most recent book published when the hire date is before Jan 1, 1992? If there is no publish date, it will set the hire date to the current date and time. [Check all correct answers]

❑ a.
```
update employee  set hire_date = isnull((
     select max(pubdate)
  from titles t
  where  employee.pub_id = t.pub_id
  and hire_date <'jAN 1 1992' ),getdate())
```

❑ b.
```
update [employee]  set [hire_date] = isnull((
     select max([pubdate])
  from [titles] t
  where  employee.[pub_id] =
     t.[pub_id]),getdate())
  where [hire_date]  < 'Jan 1 1992'
```

❑ c.
```
update employee  set hire_date = isnull((
     select max(pubdate)
   from titles t
  where  employee.pub_id = t.pub_id),getdate())
  where hire_date  < 'Jan 1 1992'
```

❑ d.
```
update [employee]  set [hire_date] = isnull(
     max([pubdate]) ,GETDATE())
  from [titles] t
  where  employee.[pub_id] = t.[pub_id]
  and [hire_date]  > 'Jan 1 1992'
```

❑ e.
```
update employee  set hire_date =
     isnull(pubdate,getdate())
  from titles t
  where  employee.pub_id *= t.pub_id
  and hire_date  < 'Jan 1 1992'
  and t.pubdate = ( select max(pubdate) from
     titles t2
  where t2.pub_id =employee.pub_id)
```

Answers b and c are correct. Both answers b and c perform the same SQL—
they calculate the maximum pubdate for the publisher that the employee works
for. If there are no books published, the pubdate will be the current date. Then
answers b and c assign the pubdate to the hire date. This modification is only
performed if the hire date is less than 'Jan 1 1992'. Answer a is a valid statement, but there is no **WHERE** clause limiting which rows in the **employee**
table are updated, so it will update every row in the **employee** table. Answer d is
an invalid SQL statement, because there is an aggregate function in the **SET**
clause. Answer e is an invalid SQL statement—**titles** is part of an inner TSQL
join and an outer TSQL join.

Question 3

Which answers are true regarding the following SQL? [Check all
correct answers]

```
declare @a varbinary(16)
select @a = textptr(logo) from pub_info
updatetext pub_info.logo @a 3 10 '000123'
```

❏ a. The statement will fail, because you cannot use
UPDATETEXT with an image column.

❏ b. The statement will fail, because 10 characters are being
replaced with 6 characters.

❏ c. The statement will fail, because the variable **@a** is a
VARBINARY, not a **BINARY**.

❏ d. The statement will remove 10 bytes starting with byte 3
and insert the bytes for '000123.'

❏ e. None of the above.

Answer d is correct, because the starting byte value is 3, the length to replace
value is 10, and the value to replace with is "000123." Answer a is incorrect,
because an **UPDATETEXT** can modify any BLOB data type. Answer b is
incorrect, because you can reduce the size of a text/image column with the
UPDATETEXT statement. Answer c is incorrect, because the text pointer
variable can be a **BINARY** or **VARBINARY** of at least 16 bytes long.

Question 4

> Which answers are true about the following SQL statements?
> [Check all correct answers]
>
>
>
> ```
> select * into #pubs1 from authors where au_id >
>     '123-45-6789'
> select * into #pubs1 from authors where
>     au_fname like 'A%'
> ```
>
> ❏ a. A table will be created in the current database.
>
> ❏ b. A table will be created in tembdb.
>
> ❏ c. The statements will only work if the **'Select Create'**
>   database option is turned on.
>
> ❏ d. The table created will only have the rows from the first
>   **SELECT** statement.
>
> ❏ e. None of the above.

Answer e is correct. The other answers are all false, because when the second
SELECT INTO is compiled, the **#pubs1** table will already exist. This will
stop the batch from running.

Need To Know More?

 Amo, William C. *Transact-SQL*, IDG Books Worldwide, Foster City, CA, 1998. ISBN 0-7645-8048-5. Chapter 6 describes inserting and updating data. Chapter 11 describes how to modify text and image data.

 Coffman, Gayle. *SQL Server 7: The Complete Reference*, Osborne/McGraw-Hill, Berkley, CA, 1999. ISBN 0-07-882494-X. Chapter 21 provides a complete T-SQL reference on the commands used to modify data.

 MS SQL Server Books Online contains a complete DML reference you can find information either in the table of contents under Accessing and Change Data or you can look in the index for specific SQL statements.

 Search the TechNet CD or its online version at **www.microsoft.com**.

 www.microsoft.com/sql
Find up-to-date information about using SQL Server here.

Session Configuration

Terms you'll need to understand:

- √ Configuration option
- √ Deadlock
- √ Lock timeout
- √ Quoted identifier
- √ Arithmetic overflow
- √ Query governing
- √ Implicit transaction
- √ Transaction isolation level

Techniques you'll need to master:

- √ Using the **SET** command to control a session's behavior
- √ Listing a session's configuration options
- √ Setting the default configuration options

In previous chapters, we have covered how different commands behave in SQL Server. SQL Server increases your flexibility by giving you the option to change the way SQL statements are processed during any session with the **SET** statement. In this chapter, we'll cover the use of the **SET** statement to configure SQL Server connection behavior, viewing configured options, and setting default connection options.

SET Statement

The **SET** statement affects SQL Server's behavior for the duration of a connection. You can use the **SET** statement to customize how results display, change SQL Server's behavior, show processing statistics, and provide diagnostic aids for debugging TSQL. Microsoft divides the **SET** statement into the following seven categories:

➤ **Date and time statements** Sets date and time behavior

➤ **Locking statements** Sets locking behavior

➤ **Miscellaneous statements** Sets behavior not part of any other category

➤ **Query-execution statements** Sets query execution behavior

➤ **SQL-92 settings statements** Sets ANSI standard behavior

➤ **Statistics statements** Displays information about execution

➤ **Transaction statements** Sets transaction's behavior

 When executing a stored procedure, the current **SET** options will apply to the stored procedure. If you set an option inside the procedure, after the stored procedure is done executing, the option will revert to the value it had before calling the stored procedure.

The next few sections address Microsoft's seven types of **SET** statements.

Data And Time Statements

The date and time **SET** statements are used to control the format of date and time data. SQL Server provides two functions to control date format—**SET DATEFIRST** and **SET DATEFORMAT**.

SET DATEFIRST

With the **SET DATEFIRST** statement, you can control which day is the first day of the week. The syntax for **SET DATEFIRST** is

```
SET DATEFIRST number
```

Table 8.1	DATEFIRST values.
Value	**Meaning**
1	Monday
2	Tuesday
3	Wednesday
4	Thursday
5	Friday
6	Saturday
7	Sunday

where *number* is from one through seven. Table 8.1 contains the definitions of the numbers used in the **SET DATEFIRST** statement.

By default, the first day of the week is set to Sunday, 7. When using the **DATEPART** function, to retrieve the day of the week, the number returned is based on the current setting for the first day of the week. (Note: Chapter 6 covers the **DATEPART** function in more detail.) For example, using the default configuration, the day of the week for Friday is six. If you change the first day of the week to Monday, the day of the week for Friday will be five.

 To find out which day of the week is currently set to be the first day of the week, you can use the **@@DATEFIRST** function.

SET DATEFORMAT

The **SET DATEFORMAT** statement specifies the format of date values in character strings used by SQL Server. Keep in mind that **SET DATEFORMAT** does not affect the format of date values being returned, or converted from date to character. **DATEFORMAT** only affects character values being converted to date values. The syntax for **SET DATEFORMAT** is:

```
SET DATEFORMAT {format | @format_var}
```

Table 8.2 lists **SET DATEFORMAT**'s valid formats.

When converting a string into a **DATETIME** field, the date format specifies the order of the day, month, and year in the string. If your date format is set to **mdy**, then **01/07/1999** is January 7, 1999. If you change the date format to

Table 8.2	Valid date formats for SET DATEFORMAT.	
Format	**Description**	**Example**
mdy	Month then day then year	07/30/98
myd	Month then year then day	07/98/30
dym	Day then year then month	30/98/07
dmy	Day then month then year	30/07/98
ymd	Year then month then day	98/07/30
ydm	Year then day then month	98/30/07

dmy, then **01/07/1999** is July 1, 1999. The default value when the SQL Server is configured to use US-English is **mdy**.

 The date format does not affect dates that are formatted as numeric. Numeric date values are always treated as **ymd**. For example, the value 19990730 will be July 30, 1999.

Locking Statements

The locking **SET** statements control how SQL Server handles locks. Using locking **SET** statements, you can control deadlocks and how long a connection will wait for a lock to complete.

SET DEADLOCK_PRIORITY

The **SET DEADLOCK_PRIORITY** statement controls how SQL handles deadlocks. A deadlock occurs when two connections have resources locked, and they need to access the other connections resources. The syntax for **SET DEADLOCK_PRIORITY** is:

```
SET DEADLOCK_PRIORITY { LOW | NORMAL | @var }
```

As you can see in the syntax, you can change your connection deadlock priority to either **LOW** or **NORMAL**. The priority can also be in a variable, @var, that contains either **LOW** or **NORMAL**. A **LOW** priority means that SQL Server will increase the likelihood that your connection will be chosen as the deadlock victim. A **NORMAL** priority setting means that SQL Server will perform its normal deadlock processing with your connection having the same standard likelihood of being chosen as the deadlock victim. The default deadlock priority is **NORMAL**.

SET LOCK_TIMEOUT

By default, connections waiting for locked resources will wait until the resources are released. With the **SET LOCK_TIMEOUT** command, you can change this behavior by specifying how many milliseconds the current connection will wait for locked resources before it times out. The syntax for **SET LOCK_TIMEOUT** is:

```
SET LOCK_TIMEOUT milliseconds_to_wait
```

If you set the **LOCK_TIMEOUT** to -1, SQL Server will perform its standard locking behavior, with connections waiting for locks never timing out. Setting **LOCK_TIMEOUT** to any positive number sets the number of milliseconds that SQL Server will wait. To see what the timeout value is set to, you use the **@@LOCK_TIMEOUT** function.

Miscellaneous Statements

The miscellaneous **SET** statements incorporate all the **SET** statements that Microsoft does not include in any other category. Some of the types of **SET** statements in this category are those with null behavior, cursor behavior, and identity behavior.

SET CONCAT_NULL_YIELDS_NULL

The **SET CONCAT_NULL_YIELDS_NULL** determines SQL Server's behavior when you concatenate a string with a **NULL**. The syntax for **CONCAT_NULL_YIELDS_NULL** is:

```
SET CONCAT_NULL_YIELDS_NULL {ON | OFF}
```

If **CONCAT_NULL_YIELDS_NULL** is turned on, then, when you concatenate a string with a **NULL**, you will get a **NULL** as the result. If **CONCAT_NULL_YIELDS_NULL** is turned off, the database option **CONCAT NULL YIELDS NULL** will determine the behavior. If both the database and connection options are set to off, a string concatenated with a **NULL** will yield a **NULL**. If the connection's **CONCAT_NULL_YIELDS_NULL** options is turned off and the database **CONCAT_NULL_YIELDS_NULL** is turned on, you will get a **NULL** as the result when you concatenate a string with a **NULL**. The default behavior is that the **CONCAT_NULL_YIELDS_NULL** connection option is turned on.

SET CURSOR_CLOSE_ON_COMMIT

The **SET CURSOR_CLOSE_ON_COMMIT** statement determines the behavior of a cursor when a **COMMIT** is issued. The syntax is:

```
SET CURSOR_CLOSE_ON_COMMIT { ON | OFF }
```

If the **SET CURSOR_CLOSE_ON_COMMIT** is turned on, then cursors are closed whenever the connection issues a **COMMIT** or a **ROLLBACK**. (See Chapter 11 for details on cursors.) When the value is set to **OFF**, the database option **CURSOR CLOSE ON COMMIT** will be used to determine the behavior of cursors when a **COMMIT** or **ROLLBACK** is issued. If both the connection option **CURSOR_CLOSE_ON_COMMIT** and the database option **CURSOR CLOSE ON COMMIT** are set to **OFF**, the cursors will stay open when a **COMMIT** is issued. If either the connection option **CURSOR_CLOSE_ON_COMMIT** or the database option **CLOSE CURSOR ON COMMIT** are set to **ON**, a rollback will close all cursors except cursors that are defined to be **INSENSITIVE** or **STATIC**.

Microsoft's OLE-DB driver, ODBC driver, and DB-Library automatically turn off **SET CURSOR_ON_COMMIT**.

SET FIPS_FLAGGER

The **SET FIPS_FLAGGER** statement is used to check SQL for compliance with the ANSI SQL-92 standard. The **FIPS_FLAGGER** option turns on the FIPS flagging capability of SQL Server. When the **FIPS_FLAGGER** is set, any SQL statement in violation of the ANSI SQL-92 standard for the level of the flag will generate an error message. The syntax for **SET FIPS_FLAGGER** is:

```
SET FIPS_FLAGGER { ENTRY | INTERMEDIATE | FULL | OFF }
```

By default, the **FIPS_FLAGGER** is set to **OFF**, and SQL Server will not check for TSQL that violates ANSI SQL-92. If **FIPS_FLAGGER** is set to **ENTRY, INTERMEDIATE,** or **FULL**, SQL Server will check your TSQL for violations of the corresponding level of ANSI SQL-92. The default value for this flag is off.

SET IDENTITY_INSERT

By default, you cannot insert or update an explicit value into an identity column. The **SET IDENTITY_INSERT** statement allows you to specify a value for an identity column. The syntax for **SET IDENTITY_INSERT** is:

```
SET IDENTITY_INSERT table_name { ON | OFF}
```

When the **IDENTITY_INSERT** is turned on for a table, you can modify the table's identity column. Only one table per database can have the **IDENTITY_INSERT** option turned on at a time. When the **IDENTITY_INSERT** is turned off, you cannot modify the table's identity column.

If an identity column has a value assigned that is larger than the current maximum value for the column, identity values for new rows will be generated starting at the new value.

SET LANGUAGE

The **SET LANGUAGE** statement allows you to specify a different language for a connection. The selected language will determine **DATETIME** formats and the language used for system messages. The syntax for **SET LANGUAGE** is:

```
SET LANGUAGE {language | @var}
```

The *language* parameter can be any language that is listed in the system table syslanguages in the **MASTER** database.

SET OFFSETS

The **SET OFFSETS** statement is used in conjunction with DB-Library applications to find keywords in SQL. This statement is not covered on the exam.

SET PROCID

The **SET PROCID** statement is used in conjunction with DB-Library applications to return stored procedures' IDs to the calling DB-Library application.

SET QUOTED_IDENTIFIER

The **SET QUOTED_IDENTIFIER** statement instructs SQL Server to follow the ANSI SQL-92 quotation mark rules. When **SET QUOTED_IDENTIFIER** is turned on, double quotes are treated as object identifiers, and single quotes are used for literal strings. When **SET QUOTED_IDENTIFIER** is set to **OFF**, you can use either single or double quotes for literal strings, and you can not use any quotes for object identifiers. The syntax for **SET QUOTED_IDENTIFIER** is:

```
SET QUOTED_IDENTIFIER { ON | OFF }
```

If you are using DB-Library, **QUOTED_IDENTIFIER** defaults to **OFF**. For ODBC and OLE-DB applications, **QUOTED_IDENTIFIER** defaults to **ON**.

Query-Execution Statements

The query-execution **SET** statements affect how SQL statements are processed. For example, you can use query-execution statements to control the number of rows, determine whether a statement will run, and control what to do when various arithmetic conditions arise.

SET ARITHABORT

The **SET ARITHABORT** statement determines SQL Server processing when either an arithmetic overflow or a division by zero occurs. An arithmetic function causes you to try and set a column to a value that does not fit in its date type. The syntax for **SET ARITHABORT** is:

```
SET ARITHABORT { ON | OFF }
```

If **ARITHABORT** is set to **OFF**, SQL Server will generate a warning message and continue processing when a division by zero or an arithmetic overflow occurs. If you set **ARITHABORT** to **ON**, SQL Server will terminate a query or batch when a division by zero or an arithmetic overflow occurs.

> Note: SQL Server will generate a NULL in calculation for the division by zero or arithmetic overflow conditions.

SET ARITHIGNORE

The **SET ARITHIGNORE** statement determines which SQL Server error message is generated when an arithmetic overflow or a division by zero occurs in **SELECT** statements. The syntax for **SET ARITHIGNORE** is:

```
SET ARITHIGNORE { ON | OFF }
```

If **ARITHIGNORE** is set to **OFF**, SQL Server will generate a warning when a division by zero or an arithmetic overflow occurs. If you set **ARITHIGNORE** to **ON**, SQL Server will not generate an error message when a division by zero or arithmetic overflow occurs.

SET FMTONLY

The **SET FMTONLY** statement enables you to configure SQL Server to only return column information to a client. The syntax is:

```
SET FMTONLY { ON | OFF}
```

When **SET FMTONLY** is turned off, SQL Server will parse and execute the SQL statements. This will return data and column information to the client. If you turn on **SET FMTONLY**, SQL Server will only parse the SQL statement. This will only return the column information to the client. When executing a stored procedure, you will get the column information for every **SELECT** statement in the procedure.

SET NOCOUNT

The **SET NOCOUNT** statement is used to stop SQL Server from sending the number of rows affected by a SQL statement back to the client after every SQL statement. The syntax is:

```
SET NOCOUNT { ON | OFF }
```

When **SET NOCOUNT** is turned on (the default behavior), SQL Server will tell the client the number of rows, affected by a SQL statement, rowcount, for every SQL statement executed. When **SET NOCOUNT** is turned off, SQL Server will tell the client the number of rows affected by a SQL statement.

 The **SET NOCOUNT** statement has no effect on the **@@ROWCOUNT** function. The **@@ROWCOUNT** function will return the number of rows affected by the previous SQL statement, even if **SET NOCOUNT** is turned on.

SET NOEXEC

The **SET NOEXEC** statement is used to stop SQL statements from running. **SET NOEXEC** is often used in conjunction with other **SET** statements to analyze SQL statements. The syntax is:

```
SET NOEXEC { ON | OFF }
```

When **SET NOEXEC** is turned on, no SQL statement except **SET NOEXEC** will be executed. When the **SET NOEXEC** is turned off, all SQL statements will execute as normal.

SET NUMERIC_ROUNDABORT

The **SET NUMERIC_ROUNDABORT** statement controls SQL Server's behavior when arithmetic rounding of a value causes a query to lose precision. The syntax is:

```
SET NUMERIC_ROUNDABORT { ON | OFF }
```

The default for **SET NUMERIC_ROUNDABORT** is **OFF**, which means that no errors or warnings are generated when there is a loss of precision. If

SET ARITHABORT is turned off and SET NUMERIC_ROUNDABORT is turned on, a warning will be returned when there is a loss of precision. If SET ARITHABORT is turned on and SET NUMERIC_ROUNDABORT is also turned on, an error will be returned when there is a loss of precision.

SET PARSEONLY

The **SET PARSEONLY** statement is used to configure SQL Server to check the syntax of SQL statements. The syntax for **SET PARSEONLY** is:

```
SET PARSEONLY { ON | OFF }
```

If **SET PARSEONLY** is turned on, SQL Server will only check the syntax of SQL statements—SQL Server will not check whether objects exist. When **SET PARSEONLY** is turned on, the only statement that will execute is **SET PARSEONLY OFF**. The **SET PARSEONLY** statement cannot be in a stored procedure, and it cannot be in a batch with any other SQL statements.

SET QUERY_GOVERNOR_COST_LIMIT

The **SET QUERY_GOVERNOR_COST_LIMIT** statement allows you to limit the queries that can run based on the amount of work SQL Server estimates the statement will take. This is called *query governing*. The syntax is:

```
SET QUERY_GOVERNOR_COST_LIMIT  int_value
```

If the *int_value* is set to zero, all queries will run, regardless of the estimated cost (cost refers to the amount of resources required to run a query). If *int_value* is any positive integer, any query that SQL Server estimates will cost more (or use more resources) than the *int_value* will not be allowed to run. The default value for **QUERY_GOVERNOR_COST_LIMIT** is 0.

SET ROWCOUNT

The **SET ROWCOUNT** statement allows you to limit the number of rows affected by a SQL statement. The syntax is:

```
SET ROWCOUNT int_value
```

If *int_value* is zero, you are not placing artificial limits on the rows affected. If *int_value* is any positive integer, when a SQL statement affects *int_value* row, processing will stop. That is, a **SELECT** will stop returning rows. Any data modification statement (**INSERT, UPDATE, DELETE**) will stop modifying rows when the row count limit is reached.

SET TEXTSIZE

The **SET TEXTSIZE** statement is used with text and image data types to specify the number of bytes returned with a **SELECT** statement. The syntax is:

```
SET TEXTSIZE {int_value | @int_var }
```

The *int_value* is a nonnegative integer, specifying the number of bytes to return when selecting text or image columns. When you select data from a text or image column, you will only get the **TEXTSIZE** number of bytes returned to a client program. The maximum text size is 2GB. A value of **0** will set the **TEXTSIZE** to 4K, which is the default **TEXTSIZE**. Setting the **TEXTSIZE** sets the value for the **@@TEXTSIZE** function.

> *Note: When connecting to SQL Server with Microsoft's ODBC driver or OLE-DB driver, the textsize will automatically be set to 2,147,483,647 bytes.*

SQL-92 Settings Statements

Microsoft's TSQL behavior normally does not follow ANSI SQL behavior. SQL Server gives you the capability to have standard ANSI behavior for SQL.

SET ANSI_DEFAULTS

The **SET ANSI_DEFAULTS** statement is used to turn on and off SQL ANSI behavior as a group. The syntax is:

```
SET ANSI_DEFAULTS { ON | OFF }
```

When you turn on **SET ANSI_DEFAULTS**, the following **SET** options are turned on:

➤ ANSI_NULL_DFLT_ON

➤ ANSI_NULLS

➤ ANSI_PADDING

➤ ANSI_WARNINGS

➤ CURSOR_CLOSE_ON_COMMIT

➤ IMPLICIT_TRANSACTIONS

➤ QUOTED_IDENTIFIER

When you turn off **SET ANSI_DEFAULTS, ANSI_NULL_DFLT_OFF** is turned on, and the following options are turned off:

- ➤ ANSI_NULLS
- ➤ ANSI_PADDING
- ➤ ANSI_WARNINGS
- ➤ CURSOR_CLOSE_ON_COMMIT
- ➤ IMPLICIT_TRANSACTIONS
- ➤ QUOTED_IDENTIFIER

SET ANSI_NULL_DFLT_OFF

The **SET ANSI_NULL_DFLT_OFF** statement works in conjunction with the **SET ANSI_NULL_DFLT_ON** statement to determine the nullability of new columns. The syntax is:

```
SET ANSI_NULL_DFLT_OFF { ON | OFF }
```

If both **ANSI_NULL_DFLT_OFF** and **ANSI_NULL_DFLT_ON** are turned off, the database option **ANSI NULL DEFAULT** determines whether columns allow nulls when a null is not specified for the column when a table is created. When the **ANSI_NULL_DFLT_OFF** is turned on, columns that do not have nullability specified will not allow nulls—this is SQL Server's default behavior. Only one of **ANSI_NULL_DFLT_OFF** and **ANSI_NULL_DFLT_ON** can be turned on at a time. If you turn one statement on, the other one will be turned off automatically.

 You should always specify columns to be either **NULL** or **NOT NULL** when creating tables. Otherwise, you cannot guarantee the behavior of the **CREATE TABLE** statement.

SET ANSI_NULL_DFLT_ON

The **SET ANSI_NULL_DFLT_ON** statement is used to set the ANSI standard behavior for **CREATE TABLE** statements that do not specify the nullability of a column. The syntax is:

```
SET ANSI_NULL_DFLT_ON { ON | OFF }
```

The **ANSI_NULL_DFLT_ON** works in conjunction with the **ANSI_NULL_DFLT_OFF** statement (as discussed in the previous section).

SET ANSI_NULLS

In the ANSI standard, comparing a *column_name* to a **NULL** will always be false, even if the *column_name* contains a **NULL**. The **SET ANSI_NULL** statement enables you to specify how SQL Server will behave when checking whether columns equal a **NULL** value. The syntax is:

```
SET ANSI_NULLS { ON | OFF }
```

When **ANSI_NULLS** is turned on, comparing a column to a null will always be null. When **ANSI_NULLS** is turned off, SQL Server will evaluate comparing a column containing a null to a null value to true. For example, if **ANSI_NULLS** is turned off, the following statement will return all rows that do not have a spouse:

```
SELECT * FROM Person WHERE SpouseName = NULL
```

If **ANSI_NULLS** is turned on, the previous statement will never return any rows. The ANSI standard way to compare a column to a null is to use the **IS NULL** and **IS NOT NULL** statements. The following statement will return all rows from the **Person** table, independent of the value for **ANSI_NULLS**:

```
SELECT * FROM Person WHERE SpouseName IS NULL
```

SET ANSI_PADDING

The **SET ANSI_PADDING** statement controls how SQL Server stores **CHAR, VARCHAR, BINARY**, and **VARBINARY** columns that either end in blanks or are shorter than the maximum column length. The syntax is:

```
SET ANSI_PADDINGS { ON | OFF }
```

If ANSI_PADDING is set to OFF:

➤ **CHAR** Values are padded with spaces to the column width.

➤ **VARCHAR** Values have trailing spaces removed, and strings containing only spaces are set to a single space.

➤ **VARBINARY** Values have trailing zeros removed.

If ANSI_PADDING is turned ON:

➤ **CHAR** Columns are padded with spaces to the column width.

➤ **VARCHAR** Columns are neither truncated nor padded.

➤ **VARBINARY** Columns are neither truncated nor padded.

*Note: Microsoft recommends that **ANSI_PADDING** always be set to **ON**.*

SET ANSI_WARNINGS

The **SET ANSI_WARNINGS** statement is used to specify ANSI standard behavior for error conditions. The syntax is:

```
SET ANSI_WARNINGS { ON | OFF }
```

If **ANSI_WARNINGS** is turned on, the following conditions will have ANSI standard behavior:

➤ A **NULL** value in any row used in an aggregate function will generate a warning message.

➤ A divided by zero or arithmetic overflow will roll back the statement and generate an error message

Although the **ANSI_WARNINGS** statement defaults to **OFF**, Microsoft's SQL Server OLE-DB driver and ODBC driver automatically turn on **ANSI_WARNINGS**.

Statistics Statements

The statistics statements are used to help analyze queries. With these statements, you can see how much work SQL Server will do to process a query.

SET FORCEPLAN

The **SET FORCEPLAN** statement is used to force SQL Server to perform joins in the order that they show up in the **FROM** clause. The syntax is:

```
SET FORCEPLAN { ON | OFF }
```

When **FORCEPLAN** is **OFF**, SQL Server will determine the optimal order to perform a join. When **FORCEPLAN** is **ON**, the tables will be joined in the order that they are listed in the **FROM** clause. The **FORCEPLAN** statement does not affect the results of a SQL statement—only SQL Server's internal processing will be affected.

SET SHOWPLAN_ALL

The **SET SHOWPLAN_ALL** statement instructs SQL Server to retrieve execution information about each SQL statement. The syntax is:

```
SET SHOWPLAN_ALL { ON | OFF }
```

When **SHOWPLAN_ALL** is turned on, SQL Server will return the SQL statement being executed and information about what the SQL Server is doing to process the statement.

 Using the **SHOWPLAN_ALL** statement is similar to using **SHOWPLAN** in earlier versions of SQL Server.

The **SHOWPLAN_ALL** statement cannot be called from inside a stored procedure. When using **SHOWPLAN_ALL**, it must be the only statement in the batch.

SET SHOWPLAN_TEXT

The **SET SHOWPLAN_TEXT** statement tells SQL Server to retrieve execution information about each SQL statement. The syntax is:

```
SET SHOWPLAN_TEXT { ON | OFF }
```

When **SHOWPLAN_TEXT** is turned on, SQL Server will return the SQL statement being executed and information about what SQL Server is doing to process the statement. The only SQL statement that will execute when **SHOWPLAN_TEXT** is on is the **SHOWPLAN_TEXT OFF** statement.

 Using the **SHOWPLAN_TEXT** statement is similar to using the **SHOWPLAN** followed by a **NOEXEC** in earlier versions of SQL Server.

The **SHOWPLAN_TEXT** statement cannot be called from inside a stored procedure. When using **SHOWPLAN_TEXT**, it must be the only statement in the batch.

SET STATISTICS IO

The **SET STATISTICS IO** statement causes SQL Server to return information about the amount of disk activity performed by a SQL statement. The syntax is:

```
SET STATISTICS IO { ON | OFF }
```

When the **STATISTICS IO** option is turned on, SQL Server will return information about all database reads generated by a SQL statement. SQL Server will not return information about disk writes.

SET STATISTICS TIME

The **SET STATISTICS TIME** statement causes SQL Server to return the number of milliseconds to execute a SQL statement. The syntax is:

```
SET STATISTICS TIME { ON | OFF )
```

When the **STATISTICS TIME** option is turned on, SQL Server will return the number of milliseconds to parse, compile, and execute each SQL statement.

Transaction Statements

The transaction **SET** statements control how SQL Server handles transactions. Some of the items covered are whether SQL Server treats each SQL statement as its own transaction and the transaction isolation level.

SET IMPLICIT_TRANSACTIONS

The **SET IMPLICIT_TRANSACTIONS** statement causes SQL Server to implicitly begin transactions. The syntax is:

```
SET IMPLICIT_TRANSACTIONS { ON | OFF }
```

When **IMPLICIT_TRANSACTIONS** is set to **ON**, SQL Server will automatically begin a transaction when one of the following SQL statements are issued and a transaction is currently not in progress:

➤ ALTER TABLE

➤ CREATE

➤ DELETE

➤ DROP

➤ FETCH

➤ GRANT

➤ INSERT

➤ OPEN

➤ REVOKE

➤ SELECT

➤ TRUNCATE TABLE

➤ UPDATE

When **IMPLICIT_TRANSACTIONS** is set to **OFF** (SQL Server's default mode), you must explicitly issue a **BEGIN TRANSACTION** statement. See Chapter 13 for the information on the **BEGIN** statement.

SET REMOTE_PROC_TRANSACTIONS

The **SET REMOTE_PROC_TRANSACTIONS** statement affects SQL Server's behavior when a remote procedure call is made. The syntax is:

```
SET REMOTE_PROC_TRANSACTIONS { ON | OFF }
```

When **REMOTE_PROC_TRANSACTIONS** is turned on, SQL Server will start a distributed transaction whenever a remote procedure call (RPC) is made. Microsoft Distributed Transaction Manager (MS DTC) will start and manage the RPC's transaction. When **REMOTE_PROC_TRANSACTIONS** is turned off, an RPC does not start a distributed transaction.

SET TRANSACTION ISOLATION LEVEL

The **SET TRANSACTION ISOLATION LEVEL** statement controls SQL Server's locking behavior. The syntax is:

```
SET TRANSACTION ISOLATION LEVEL { READ COMMITTED |
        READ UNCOMMITTED | REPEATABLE READ | SERIALIZABLE }
```

Only one value for **TRANSACTION ISOLATION LEVEL** can be set at a time. SQL Server's default value is **READ COMMITTED**. The **TRANSACTION ISOLATION LEVEL** settings are described as follows:

➤ **READ COMMITTED** Removes the ability to perform *dirt reads* (read data changes that have not been committed to the database). The only data that can be accessed is data that is not locked by another connection.

➤ **READ UNCOMMITTED** Allows you to read through other people's locks. You will be able to read data changes that have not been committed to the database.

➤ **REPEATABLE READ** Causes SQL Server to hold locks and stop other users from updating data that is used in your SQL Statement. But, **REPEATABLE READ** does not stop other rows from being added to the table. These new rows are called *phantom rows* and will show up when you reread the data.

➤ **SERIALIZABLE** Represents the most restrictive isolation level. **SERIALIZABLE** stops other users from modifying the data you read, and it also stops other users from adding data that would have been included in the SQL statement you executed.

SET XACT_ABORT

The **SET XACT_ABORT** statement controls SQL Server's behavior when a runtime error occurs. The syntax is:

```
SET XACT_ABORT { ON | OFF }
```

When **XACT_ABORT** is turned on, SQL Server will abort transactions when a runtime error occurs. When **XACT_ABORT** is turned off, SQL Server will only abort the SQL statement that causes the runtime error.

Viewing User-Configuration Options

After setting the connection options with the **SET** statement, it is sometimes useful to view which options are in effect. You can view configuration settings by using the **DBCC USEROPTIONS** statement or the **@@OPTIONS** function.

DBCC USEROPTIONS

The **DBCC USEROPTIONS** command returns all the **SET** options for the current connection. The **DBCC USEROPTIONS** syntax is:

```
DBCC USEROPTIONS
```

You can use the **DBCC USEROPTIONS** command to return the connection's configured options in a standard table format. The table shows a column for each option that is set and a column for the configured value of the option. **DBCC USEROPTIONS** will not show what **DBCC** options have been set. Any user can run the **DBCC USEROPTIONS** statement.

The following **DBCC USEROPTIONS** example assumes that no options have been set, and it displays all default values for the connection:

```
Set Option                        Value
-------------------------------   -------------------------
textsize                          64512
language                          us_english
dateformat                        mdy
datefirst                         7
ansi_null_dflt_on                 SET
```

As shown in the previous example, only options that have been explicitly set will appear in the results of a **DBCC USEROPTIONS** statement. For example, looking at the results, you do not see a row for **ROWCOUNT** or **TRANS-ACTION ISOLATION LEVEL**. The next example illustrates a **DBCC USEROPTIONS** statement after the **SET** statement is used to set the **ROWCOUNT** and **TRANSACTION ISOLATION LEVEL** statements:

```
SET ROWCOUNT 100
SET TRANSACTION ISOLATION LEVEL READ UNCOMMITTED
DBCC USEROPTIONS
```

This setting changes the results of the **DBCC USEROPTIONS** to the following:

```
Set Option                         Value
-------------------------------    ------------------------
textsize                           64512
rowcount                           100
language                           us_english
dateformat                         mdy
datefirst                          7
ansi_null_dflt_on                  SET
isolation level                    read uncommitted
```

The results of the **DBCC USEROPTIONS** statement now have a row for **ROWCOUNT** and for **ISOLATION LEVEL**. An important detail to note in the preceding examples is that the name of the option that was configured using the **SET** statement does not always match the name used for the option in the **DBCC USEROPTION**; the **TRANSACTION ISOLATION LEVEL** option is listed as isolation level.

@@OPTIONS

The **@@OPTIONS** function returns a bit mask that lists which **SET** options are turned on for the current connection. The one main limitation of the **@@OPTIONS** command is that not all options affect the bit mask that is returned. Table 8.3 lists the bit that is set in the bit mask and the option that is associated with the bit.

The bit is the bit position from the right in the result of the **@@OPTIONS** command. The decimal value is the number that corresponds to two to the power of the set bit. The option is the **SET** option that is turned on if the bit is set. The only special case is that the **ANSI NULL DEFAULT** option has a value for both on (bit 10) and off (bit 11). The following example shows the use of the **@@OPTIONS** function:

```
IF @@OPTIONS & 64 != 0
    SELECT 'ARITHABORT IS SET'
```

Bit	Decimal Value	Option
0	1	DISABLE DEFAULT CONSTRAIN CHECK
1	2	IMPLICIT TRANSACTIONS
2	4	CURSOR CLOSE ON COMMIT
3	8	ANSI WARNINGS
4	16	ANSI PADDING
5	32	ANSI NULLS
6	64	ARITHABORT
7	128	ARITHIGNORE
8	256	QUOTED IDENTIFIER
9	512	NOCOUNT
10	1024	ANSI NULL DEFAULT ON
11	2048	ANSI NULL DEFAULT OFF

Table 8.3   @@OPTIONS bits.

The preceding example uses the bitwise **AND** function (&) to check if the sixth bit, 64 decimal, is set. If the bit is set, the **ARITHIGNORE** option is turned on.

Default User-Configuration Options

When users connect to SQL Server, they will get the default SQL Server user options. These default options can be set with the **SP_CONFIGURE** command. The syntax is:

```
sp_configure 'user options', option_bitmask
```

When configuring default user options, you use a bit mask specifying what options to turn on. Any bit not specified will cause the option to be turned off. Table 8.3 lists the bits and the associated options that the bit controls. Even though **ANSI_NULL_DFLT_ON** and **ANSI_NULL_DFLT_OFF** are set with separate bits, you cannot turn on both **ANSI_NULL_DFLT_ON** and **ANSI_NULL_DFLT_OFF**.

You cannot change the default values for all connection configuration options. The only options you can change values for are the ones listed in Table 8.3.

Practice Questions

Question 1

Which of the following **SET** statements can be used to stop SQL statements from affecting any rows? [Check all correct answers]

❏ a. set showplan on

❏ b. set noexec on

❏ c. set parseonly on

❏ d. set rowcount 0

❏ e. set query_governor_cost_limit 0

Answers b and c are correct. The **SET NOEXEC ON** statement will stop any
statement from executing except the **SET NOEXEC** statement. Likewise, the
SET PARSEONLY ON statement will cause SQL Server to parse the statement, checking for syntax errors. Answer a is incorrect, because **SET
SHOWPLAN** was used in previous versions of SQL Server to show the query
execution plan. With SQL Server 7, **SET SHOWPLAN** is replaced with the
SET SHOWPLAN_TEXT and **SET SHOWPLAN_ALL**. Answer d is incorrect, because the **SET ROWCOUNT 0** statement instructs SQL Server to
return all rows. Answer e is incorrect, because the **SET QUERY_GOVERNOR_
COST_LIMIT 0** statement turns off the query governor—it doesn't cause
processing to stop.

Question 2

If the current default user options only have ANSI WARNINGS and
NOCOUNT turned on, which of the following SQL statements will also
set the QUOTED IDENTIFIER and IMPLICIT TRANSACTIONS as default
options?

○ a.
```
sp_configure 'user options', 778
```

○ b.
```
set default_option, 'quoted_identifier', on
set default_option, 'implicit_transactions', on
```

○ c.
```
sp_configure 'user options',+258
```

○ d.
```
set quoted_identifier on
set implicit_transactions on
```

○ e. None of the above

Answer a is correct, because it sets **ANSI WARNINGS (8), NOCOUNT
(512), QUOTED IDENTIFIER (256),** and **IMPLICIT TRANSACTIONS
(2).** When you add the decimal numbers associated with the bits together, you
get 778. Answer b is incorrect, because there is not a set **default_option** statement. Answer c is incorrect, because 258 sets, **QUOTED IDENTIFIER (256)**
and **IMPLICIT TRANSACTIONS (2),** a value set in with the **sp_configure**
'user options' only sets the options specified in the statement. When setting
user options, any option not specified will be turned off, so answer c will turn
off the **ANSI WARNINGS** and **NOCOUNT.** Answer d is incorrect, because
it will only turn on the **QUOTED IDENTIFIER** and **IMPLICIT TRANS-
ACTION** for the current connection.

Question 3

> Which of the following SQL statements will show you the value that all the current user options are set to?
>
> ○ a. dbcc useroptions
>
> ○ b. select @@options
>
> ○ c. sp_configure
>
> ○ d. sp_options
>
> ○ e. None of the above

Answer e is correct; none of the SQL statements are correct. Answer a is incorrect, because it will not return values for all user options. **DBCC USEROPTIONS** does not return values for options that are set to the standard value, nor does it show options for all user options. Answer b is incorrect, because it will only show the settings for the 12 options that are listed in Table 8.3. Answer c is incorrect, because it will return the server configuration. Answer d is not a valid SQL statement, so it will not return any options.

Question 4

> The following statement
>
> ```
> set lock_timeout 0
> ```
>
> will have which of the following effects when the connection has to wait for a lock?
>
> ○ a. The connection will perform the default behavior and wait until the locked resource is released.
>
> ○ b. The connection will immediately return with an error stating that the lock time period has been exceeded.
>
> ○ c. The **SET** statement is invalid, so it will have no effect on the lock.
>
> ○ d. The connection will force the locked resources to immediately be released by the other connection.

Answer b is correct—the **SET** statement will set the timeout period to zero milliseconds. Answer a is incorrect, because, unlike other **SET** statements, setting the **SET LOCK_TIMEOUT** to zero will not set the option to the default value. You set the **LOCK_TIMEOUT** to -1 to make the connection wait forever on locks. Answer c is incorrect, because the statement is a valid SQL statement. Answer d is incorrect, because there is no SQL statement that will cause the behavior specified in answer d.

Need To Know More?

 Amo, William C. *Transact-SQL*, IDG Books Worldwide, Foster City, CA, 1998. ISBN 0-7645-8048-5. Chapter 4 contains information about some of the more common session configuration options.

 Coffman, Gayle. *SQL Server 7: The Complete Reference*, Osborne/McGraw-Hill, Berkley, CA, 1999. ISBN 0-07-882494-X. Chapter 21 provides a complete T-SQL reference.

 MS SQL Server Books Online provides information on setting configuration options look in the index for "set".

 Search the TechNet CD or its online version at **www.microsoft.com**.

 www.microsoft.com/sql
Find up-to-date information about using SQL Server here.

Indexes

· ·

Terms you'll need to understand:

√ Index

√ B-tree

√ Clustered index

√ Nonclustered index

√ Page

√ Unique

Techniques you'll need to master:

√ Choosing clustered versus nonclustered indexes

√ Converting from a logical to a physical model

√ Choosing indexes for performance

An *index* is a physical database object, structured as a b-tree, which is used by the optimizer to access data faster than a table scan. As an ancillary benefit, indexes are also used to enforce uniqueness on a key, which means that no duplicates are allowed for a specific key value in a column. SQL Server uses two types of indexes—clustered and nonclustered.

Clustered And Nonclustered Indexes

SQL Server enables you to use clustered or nonclustered indexes. When you define a clustered index on a table, you instruct the server to physically sort, or cluster, the data in the order of the columns in which you are defining the index. Because creating a clustered index physically sorts data, each table can have only one clustered index (therefore, you can only cluster a table one way).

But a single index can rarely fulfill all your needs. When you use a database, you frequently need to access data in many different ways. This means that you need to have many indexes on a table, so you can access the data in a variety of ways. As mentioned earlier, you can only physically sort data one way, and, therefore, you can have only one clustered index. Fortunately, SQL Server has a mechanism for accessing data stored in sequences other than the sorted order. That's where nonclustered indexes come into play, providing indexing based on the key value in each row. SQL Server enables you to create a total of 249 nonclustered indexes.

There are many physical differences between clustered and nonclustered indexes. In the upcoming sections, we'll look at the physical mechanisms for each types of index.

Clustered Index Mechanisms

One of the primary characteristics of a clustered index is that there is one index entry per *page* of data. A page of data refers to the physical storage representation of the data, 8K. After the server identifies the correct page (either by traversing the index or scanning the table), it must then find the row on the page. Because clustered indexes allow you to zero in on the first result row and then scan the table (rather then re-traversing the index) for the rest of the rows without returning to the index level, clustered indexes tend to be an excellent first choice for retrieving data ranges. This includes foreign keys (joins), lists of names, and any other data collection that references sequential keys.

For performance reasons, you should keep as many index entries on a page as you can and index widths (the number of bytes in an index) as narrow as possible. In SQL Server, indexes can be up to 900 bytes wide and use up to 16 columns of data, but you should try to keep your index's parameters much lower than that to maximize the number of index entries on a page.

The clustered index and data also share a row in sysindexes (which exists in every database). When the server needs to find space to allocate for a table, it looks in the segment column of sysindexes. This is mostly outmoded with SQL Server 7.

You've probably seen binary trees in some data structures course or another—effectively, they exist to shorten searches. You start at the root, and traverse the tree until you find the index you're looking for. Let's take a look at a b-tree structure for a clustered index. In Figure 9.1, you can see that there's an index on the **last_name** column.

Index entry searches always start from the *root page*, which is the starting point for any tree traversal. For example, let's assume that you're trying to find the "Baker" row. First, you enter the index from the root and find that "Baker" is between "Albert" and "Jones" (keep in mind that SQL Server *between*s are inclusive). Therefore, you follow the "Albert" pointer to the next index level.

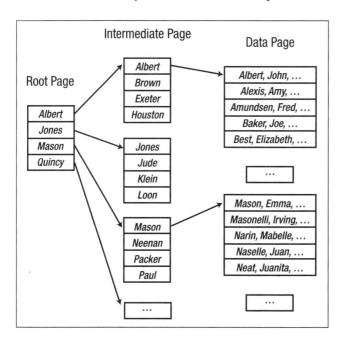

Figure 9.1 Clustered index b-tree structure.

Again, you look for "Baker," which is between "Albert" and "Brown." Next, follow the "Albert" pointer to the next index level. In this case, the next index level is the data page, which you can scan for the "Baker" row(s).

Due to their setup, clustered indexes generally tend to be one IO faster than a random row retrieval (single-row lookup) for a corresponding nonclustered index. This is a rule of thumb and certainly not cast in stone. It is largely due to the effect of the number of pointers that are needed for each index type, and their corresponding widths. At times, a clustered index might be two IOs faster, or it might not provide any speed difference at all. Normally, though, clustered indexes are a bit faster than nonclustered indexes for most queries. Of course, when necessary, using nonclustered indexes usually beats the alternative—no index. With that in mind, let's take a closer look at nonclustered index mechanisms.

Nonclustered Index Mechanisms

Nonclustered indexes are very similar in appearance to clustered indexes.

The first characteristic of the nonclustered index is that there is one index entry per *row* of data. When a row is identified, it is accessed directly. A row ID is stored for every row in the table. Because the nonclustered index has a pointer per row, and because the pointer structures are larger than the corresponding clustered index pointer structures (they contain a row ID, not just a page ID), nonclustered indexes tend to be much larger than clustered indexes proportional to the number of rows on a page, because you have pointers per row for the nonclustered index and pointers per page for the clustered index.

Let's take a look at a b-tree structure for a nonclustered index. In this example, let's say that you have an index on the **first_name** column, and you want to find all the "Amy" entries (see Figure 9.2).

As mentioned earlier, index entries always start from the root page. Therefore, you first enter the index from the root. You find that "Amy" is between "Amy" and "George" (remember, SQL Server *between*s are inclusive). Therefore, you follow the "Amy" pointer to the next index level. Again, you look for "Amy." It is between "Amy" and "Bob," so you follow the "Amy" pointer to the next index level. In this case, the next index level is the leaf level of the nonclustered index. At the leaf level, you find entries with row pointers for each result row. In this example, you end up with two entries for "Amy." Note that you have two row pointers, one for each "Amy," and that you will need to request one page for each of the entries.

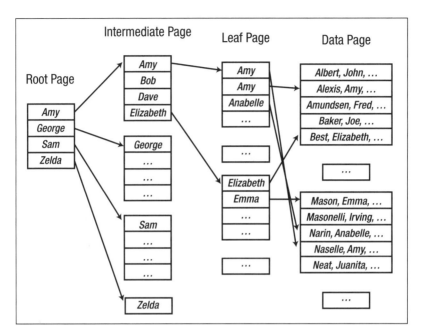

Figure 9.2 Nonclustered index b-tree structure.

The SQL Server optimizer can take advantage of a special index retrieval technique, called *index covering*. Index covering treats the leaf level of a nonclustered index as the data level of a clustered index. Index covering can dramatically speed up specific types of queries which only need the data that is actually in the index. For example, if you are indexed on titles (title, qty_sold) and you issue "select title, sum(qty_sold) from titles group by title," then all information needed for the query can be found in the index, and the server does not need to read the base page. This is a common performance and tuning trick.

You should not create indexes prior to loading data unless you have no choice, as you will experience a period of time wherein your index statistics will be out of date. When you do create your indexes, you have some other things to consider.

Creating Indexes

For better performance, you should create the clustered index before you create nonclustered indexes. Clustered index creation requires the physical sort of a table, and nonclustered indexes have page and row pointers, which have to be adjusted when rows move.

Note: When you create a clustered index, you need free space within your database. You'll need enough space for a sorted copy of the table plus the index, or from 120 to 150 percent of the size of the table in additional disk space.

Here is simplified syntax for creating an index:

```
create [unique] [clustered | nonclustered] index
    IndexName on TableName (column [, ...] )
```

The parameters of the code are as follows:

➤ **Unique** Specifies that there will be no duplicate keys allowed in the table. This is customary for primary key columns. The default is nonunique.

➤ **Clustered** Specifies to create a clustered index.

➤ **Nonclustered** Specifies to create a nonclustered index. The default is nonclustered.

➤ **IndexName** Specifies the index's name. **IndexName** must be unique for the table.

➤ **Column** Specifies which columns to access in the index. The limit is 16 columns, with a total of 900 bytes.

The following code creates a clustered index named **name_index**:

```
create unique clustered index name_index on
    authors (au_lname, au_fname)
```

The preceding code will create a unique, clustered index on the **authors** table, indexing first on the **au_lname** column and secondarily on the **au_fname** column. Following is another code snippet. This time, the code creates a nonclustered table named **fname_index**:

```
create index fname_index on authors (au_fname, au_lname)
```

This time, the code will create a nonunique, nonclustered index on the **authors** table, indexing on the **au_fname** and **au_lname** columns.

Note: If you create a clustered index on a table that already has nonclustered indexes, SQL Server will automatically rebuild all non-clustered indexes, because the page and row positions will have changed.

Indexes are database objects like any other, and as such, need to be maintained periodically.

Index Management

To change an index for a table, you must drop it and then re-create it with a new definition. Dropping and re-creating indexes is frequently performed in production environments for the purpose of reapplying fill factors or rebuilding index structures if they have become skewed or out of balance over time. In those instances, rebuilding an index is done for performance reasons, not because it's required.

The following syntax will drop an index for a table.

```
drop index TableName.IndexName
```

This will remove the index structure from the database, remove all entries from system tables, and release the pages that were in use.

To get information on the indexes that are currently defined for a table, you can use **sp_help** or **sp_helpindex**, as follows:

```
sp_helpindex titles
go

index_name        index_description                          index_keys
------------------------------------------------------------------------
------------------------------------------------------------------------
------------------------------------------------------------------------
------------------------------------------------------------------------
------------------------------------------------------------------------
------------------------------------------------------------------------
UPKCL_titleidind  clustered, unique, primary key located on PRIMARY
title_id
titleind          nonclustered located on PRIMARY                  title
```

 All index information and properties can be managed within SQL EM.

Notes On Indexes

Finally, before wrapping up this chapter, there are a few items that you need to be aware of regarding indexes. Following is a quick list of index specifics that you should be familiar with before taking the exam:

➤ When an index is defined as unique, no two rows may have the same index value (null counts as one value). The uniqueness check is performed at index creation, on insert and update.

➤ Index selection should be a performance decision, not a decision based on primary key or other values. Often, a clustered index is used for the primary key. This is not always the best performance selection.

➤ For physical data placement purposes, it is a good idea to have a clustered index on most tables.

➤ As the number of indexes increases (over five) the update overhead to maintain the indexes gets excessive.

➤ In an executive information system (EIS) where there is virtually no realtime update, the only constraint on the number of indexes is disk space.

➤ An online transaction processing (OLTP) system usually is configured with as few indexes as possible to speed **UPDATE**, **INSERT**, and **DELETE** processes.

Practice Questions

Question 1

What are the characteristics of a clustered index? [Check all correct answers]

❏ a. Physically sorts data in clustered index order.

❏ b. Tends to be smaller than nonclustered indexes.

❏ c. Should be clustered on primary keys.

❏ d. Tends to be one IO faster than a nonclustered index.

Answers a, b, and d are correct, as they define a clustered index; c is a physical design decision, which is not always a good one.

Question 2

What are the characteristics of a non–clustered index? [Check all correct answers]

❏ a. Physically sorts data in clustered index order.

❏ b. Tends to be small compared to clustered indexes.

❏ c. Should be clustered on primary keys.

❏ d. Tends to be one IO faster than a nonclustered index.

❏ e. None of the above.

Answer e is correct. Answer a, b, and d are incorrect, because those are clustered index characteristic. Answer c is incorrect, because that is a physical design decision, not an index characteristic.

Question 3

> If you are designing an EIS (executive information system) or a DSS (decision support system), what is true about index selection?
>
> ○ a. Avoid clustered indexes.
>
> ○ b. Avoid nonclustered indexes.
>
> ○ c. The number of indexes you choose is largely irrelevant.
>
> ○ d. The number of indexes you choose should be minimal.
>
> ○ e. You ignore, for the most part, update ramifications.

Answer c is correct, because only updates have negative implications on the overall number of indexes. Answer a is incorrect, because clustered indexes provide quick access to the data. Answer b is incorrect, because in a query system, you need lots of indexes, and you can have only one clustered index. Answer d is incorrect for the same reason as b. Answer e is correct, because neither system has users performing updates.

Question 4

> If you are designing an OLTP (online transaction processing) system, what is true about index selection?
>
> ○ a. Avoid clustered indexes.
>
> ○ b. Avoid nonclustered indexes.
>
> ○ c. The number of indexes you choose is largely irrelevant.
>
> ○ d. The number of indexes you choose should be minimal.
>
> ○ e. You ignore, for the most part, update ramifications.

Answer d is correct. Answer a is incorrect, because clustered indexes provide quick access to the data. Answer b is incorrect, because you need indexes to access the data, and you can have only one clustered index. Answer c is incorrect, because updates have negative implications on the overall number of indexes (it takes longer to update many indexes). Answer e is incorrect, because that is what you are doing, principally.

Question 5

> Which statement is true about clustered indexes?
>
> ○ a. Clustered indexes are the quickest way to resolve any query.
>
> ○ b. Clustered indexes are always faster than nonclustered indexes.
>
> ○ c. Clustered indexes are always faster than table scans.
>
> ○ d. None of the above.
>
> ○ e. All of the above.

Answer d is correct. Answer a is incorrect, because index covering or a table scan may be faster than a clustered index. Answer b is incorrect, because it is often slower than nonclustered index covering. Answer c is incorrect, because if the index isn't useful, or you are going after all of the data, a table scan is faster.

Question 6

> Which statement is true about nonclustered indexes?
>
> ○ a. Nonclustered indexes are the quickest way to resolve any query.
>
> ○ b. Nonclustered indexes are always faster than clustered indexes.
>
> ○ c. Nonclustered indexes are always faster than table scans.
>
> ○ d. None of the above.
>
> ○ e. All of the above.

Answer d is correct. Answer a is incorrect, because index covering may be faster than a clustered index, but this only helps specific types of queries. Answer b is incorrect, because it is usually slower than clustered index access. Answer c is incorrect, because if you are going after more than a small percentage of data, the cost of bouncing in and out of the index structure, as well as the large quantity of logical page requests, will make a table scan faster.

Need To Know More?

 Amo, William C. *Transact-SQL*, IDG Books Worldwide, Foster City, CA, 1998. ISBN 0-7645-8048-5. Chapter 5 contains information about indexes.

 Coffman, Gayle. *SQL Server 7: The Complete Reference*, Osborne/McGraw-Hill, Berkley, CA, 1999. ISBN 0-07-882494-X. Chapter 21 provides a complete T-SQL reference.

 MS SQL Server Books Online contains a complete DML reference you can find information either in the table of contents under Accessing and Change Data or you can look in the index for information about "indexes".

 Search the TechNet CD or its online version at **www.microsoft.com**.

 www.microsoft.com/sql
Find up-to-date information about using SQL Server here.

Rules, Defaults, And Views

10

. . . .

Terms you'll need to understand:

√ Bind

√ Rule

√ Default

√ View

Techniques you'll need to master:

√ Creating rules and defaults

√ Binding rules and defaults to columns

√ Creating and using views

Rules, defaults, and views are used to restrict or change access to a SQL Server table's data. You can use rules, defaults, and views to enforce simple domain restrictions; you'll be using triggers for complex domain restrictions. Each of these different database objects (views, rules, and defaults) exist in and of themselves; they do not have to be attached to a table to have significance. Briefly, rules, defaults, and views can be defined as follows:

➤ **Rule** A standalone database object that can be bound to table columns in a database, which constrains its domain.

➤ **Default** A standalone database object that can be bound to table columns in a database, which places a value in a column if it is explicitly excluded in an **INSERT** statement.

➤ **View** A standalone database object that is a pre-parsed query tree for any **SELECT** statement.

This chapter takes a look at these three key database objects.

Rules

A rule is an expression that is evaluated when a row is inserted or updated. If the rule is **FALSE**, the **INSERT** or **UPDATE** that caused the rule to fire will be rolled back (in other words, the rule will be removed from the database).

The complete syntax used to create a rule is:

```
CREATE RULE RuleName
@variable operator expression
  [{and|or} ...]
```

Rule definition is best explained by example. Following is an example of a rule:

```
CREATE RULE AgeRule
AS @age between 16 and 21
```

In the preceding example, the **@age** variable denotes where the column value will be substituted. The name of this variable has no effect on the execution and evaluation of the rule.

Using the preceding AgeRule rule, Table 10.1 shows the result of inserting various values into the age column. Note that the row will only be inserted if the expression evaluates to **TRUE** (remember, a **BETWEEN** is inclusive).

To drop a rule, use the **DROP RULE** statement, as follows:

```
DROP RULE RuleName
```

Table 10.1 Inserting values into AgeRule.	
Value	**Evaluates As**
6	FALSE
20	TRUE
30	FALSE

When a rule is dropped, it is deleted from the database. To use a rule, you have to associate it to a column. We call that binding it to a column.

Binding A Rule To A Column

SQL Servers enforce rules by using the stored procedure **sp_bindrule**. The following code shows the syntax for binding a rule to a column in a table by using the **sp_bindrule** stored procedure:

```
sp_bindrule RuleName, 'TableName.ColumnName'
```

> *Note: Single or double quotes are required around the table and column names because of the special character in the argument—the period.*

In the preceding example, the *sp_bindrule* stored procedure instructs the server to tie the rule named **RuleName** to the column named **ColumnName**. The net effect is that if a rule is bound to a table, then no additional data that violates the rule can be entered into the table.

> *Note: When you bind a rule to a table, the rule will not be applied to data that is already stored in the database.*

After a rule is bound to a column, the rule is always enforced. If a rule is bound over a previous rule, the new rule takes effect immediately. If you want to remove a rule binding from a column, you use **sp_unbindrule**, like this:

```
sp_unbindrule 'TableName.ColumnName'
```

When you use **sp_unbindrule**, you do not need to specify the rule name, because the server already knows which rule is bound to the table.

You can bind and unbind rules to or from columns or data types by clicking on the appropriate tab in the Rules Property dialog (by right mouse clicking on the rule).

Rule Limitations

When using rules, you must work within some specific rule limitations. Keep the following points in mind when you use rules:

➤ A rule can only deal with constants, SQL Server functions, and edit masks. In other words, a rule cannot perform complex tasks.

➤ A rule cannot perform a table lookup. If the business rule has a level of complexity that requires a table lookup, you can use a trigger or a declarative constraint.

➤ Rules cannot compare against other columns in the table. Again, if this is a requisite, use a constraint.

➤ Only one rule can be bound per column. A second rule can be applied with a constraint or by building all of the logic into a trigger.

➤ If an existing rule is bound to a column, it will be replaced by a new rule. SQL Server treats this as having a stack, with a permitted depth of one.

➤ The values in a rule should be compatible with the data type of the column it is bound to. If there is a conflict, performance will slow down or a runtime problem will occur, depending on whether there is an implicit datatype conversion available.

➤ A rule cannot be retroactively applied to an existing data in a table, but it can be applied when an existing row is updated.

➤ A rule cannot be dropped if it is bound to a column or user-defined data type. You must first unbind the rule from all columns and data types.

➤ Rules are not applied during a BCP in. If rules need to be applied, use a front-end other than BCP (for example, write a C program).

➤ Microsoft no longer recommends the use of rules. Rules are left for backward compatibility. Instead, Microsoft recommends using constraints, as discussed in Chapter 5.

Similar in utilization to rules, defaults are also separate database objects that may be directly bound to columns.

Defaults

A default is used to insert values into columns when you exclude the columns from your **INSERT** statement. Here's the syntax used to create a default:

```
CREATE DEFAULT DefaultName
  AS ConstantExpression
```

When you insert a row into a table that has a default and fail to supply a value for the column on which the default is applied, the default is used as the insertion value for that column in that row.

> *Note: If you supply null as a value for the column, null will be inserted into the table, because null is considered to be a value.*

The following example creates a default for **Age**:

```
CREATE DEFAULT AgeDefault
AS 18
```

In the preceding example, a default called AgeDefault is created. When it is applied, the value 18 will be placed in the column.

A default is a standalone database object that can be bound to one or more columns in database tables. Further, a default should have the same data type as the column to which it is bound.

To drop a default, you should use the **DROP DEFAULT** statement, using the following syntax:

```
DROP DEFAULT DefaultName
```

When you drop a default, the object is permanently removed from the database. You instruct the server to use a default for the column by binding it to a column.

Binding A Default To A Column

To instruct a server to enforce a default, you use the **sp_bindefault** stored procedure. The following code snippet shows the syntax for binding a default to a column in a table:

```
sp_bindefault DefaultName, 'TableName.ColumnName'
```

 Single or double quotes are required around the table and column names, because of the special character in the argument— the period.

The **sp_bindefault** stored procedure instructs the server to tie the default named **DefaultName** to the column named **ColumnName**.

*Note: When you use the **sp_bindefault** stored procedure, the default will not be applied to data that already exists in the database.*

After a default is bound to a column, it is always enforced. If a default is bound over a previous default, the new default takes effect immediately. To remove a default binding from a column, you use **sp_unbindefault**, like this:

```
sp_unbindefault 'TableName.ColumnName'
```

When you use **sp_unbindefault**, you do not need to specify the default name, as the server already knows which default is bound to the column. You can bind and unbind defaults to or from columns or data types by clicking on the appropriate tab in the Defaults Property dialog of SQL EM.

Default Limitations

Defaults have very limited application and include the following restrictions:

➤ A default can set only one constant or SQL Server function value—there is no logic capability.

➤ A default cannot make a decision or perform a table lookup. You should use a trigger if decision-making or table-lookup tasks are necessary.

➤ Only one default can be applied per column. This makes sense, because a column can only have one value.

➤ Attempting to bind a second default to a column that already has a default will generate an error message.

➤ You must ensure that the data type of a default's value is compatible with the column data type. This is tested at execution time, not creation time.

➤ A default will not be retroactively applied to existing data in a table. Instead, write an **UPDATE** statement that will modify all rows that have a **NULL** column value.

➤ You must ensure that defaults are consistent with any rule or constraint on the column. Without this consistency, insertions that use the default will fail.

➤ A default is applied before a rule is applied. (Therefore, if a rule requires a value in a column, the default can be used to circumvent any potential insertion failure.)

➤ Defaults are applied during bulk copies, but not retroactively against data in the table.

➤ A default cannot be dropped if it is bound to a column or user-defined data type. You must unbind the default from all columns or data types before dropping it.

Views

A view is a logical way of looking at physical data stored in a database. The complete view creation syntax is as follows:

```
create view view_name [ (col_name, ...) ]
[with encrypt]
as SelectStatement
[ with check option ]
```

From a practical standpoint, a view is a pre-parsed **SELECT** statement that can be treated as if it is a table. In actuality, a view is not a physical table, but a logical table. In other words, a view changes the way data is perceived, without changing the underlying database object. As you will see, in most instances, including **SELECT** statements, a view can be treated as any other table.

You can use a view to restrict access to rows or columns, hide joins, or simplify SQL by pre-coding aggregates, groups, or other complex tasks. View columns inherit the column names from the base table(s) unless you explicitly name the columns. Note that if you are using aggregates, you will need to explicitly name the columns.

View options enable you to control how users can access your view. For example, you can use the Encrypt option to restrict anybody except the creator of the view from accessing the code. In other words, when the Encrypt option is used, nobody but the owner of the view can look at the underlying SQL. Also, you can use the With Check Option to specify that users can only insert and update rows through the view if they are also able to retrieve that row by selecting from the view.

The following example creates a view called FLAuthorsView, which will look like a table, act like a table, and can be treated as a table:

```
CREATE VIEW FLAuthorsView
AS
select * from authors where state = 'FL'
```

You can select from the FLAuthorsView table, like this:

```
Select * from FLAuthorsView
```

The preceding **SELECT** statement will return a list of all columns and rows from the **authors** table, but only if the author lives in Florida.

If you try to insert into the view and the With Check Option is turned on, the **INSERT** will fail if the author does not live in Florida. That is, if an **INSERT** statement violates the view, the With Check Option prohibits the insert.

The following code creates a view that contains only two columns from the authors table, the author's first and last name.

```
create view author_name as
  select last = au_lname, first = au_fname
  from authors
```

If you use column headings, as in the preceding example, the column headings will become the column names in the view.

 When you create a view, ensure that your column headings follow the basic SQL Server naming conventions.

The next example retrieves all rows and columns from the author_name view:

```
select * from author_name
```

To remove a view, use a **DROP** statement with the following syntax:

```
drop view view_name
```

The following code drops the author_name view:

```
drop view author_name
```

When you drop a view, the view definition is removed from the database.

 Note that as with all **DROP** statements, there is no "undrop," so do not lightly drop an object if you have no way to re-create it.

Views can be used for a variety of security purposes, from restricting columns from read access (vertical security), to row-level access (horizontal security).

Views As Security: Vertical

You can use a view to limit access to selected columns in a base table by limiting the select list to the columns you want your users to have access to. In the following example, users can select from three of the four columns in the **titleauthor** table—users will not have access to the **royalty** column:

```
create view ta_limited as
  select au_id, title_id, au_ord from titleauthor
```

When a user uses the ta_limited view instead of the underlying table, the user can perform any action with the underlying table except access the **royalty** column. The following is the output from the preceding code:

au_id	title_id	au_ord	royaltyper
172-32-1176	PS3333	1	100
213-46-8915	BU1032	2	40
213-46-8915	BU2075	1	100
...			
998-72-3567	PS2106	1	100

You may now grant a user permission to select from this view, without granting select permission from the base table. The ta_limited view can now be used to join titles and authors, as shown here:

```
select *
from authors a, titles t, ta_limited ta
where a.au_id = ta.au_id and t.title_id = ta.title_id
```

The example selects the title and author name columns using the ta_limited view. A user will not see the **royaltyper** column through the ta_limited view.

You can grant access to a view and not to the underlying table if you own both the view and the table. This technique can be used to restrict access to parts of a table without using column-level protections, which would make using SELECT * statements impossible.

Views As Security: Horizontal

You can use a view to limit access to specific rows in a base table by using a WHERE clause to restrict which rows are displayed in a view. For example, the following view will only allow the user of the view to access publishers in California:

```
create view cal_publishers as
  select *
  from publishers
  where state = "CA"
```

The following **SELECT** retrieves all rows and columns from the view created by the preceding code:

```
select * from cal_publishers
```

Note that the preceding code looks just like a **SELECT** from a table.

Views To Ease SQL

Views can be used to simplify queries or to hide complex joins or denormalized tables from end users. For example, the following code will create a view to handle a three-way join:

```
create view titles_and_authors as
  select title, au_lname, au_fname, type
  from titles t, ta_limited ta, authors a
  where t.title_id = ta.title_id  and a.au_id = ta.au_id
```

This view contains the ta_limited view, which was created earlier.

The following code snippet will retrieve all rows and columns from the titles_and_authors view:

```
select *  from titles_and_authors
  where type = "business"
```

INSERT, UPDATE, DELETE, And Views

SQL Server allows you to insert into, update, and delete from views. An **INSERT** will add rows to the base table. An **UPDATE** or **DELETE** will modify rows in the base table. For example, the following code snippet deletes rows from the table underlying the view:

```
delete author_name
  where last = "Smith" and first = "Joseph"

update cal_publishers
  set pub_name = "Joe's Books and Magazines"
  where pub_id = "1389"
```

Both SQL statements modify the underlying tables.

When a view includes columns from more than one table, you cannot delete rows from the view or update columns from more than one table in a single **UPDATE** statement. For example, the following is not permitted:

```
update titles_and_authors
  set type = "mod_cook", au_fname = "Mary"
  where title = "The Gourmet Microwave"
```

This limitation can pose a problem, because you can only modify one underlying base table. To work around this limitation, you can update each table in turn, like this:

```
update titles_and_authors
 set type = "mod_cook"
 where title = "The Gourmet Microwave"
update titles_and_authors
 set au_fname = "Mary"
  where title = "The Gourmet Microwave"
```

Inserts are not allowed into views unless all underlying columns in the base table not included in the view either are defined to allow **NULL** values, or have a default defined on the columns.

Inserts are allowed on views containing joins, as long as all columns being inserted into the view belong to a single base table. Therefore, you cannot update, delete, or insert into a view containing the **DISTINCT** clause, because the **DISTINCT** creates a temporary work table. In that situation, you would be modifying the work table rather than the actual base table.

With Check Option

In previous releases of SQL Server, a user could insert or update a row to create a row that users could not retrieve with a **SELECT** statement. Following is an example of a row that violates the restrictions on this view:

```
insert into cal_publishers
 (pub_id, pub_name, city, state)
values
 ("1234", "Joe's Books", "Canton", "OH")
/* update creates an "invisible" row */
update cal_publishers
 set state = "OH"
```

In SQL Server 7, the **With Check Option** flag prevents users from inserting or updating rows in a way that will subsequently not meet the view criteria. The syntax for the **With Check Option** is as follows:

```
create view view_name [ ( colname, ... ) ]
  as select_statements
  [with check option]
```

The following view uses the **With Check Option** to only allow users to select, modify, and insert rows that fit the view:

```
create view cal_publishers as
  select *
  from publishers
  where state = "CA"
  with check option
```

Getting View Information

You can list all objects in a database, including views and tables, by using **sp_help**. But this approach can create an unwieldy list. To retrieve a list of just the views defined on a database's tables, run the following **SELECT** statement:

```
select name from sysobjects
  where type = "V"
```

To view a list of columns in a view, use the following:

```
sp_help view_name
```

To see the SQL that creates a view, use the following:

```
sp_helptext view_name
```

ALTER VIEW

Views can be edited by using the **ALTER VIEW** statement. The **ALTER VIEW** statement modifies an existing view without affecting dependent stored procedures or triggers and without changing permissions. Previously, the only way to modify a view was to drop and re-create it. This would change the object ID, forcing recompilation of stored procedures and triggers that depended on the view. You would also have to grant permissions again, because permissions are removed when the objects are dropped. The **ALTER VIEW** syntax follows:

```
ALTER VIEW view_name [(column [, ...n])]
  [WITH ENCRYPTION]
AS
select_statement
  [WITH CHECK OPTION]
```

ALTER VIEW is a new feature available in SQL Server 7 that enables you to modify an existing view without having to drop and re-create the view.

The following describes the **ALTER VIEW** arguments:

➤ *n* Acts as a placeholder indicating the *column* can be repeated *n* number of times.

➤ **ENCRYPTION** Encrypts the **syscomments** entries that contain the text of the **CREATE VIEW** statement. This means that users other than the object owner will not be able to access the view's underlying code.

➤ **CHECK OPTION** Verifies that all data modified still sticks to the criteria set within the *select_statement* defining the view.

Note: Column permissions are maintained only when the columns have the same name before and after the ALTER VIEW statement is executed.

Further, if the previous view was created using **WITH ENCRYPTION** or **CHECK OPTION**, these options are enabled only if they are included in **ALTER VIEW**. In other words, you can inadvertently turn the **WITH ENCRYPTION** or **CHECK OPTION** options off if not explicitly stated.

A view actively in use cannot be modified. If you attempt to do so, Microsoft SQL Server takes an exclusive schema lock on the view. When the lock is granted (meaning that there are no active users of the view), the SQL Server deletes all copies of the view from the procedure cache. Any existing plans referencing the view are still in the cache, but will be automatically recompiled the next time they are invoked.

Finally, **ALTER VIEW** permissions default to members of the db_owner and db_ddladmin roles, and the owner of the view. These permissions are non-transferable.

Notes On Views

The exam incorporates many topics related to views. Some important points to remember when working with views include:

➤ Views can only be created in the database that you are using, though the view can be accessed from other databases by fully qualifying the name of the view.

➤ You must specify column names for every column in a view if one of the following is true:

➤ Any column in the view is derived from a constant, built-in function, or arithmetic expression. Note that you can name the columns in the **SELECT** statement.

➤ Two or more columns in the view would otherwise have the same name.

➤ You want to rename a column.

➤ Views can have up to 1,024 columns. This is a change from the earlier, 255-column limit.

➤ To update a column in a row through the view, the **UPDATE** statement must modify only one base table within the view at a time (it can reference multiple tables, but only one can be updated).

➤ Views cannot include the following:

➤ **SELECT INTO**

➤ **COMPUTE**

➤ **ORDER BY** (but you can use **ORDER BY** when selecting from the view)

➤ References to a temporary table

Views can contain the following: aggregate functions and groupings, joins, other views, A **DISTINCT** clause, and unions (this last category is relatively new).

Practice Questions

Question 1

> How are business rules currently enforced at the database level? [Check all correct answers]
>
> ❑ a. By defining a rule at the database level.
>
> ❑ b. By defining a default.
>
> ❑ c. By using declarative constraints.
>
> ❑ d   This has to be handled programmatically.
>
> ❑ e. None of the above.

Answers a and c are the correct answers, although answer c is the preferred method. Answer b is incorrect, because defaults do not enforce business rules. Answer d is incorrect, because you can create a rule. Answer e is incorrect, because the correct answer is provided.

Question 2

> What step is necessary to instruct the server to use a rule for a row?
>
> ○ a. The create rule statement
>
> ○ b. The bind rule statement
>
> ○ c. sp_bindrule
>
> ○ d. sp_bindefault
>
> ○ e. None of the above

Answer e is correct, because a rule is not enforced for a row, it is enforced on a column within a role. Answer b is incorrect, because there is no bind rule statement. Answer d is incorrect, because it refers to defaults.

Question 3

How many rules can be enforced on a row in a table?

○ a. None

○ b. One per table

○ c. One per column in the table

○ d. 16

○ e. None of the above

Answer c is the correct answer, because that is a predefined limitation.

Question 4

How long does a rule persist in a database?

○ a. Until the session is terminated.

○ b. Until the rule is dropped.

○ c. Until a new rule is created.

○ d. Until a constraint replaces the rule.

○ e. None of the above.

Answer b is the correct answer, because a rule is a permanent database object.

Question 5

A rule can be dropped:

○ a. By the owner of the rule.

○ b. By using the drop rule statement.

○ c. If it is not bound to a database object.

○ d. All of the above.

○ e. None of the above.

Answer d is correct.

Question 6

A default is used [Check all correct answers]:

- ❑ a. To modify existing data in a database.
- ❑ b. To place a value in a column that is inserted null.
- ❑ c. To place a value in a column that was included in the column list in the insert statement.
- ❑ d. Commonly in current MS SQL Server applications.
- ❑ e. None of the above.

Answer b is correct. Answer a is incorrect, because no existing data is affected. Answer c is incorrect, because excluded values are addressed. Answer d is incorrect, because Microsoft no longer recommends separate user objects. Answer e is incorrect, because the correct answer is provided.

Question 7

The preferred method of defaulting a value in a column is:

- ○ a. To use a constraint.
- ○ b. To use a default.
- ○ c. Write the application code correctly.
- ○ d. None of the above.
- ○ e. All of the above.

Answer a is correct, because it is Microsoft's current recommendation. Answer d is incorrect, because the correct answer is provided. Answer e is incorrect, because answers b and c are not preferred methods of defaulting a value in a column.

Question 8

> If you bind a rule or default over an existing rule or default:
>
> ○ a. You will get a runtime error.
>
> ○ b. The first rule or default to be bound will take effect.
>
> ○ c. The last rule or default to be bound will take effect.
>
> ○ d. The action is different for rules and defaults.
>
> ○ e. None of the above.

Answer c is the correct answer, because only one may exist, and it will be the one most recently defined. Answer e is incorrect, because the correct answer is provided.

Question 9

> A view can be used: [Check all correct answers]
>
> ❑ a. To simplify code.
>
> ❑ b. As horizontal security.
>
> ❑ c. As vertical security.
>
> ❑ d. To hide data.
>
> ❑ e. To hide underlying database changes.

Answers a, b, c, d, and e are correct. These are all valid applications of views.

Question 10

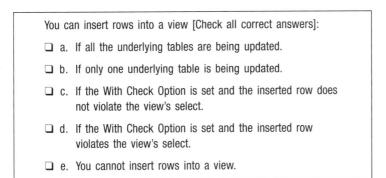

You can insert rows into a view [Check all correct answers]:

❑ a. If all the underlying tables are being updated.

❑ b. If only one underlying table is being updated.

❑ c. If the With Check Option is set and the inserted row does not violate the view's select.

❑ d. If the With Check Option is set and the inserted row violates the view's select.

❑ e. You cannot insert rows into a view.

Answers b and c are correct, because these are view restrictions. Answer a is incorrect, because the opposite is true. Answer d is incorrect, because the opposite is true. Answer e is incorrect, because no such restriction exists.

Need To Know More?

 Amo, William C. *Transact-SQL*, IDG Books Worldwide, Foster City, CA, 1998. ISBN 0-7645-8048-5. Chapter 5 contains information about rules and defaults. Chapter 10 contains information about views.

 Coffman, Gayle. *SQL Server 7: The Complete Reference*, Osborne/McGraw-Hill, Berkley, CA, 1999. ISBN 0-07-882494-X. Chapter 21 provides a complete T-SQL reference.

 MS SQL Server Books Online contains a complete DML reference you can find information either in the table of contents under Accessing and Change Data or you can look in the index for information about "rules", "defaults", and "views".

  Search the TechNet CD or its online version at **www.microsoft.com**.

 www.microsoft.com/sql
Find up-to-date information about using SQL Server here.

Transact-SQL Programming

Terms you'll need to understand:

√ Batch

√ Comments

√ Cursor

√ Stored procedure

√ Variable

Techniques you'll need to master:

√ Understanding Transact-SQL programming

√ Applying message handling techniques

√ Using error handling techniques

The ANSI-standard SQL provides a language with which users can create database structures, modify databases, and retrieve information from the database. The standard is not sufficient for programming. Programming requires additional functionality, from control of flow statements to modularity. For this, SQL Server provides extensions that are referred to as Transact-SQL, or T-SQL.

This chapter presents examples of the T-SQL language's components, from the definition of a batch to the idiosyncrasies of the individual statements. While this chapter can't comprehensively cover every T-SQL statement, many examples are provided for you to review. Specifically, we'll look at the following constructs:

➤ Batches

➤ Comments

➤ Variables

➤ T-SQL statements

➤ Cursors

➤ Stored procedures

Batches

A *batch* is a packet of information that is shipped from the client to the server. Batches are the basis of your SQL Server programs. After you make a connection, you start submitting batches to a SQL Server. A transaction (see Chapter 13 for more information on transactions) can span batches.

A batch can consist of a single SQL statement or many SQL statements. For example, the following batch performs two **SELECT** statements:

```
Select * from authors
Select * from titles
```

Both of these statements are shipped to the server and executed, and the results are returned together. Statements in a batch are parsed, compiled, and executed as a group. If there are any syntax errors, the entire batch will fail. Finally, if a stored procedure is not the first statement in a batch, the stored procedure must be preceded by the keyword **exec**. For example:

```
exec sp_who
```

Comments

Any good programmer knows that programs need comments; otherwise, the programmer will have to maintain the programs forever. There are a few basic ways to write comments. You can write multiline or single-line comments. Typically, you use multiline comments when you are introducing a program with description, version, and so forth. On the other hand, single-line comments usually comment on a single line of code. Single-line comments can be placed on their own line or on a code line. Following are examples of multiline and single-line comments:

```
/* this multiline
comment is used for a host
of purposes */
-- a single-line comment can be on its own line
select getdate()      -- or it can appear on a code line
```

 When programming, if you get errors which are not easily explained, double-check to make sure you have terminated all of your multiline comments.

Variables

SQL Server supports two types of variables, Local and Global. Local variables exist only in the session that creates them. Global variables, which Microsoft is moving into functions, are used for information about the server as a whole.

Local Variables

When you have information that is too ephemeral for tables, you should use *local variables*. Local variables are defined using the **DECLARE** statement. They only last for the duration of the batch. Therefore, when the batch is finished, you can no longer access the value in the variable.

Variables are set using either the **SELECT** or **SET** statement, which can be used interchangeably if you are assigning one variable. The **SELECT** statement can assign many variables at one time. In the following example, two variables are declared with the same **DECLARE** statement. One variable is set using **SELECT** and the other uses a **SET** statement. Finally, both variables are retrieved:

```
Declare @today datetime, @counter int
Select @counter = 1
Set @today = getdate()
Select @counter, @today
```

The result of the preceding batch will be a display of the defined variables. Note that **getdate()** is a built-in function that returns the current date and time.

 It is more efficient to set multiple variables in a single **SELECT** statement and to declare multiple variables in a single **DECLARE**.

Microsoft recommends setting variables to constants with the **SET** statement, rather than the **SELECT** statement. The **SET** will be slightly faster.

Global Variables

Global variables are used by the server to track server-wide and session-specific information. They cannot be explicitly set or declared. Some are modified as the result of SQL statements. Table 11.1 presents a few global variables that you might encounter, both on the exam and in real-life situations.

The following example uses the **@@version** global variable to check the version of the server:

```
select @@version
go
-------------------------------------------------------------
Microsoft SQL Server  7.00 - 7.00.517 (Intel X86)
    Jun 19 1998 17:06:54
    Copyright (c) 1988-1998 Microsoft Corporation
    Enterprise version on Windows NT
```

T-SQL Statements

Transact SQL (T-SQL) is used to supplement the ANSI standard, which does not support messaging or control of flow statements. Essentially, anything you would consider to be programming will be T-SQL.

PRINT Statement

The **PRINT** statement is used to send messages of up to 1,024 characters back to the client's message handler. Keep in mind that a message handler is not the same as an error handler. Typically, a message handler looks like a pop-up box

Table 11.1 Common global variables.

Global Variable	Description
Rowcount	Number of rows processed by the preceding command
@@error	Error number reported for last SQL statement
@@trancount	Transaction nesting level
@@servername	Name of local SQL Server
@@version	SQL Server version number, date, and processor level
@@spid	Current process id
@@identity	Last identity value used in an insert
@@nestlevel	Number of levels nested in a stored_procedure or trigger
@@fetch_status	Status of previous fetch statement in a cursor

on the front end, and an error handler causes an interrupt in the program logic. In the following example, the **PRINT** statement simply returns the text in quotes to the client's message handler:

```
print "This is a message"
```

In the next example, the **PRINT** statement will print the concatenation of the text "Hello" to the username returned by the server:

```
/* send a variable to the message handler
** the variable needs to be of a character type */
declare @msg varchar(30)
select @msg = "Hello " + user_name()
print @msg

print convert(char,123)
```

RAISERROR

The **RAISERROR** statement is used to pass error conditions, messages, and codes programmatically to the client front end. The predefined messages cannot exceed 8,000 characters, and ad hoc error messages cannot exceed 14,000 characters. The **RAISERROR** syntax, shown in the following code snippet, allows you to use a predefined message or define one on the fly:

```
raiserror ({error_number | character_string},
    severity, state [, arg_list] ) [WITH option]
```

Error numbers must be greater than 50 and less than 2,147,483,647. Ad hoc messages automatically raise an error number of 50,000. An error number is the ID of the user-defined message in the sysmessages table. The following example will generate an ad hoc message with an argument list:

```
declare @tab_name varchar(30),
    @count int
select @tab_name = "authors"
select @count = count(*) from authors
raiserror ("%d rows exist in table '%s'", 16, 1,
    @count, @tab_name)
/* same thing but in left justified hex with a width of 10
** and having the 0x
*/
raiserror ("%-#10x rows exist in table '%s'", 16, 1,
```

You can (and should) standardize and reuse your error messages by defining them to the database. The syntax for adding messages to your database is as follows:

```
sp_addmessage message_number, severity, message_text
    [, language[, [FALSE|TRUE] [, REPLACE]]]
```

In the preceding syntax example, severity is the same as the **RAISERROR** severities, and message_text is up to 255 characters, which can include place-holders. **FALSE|TRUE** indicates whether the error message is to be recorded in the SQL Server error log. The default language is **NULL**, which will default to the session's language. Finally, **REPLACE** overwrites the existing message.

After a message has been added, it can be dropped using the **sp_dropmessage** stored procedure or changed using the **sp_altermessage** stored procedure, as follows:

```
sp_dropmessage msg_number,language
sp_altermessage msg_number, WITH_LOG, {true | false}
```

Following is an example that declares and uses a defined message:

```
exec sp_addmessage 52345, 16, 'Row not found'
exec sp_addmessage 55555, "No rows exist in table '%1!'"

/* To use these messages, use raiserror
** without specifying a message string */
raiserror (52345, 16, 1)
```

```
declare @tab_name varchar(30)
select @tab_name = "authors"
raiserror (55555, 16, 1, @tab_name)

/* drop a user defined message */
exec sp_dropmessage 66666
```

You can manage messages in SQL EM by choosing the Tools|Manage SQL
Server Messages option on the Server menu. Select the Message tab, and then
click on the New button. (See Figure 11.1.)

Conditional Execution Statements

Conditional execution means that statements will only be performed (executed)
if specific criteria (conditions) are met.

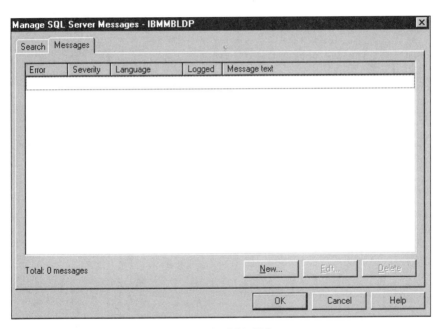

Figure 11.1   Managing messages in SQL EM.

IF...ELSE

The **IF...ELSE** construct identifies statements that are to be conditionally executed. This construct is common across most programming languages. The syntax for using the **IF...ELSE** statement is as follows:

```
if boolean_expression
    {statement | statement_block}
[else
    {statement | statement_block}]
```

The following example of an **IF...ELSE** statement checks for the average price of business books and returns a message:

```
if (select avg(price) from titles
    where type = "business") > $19.95
    print "The average price of business books is greater than
$19.95"
else
    print "The average price of business books is less than $19.95"
```

A subset of the **IF** statement is the existence check, **IF EXISTS**.

IF EXISTS

The existence check is used to find out whether any instances of a condition exist. **IF EXISTS** is used to replace the **count(*) > 0** for an existence check, because as soon as the first matching row is found, it stops processing the **SELECT**. The next example finds out if there are any authors named Smith. The code doesn't find out how many there are—it just finds out whether there are any Smiths:

```
declare @lname varchar(40)
select @lname = "Smith"
if exists (select * from titles
    where au_lname = @lname)
    print "Author's name found !"
else
    print "Authors name not found !"
```

If the Boolean expression contains a **SELECT** statement, the **SELECT** statement must be enclosed in parentheses. There are no limits to the number of nesting levels for **IF** statements. **IF EXISTS** is useful when performing referential integrity checks.

The **IF** condition affects exactly one succeeding statement or statement block. This is a good way to make a mistake that is difficult to catch.

BEGIN...END

To create a statement block, you use a **BEGIN...END** construct. Everything between the **BEGIN** and the **END** is part of the block. **BEGIN...END** statements must be nested syntactically. The next example checks to see if a Smith exists, and takes action based on the results:

```
if exists (select * from authors
    where au_lname = "Smith")
    begin
        print "Smith exists"
        exec found_proc
    end
else
    begin
        print "Smith not found"
        exec not_found_proc
    end
```

If a Smith exists, the **found_proc** will be executed, otherwise the **not_found_proc** will be executed.

CASE Statements

In situations where you might have a host of **IF** statements, Microsoft SQL Server provides a **CASE** statement. A **CASE** statement enables multiple possible conditions to be managed within a single **SELECT** statement, because it can replace any expression. The syntax for the **CASE** statement follows:

```
case expression
    when expression1 then expression2
    [...]
    [else expressionN]
    END
/*  or  */
case  when Boolean_expression1 then expression1  [[when
    Boolean_expression2
  then expression2] [...]] [else expressionN]  END
```

The next example uses the **CASE** statement to fill in the type of book and category of sales:

```
select substring (title, 1, 20),
   case    type
      when 'popular_comp' then ' Computer book'
      when 'mod_cook'  then ' Cook book'
      when 'trad_cook'  then ' Cook book'
         else 'Unknown book'
   end,
'Sales are ' +
   case
      when ytd_sales < 5000 then "Poor"
      when ytd_sales between 5001 and 10000 then "Good"
      when ytd_sales > 10000 then "Awesome"
      else "unknown"
   end
from titles


-------------------- --------------- ----------------
The Busy Executive's Unknown book   Sales are Poor
Cooking with Compute Unknown book   Sales are Poor
You Can Combat Compu Unknown book   Sales are Awesome
Straight Talk About  Unknown book   Sales are Poor
Silicon Valley Gastr Cook book      Sales are Poor
The Gourmet Microwav Cook book      Sales are Awesome
The Psychology of Co Unknown book   Sales are unknown
But Is It User Frien Computer book  Sales are Good
Secrets of Silicon V Computer book  Sales are Poor
Net Etiquette        Computer book  Sales are unknown
Computer Phobic AND  Unknown book   Sales are Poor
Is Anger the Enemy?  Unknown book   Sales are Poor
Life Without Fear    Unknown book   Sales are Poor
Prolonged Data Depri Unknown book   Sales are Poor
Emotional Security:  Unknown book   Sales are Poor
Onions, Leeks, and G Cook book      Sales are Poor
Fifty Years in Bucki Cook book      Sales are Awesome
Sushi, Anyone?       Cook book      Sales are Poor
```

Without the **CASE** statement, the preceding process might otherwise require a temporary table.

WHILE Loops

To execute statements multiple times, use the **WHILE** construct. The **WHILE** statement evaluates the expression first, and, if it is **TRUE**, executes the code. The syntax for a **WHILE** statement follows:

```
while boolean_condition
   [{statement | statement_block}]
```

```
[break]
[continue]
```

The **BREAK** statement unconditionally exits the **WHILE** loop and continues processing with the first statement after the **END** statement. The **CONTINUE** reevaluates the Boolean condition and begins processing from the top of the loop if the condition is **TRUE**. The following example loops until the average price equals or exceeds $25:

```
while (select avg (price) from titles) < $25
   begin
      update titles set price = price * 1.05
      /* if fewer than 10 books are less than
      ** $15, continue processing */
      if (select count(*) from titles
         where price < $15) < 10
         continue
      else
      /* If maximum price of single book exceeds
      ** $50, exit loop */
      if (select max(price) from titles) > $50
         break
   end
```

 Note the dollar sign ($) in the code. This helps the parser identify that the argument is a money type.

GOTO Statement

There is yet another way to repeat execution, and that is with the **GOTO** statement. Beware, though, that if you use **GOTO**, other programmers will make fun of you (the **GOTO** fell out of favor years ago). The following example uses the **GOTO** statement:

```
declare @counter tinyint
select @counter = 0
top:
select @counter = @counter + 1
print "Structured programming scoffs at the goto"
if @counter <= 10
goto top
```

In this example, **top:** is a label. If the counter is less than or equal to 10, control transfers back to the **top:** label.

WAITFOR Statement

The **WAITFOR** statement is used to cause a query to pause for a period of time or until an event occurs. It is also called an event handler. The **WAITFOR** syntax is as follows:

```
waitfor {delay "time" | time "time"}
```

The **delay** pauses a batch or process for the specified amount of time, up to a maximum of 24 hours. If instead you specify **time,** the process waits until the specified time of day before it executes. The time specified for delay and time is in **hh:mi:ss** format—you cannot specify dates. The following examples are documented by inline comments:

```
/* Pause until 10pm */
waitfor time "22:00:00"

/* Display the current logins every 30 seconds */
while 1 < 2
begin
    waitfor delay "00:00:30"
    exec sp_who
end
```

RETURN Statement

To unconditionally exit a batch, use the **RETURN** statement. You can also pass a return code if desired (note that this is only useful when returning from a stored procedure). The syntax for the **RETURN** statement is as follows:

```
Return {integer}
```

The following examples show uses of the **RETURN** statement.

```
select * from authors
print "finishing now"
return

/* return can be used with a conditional statement
** to terminate processing */
if not exists (select * from inventory
    where item_num = @item_num)
    begin
        raiserror ("Not found", 16, 1)
        return
    end
```

```
print "No error found"
return
```

SET Options

SET options affect the way a server handles specific conditions. The syntax for using **SET** is as follows:

```
set condition {on | off | value}
```

The following examples show several session **SET** statements.

```
set rowcount 100
set statistics io on
set statistics time on
set nocount on
set showplan on
set noexec on
set parseonly on
```

Options are set at the session or procedure level. They are not retained between sessions. Option settings made within stored procedures are returned to their prior value upon exit.

Cursors

Cursors allow an application to take action on individual rows of a query result set one at a time, rather than on the entire result set. SQL was designed as a set-oriented processing language. Some business rules require performing actions on a row-by-row basis. Note that this should be avoided if possible. Because SQL is a set-processing language, row-by-row processing is a performance hit.

Let's say that you want to increase the price of books whose prices are less than or equal to $15 by 15 percent, and you want to decrease the price of books whose prices are greater than $15 by 10 percent. Execute the following **UPDATE** statement:

```
update titles set price = price * $1.15
   where price <= $15.
update titles set price = price * $.90
   where price > $15.
```

In the preceding example, what happens to a book priced at $14.95? Will it move in both directions? With a cursor, you can look at the price for each row and update it accordingly.

SQL Server recognizes two main types of cursors: T-SQL (back-end cursors) and API (front-end cursors). T-SQL cursors are cursors that are completely performed within T-SQL. These are often called back-end cursors, or language cursors. API cursors are cursors that are created through a database API. These are often called front-end cursors, or client cursors. Even though you can define a language cursor that executes T-SQL cursor statements, it is not recommended that you mix cursor types. This section focuses on the features of T-SQL cursors.

Cursor Steps

Whether you use T-SQL or API cursors, using them requires the same basic steps:

1. Associate the cursor with a result set, and define the characteristics of the cursor.

2. Populate the cursor by executing T-SQL.

3. Fetch the rows you want to process.

4. Perform your row-by-row processing.

5. Close the cursor.

T-SQL Cursor Types

T-SQL cursors come in three main types:

➤ **Dynamic Cursors** Cursors wherein data changes show up as the cursor scrolls. Dynamic cursors make the least use of server resources outside of the database. They also make the least use of tempdb.

➤ **Static Cursors** Cursors that are isolated from data changes. The server stores the entire cursor result set in tempdb when the first fetch is performed.

➤ **Keyset Cursors** Cursors wherein most data changes will show up, although new rows will not show up. The server stores the keys for the rows returned in tempdb when the cursor is opened. Keyset cursors make moderate use of tempdb. New rows will not show up. Rows deleted by other users show up as errors.

T-SQL Cursor Usage

Here are the steps in cursor utilization. Make sure you do everything in the proper order.

1. Declare the cursor.

2. Open the cursor.

3. Fetch rows as needed.

4. Modify or delete rows from the cursor.

5. Continue fetching rows until processing is complete.

6. Close the cursor.

7. Deallocate the cursor.

Declaring Cursors

The following is complete syntax for declaring a cursor.

```
declare cursor_name  cursor [LOCAL | GLOBAL]
[FORWARD_ONLY | SCROLL][STATIC | KEYSET | DYNAMIC]
[READ_ONLY | SCROLL_LOCKS | OPTIMISTIC]
  for select_statement
    [for  update [of column_list] } ]
```

The following example shows a cursor that will walk the authors table, one row at a time, reading only rows that have the value "Los Angeles" in the city column.

```
declare authors_curs cursor for
  select * from authors where city = "Los Angeles"
  for read only
```

This cursor accesses the authors table, and lists the authors who live in Los Angeles. Further, the code specifies that the cursor is not updateable.

Cursor_name follows the standard database object naming conventions. Declaring a cursor with the **INSENSITIVE** keyword causes the server to make a copy of the affected data into a temporary worktable. The contents of the worktable are what you actually see. As you fetch rows in the cursor, only the underlying data in the actual table changes.

You can use this mechanism to take a snapshot of data at a particular moment in time, then use a cursor to process and report on that data. Insensitive cursors cannot be updated.

The **SCROLL** option declares the cursor to be scrollable, allowing for first, last, and backward fetches.

ANSI **SELECT** can be any valid ANSI **SELECT** statement. T-SQL **SELECT** can be any valid T-SQL **SELECT** with the following conditions:

➤ You cannot have a **SELECT INTO, COMPUTE, COMPUTE BY,** or **FOR BROWSE.**

➤ If a **GROUP BY, HAVING, DISTINCT,** or **UNION** is used, the cursor will become a **STATIC CURSOR.**

➤ If all the tables used in the cursor do not have a unique index, the cursor will become a **STATIC CURSOR.**

➤ If all of the columns used in the **ORDER BY** are not part of a unique index, a **DYNAMIC CURSOR** will be converted to a **KEYSET** or **STATIC CURSOR.**

The remaining arguments included in the **DECLARE** syntax are:

➤ **LOCAL** Specifies that the cursor is local to the batch, stored procedure, or trigger declaring the cursor. At the end of a procedure or trigger, local cursors are automatically de-allocated. If the cursor is passed as an output parameter, it will not be de-allocated until the last variable referencing it is de-allocated.

➤ **GLOBAL** Specifies that the cursor can be referenced anywhere by the connection. It must be explicitly de-allocated, or it will go away when the connection is broken.

➤ **FORWARD_ONLY** Specifies that the cursor can only be scrolled from first to last. If it is used without specifying **STATIC | KEYSET | DYNAMIC,** the cursor is a **DYNAMIC** cursor. **FORWARD_ONLY** is the default unless **STATIC | KEYSET | DYNAMIC** is specified, then **SCROLL** is the default.

➤ **STATIC** Makes a read-only static cursor.

➤ **KEYSET** Defines the cursor as a keyset cursor.

➤ **DYNAMIC** Defines the cursor as a dynamic cursor.

➤ **READ_ONLY** Specifies that the cursor is a read-only cursor.

➤ **SCROLL_LOCKS** Specifies that updates and deletes where current are guaranteed to be successful, and locks are held until the next row is fetched.

➤ **OPTIMISTIC** Specifies that updates and deletes using the **WHERE CURRENT** statement are not guaranteed to be successful, and locks are not held until the next row is fetched.

➤ **FOR READ ONLY** Specifies that no data can be updated with **UPDATE WHERE CURRENT (ANSI).**

➤ **FOR UPDATE** Serves as the default cursor mode, if none is stated.

➤ **COLUMN_LIST** Contains a list of updateable columns.

SQL Server allows all users to declare and use cursors. Once declared, the cursor is ready to be opened.

Opening Cursors

Opening a cursor begins the processing of a **SELECT** statement and prepares the cursor for rows to be fetched. The syntax used to open a cursor is:

```
open {{ [global] cursor_name }|@cursor variable}
```

GLOBAL specifies that the cursor_name is a global cursor. If a local and global cursor both exist with the same name, you must specify the **GLOBAL** option to open the **GLOBAL** cursor. The **cursor_name** variable specifies the name of the cursor to open. The **cursor_variable** is a variable containing the cursor name. Following is an example of opening a cursor:

```
declare authors_curs cursor for
  select * from authors
    where city = "Los Angeles"
  for read only
open authors_curs
```

The preceding code opens the defined cursor.

Only a declared cursor can be opened. For insensitive or static cursors, the number of rows in the cursor result set must be less than the maximum number of rows in a SQL Server table. The **@@cursor_rows** global variable contains the number of rows retrieved by the last open cursor command. Once a cursor is opened, the next step is to begin retrieving rows.

Fetching Rows

Use the **FETCH** command to retrieve a specific row from a cursor. A cursor must be opened before it can be fetched. Following is the syntax for fetching a row with a cursor:

```
fetch [navigation_option from] {{[GLOBAL] cursor_name } |
@cursor_variable } [into variable_list]
```

GLOBAL, **cursor_name**, and **@cursor_variable** behave the same as they do for the open cursor. The following navigation options are available if the **SCROLL** keyword is specified when the cursor is declared:

➤ **FIRST** Moves the current cursor position to the first row of the result set.

➤ **LAST** Moves the current cursor position to the last row of the result set.

➤ **NEXT** Moves the cursor one row forward in the current cursor set, which is the default action with a fetch.

➤ **PRIOR** Moves the cursor one row backward in the current cursor set.

➤ **ABSOLUTE n** Moves the cursor to the nth row from the top if **n** is a positive number. If **n** is a negative number, moves the cursor to the last row in the cursor set, and counts backward **n** rows. If **n** is **0**, no rows are returned.

➤ **RELATIVE n/-n** Moves the cursor **n** rows forward from its current position if **n** is a positive number. If **n** is a negative number, moves the cursor backward **n** rows. If **n** is **0**, the current row is returned.

➤ **absolute** and **relative** Indicates that the cursor can accept integer variables or stored procedure parameters as arguments.

In the following example, the cursor is declared, opened, and data is accessed:

```
declare authors_curs cursor scroll for
  select au_lname, au_fname from authors
    where state = "CA"
  for read only

open authors_curs
fetch NEXT from authors_curs

declare @lname varchar(40)
declare @fname varchar(20)

/* fetch next row into local variables */
fetch NEXT from authors_curs into @lname, @fname

/* fetch 10th row away from current row */
fetch RELATIVE 2 from authors_curs

close  authors_curs
deallocate authors_curs
```

If the cursor is not a scrollable cursor, you can only do a **FETCH NEXT**. If a variable list is supplied, the columns must match the select list. If a variable list

Table 11.2   Global variables for use with cursors.

Global Variable	Description
@@cursor_rows	The number of qualifying rows in the last-opened cursor:
	-# = the number of rows currently in the keyset if the cursor is being populated asynchronously.
	# = the number of rows if the cursor is fully populated.
	0 = no cursors are open.
@@fetch_status	Results of the fetch statement.
	0 = successful fetch.
	-1 = fetch failed, or row request is not in range.
	-2 = the row returned is no longer in the table (it has been deleted since the cursor was opened).

is not supplied, the result is returned immediately. Table 11.2 lists global variables you can check while you are working with cursors.

In the following example, the **@@fetch_status** variable is used to set up the **WHILE** loop for processing cursors:

```
declare title_curs cursor for
    select title, type, price, ytd_sales
        from titles
    for read only

declare @type varchar(30),
        @price money,
        @title varchar(80),
        @total_sales int
open title_curs
fetch title_curs into @title, @type, @price,
    @total_sales
while @@fetch_status = 0
/*process rows while there are rows to fetch*/
    begin
    if @type = "business"
        select Title = @title,
        "Net Profit" = (@price * .5) * @total_sales
    else
        select Title = @title,
        "Net Profit" = (@price * .7) * @total_sales
    fetch title_curs into @title, @type, @price,
        @total_sales
    end
```

```
if @@fetch_status = -2
  /* exited while loop due to fetch error */
  raiserror ("Row fetched has been deleted", 16, 1)
close title_curs
deallocate title_curs
```

Modifying Rows With Cursors

You can modify rows using the **WHERE CURRENT OF** keywords to **UP-DATE** and **DELETE** rows through a cursor, as follows:

```
update table_name
  set column_name = expression [ , ... ]
  [from table_name [, table_name] ]
  where current of cursor_name
    [ {and | or} ... ]

delete [from] table_name
  [from table_name [, table_name] ]
  where current of cursor_name
    [ {and | or} ... ]

/* update author phone number to new area code */
update authors
  set phone = stuff(phone, 1, 3, "310")
  where current of authors_curs

/* delete current author */
delete authors
  where current of authors_curs
```

You cannot delete from a multitable cursor (that is, a cursor declared with a **JOIN** clause or a view containing a **JOIN**). But, you can update a multitable cursor if the update affects only one table. A delete removes a row from a table. An update does not modify the cursor position, allowing a row to be updated more than once within a cursor. An **UPDATE** or **DELETE** statement on a **READ ONLY** cursor will generate an error indicating that the cursor is read only.

Closing Cursors

Closing a cursor deactivates the cursor, effectively removing its result set. To close a cursor, use the following syntax:

```
close {{[GLOBAL] cursor_name}|{@cursor_variable}}
```

The following example closes a cursor:

```
close authors_curs
```

The close stops cursor processing. A cursor can be reopened, which resets all pointers.

De-allocating Cursors

De-allocating a cursor removes the cursor reference. You can de-allocate a cursor even if its transactions are not committed. Following is the syntax for de-allocating a cursor:

```
deallocate {{GLOBAL} cursor_name }|{@cursor_variable}
```

The following example de-allocates a cursor:

```
deallocate author_curs
```

The preceding example frees the name for use by another **DECLARE CURSOR** statement. If this is the last reference to the cursor, it frees any memory used by the cursor structure. To reopen the cursor, you will need to declare it again.

Stored Procedures

Stored procedures are programs that reside in the database and can be executed from the client. Stored procedures are a batch of SQL statements compiled together.

One advantage of stored procedures is improved performance due to reduced network traffic. With 7, regular SQL statement execution plans can be reused so it no longer is a significant performance improvement to have stored procedure execution plans precompiled.

The advantages of stored procedures include modular programming and testing, and restricted, function-based access to tables. This can shield users from knowing underlying table structures, reduce operator error, enforce consistency, and automate complex or sensitive transactions. Stored procedures are permanent database objects, and you can create them as follows:

```
create proc[edure] procedure_name [; number]
[ @parm datatype  [Varying] [= default ] [output]
[ , ... ]
]
[With  {RECOMPILE|ENCRYPTION|RECOMPILE|ENCRYPTION} ]
[For Replication]
as
SQL statements
[return [status_value]]
```

A description of the arguments available when creating stored procedures follows:

➤ **procedure_name** Follows the standard object naming rules:

> ➤ In a database for an object owner and procedure name, a number must be unique.

> ➤ Local temporary procedure names start with a number sign (#).

> ➤ Global temporary procedure names start with double number signs (##).

➤ **number** Groups together procedures to drop as a unit (frequently used in conjunction with application releases).

➤ **@parm** Represents a parameter passed in and/or out of the procedure. You can have up to 1,024 parameters. Parameters are nullable. They cannot be used in place of database objects in the procedure unless they are used in an **EXEC** statement. Parameter data types can be either system data types or user-defined data types. Note that rules, defaults, and column properties do not apply to parameters defined with user-defined data types. Data type can be any SQL Server data type. This includes text, image, and cursor data types. If using a cursor data type, the varying and output options are mandatory.

➤ **Varying** Specifies a result set is returned in the parameters. It can only be used with cursor data type.

➤ **Default** Supplies a default value for the parameter. It can be any constant value or **NULL**.

➤ **Output** Indicates that the parameter can be returned to the caller. Any data type except text and image can be an output parameter. The cursor data type must be output.

➤ **RECOMPILE** Specifies that SQL Server does not cache execution plans. The **ENCRYPTION** option indicates that the syscomment table is encrypted (this hides text from curious but unauthorized eyes).

➤ **For Replication** Indicates that the procedure is used with replication. Note that this is mutually exclusive with the **RECOMPILE** option.

➤ **SQL Statements** Represents any number of SQL statements that make up the body of the procedure, up to the maximum size of 128K.

In addition to being aware of the available stored procedure arguments, there are a number of limitations that you need to keep in mind when working with stored procedures:

➤ Permanent procedures can only be created in the current database.

➤ The **CREATE PROCEDURE** statement must be the only statement in the batch.

➤ Object references are resolved at execution time, not creation time.

➤ Temporary procedures are automatically dropped when the user that created it disconnects.

➤ Global temporary procedures can be executed by other users.

➤ Procedures cannot contain **ALTER TABLE, CREATE INDEX, CREATE TABLE,** all DBCC statements, **DROP TABLE, DROP INDEX, TRUNCATE TABLE,** or **UPDATE STATISTICS** statements.

Following is an example of a stored procedure that lists each title with its publisher.

```
create proc pub_titles
as
select t.title, p.pub_name
    from publishers p, titles t
    where p.pub_id = t.pub_id
return
go
/* example of a procedure with a cursor parameter */
CREATE PROCEDURE acur
    @auth_cur cursor varying output,
    @state char(2)  = "CA",
    @ctype int = 1   ·
AS
if (@ctype = 1)
    set @auth_cur = cursor SCROLL for
        select au_lname
        from authors where state = @state
else
    set @auth_cur = cursor SCROLL for
        select au_lname, au_fname from authors

open @auth_cur
```

As mentioned earlier in this chapter, procedures are called using the **EXECUTE** keyword. You must use the **EXECUTE** keyword if the call to the stored procedure is not the first statement in the batch. All parameters without defaults must be passed into the procedure. The syntax for using the **EXECUTE** keyword is:

```
[exec[ute]] [@return_status = ] proc_name [;number ]
    [@parm list] [with recompile]
```

In the preceding syntax:

➤ **@return_status** Stores the return value from the procedure.

➤ **number is to s** Specifies a numbered procedure. If this argument is not present, the highest numbered version is executed.

➤ **@parm_list** Specifies the parameter list for the procedure. Parameters can be specified by name (parmname = value). Parameters can be specified by position, but once you specify a parameter by name, the rest of the parameters must be specified by name. To skip a parameter in the middle of the parameter list, you have to pass the rest of the parameters in by name.

➤ **with recompile** Indicates to recompile the procedure.

The next two lines of code both execute a procedure called pub_titles. Note that only the second needs the **EXEC** keyword, as the first statement in a batch does not need one:

```
pub_titles -- procedure is first in the batch
exec pub_titles
go
```

To drop a stored procedure, use the following syntax:

```
drop proc proc_name [,proc_name[, . . . ] ]
```

A stored procedure is a permanent database object, so it must be explicitly removed from the database. The **DROP PROC** statement removes one or more procedures. It removes all the number procedures—a procedure group—for **proc_name**.

You cannot drop an individual procedure from a procedure group.

The historical method of modifying a stored procedure is to drop the procedure, re-create the procedure, and then regrant any permissions on the procedure. New with version 7, you can use the **ALTER** statement to modify a stored procedure, as follows:

```
alter proc[edure] procedure_name [; number]
[ @parm datatype  [Varying] [= default ] [output]
[ , ... ]
]
[With  {RECOMPILE|ENCRYPTION|RECOMPILE|ENCRYPTION} ]
[For Replication]
```

```
as
SQL statements
[return [status_value]]
```

The **ALTER** statement behaves the same as a **CREATE PROCEDURE** statement. The **ALTER** statement does not change dependencies or permissions, and you cannot alter a procedure that does not exist.

In addition to altering procedures, you can rename them. To rename procedures, use **sp_rename**, as follows:

```
sp_rename proc, newname
```

Finally, to display text of a stored procedure in the database in which it was created, use **sp_helptext**, like this:

```
sp_helptext procedure_name
```

The **sp_help** procedure reports parameters' names and data types for a stored procedure.

You can create, drop, and modify stored procedures by using the stored procedure property in SQL EM. Click on the OK or Apply button to execute the SQL displayed in the window. The SQL EM window is shown in Figure 11.2.

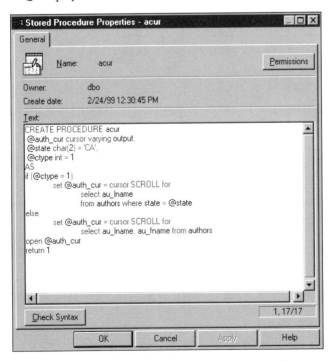

Figure 11.2 Creating a procedure using SQL EM.

Practice Questions

Question 1

> Which are characteristics of a batch? [Check all correct answers]
>
> ❑ a. A batch is always a transaction.
>
> ❑ b. A batch can be a transaction.
>
> ❑ c. A batch can be part of a transaction.
>
> ❑ d. A single syntax error in a batch will cause an entire batch to fail.
>
> ❑ e. SQL Server does not support batch processing.

Answers b and c are correct, because a batch can be a transaction or part of a transaction. Answer d is also correct, because a batch is parsed as a unit. Answer a is incorrect, because transactions are batch-independent. Answer e is incorrect and misleading, because a batch is not necessarily related to batch processing.

Question 2

> Which are valid applications of procedures? [Check all correct answers]
>
> ❑ a. Passing parameters
>
> ❑ b. Managing transactions
>
> ❑ c. Reducing network traffic
>
> ❑ d. Modularizing applications
>
> ❑ e. Managing a cursor

Answers a, b, c, d, and e are correct.

Question 3

> What is the maximum stored procedure size?
>
> ○ a. 128 SQL statements
>
> ○ b. 128K
>
> ○ c. 64 SQL statements
>
> ○ d. 64K
>
> ○ e. There is no size limit on a stored procedure

Answer b is correct. Answers a and c are wrong, because we do not measure size in SQL statements. Answer d is wrong, because it is too small. Answer e is wrong, because the size is limited.

Question 4

> When is using a cursor a good idea? [Check all correct answers]
>
> ❑ a. Never, because it causes a performance hit.
>
> ❑ b. When there is no set-processing method of solving a business problem.
>
> ❑ c. When you are defeated in your attempts to write set-processing code.
>
> ❑ d. When you are too lazy to write set-processing code.
>
> ❑ e. None of the above.

Answer b is correct. Answer a is incorrect, because sometimes you must process row-wise for business reasons. Answer c is incorrect, because you should fix the problem, not work around it. Answer d is incorrect, because being lazy is not a good reason to not do something.

Question 5

What is the WAITFOR statement?

○ a. An event handler

○ b. An error handler

○ c. A deadlock avoidance mechanism

○ d. A programming technique no longer supported in SQL Server 7

○ e. None of the above

Answer a is correct. Answer b is incorrect, because an error handler is an interrupt. Answer c is incorrect, because this may even cause deadlocks if there is an open transaction. Answer d is incorrect, because the statement still exists.

Need To Know More?

 Amo, William C. *Transact-SQL*, IDG Books Worldwide, Foster City, CA, 1998. ISBN 0-7645-8048-5. Chapter 13 describes how to use triggers. Chapter 15 contains information about stored procedures and control flow statements.

 Coffman, Gayle. *SQL Server 7: The Complete Reference*, Osborne/McGraw-Hill, Berkley, CA, 1999. ISBN 0-07-882494-X. Chapter 21 provides a complete T-SQL reference.

 MS SQL Server Books Online contains a complete DML reference you can find information either in the table of contents under Accessing and Change Data or you can look in the index for "stored procedures" or the specific SQL statements.

 Search the TechNet CD or its online version at **www.microsoft.com**.

 www.microsoft.com/sql
Find up-to-date information about using SQL Server here.

Triggers

Terms you'll need to understand:

- ✓ Trigger
- ✓ Inserted table
- ✓ Deleted table
- ✓ Transaction log

Techniques you'll need to master:

- ✓ Defining triggers
- ✓ Modifying triggers
- ✓ Knowing trigger limitations

A *trigger* is a special case of stored procedure that is automatically executed, or *fired*, when table data is modified. Triggers are used for a variety of purposes, from data validation to enforcing complex business rules. One particularly useful feature of triggers is that they have access to before- and after-modification images of a row; therefore, you can compare the two rows and make decisions accordingly.

On the exam, you'll be expected to know what triggers are and how to create, use, and manipulate them. Therefore, in this chapter, we'll review how to use triggers as well as how to create, delete, and modify triggers. Further, we'll look at some code samples that illustrate typical trigger applications.

Using Triggers

Triggers are used for a variety of purposes, including:

➤ **Enforcing referential integrity** Triggers are used to maintain RI (referential integrity) that is too complex to define at table-definition time. This includes the ability to cascade updates and deletes of primary keys.

➤ **Complex domain enforcement** If necessary, triggers can be used to check values in other tables or databases, or to check before and after images of data.

➤ **Enforcing complex business rules** Triggers can be used to perform tasks such as initiating purchase orders if inventory falls low or putting a hold on a shipment if payments have fallen behind.

➤ **Complex defaults** Triggers enable you to base column defaults on a decision-making process. This is useful, because user-defined defaults only allow you to set one specific default for a column.

➤ **Maintaining duplicate data** A trigger can be used to enforce data consistency. This might be helpful if you have logically segmented your data or if you are maintaining duplicate data for performance reasons (such as to obtain summary information).

Firing Triggers

Triggers are a mechanism assigned to a table that fire in response to specific DML commands. In other words, if you execute a statement that modifies a row containing a trigger, the trigger will always execute. Because the trigger is part of the same transaction, it can roll back the statement or the entire transaction. This gives you the ability to control table modifications with logic bound to the table.

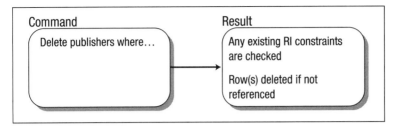

Figure 12.1   A data modification command without a trigger.

To further clarify, let's look at an example using a **DELETE** command to remove rows from the **publishers** table. Figure 12.1 shows how a **DELETE** command works without a trigger.

Referring to Figure 12.1, when you delete a table row, any corresponding referential integrity constraints that are part of the **publishers** table might come into play. If an RI constraint exists, the constraint will be checked. If the constraint is not violated (or does not exist), the row will be deleted. If this is not part of a separate transaction, the transaction commits at this time.

In contrast, Figure 12.2 shows how a data modification command works if a trigger is used. In Figure 12.2, first any constraint is checked. If the constraint is not violated (or does not exist), the row will be deleted. Then, before the transaction completes, the trigger is executed, and it makes a commit or rollback decision.

 Triggers are executed exactly once for a single data modification statement, regardless of the number of rows that are affected (this includes statements that affect none of the rows in a table, as well as statements that affect all the rows in a table).

So far, we've reviewed how triggers are used and when they are fired. Now, let's look at how triggers are created.

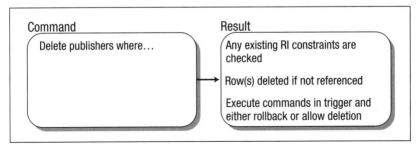

Figure 12.2   A data modification command using a trigger.

Creating Triggers

You can include three types of triggers in a table: insert, update, and delete, or any combination of the three. There is no longer a limitation on the quantity of triggers on a table.

 Note that this behavior is new to SQL Server. Earlier SQL Server releases (before version 7) would allow only one iteration of each trigger type.

Following is the syntax used to create a trigger:

```
create trigger trigger_name
  on table_name
  [WITH ENCRYPTION]
  for {insert | update | delete} [, ...]
  [WITH APPEND]
  [NOT FOR REPLICATION]
  as
[SQL_Statements]
[return]
```

The values in the trigger creation syntax are defined as follows:

➤ **Trigger_name** Specifies a valid object name, with the owner name being optional (for example, mytrigger or dbo.mytrigger).

➤ **Table_name** Specifies the name of the table for the trigger to fire against. Note that this is only one table at a time.

➤ **INSERT|UPDATE|DELETE** Specifies which data modification statements will cause the specific trigger to fire. You can specify one, two, or all three options. If more than one option is specified, separate each with a comma (such as **insert, update, delete**).

➤ **WITH APPEND** Specifies that this trigger is added to the list of triggers fired for the action(s). SQL Server can be configured so the append action takes place automatically. If SQL Server is not so configured, a create trigger drops the existing trigger for the action(s).

➤ **NOT FOR REPLICATION** Specifies that this trigger is not executed during replication.

The following code creates a trigger that prints a message every time a row is inserted into the **titles** table:

```
create trigger titles_trigger
on titles
for insert
as
print "title inserted"
return
```

There are a variety of minor quirks to keep in mind when creating triggers, including:

➤ If you qualify a trigger's owner, the table owner must also be qualified (this is a language syntax feature).

➤ While triggers look and feel like stored procedures in many ways, triggers do not take parameters and cannot be explicitly called or executed.

➤ The **CREATE TRIGGER** statement must be the first statement in a batch.

➤ A trigger cannot be created on a view. Triggers are only relevant against the base tables. However, you can create a view on tables that have triggers.

➤ Triggers are not fired when a **TRUNCATE TABLE** statement is executed. The **TRUNCATE TABLE** statement is unlogged, and the trigger needs access to the log information.

➤ **WRITETEXT** statement does not fire triggers. The **WRITETEXT** statement is unlogged.

➤ In order to create a trigger, you must be the object owner, or have the db_owner or db_ddladmin roles.

Further, the following SQL statements are not permitted in triggers:

➤ Any **CREATE** command

➤ Any **DROP** command

➤ ALTER TABLE/DATABASE

➤ DENY

➤ GRANT

➤ REVOKE

➤ SELECT INTO

➤ TRUNCATE TABLE

➤ UPDATE STATISTICS

➤ RECONFIGURE

➤ LOAD/RESTORE DATABASE/TRANSACTION

After creating triggers, you might later find that you need to remove triggers.

Removing Triggers

Triggers are removed by using the **DROP TRIGGER** statement with the following syntax:

```
drop trigger trigger_name [,trigger_name [,. . . ] ]
```

The preceding code snippet drops a specific trigger. If you are replacing a trigger, the **DROP TRIGGER** statement is not required. To replace a trigger, simply do not use the **WITH APPEND** option at creation time.

 Keep in mind that if you drop a table, all underlying triggers are dropped.

An alternative to removing triggers is to modify an existing trigger.

Modifying Triggers

Historically, the typical approach to modifying a trigger is simply to drop and re-create the trigger. Alternatively, in SQL Server 7, you can use the **ALTER TRIGGER** statement. The syntax for using the **ALTER TRIGGER** statement is as follows:

```
alter trigger trigger_name
  on table_name
  [WITH ENCRYPTION]
  for {insert | update | delete} [, ...]
  [WITH APPEND]
  [NOT FOR REPLICATION]
  as
[SQL_Statements]
[return ]
```

The **ALTER TRIGGER** statement behaves the same as the **CREATE TRIGGER** statement. **ALTER TRIGGER** exists primarily for command consistency, because all the other object creations now permit alter syntax.

There are special views of the log, called the inserted and deleted tables, which give you access to before and after images of the data.

Deleted And Inserted Tables

The **inserted** and **deleted** tables are special views in the transaction log, which are only accessible while the trigger is firing, and only accessible by the trigger. These tables reflect the changes made in the table by the statement that caused the trigger to execute.

The structure of the **inserted** and **deleted** tables exactly matches the structure of the table the trigger is created on. The **inserted** table contains the new rows that resulted from an **INSERT** or **UPDATE**. The **deleted** table contains rows that were removed as the result of a **DELETE** or **UPDATE**.

SQL Server typically treats an **UPDATE** as a **DELETE** followed by an **INSERT**. The deletes and inserts are placed into the **inserted** and **deleted** tables. These tables can be used inside a trigger to determine which event caused the trigger to fire. You'll have rows in the inserted table on insert or update, and rows in the deleted table on delete or update. Often, a trigger will join to the **inserted** and **deleted** tables to maintain foreign keys and RI.

> Note: **Inserted** and **deleted** tables can only be seen inside the trigger for which they were created—this specifically excludes nested triggers (nested triggers are discussed in more detail later in this chapter).

To further clarify, let's look at an example that illustrates the use of the deleted table. In this example, a specific row is deleted from the **publishers** table (see Figure 12.3). When the trigger fires, the transaction has not yet committed. The trigger can see the deleted table and, therefore, look at the information that was deleted. The trigger can, for example, choose not to allow the deletion of a publisher if there is an outstanding order for a book published by the publisher.

Figure 12.4 illustrates what happens when a row is updated. At update time, the trigger will see the updated table, as always. The deleted table will contain the "before" image of the row, and the inserted table will contain the "after" image of the row. Note that all three of these tables are identically structured.

Viewing Deleted And Inserted Tables In Action

This section illustrates how deleted and inserted tables are used. You are to write a delete trigger for the publishers table that will cascade deletions to the **titles** table.

titles

title id	title	type	pub id	...
BU1032	The Busy Executive's...	business	1389	...
BU1111	Cooking With Comput...	business	1389	...
BU2075	You Can Combat Com...	business	0736	...
...	...	...	...	...

1. Command executes:

```
insert titles
  values ("BU1234", "Tuning SQL Server", "business", "0877", …
```

2. The trigger sees:

titles

title id	title	type	pub id	...
BU1032	The Busy Executive's...	business	1389	...
BU1111	Cooking With Comput...	business	1389	...
BU1234	Tuning SQL Server	business	0877	...
BU2075	You Can Combat Com...	business	0736	...
...	...	...	...	...

deleted

title id	title	type	pub id	...

inserted

title id	title	type	pub id	...
BU1234	Tuning SQL Server	business	0877	...

Figure 12.3 An update trigger example.

Cascading deletes means that any rows in the titles table that depend on the publisher being deleted will also be deleted.

Remember to check the number of rows affected (via **@@rowcount**) because the **DELETE** statement itself causes the trigger to fire exactly once whether any rows were deleted or not. The following trigger will cascade deletes from the primary to the secondary(ies).

salesdetail

stor id	ord num	title id	qty	discount
7896	234518	TC3218	75	40.0
7896	234518	TC7777	75	40.0
7131	Asnan432	TC3218	50	40.0

1. Command executes:

```
Update salesdetail
  set qty = 100
  where stor id = 7896
  and ord num = 234518
  and title id = TC3218
```

2. The trigger sees:

salesdetail

stor id	ord num	title id	qty	discount
7896	234518	TC3218	100	40.0
7896	234518	TC7777	75	40.0
7131	Asnan432	TC3218	50	40.0

deleted

stor id	ord num	title id	qty	discount
7896	234518	TC3218	75	40.0

inserted

stor id	ord num	title id	qty	discount
7896	234518	TC3218	100	40.0

Figure 12.4   Update trigger example.

Listing 12.1   Cascading delete trigger.

```
create trigger cascade_del_trigger
on publishersfor delete
as

if @@rowcount = 0   -- no rows deleted
  return
```

```
/* cascade delete of pub_id(s) to related */
/* rows in titles table */
delete titles
  from titles t, deleted d
  where t.pub_id = d.pub_id

if @@error != 0
  begin
  print "Error occurred deleting related titles" rollback tran
  end

return
```

Figure 12.5 shows what happens when a row is inserted into the **publishers** table. When a row is inserted, the insert trigger "sees" an empty deleted table

publishers

pub id	pub name	city	state
0736	New Age Books	Boston	MA
0877	Binnet & Hardley	Washington	DC
1389	Algodata Infosystems	Berkeley	CA

1. Command executes:

```
delete publishers where pub_id = "0736"
```

2. The trigger sees:

publishers

pub id	pub name	city	state
0877	Binnet & Hardley	Washington	DC
1389	Algodata Infosystems	Berkeley	CA

deleted

pub id	pub name	city	state
0736	New Age Books	Boston	MA

inserted

pub id	pub name	city	state

Figure 12.5 Results of inserting a row into the **publishers** table.

and an inserted table containing the new row(s). Note that the deleted and inserted tables are identical in structure to the base table.

Handling Multirow INSERTs And UPDATEs

SQL Server allows multirow inserts in a single INSERT statement via the INSERT...SELECT syntax. If you are inserting or updating multiple foreign key values, the trigger will need to compare the count of the inserted or updated rows against a count of the rows that are valid keys. This comparison will verify that the modified rows have corresponding keys (verification can also be accomplished by using declarative constraints as discussed in Chapter 6).

You can determine referential integrity by using the **count(*)** aggregate with a join between the inserted table and the primary key table. For example, you can compare the value of the **select count(*)** against the value of **@@rowcount** at the beginning of the trigger. **@@rowcount** must be checked (and preferably stored in a local variable) before any operations are performed within the trigger that can affect **@@rowcount**. This is because every other SQL statement, including the one that initially checks the value of **@@rowcount**, will change the value of **@@rowcount**.

If the number of rows in the inserted table that join successfully with rows in the primary key table doesn't equal the total number of rows inserted or updated, at least one of the rows is invalid. The following code fragment shows how to verify referential integrity in a trigger:

```
create trigger tr1
on ...
for insert, update
as
declare @rows int
select @rows = @@rowcount
...
if (select count(*) from inserted i, pkey_tab p
   where i.fkey = p.pkey) != @rows
/* At least one of the inserted/updated rows
   does not match a primary key */
/*  begin error processing */
...
```

Checking Columns For Modification

Any INSERT or UPDATE performed on a table will cause the corresponding insert or update trigger to fire. If the trigger is designed to maintain referential integrity, you might only be concerned with updating or inserting a primary or foreign key column. The IF UPDATE test provides a mechanism to find out whether a specific column has been modified or inserted. The following code snippet shows **if update** syntax:

```
if update (col_name)
    [ { and | or } update (col_name) ...]
```

The **IF UPDATE** test will be **True** when one of the following conditions is true:

➤ A non-null value has been inserted into the column.

➤ The column was named in the **SET** clause of an **UPDATE** statement.

You can use the **columnsupdated()** function to determine whether specific columns were modified as part of an **INSERT** or **UPDATE** statement. The following code snippet shows the **columns_updated** operator:

```
IF (COLUMNS_UPDATED() {bitwise_operator} updated_bitmask)
{ comparison_operator} column_bitmask [
```

The preceding code shows the syntax for a column check that can be performed in **INSERT** or **UPDATE** triggers to see if multiple columns were updated. The individual parameters are:

➤ **bitwise_operator** Specifies which operator to use in the comparison.

➤ **updated_bitmask** Specifies the columns that are updated.

➤ **column_bitmask** Specifies which columns are to be checked.

➤ **comparision_operator** Specifies which operator to use when checking columns.

➤ = Means that all the columns in the mask need to be updated.

➤ > Means that not all the columns in the mask were updated.

At this point, we've reviewed the theory behind insert, delete, and update triggers in a fair amount of detail. Now, let's review some examples. We'll start by looking at a typical insert trigger example, then we'll review a conditional insert trigger example, and finally we'll look at an update example.

Insert Trigger Example

In Listing 12.2, we will verify the referential integrity of the titles row(s) inserted into *titles* against the *publishers* table, and roll back the insert transaction if any rows violate RI.

Listing 12.2   Insert trigger that checks referential integrity.

```
create trigger tr_titles_i
on titles
for insert
as
declare @rows int  -- create variable to hold @@rowcount
select @rows = @@rowcount


if @rows = 0       -- no rows inserted, exit trigger
return

/* check if pub_id was inserted and if all pub_ids
   inserted are valid pub_ids in the publishers table */
if update(pub_id)  -- was an explicit pub_id inserted?
  and (select count(*)
    from inserted i, publishers p
    where p.pub_id = i.pub_id ) != @rows
  begin
    raiserror ("Invalid pub_id inserted", 16, 1)
    rollback transaction
  end

return
```

The next section expands on the preceding example and explains how you can verify the referential integrity of the **titles** row(s) inserted into the **titles** table by comparing the foreign keys to the primary keys in the **publishers** table.

Conditional Insert Trigger Example

Remove any rows from **titles** that violate RI, and allow the other rows to remain in the table. Listing 12.3 shows the implementation of a conditional insert trigger that accomplishes the desired goal.

Listing 12.3   The solution to the conditional insert trigger example.

```
create trigger tr_titles_i
on titles
for insert
as
declare @rows int  -- create variable to hold @@rowcount
select @rows = @@rowcount
```

```
if @rows = 0        -- no rows inserted, exit trigger
return

/* check if pub_id was inserted and if all pub_ids
   inserted are valid pub_ids in the publishers table
   delete any invalid rows from titles */
if update(pub_id)  -- was an explicit pub_id inserted?
  and (select count(*)
    from inserted i, publishers p
    where p.pub_id = i.pub_id ) != @rows
  begin
  delete titles
    from titles t, inserted i
    where t.pub_id = i.pub_id
    and i.pub_id not in
      (select pub_id from publishers)
  raiserror ("Some Invalid pub_id(s) not inserted", 16, 1)
  end

return
```

Update Trigger Example

In this example, when a **sales** row is inserted or updated, we will update the corresponding summary value, *ytd_sales*, in the *titles* table. Listing 12.4 shows how you can accomplish updating corresponding summary values.

Listing 12.4   Updating corresponding summary values.

```
create trigger tr_total_sales
on sales
for update, insert
as
declare @rows int  -- create variable to hold @@rowcount
select @rows = @@rowcount
if @rows = 0        -- no rows inserted, exit trigger
   return
if exists (select * from deleted) and @rows > 1
  begin
  print "Multi-row updates to sales not allowed!"
  rollback tran
  return
  end
/* update the ytd_sales in titles with qty
** in modified sales rows */
if update(qty)
  begin
```

```
     update titles set ytd_sales = isnull(ytd_sales, 0)
/* use isnull function in case of no value */
/* use subqueries to get total inserts and deletions */
   + (select isnull(sum(i.qty), 0)
     from inserted i
     where i.title_id = titles.title_id)
   - (select isnull(sum(d.qty), 0)
     from deleted d
     where d.title_id = titles.title_id)
   end
return
```

Triggers During Transactions

As mentioned earlier, a trigger is an integral part of the statement that fires the trigger and the transaction in which the statement occurs. A **ROLLBACK TRAN** inside a trigger rolls back all work to the outermost **BEGIN TRAN**, completes processing in the trigger, and then aborts the current batch. For example, the following trigger is called when a row is inserted into the **titles** table.

```
create trigger tr_titles_i on titles for insert as
declare @rows int  -- create variable to hold @@rowcount
select @rows = @@rowcount
if @rows = 0 return
if update(pub_id) and (select count(*)
   from inserted i, publishers p
   where p.pub_id = i.pub_id ) != @rows
   begin rollback transaction
     raiserror ("Invalid pub_id inserted", 16, 1)
   end
return
/* transaction inserts rows into a table */
begin tran add_titles
insert titles (title_id, pub_id, title)
   values ('BU1234', '0736', 'Tuning SQL Server')
insert titles (title_id, pub_id, title)
   values ('BU1235', 'abcd', 'Tuning SQL Server')
insert titles (title_id, pub_id, title)
   values ('BU1236', '0877', 'Tuning SQL Server')
commit tran
```

Based on the preceding code, how many rows are inserted if 'abcd' is an invalid **pub_id**? No rows will be inserted, because unlike a **ROLLBACK TRAN** in a procedure, a **ROLLBACK TRAN** in a trigger aborts the rest of the batch.

There are a variety of "gotchas" to be aware of regarding triggers used in a transaction:

➤ Statements subsequent to a **ROLLBACK TRAN** in a trigger will be executed. The rollback is for transaction control, not process flow. (This is a common error.)

➤ Remember to **RETURN** following a **ROLLBACK TRAN** in a trigger to prevent unwanted results; this action is required because odd problems can occur in certain front-end client programs.

➤ Do not issue **BEGIN TRAN** statements in a trigger—you are already in a transaction, so **BEGIN TRAN** is redundant. You can set a savepoint in a trigger and roll back to the savepoint (as discussed in the next section). Only the statements in the trigger subsequent to the savepoint will be rolled back.

➤ The transaction will still be active until subsequently committed or rolled back, and the batch will continue.

➤ Do not roll back to a named transaction within a trigger. This will generate a runtime error, roll back all work, and abort the batch.

➤ For best results, do not include **BEGIN TRAN** or **ROLLBACK TRAN** (note that this includes **ROLLBACK TRAN** to savepoints) statements in triggers.

Using Savepoints In Triggers

To avoid a trigger from arbitrarily rolling back an entire transaction, use the **SAVEPOINT** command inside the trigger. You can define a savepoint and optionally roll back to the named savepoint in the trigger. If you do, you should issue a **RAISERROR** and **RETURN** immediately, to pass the error code back to the calling process.

The calling process can check the error status and take appropriate action—it can roll back the transaction, roll back to a savepoint, or ignore the error and commit the data modification.

Listing 12.5 shows a trigger on the **titles** table that assumes a transaction is already in place.

Listing 12.5　Insert trigger example using savepoint transaction processing.

```
/* trigger on the titles table called on insert */
create trigger tr_titles_i on titles for insert as
```

```
declare @rows int  -- create variable to hold @@rowcount
select @rows = @@rowcount
if @rows = 0 return
save tran titlestrig
if update(pub_id) and (select count(*)
  from inserted i, publishers p
  where p.pub_id = i.pub_id ) != @rows
  begin
    rollback transaction titlestrig
    raiserror ("Invalid pub_id inserted", 16, 1)
  end
return
```

The code in Listing 12.6 uses an **INSERT** statement to fire the trigger shown in Listing 12.5.

Listing 12.6   Inserting into the titles table and calling the trigger.

```
/* transaction inserts rows into a table */
begin tran add_titles
insert titles (title_id, pub_id, title)
  values ('BU1234', '0736', 'Tuning SQL Server')
if @@error = 50000
  begin
  rollback tran add_titles
  return
  end
insert titles (title_id, pub_id, title)
  values ('BU1235', 'abcd', 'Tuning SQL Server')
if @@error = 50000
  begin
  rollback tran add_titles
  return
  end
insert titles (title_id, pub_id, title)
  values ('BU1236', '0877', 'Tuning SQL Server')
if @@error = 50000
  begin
  rollback tran add_titles
  return
  end
commit tran
```

Here, we have inserted rows into a table that has an insert trigger. After each insert, we check the value of @@error to see whether the trigger performed a rollback. If it did, we roll back the entire transaction.

When a trigger modifies a table that itself has a trigger, the trigger on a called table usually fires. This is called "nested triggers."

Nested Triggers

For example, if trigger A performs an **INSERT, UPDATE,** or **DELETE** on another table that has a trigger (trigger B) defined for the action performed by trigger A, then trigger B will also fire. This illustrates the concept of nested triggers, which is the default server behavior.

Triggers are limited to 32 levels of nesting. If you think the 32-level limitation for nesting triggers might be an issue in your application (under most circumstances, this limitation shouldn't present a problem), you can check the global variable **@@nestlevel** to avoid exceeding the limit or call the **NEST_LEVEL()** function.

Nested triggers cannot see the contents of other triggers' inserted and deleted tables—nested triggers can only see the inserted and deleted tables for the trigger that caused the nested trigger to fire. A system administrator can disable trigger nesting at the server level by using the **sp_configure** stored procedure. Triggers typically are not *recursive*. That is, they will not fire if the trigger modifies its own table, though you might turn on self-recursion.

Data modification statements inside a trigger do not affect the values of the inserted or deleted tables for that trigger. This means that you can replace the values in the base table without causing recursive looping. If more than one trigger is defined for a given action on a table, the triggers are fired in the order in which they are defined. If order is important, it might be easier (and wiser) to use only one trigger.

Triggers will not override existing permissions. Instead, they take advantage of the current permission scheme. If a user does not have permission to update a table directly, then the user cannot update the table via a trigger on another table that the user has update permission on.

Triggers cannot be defined on temporary tables or on views. If you are modifying data through a view, any triggers on the underlying tables will be executed. Triggers can execute stored procedures, including remote stored procedures.

Cursors can be used in triggers, though this is not a recommended practice, because triggers are executed frequently and cursors are slow. Some uses for cursors in triggers include custom logging, maintaining duplicate data, and performing actions in individual rows in the inserted/deleted tables.

Trigger overhead, like stored procedure overhead, is relatively low.

An insert trigger will not fire during a slow BCP load (Bulk Copy Program). A delete trigger will not fire on a **TRUNCATE TABLE** command. Output from the trigger is returned to the calling program, though this is not a recommended practice. *Do not* use **SELECT** statements that return result sets to the end user within a trigger. An application issuing an **INSERT** command will most likely not be expected or coded to process result rows. Return information from triggers via **PRINT** or **RAISERROR**.

You may want to look at the trigger's text.

Examining Triggers

To list all tables and their triggers, you can use the following **SELECT** statement:

```
select name, user_name(uid),
  "insert trigger" = object_name(instrig),
  "update trigger" = object_name(updtrig),
  "delete trigger" = object_name(deltrig)
 from sysobjects
  where type = "U"
  order by name
```

The above code displays user tables and their triggers.

To display the text of the SQL that created the trigger, use the following code:

```
sp_helptext trigger_name
```

To list all objects referenced within a trigger, use the following code:

```
sp_depends trigger_name
```

To list all triggers and stored procedures that reference a table, use the following code:

```
sp_depends table_name
```

Finally, you can create, drop, modify, and view triggers using SQL EM by selecting the table, opening the Manage menu, and then clicking on the task->Manage Triggers option. Figure 12.6 shows a trigger being created using SQL EM.

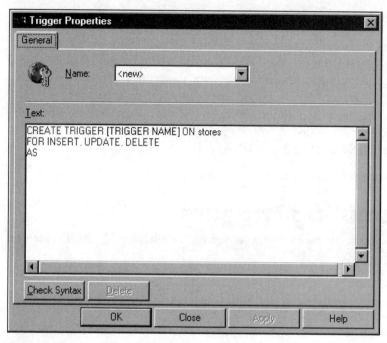

Figure 12.6 Creating a trigger with SQL EM.

Practice Questions

Question 1

> What are triggers used for? [Check all correct answers]
>
> ❏ a. Enforcing referential integrity by defining a default
>
> ❏ b. Complex domain enforcement
>
> ❏ c. Enforcing complex business rules
>
> ❏ d. Enforcing complex defaults
>
> ❏ e. Maintaining duplicate data

Answers a, b, c, d, and e are correct.

Question 2

> When is a trigger fired? [Check all correct answers]
>
> ❏ a. When the trigger fire statement is executed
>
> ❏ b. Before data modification
>
> ❏ c. Before constraint validation
>
> ❏ d. After the transaction completes
>
> ❏ e. After constraint validation, but before the transaction commits

Answer a is correct. Answers b and c are incorrect, because these are performed first. Answer d is incorrect, because in that case the trigger could not roll back the transaction. Answer e is correct, but misleading.

Question 3

How many triggers can exist on a table?

○ a. None

○ b. No effective limit

○ c. Three

○ d. One for each type of data modification statement

○ e. None of the above

Answer b is correct, because there is currently no limit on the number of triggers that can exist on a table. Answer a is incorrect, because triggers can exist on a table. Answers c and d are incorrect, although the answers specify previous trigger limitations in earlier versions of SQL Server.

Question 4

How long does a trigger persist in a database? [Check all correct answers]

❑ a. Until the session is terminated

❑ b. Until it is dropped

❑ c. Until a new trigger is created without the append option

❑ d. Until another trigger replaces it

❑ e. Until the table it is created for is dropped

Answers b, c, d, and e are correct. Answer a is incorrect, because a trigger is a persistent database object.

Question 5

What are the inserted and deleted tables?

○ a. Temporary tables located in the tempdb database

○ b. Special views of the transaction log

○ c. Separate database tables

○ d. All of the above

○ e. None of the above

Answer b is correct, because inserted and deleted tables are special views of the transaction log. Answer a is incorrect, because they are not temporary tables. Answer c is incorrect, because they are views of the log.

Question 6

When can you access the inserted and deleted tables?

- ○ a. You cannot access these tables, because they are log tables
- ○ b. Only within the transaction in which they are created
- ○ c. Only within the trigger that is firing
- ○ d. In the trigger in which it fires and in any nested trigger fired from the trigger
- ○ e. All of the above

Answer c is correct, because these tables are only accessible through the trigger.

Question 7

What is the structure of the inserted and deleted tables? [Check all correct answers]

- ❑ a. Predefined
- ❑ b. Set by server defaults
- ❑ c. Identical to each other
- ❑ d. Identical to the base table
- ❑ e. None of the above

Answers c and d are correct. Answer b is incorrect, because there are no defaults.

Question 8

What are the contents of the inserted and deleted tables? [Check all correct answers]

❑ a. The inserted table contains all rows inserted or updated.

❑ b. The deleted table contains all rows deleted or updated.

❑ c. The inserted table contains only rows inserted.

❑ d. The deleted table contains only rows deleted.

❑ e. None of the above.

Answers a and b are correct. Answer c is incorrect, because it also contains rows updated. Answer d is incorrect, because it also contains rows updated.

Need To Know More?

 Amo, William C. *Transact-SQL*, IDG Books Worldwide, Foster City, CA, 1998. ISBN 0-7645-8048-5. Chapter 15 contains information about triggers.

 Coffman, Gayle. *SQL Server 7: The Complete Reference*, Osborne/McGraw-Hill, Berkley, CA, 1999. ISBN 0-07-882494-X. Chapter 21 provides a complete T-SQL reference.

 MS SQL Server Books Online look in the index for information about "triggers".

 Search the TechNet CD or its online version at **www.microsoft.com**.

 www.microsoft.com/sql
Find up-to-date information about using SQL Server here.

13

Transactions

. . . .

Terms you'll need to understand:

✓ Commit

✓ Deadlock

✓ Distributed Transaction Coordinator

✓ Lock

✓ Recovery

✓ Rollback

✓ Transaction

✓ Transaction log

Techniques you'll need to master:

✓ Managing transactions

✓ Using transaction control statements

✓ Understanding transaction flow

✓ Knowing transaction limitations

✓ Using distributed transactions

✓ Understanding the transaction log

✓ Locking transactions

Transactions are one of the most important concepts to understand when building a SQL Server application. A transaction is intrinsic to the nature of an RDBMS, because it is what guarantees data consistency in all situations.

The Nature Of Transactions

A transaction is a SQL statement or group of SQL statements that needs to succeed or fail as a group. It is a logical unit of work with the following properties:

➤ **Atomicity** Acts as a standalone unit of work.

➤ **Consistency** Ensures data and internal data structures are consistent.

➤ **Isolation** Enables two transactions to access the same data, independent of the changes being made by the other transaction.

➤ **Durability** Specifies that the transaction's effects are permanent, until another transaction modifies them.

A classic transaction example is an ATM transfer. Let's say that you want to use an ATM to transfer $5,000 from your savings account into your checking account. The program will subtract $5,000 from your savings account, and subsequently add $5,000 to your checking account. As the code is processing, right after the money is subtracted from your savings account, but before it is added to your checking account, the power goes down at the ATM. The question: Is the $5,000 returned to your savings account, placed into your checking account, or missing forever?

If the two statements are bundled together into a transaction, you have no problem. You are guaranteed that both will finish, or neither will finish. If not, you are at risk of having only one execute.

Now, let's look at a less classic, but more common example of when you need transaction control. In this example, let's say that you issue a single **UPDATE** statement that affects many rows. Halfway through the update, a failure occurs (such as a power outage, the SQL Server shuts down, or the physical server crashes). What happens when the data becomes available again? Will the update finish? It will not. It will be rolled back.

In a client/server system, once a connection is broken, the connection is not reestablished. Instead, you get a new connection. The server has no way of associating the old connection with the new one. As a result, SQL Server does not try to roll incomplete transactions forward. Therefore, in the preceding example, the **UPDATE** would be interrupted, and you would have to re-execute the **UPDATE** statement.

This chapter is not especially long, but it presents a number of definitions that are crucial to understanding SQL Server, and therefore, performing well on the test.

By default, any SQL statement is a transaction. Further, most SQL statements can be grouped into a single transaction.

Transactions are used for a variety of purposes, including:

➤ Enforcing business rules or referential integrity

➤ Managing discrete units of work

➤ Enforcing data consistency, particularly of redundant or summary data

SQL Server provides transaction management for all user databases. To this end, SQL Server implements a variety of components, including:

➤ Transaction control statements

➤ Write-ahead transaction logs

➤ Automatic recovery processes

➤ Automatic locking processes

We'll address these in the next section.

Transaction Control Statements

Transaction control statements are used to define individual units of work. Table 13.1 shows SQL Server's transaction control statements and their uses. Keep in mind that transaction control statements don't have an effect on process flow.

Listing 13.1 shows a sample transaction demonstrating **BEGIN TRAN/ COMMIT TRAN** pairs to combine multiple SQL statements into a single logical unit of work.

Listing 13.1   Sample transaction.

```
begin tran
  update savings_account
  set balance = balance - $5000
  where account_number = @sav_account
  if @@error != 0
  begin
    rollback tran
```

```
   return
end
update checking_account
set balance = balance + $5000
where account_number = @chk_account
if @@error != 0
begin
   rollback tran
   return
end
commit tran
```

In Listing 13.1, **BEGIN TRAN** informs the server that a transaction has started. This means that until the server is informed that the transaction has completed (by using the **COMMIT TRAN**), no changes are permanent. Therefore, if the server crashes after the first update, the transaction will be *rolled back*. Rolled back means that the effects of the transaction will be undone; the data in the server will be as if no changes have taken place. In order to ensure consistency across other transactions, the code in Listing 13.1 locks the information that has been modified until the transaction completes. *Locked* means that no process will be able to access the information until the transaction releases it (by committing or rolling back the transaction).

Table 13.1 Transaction control statements and their uses.	
Syntax	**Use**
BEGIN TRAN[saction] [*transaction_name* | *@tran_variable*]	Defines the beginning of a transaction, and causes the server to log a **BEGIN TRAN** record.
COMMIT TRAN[saction] [*transaction_name* | *@tran_variable*]	Informs the server that the current transaction is complete, causes the server to log a **COMMIT TRAN** record, and makes the data changes permanent.
COMMIT WORK	Works like a commit transaction, but has no transaction name. This is the ANSI-92 syntax.
ROLLBACK TRAN[saction] [*transaction_name* | *savepoint_name* | *@tran_variable*]	Informs the server to undo all data changes since the last defined save point or to the beginning of the transaction.
ROLLBACK WORK	Works like a rollback transaction, but has no transaction name. This is the ANSI-92 syntax.
SAVE TRAN[saction] *transaction_name* | *@tran_variable*	Logs a point to which the server can roll back to, other than to the beginning of a transaction (to enable a partial rollback). The transaction remains active.

Only the process that owns a lock will be able to look at the locked, modified page.

If any errors occur during the transaction, or if logic requires it, you can issue the **ROLLBACK TRAN** statement.

 Note that the **ROLLBACK TRAN** statement does not have any effect on a program's flow. Therefore, you would have to issue a **RETURN** statement subsequent to the rollback.

Note that the transaction control statements do not have an effect on the flow of the logic or the transaction.

Transaction Flow

Transaction flow is most easily demonstrated by referring to some sample code. Consider Figure 13.1.

In Figure 13.1, the transaction begins when the first line of code executes. The server tracks this by updating the **@@trancount** global variable. **@@trancount** has a value of **0** if the transaction is open, or **1** or greater depending on the nesting level of the transaction if it is open.

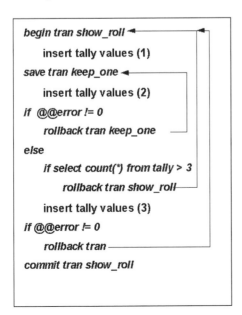

Figure13.1   Here's an example of transaction flow.

You can check the **@@trancount** value programmatically if you want to determine whether a transaction is open.

After the transaction is opened, the insert adds a row to the table *tally*. This added row is in the table and can be queried by the process that opened the transaction but not by any other process. It is not a permanent object of the database until the transaction is committed.

The **SAVE TRAN** is used as a bookmark. It has no effect on **@@trancount** and does not affect the transaction nesting level. It can be used later, by a rollback to the save point. Note that the number of rollbacks, commits, and **BEGIN TRAN** statements do not need to match up the way a begin/end pair traditionally (and syntactically) match up. You need a rollback or commit to end a transaction, but you can have several commits and/or rollbacks for the purpose of simplifying your logic.

Regardless of the number of **BEGIN TRAN** statements you nest, the nesting is syntactic only. In other words, only one transaction is really active. This open transaction will be made permanent in the database only by the outermost commit. SQL Server keeps track of this by decrementing **@@trancount** by one for each commit. Note that while a commit only decrements **@@trancount**, an unqualified rollback will roll back to the outermost transaction. If the **@@trancount** global variable never makes it back to zero, the transaction never completes, and the transaction rolls back. The locks are maintained until the transaction completes, one way or the other.

There are, however, some things a transaction can't do.

Transaction Limitations

SQL Server transactions are subject to a number of limitations. For example, transactions are server-specific (that is, they do not span servers). If you need a multiserver transaction, you need to use the Distributed Transaction Coordinator, which exists for that purpose.

Another limitation involves remote procedure calls. Remote procedure calls are stored procedures that span servers, so they are not local to the server. Therefore, remote procedures cannot be managed by the local transaction log. This means that they cannot be rolled back by a local process (again, you will need to use the Distributed Transaction Coordinator).

Finally, some Data Definition Language (DDL) cannot be used in transactions. The official list is:

➤ ALTER/CREATE/DROP DATABASE

➤ DUMP/LOAD DATABASE/TRANSACTION

➤ UPDATE STATISTICS

Distributed transactions—transactions that span two or more databases—come with their own set of rules and limitations.

Distributed Transactions

As mentioned, a distributed transaction is a transaction that spans two or more databases. If both databases are on the same server, the Distributed Transaction Coordinator steps aside and lets the SQL Server manage the transaction. If the databases reside on different servers, the Distributed Transaction Coordinator creates a two-phase commit across the transaction logs.

Distributed transactions are managed with a *two-phase commit*. The first phase is called a prepare phase, in which a *prepare to commit* command is sent to all associated servers by the transaction manager. Phase two is the commit phase, in which the transaction manager sends a notification of success to all servers after phase one completes successfully. If anything fails, all components of the transaction are rolled back on all servers.

In addition to the two-phase commit, additional transaction control commands exist to help you manage distributed transactions. The following syntax shows the commands you can use with distributed transactions:

```
Begin distributed tran[saction]
[transaction name| transaction variable]
```

This instructs the server to start the Distributed Transaction Coordinator.

Distributed transactions are committed by the same **COMMIT TRAN** statement that terminates any other transaction. A commit or rollback for a distributed transaction must be issued on the server that the *begin distributed transaction* command is issued on. This is called the *controlling server*. Servers can be added into the distributed transaction by either the server initiating the transaction directly or by any other server in the transaction. Added servers are called *coordinating servers*. Note that coordinating servers do not ask to be part of the transaction—they are requested to take part.

 Distributed transactions can only call stored procedures on the distributed servers. The coordinating server can use either stored procedures or inline SQL.

The next crucial piece of transaction management is the transaction log.

Transaction Log

Each SQL Server maintains a transaction log that keeps a record of all data modifications in a database. This transaction log is not in a format that is readable or modifiable by a user process. For some operations, such as **CREATE INDEX**, the information is not logged, but the page utilization is logged and the page allocations are maintained.

 The transaction log is now a separate file from the database. Prior to SQL Server 7, the transaction log was a database table, called syslogs. This change is a major departure from previous versions of SQL Server.

Transaction logging provides forward and backward recovery. Recovery automatically takes place when the server is started, and it synchronizes the data with the log (the data and log can become out of synch during the process of flushing data from cache to disk).

The transaction log also provides a record of changes for your current transaction, thereby enabling you to roll back a transaction. This allows you to change data back to the way it was before you altered it.

What precisely happens during transaction logging?

Transaction Logging Sequence Of Events

The process of transaction logging exists to guarantee transactional integrity. First, the **BEGIN TRAN** is written to the log in cache, which tracks a unique transaction number and a sequence number for the transaction. Next, log pages are modified in cache (SQL Server has a write-ahead transaction log). Data pages are then modified in cache. Finally, the **COMMIT TRAN** is written to the log in cache, and the log cache is flushed to disk. Note that the data pages do not need to be pushed to disk, because, at recovery, the server can re-create data pages from the log pages.

Checkpoints

A checkpoint is the process of writing all *dirty data pages* from cache to disk. Dirty data pages are pages in cache that have been modified, but the modifications are not reflected on the disk. Log pages are written to disk first, followed by data pages. Finally, the checkpoint marker is written to disk. The checkpoint marker is a mechanism that reduces recovery time, as the database on disk is fully synchronized (log and data) at the conclusion of the checkpoint. A checkpoint will occur under several circumstances:

➤ A server recovery interval has been exceeded.

➤ A server has no space left in cache and needs to age-out dirty pages.

➤ A DBO issues the checkpoint command.

➤ A transaction log is dumped.

Transactions lock rows, pages, or tables to make sure that nobody modifies or views transactions in progress.

Locking In Transactions

Objects are locked to maintain data consistency. When one process is modifying data, another process should not be using that information. As mentioned earlier in this chapter, locks are maintained until transactions are completed. There are several levels of locking used to maintain different applications under different situations, as defined by the ANSI-92 SQL standard.

ANSI-92 Isolation Levels

The ANSI-92 SQL standard defines four levels of isolation for SQL transactions. Each isolation level describes the types of actions that are not permitted at the same time. The following sections describe each ANSI isolation level. Keep in mind that the higher levels include the lower levels. Note the following alternative names for the different isolation levels.

➤ READ UNCOMMITTED ANSI level 0

➤ READ COMMITTED ANSI level 1

➤ REPEATABLE READ ANSI level 2

➤ SERIALIZABLE ANSI level 3

Isolation Level 0—READ UNCOMMITTED

Level 0 allows dirty reads. No locks are needed or acquired by the reading process. Level 0 is implemented with **NOLOCK** or the **READUNCOMMITTED** option on **SELECT** or with the **SET** statement. This locking level only guarantees that data is not physically corrupted.

Isolation Level 1—READ COMMITTED

Level 1 is the default locking level. This level prevents dirty reads. SQL Server implements this locking level with exclusive locks. SQL Server can also override a defined alternative isolation level by using the **SET LOCKIMPLEMENTS** or with the **READ COMMITTED** options on **SELECT** and **SET** statements.

Isolation Level 2—REPEATABLE READ

Level 2 prevents non-repeatable reads. Therefore, a second transaction cannot modify a row previously read within the current transaction. SQL Server implements this with the **REPEATABLE** option on **SELECT** or with **SET** statements.

Isolation Level 3—SERIALIZABLE

Level 3, the final isolation level, prevents *phantom* reads. This level prevents a transaction from reading a different set of rows satisfying a search condition than were previously read within the transaction. SQL Server implements level 3 locking with the **HOLDLOCK** and **SERIALIZABLE** option on **SELECT** or with **SET** statements.

Default Isolation Level

As mentioned, level 1 is the SQL Server default isolation level. The ANSI standard requires the ability to permit a level 3 default isolation level for transactions. You can set the default isolation level for a session by using the **SET** statement, as follows:

```
set transaction isolation level { READ COMMITTED |
   READ UNCOMMITTED | REPEATABLE READ | SERIALIZABLE }
```

When **SERIALIZABLE** is set, **HOLDLOCK** is automatically applied to all **SELECT** statements in a transaction. The transaction isolation level remains in effect for the duration of the session or until it is changed. To determine the current isolation level, execute the **DBCC USEROPTIONS** command.

All SQL Server locking is automatic. Table 13.2 lists lock granularity. Table 13.3 shows the various types of locks.

Table 13.2 Lock granularity.	
Resource	**Description**
Rid	Uses the row ID to lock an individual row.
Key	Uses a unique index (key) to lock an individual row.
Page	Uses an 8K data page or index page.
Extent	Uses a contiguous group of eight data pages or index pages.
Table	Uses an entire table, including all data and indexes.
DB	Uses an entire database.

Table 13.3 Lock types.	
Type	**Description**
Exclusive (X)	Allows only the process that owns the lock to read or write data. No other concurrent users are allowed. This lock is normally used for data modifications.
Intent Shared (IS)	Accepts requests to read data.
Intent To Write (IX)	Accepts request to modify data.
Shared (S)	Enables any process to read data, but none can write. There's no limit to concurrent users.
Shared With Intent Exclusive (SIX)	Sets concurrent locks on higher-level resources (table), but exclusive locks on some lower-level resources (pages/rows).
Schema	Applies to system tables and indexes. Schema locks are much more resource intensive and shareable than the other types of locks. Schema Modify (SCH-M) is used when a schema is being modified and a DDL is issued. Schema Shared (SCH-S) is used when queries are being compiled. Schema Shared does not block any locks.
Update (U)	Acts as a "bookmark" to help SQL Server avoid deadlocking. This lock allows shared locks, but no other update locks or exclusive locks.

Locks may escalate to improve performance when an excessive number of locks are requested on a page or in a table by a single transaction.

Lock Escalation

SQL Server will try to lock at the row level to maximize concurrency. At the same time, SQL Server will place intent-level locks on the pages and table. As row locks on a table increase by a single statement, SQL Server can escalate to a page lock when the number of rows exceeds the threshold. As page locks on a table increase by a single statement, SQL Server can escalate to a table lock when the number of pages exceeds the threshold. When a lock gets escalated, all lower-level locks are released. Lock thresholds are determined dynamically by SQL Server and have no configuration.

Here are some things to be aware of when working with locks.

Notes On Locks

If a process gets an exclusive lock on a row, page, or table, no other process can read or obtain a lock on that object until the process commits or rolls back. If a process has a shared lock, no other process can get an exclusive lock until the shared lock is released. If this becomes a problem, the server may escalate to a *demand lock*.

Locking contention between processes can adversely impact system performance. You should try to access a database via stored procedures to minimize the amount of time spent on locks.

 Try to keep transactions concise, and keep extraneous **SELECT** statements out of transactions. This will help to minimize the amount of time that locks are held. Never have an application holding a lock while waiting for user input.

Shared locks are typically released after a page or row has been read.

Overriding SQL Server's Query-Level Locking

You can override the server's locks, but do not do this frivolously. In addition to **HOLDLOCK**, MS SQL Server supports other query-definable lock overrides. By using one of the following keywords after the table name in the **FROM** clause, a query can override SQL Server's locking manager and apply the specified lock. The lock is held for the duration of the statement or the transaction that contains the statement. Available lock types include:

➤ **NOLOCK** Allows dirty reads

➤ **PAGLOCK** Locks at the page level, may escalate

➤ **ROWLOCK** Performs row-level locking

➤ **TABLOCK** Acquires a shared table lock

➤ **TABLOCKX** Acquires an exclusive table lock

➤ **UPDLOCK** Uses updates instead of shared locks

Here are some sample **SELECT** statements which are overriding the server's default locking mechanism.

```
SELECT * FROM titles NOLOCK
   WHERE title_id = "394-92-9841"

SELECT * FROM publishers TABLOCKX HOLDLOCK
```

Remember, every lock you place prevents another process from accessing the information.

Setting Index Locking Levels

You can turn off locking levels for a given index using the **sp_indexoption** command. For example, if you have a decision support system within which you have no significant updates, you might want to make the access shared-only.

You can turn off page and/or row level locking using the **sp_indexoption** stored procedure.

```
sp_indexoption index_name, option_name, value
```

In the preceding example, valid option names are **AllowRowLocks** or **AllowPageLocks**, and valid values are **TRUE** or **FALSE**. The following example shows how to turn off row-level locking by using the **sp_indexoption** command:

```
sp_indexoption 'mytable.myindex',AllowRowLocks,'FALSE'
```

This prevents row-level locking on the index called myindex on the table called mytable.

 Be very careful when using the **sp_indexoption** feature.

Practice Questions

Question 1

> When is a transaction made permanent in a database? [Check all correct answers]
>
> ❏ a. After the first commit
>
> ❏ b. After the final commit
>
> ❏ c. After any checkpoint
>
> ❏ d. When the session terminates
>
> ❏ e. All of the above

Answer b is correct. The only action that makes a transaction permanent in a database is when **@@trancount** hits zero, which indicates a final commit. Answer a is incorrect, because there may be a transaction deeper than one level. Answer c is incorrect, because a checkpoint has nothing to do with transaction nesting levels. Answer d is incorrect, because that would cause a rollback.

Question 2

> When does recovery occur?
>
> ○ a. Automatically when the server is started
>
> ○ b. Automatically when the server is stopped
>
> ○ c. Only during the recover server command
>
> ○ d. After each rolled back transaction
>
> ○ e. All of the above

Answer a is correct. Recovery occurs automatically when the server is started. Answer b is incorrect, because that is when the checkpoint occurs. Answer c is incorrect, because there is no recover server command. Answer d is incorrect, because recovery performs transaction completion.

Question 3

How many transaction isolation levels does the ANSI standards board define?

○ a. zero

○ b. one

○ c. two

○ d. three

○ e. four

○ f. None of the above

Answer e is correct. The ANSI standards board defines four levels.

Question 4

How long does a completed transaction persist in a database?

○ a. Until it is rolled back

○ b. Until it is committed

○ c. Until the locks are released

○ d. Until another transaction replaces it

○ e. None of the above

Answer e is correct.

Question 5

What lock types are supported by SQL Server? [Check all correct answers]

❑ a. Row level

❑ b. Page level

❑ c. Table level

❑ d. Database level

❑ e. Server level

Answers a, b, c, and d are correct. SQL Server supports row, page, table, and database level locks, as well as a few other locks. Answer e is incorrect, because it is not a lock type.

Need To Know More?

 Amo, William C. *Transact-SQL*, IDG Books Worldwide, Foster City, CA, 1998. ISBN 0-7645-8048-5. Chapter 16 explores transactions and the commands that affect transactions.

 Coffman, Gayle. *SQL Server 7: The Complete Reference*, Osborne/McGraw-Hill, Berkley, CA, 1999. ISBN 0-07-882494-X. Chapter 21 provides a complete T-SQL reference for the commands used to control transactions.

 MS SQL Server Books Online provides information about transactions, look in the index for "transactions".

 Search the TechNet CD or its online version at **www.microsoft.com**.

 www.microsoft.com/sql
Find up-to-date information about using SQL Server here.

Importing, Exporting, And Transforming Data

14

Terms you'll need to understand:

√ Import

√ Export

√ Transformation

√ **dtswiz** utility

Techniques you'll need to master:

√ Using the BCP program

√ Using the Data Transformation Service

When you use a database, you will need a way to add data to the database, as well as extract data from the database. SQL Server provides several ways to *import* and *export* database data. Importing means to load data into a database, and exporting means to transfer data from a database. You can also *transform* data, which means you can convert data from one format into another format. In this chapter, we'll look at using the Bulk Copy Program (BCP) and the Data Transformation Service (DTS) to import and export data to and from SQL Server.

BCP

The bcp.exe (BCP) program is used to import data into and export data from SQL Server database tables. The bcp.exe program is installed as part of the SQL Server installation, and is located in the binn directory under the SQL Server installation directory.

 When data is loaded into SQL Server, it is considered imported data. When BCP copies data into the database from a file, BCP appends the data to an existing database table. When BCP copies data from a database to a file (exporting data), BCP overwrites any existing contents of the file.

BCP is capable of reading and writing files in a wide variety of formats. The different formats that BCP can use will be covered with the parameters. The most common file format used with SQL Server is character data with tab-separated fields.

Note: Whereas previous versions of bcp.exe used dblibrary to connect to SQL Server, BCP version 7 uses ODBC to connect to a SQL Server.

When loading data into a database table with BCP, the table must already exist in the database, and you must have insert and select permissions on the table. The number of fields in the file and the order of the fields do not have to match the columns in the table. But, if they don't match, you must use a *format file*. A format file can list the columns that you want to import or export, the order of the columns, the length of the columns, and the terminator for the columns. Furthermore, the data types in the format file must be compatible with the column data types. The first line of the format file contains the BCP version number. The second line contains the number of columns to import or export. The rest of the lines in the format file contain the following seven fields in the following order:

➤ **Host field file order** The field position in the data file.

➤ **Host file data field type** The data type for the field.

➤ **Prefix length** The length of the field prefix—it must be 0, 1, 2 or 4.

➤ **Host file data length** The maximum length of the field in the data file.

➤ **Field terminate** The delimiter of the field—the common terminator is tab (\t).

➤ **Server column order** The order of the column in the SQL Server table.

➤ **Server column name** Used to list the name of the column in the SQL Server table. It does not have to be the actual column name.

BCP uses a number of parameters to control its behavior when importing and exporting data. Listing 14.1 shows the BCP utility's syntax.

Listing 14.1   BCP syntax.

```
bcp [[database_name.][owner].]table_name
    {in | out | format} data_file
    [-m max_errors] [-f format_file] [-e err_file]
    [-F first_row] [-L last_row] [-b batch_size]
    [-n] [-c] [-w] [-N] [-6] [-q] [-C code_page]
    [-t field_term] [-r row_term]
    [-i input_file] [-o output_file] [-a packet_size]
    [-S server_name] [-U login_id] [-P password]
    [-T] [-v] [-k] [-E] [-h "hint [, ...n]"]
```

Each BCP parameter behaves the same as the equivalent parameter for a BULK INSERT statement.

 If there are any special characters in a parameter, the parameter must be in quotes, like this:

```
bcp pubs..authors out au.dat -U"My Account"
```

The BCP parameters are as follows:

➤ **IN|OUT|FORMAT** Specifies the action of the BCP. If you specify the **FORMAT** option, the BCP utility will create a format file and not import or export data. You must specify the **-f** parameter if you use the **FORMAT** option. If the format action is used and neither **-n**, **-c**, **-w**, **-6**, nor **-N** are specified, BCP prompts for format information.

➤ **-m** Limits the number of errors that can occur. Any row that has an error is ignored. The default value for this option is 10 errors.

➤ **-f** Allows BCP to have finer control over what the data being loaded or exported looks like. If you specify the format file without specifying that the BCP is doing a format action, the format file must exist.

➤ **-e** Specifies an error file. All error messages and the row that caused the error are written to the error file.

➤ **-F** Specifies the first row to bulk copy. The default is to copy from the first row to the last row.

➤ **-L** Specifies the last row to bulk copy. The default is to copy from the first row to the last row.

➤ **-b** Specifies the batch size or the number of rows to bulk copy in a batch. The default is the whole file. BCP starts a new transaction for each batch. If the bulk copy aborts for any reason, all rows being inserted from the current batch are rolled back. Do not use **-b** with the **-h** "ROWS_PER_BATCH = *bb*" option.

➤ **-n** Causes a bulk copy to use the native (database) data types of the data.

➤ **-c** Causes a bulk copy to convert everything to a character data type. This option uses **char** as the storage type, no prefixes, \t (tab character) as the field separator, and \n (new line character) as the row terminator.

➤ **-w** Causes a bulk copy to convert everything to a Unicode data type. This option uses **char** as the storage type, no prefixes, \t (tab character) as the field separator, and \n (new line character) as the row terminator. The -w option cannot be used with SQL Server version 6.5 or earlier.

➤ **-N** Causes a bulk copy operation to use the native (database) data types of the data for non-character data, and Unicode characters for character data. This option offers a higher-performance alternative to the -w option and is intended for transferring data from one SQL Server to another using a data file. It cannot be used with SQL Server 6.5 or earlier.

➤ **-6** Causes a bulk copy operation to use SQL Server 6 or 6.5 data types. This option is used with the -c and -n options to load data that was generated by previous versions of BCP.

➤ **-q** Specifies that the table name contains special characters. When using this option, the full table name must be enclosed in double quotes (").

➤ **-C** Specifies a code page to use for character data. This affects columns with character values greater than 127 or less than 32.

➤ -t Specifies the field terminator. The default is \t (tab character).

➤ -r Specifies the row terminator. The default is \n (new line character).

➤ -i Specifies the name of an input response file. This file provides the responses to questions for each field when performing a bulk copy that doesn't use -n, -c, -w, -6, -N, or an input file.

➤ -o Specifies the name of a file that receives output from BCP. This does not affect where the data is stored.

➤ -a Specifies the network packet size. This option can be from 4,096 through 65,535 bytes. The default is 4,096. An increased packet size can enhance the performance of bulk copy operations. If a larger packet is requested but cannot be granted, the default is used.

➤ -S Instructs the SQL Server to connect to the network. The default is the local server. This option is required when executing BCP from a remote computer on the network.

➤ -U Specifies the login ID to use to connect to a SQL Server. It will default to the current user.

➤ -P Specifies the password for the login ID. If this option is not used and the -T option is not specified, BCP prompts for a password. If you use this option at the end of the parameter list with no password following it, BCP uses the default password, which is a database **NULL**.

➤ -T Instructs BCP to connect to a SQL Server with a trusted connection, using the security credentials of the network user. No SQL Server login or password are required.

➤ -v Reports the version number and copyright information of the BCP program and exits.

➤ -k Causes empty columns to be null during bulk copy inserts, instead of having the default values applied to the inserted columns.

➤ -E Specifies that identity columns are present in the file being imported. If -E is not given, the file being imported should not contain values for these columns, because SQL Server automatically assigns unique values. If -E is specified, SQL Server obtains the values for the identity columns from the data file.

➤ -h Specifies hints to the optimizer that are used during a bulk copy of data into a table. Table 14.1 list the BCP hints.

Table 14.1	BCP optimizer hints.
Hint	**Meaning**
ORDER (column [ASC | DESC] [,n])	Sort order of the data in the data file.
ROWS_PER_BATCH = bb	Number of rows of data per batch. Do not use with the –b parameter.
KILOBYTES_PER_BATCH = cc	Number of kilobytes of data per batch.
TABLOCK	A table-level lock is acquired for the duration of the bulk copy operation.
CHECK_CONSTRAINTS	Causes SQL Server to check table constraints during data loads.

Running BCP

When you copy data (into or out of a database) using BCP's **-n** or **-c** option, BCP only prompts you for your password, unless you supply BCP with the **-P** option. If you supply neither the **-n** nor **-c** option, BCP prompts you for information for each field in the table. Each prompt displays a default value, in brackets, which you can accept by pressing Enter. The prompts include:

➤ The file storage type, which can be a character or any valid SQL Server data type.

➤ The prefix length, which is an integer indicating the length in bytes of the following data.

➤ The storage length of the data in the file.

➤ The field terminator, which can be any character string.

After answering the questions for each field, the BCP utility will ask whether you want to save the format information in a file.

 You can perform multiple bulk copies into a table in parallel by running multiple BCPs against the same table. This can only be done if all requirements for a non-logged bulk copy (the database select into/bulkcopy option is turned on, the table has no triggers, and the table is not being replicated) are met and the table has no indexes.

Data Transformation Service

The Data Transformation Service (DTS) is used to import, export, and transform data between multiple heterogeneous data sources. You can use DTS with any data source that can be accessed with OLE DB. If any OLE DB driver is not provided for the data source, you can use Microsoft's OLE DB for ODBC to access data.

The Data Transformation Services use the DTS wizard to create a Data Transformation Package (DTP). The DTP can be run to transform data. You can call DTS directly from the SQL Server Enterprise Manager, run the dtswiz.exe program, or call the DTS Distributed Management Object (DMO).

DTS Components

DTS consists of four components:

➤ Import wizard

➤ Export wizard

➤ Package Designer

➤ COM programming interfaces

The upcoming sections take a brief look at each component.

DTS Import Wizard

The DTS Import wizard walks you through the steps of importing data into a SQL Server database. To use the DTS Import wizard, follow these steps:

1. Start the DTS wizard and click on Next.

2. In the next wizard window, choose the data source that contains the data you want to import. Then, enter any necessary parameters to make the connection; these parameters will depend on the data source. Then click on Next.

3. In the next wizard window, choose the data destination. Then, enter any necessary parameters to make the connection. Then click on Next.

4. In the next screen, choose Copy Tables to pick individual tables to copy or the Use Query option to write a SQL Statement to define the data to copy. Then click on Next.

5. If you picked the Copy Tables option, you get a screen that allows you to select the tables to copy. If you picked the Use Query option, you will need to either write the query in the next screen or use the Query Builder (click on the Query Builder button to open the Query Builder) to write the query for you. Then click on Next.

6. Indicate whether you want to run the package, save the package, create a replication package, or schedule the package. Then click on Next. If you opt to run the package, you will see the package status window. If you

save the package, you will be asked to supply the package's name, description, and server information.

7. In the next window, click on Finish to perform the options that you have selected.

DTS Export Wizard

The DTS Export wizard walks you through the steps required to export data from a SQL Server database. To use the DTS Export wizard, follow these steps:

1. Start the DTS wizard and click on Next.

2. In the next screen, choose the data source that contains the data you want to export, and enter any necessary parameters to make the connection. Click on Next.

3. In the next screen, choose the data destination, and enter any necessary parameters to make the connection. Click on Next.

4. In the next screen, choose the Copy Tables or Use Query option and click on Next.

5. If you picked the Copy Tables option, you get a screen that allows you to select the tables to copy. If you picked the Use Query option, you will need to either write the query in the next screen or use the Query Builder (click on the Query Builder button to open the Query Builder) to write the query for you. Then click on Next.

6. Indicate whether you want to run the package, save the package, create a replication package, or schedule the package. If you opt to run the package, you will see the package status window. Then click on Next. If you save the package, you will be asked to supply the package's name, description, and server information. Then click on Next.

7. Click on Finish in the final window to perform the package you have just created.

DTS Package Designer

The DTS Package Designer allows you to graphically design a DTS package. A DTS package is a set of steps to perform when transforming data. In the simplest form, a DTS package contains one import or export step defined by the DTS Import wizard or the DTS Export wizard. The DTS Package Designer is part of SQL Server Enterprise Manager. The DTS Package Designer allows you to save the DTS package in the SQL Server MSDB database, the Microsoft Repository, or a COM-structured storage file. Furthermore, you can also schedule the DTS package for later execution.

DTS COM Programming Interfaces

The DTS COM interfaces are used to create and execute DTS packages. You can access the COM interfaces through any programming language that supports OLE animation. The interfaces allow you to create custom applications using DTS packages and DTS Data Pump objects.

Transforming Data

One of DTS's more useful features is its ability to transform data. When DTS transforms data, a set of operations is defined to be run on the data at the destination. It allows new values to be calculated based on one or more source fields. This transformation can perform complex data validation, scrubbing, and enhancement during import and export.

 DTS moves schemas and data between data sources. Other database objects, such as triggers, stored procedures, rules, defaults, constraints, and user-defined data types are not converted. When using the DTS Import and Export wizards, you can specify column mappings and transformation information.

Column Mappings

The Column Mapping screen (shown in Figure 14.1) allows you to define the structure of the table you are sending data to and the mapping between columns.

You can instruct DTS to create destination tables, including dropping and re-creating a destination table if the table exists. If you do not create a destination

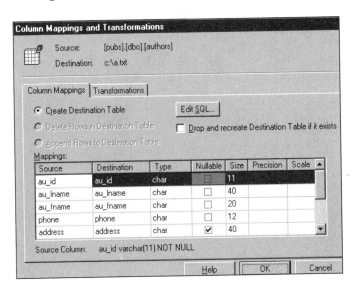

Figure 14.1   DTS Column Mapping screen.

table as part of the DTS operation, you can delete all data in the existing table or append data to the existing table.

As you can see in Figure 14.1, the Column Mapping screen allows you to change which source field is mapped to a given destination field. You can also change a field's data types; whether the field will allow nulls; and the output field's size, scale, and precision. If you use the Edit SQL option (see Figure 14.2), you can specify custom SQL for the destination table.

Transformations

The DTS Transformation screen (shown in Figure 14.3) allows you either to copy the source columns directly to the destination columns, or you can specify that DTS will run a script to perform the data transformation.

If you specify to copy the data directly, you can use the advanced options to control the transformations. The Advanced Transformation Properties screen allows you to set the flags listed in Table 14.2.

For most data transformations, the flags will provide all the functionality that you need. To perform more complex transformations, you should use the Transfer Information option on the DTS Transformation screen. Using this option, you can specify a script to be run in either Java Script, Perl Script, or Visual Basic Script. DTS will generate a default script of each type. These scripts can perform complex data transformations. Listing 14.2 shows a sample data transformation script written in Visual Basic Script.

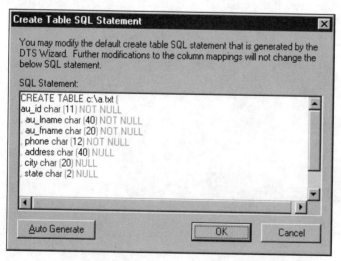

Figure 14.2 DTS Create Table SQL Statement screen.

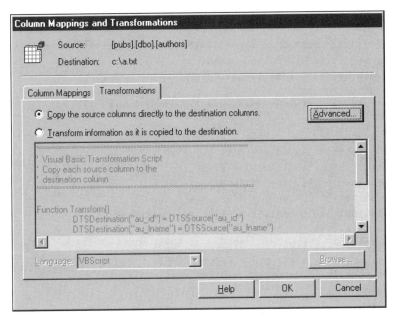

Figure 14.3   DTS Transformations screen.

Table 14.2   Data transformation flags.

Flag	Effect
Default transformation flags— all possible conversions are allowed	Allows data type conversions that do not lose data, data type promotion, and null conversions.
Require exact match between source and destination	Indicates that columns must have the same data type, size, precision, scale, and nullability in both source and destination tables. This is the strictest transformation.
Custom transformation flags	Allow you to choose any one of the following data type transformations: promotion, demotion, and NULL conversion.
Allow data type promotion	Allows numeric data types to be converted to larger numeric data types. For example, a tinyint can be converted to an integer.
Allow data type demotion	Allows numeric data types to be converted to smaller numeric data types. For example, an integer can be converted to a tinyint. If the number being converted is larger than the destination field will allow, an overflow error will be generated.
Allow NULL conversion	Allows a source column that does not permit NULL to be converted to a destination column that permits nulls.

Listing 14.2   Visual Basic data transformation script.

```
'****************************************************************
'   Visual Basic Transformation Script
'   Copy each source column to the
'   destination column
'****************************************************************

Function Transform()
    DTSDestination("au_id") = DTSSource("au_id")
    DTSDestination("au_lname") = DTSSource("au_lname")
    DTSDestination("au_fname") = DTSSource("au_fname")
    DTSDestination("phone") = DTSSource("phone")
    DTSDestination("address") = DTSSource("address")
    DTSDestination("city") = DTSSource("city")
    DTSDestination("state") = DTSSource("state")
    DTSDestination("zip") = DTSSource("zip")
    DTSDestination("contract") = DTSSource("contract")
    Transform = 1
End Function
```

dtswiz Utility

The **dtswiz** utility allows you to run the data transformation services from the command line. When running **dtswiz**, you can specify options to bypass the prompts on the DTS import, export, and data transformation screens. The syntax of **dtswiz** is as follows:

```
dtswiz [/f filename] [/i | /x] [/r provider_name]
[/s server_name] [/u login_id] [/p password] [/n]
[/d database_name] [/y]
```

Following is a description of each parameter:

➤ /f Allows you to specify a COM-structured file to store the DTS package created by the wizards.

➤ /i Specifies that you are performing an import into a SQL Server.

➤ /x Specifies that you are performing an export from a SQL Server.

➤ /r Specifies the name of the provider used to connect to the data source (when importing) or the destination (when exporting).

➤ /s Specifies the SQL Server where data is to be exported from or imported to. If you want to go from one SQL Server to another SQL Server, one of the SQL Servers has to be configured as an ODBC data source, with the server name, login, password, and database declared in the ODBC configuration.

➤ /u Specifies the SQL Server login to use when connecting.

➤ /p Specifies the password for the SQL Server login.

➤ /n Specifies that it's a trusted connection, and the /u and /p parameter will not be used.

➤ /d Specifies the SQL Server database to use.

➤ /y Specifies that the **dtswiz** program should hide the system tables and system databases.

Practice Questions

Question 1

DTS Export wizard allows you to perform which of the following? [Check all correct answers]

❑ a. Migrate data from a SQL Server to another SQL Server.

❑ b. Migrate data from a SQL Server to any ODBC data source.

❑ c. Migrate data from Oracle to SQL Server.

❑ d. Migrate data from a SQL Server to Oracle.

❑ e. None of the above.

Answers a, b, c, and d are correct. Even though it is the Export wizard, it can be used to import data into a SQL Server database from any OLE DB compliant data source. This includes any ODBC data source. Answer e is incorrect, because the correct answers are provided.

Question 2

What option is used to direct BCP to redirect the errors to a file?

○ a. -e

○ b. -o

○ c. -m

○ d. -f

○ e. None of the above

Answer a is correct. You specify -e *file_name* to redirect BCP errors to a file. Answer b is incorrect, because the -o parameter redirects standard output, not errors. Answer c is incorrect, because the -m parameter limits the number of errors BCP can hit without aborting. Answer d is incorrect, because the -f parameter specifies the first row to import or export. Answer e is incorrect, because answer a provides the correct answer.

Question 3

> What **dtswiz** parameter can be used to specify what login to use
> when connecting to a SQL Server? [Check all correct answers]
>
> ❏ a. -n
>
> ❏ b. -u
>
> ❏ c. -l
>
> ❏ d. U
>
> ❏ e. None of the above

Answer e is correct, because the correct answer is not provided. All **dtswiz**
parameters start with a slash (/), not with a dash (-). Answers a, b, c, and d are
all incorrect, because they all start with a dash (-).

Question 4

> Which of the following are true about the following BCP state-
> ment? [Check all of the correct answers]
>
> ```
> Bcp c in  -Uaaaaaa -P xyccc
> ```
>
> ❏ a. The statement will try to connect to a local server.
>
> ❏ b. The statement will fail, because the database name is
>   missing.
>
> ❏ c. The statement will connect to the user's aaaaaa default
>   database.
>
> ❏ d. The statement will prompt the user for information about
>   the file's format.
>
> ❏ e. None of the above.

Answer e is correct, because the correct answer is not provided. The first parameter after the direction -**Uaaaaaaa** will be treated as the input file name. If
it is a valid file, this statement will try to connect to the local server as the
current user with the password of **xyccc**. If the file does not exist, an error will
be generated, making answers a, b, c, and d incorrect.

Question 5

The DTS data transformation GUI can use which of the following
programming languages to directly transform data? [Check all
correct answers]

❑ a. Perl

❑ b. C

❑ c. Visual Basic

❑ d. Java

❑ e. Visual C++

Answers a, c, and d are correct. Perl, Visual Basic, and Java can all be used to
directly transform data. Answers b and e are incorrect, because C and Visual
C++ are not directly supported by the DTS data transformation GUI.

Need To Know More?

 Amo, William C. *Transact-SQL*, IDG Books Worldwide, Foster City, CA, 1998. ISBN 0-7645-8048-5. Chapter 2 describes the BCP program.

 McGehee, Brad and Matthew Shepker. *Using Microsoft SQL Server 7.0*, QUE, Indianapolis, Indiana, 1998. ISBN 0-7897-1628-3. Chapter 16 describes DTS and BCP.

 MS SQL Server Books Online provides information about loading data, look in the index for "bcp utility" or for "DTS".

 Search the TechNet CD or its online version at **www.microsoft.com**.

 www.microsoft.com/sql
Find up-to-date information about using SQL Server here.

Full-Text Search

Terms you'll need to understand:

✓ Full-text index

✓ Full-text query

✓ Full-text catalog

Techniques you'll need to master:

✓ Preparing a full-text index

✓ Creating a full-text index

✓ Performing a full-text query

In a typical relational database, like SQL Server, all data, including text, is stored in columns of a specific data type. When you search for data in a table, indexes can be implemented to allow for faster data retrieval. However, when dealing with text, it becomes questionable whether an index can be used at all.

Searching For Text

Consider the following queries that search for the word *computer*. The first example will only find titles that *begin* with the word *computer*:

```
Select title from titles where title like "Computer%"
```

Rewritten, the query could be expressed as:

```
Select title from titles where title >= "Computer"
```

This type of search argument allows for the index selection by the SQL Server optimizer. The next example will find the word *Computer* anywhere within the title column:

```
Select title from titles where title like "%Computer%"
```

This search will be very inefficient, because the server will be forced to perform a table scan. As an alternative to the preceding search techniques, you can implement a full-text search. A standard index would sort the column in ascending or descending order based on each character in the column. A full-text search allows the searching of words or phrases from within a text field, because it builds an index of the words in the text column. Before you can use a full-text search, you must complete a number of preparatory procedures.

Preparing For A Full-Text Search

Preparing for a full-text search involves a combination of enabling parameters to activate the full-text search option and declaring indexes that will be used for the search.

First, before a full-text search can be considered, the option must be enabled for the database, as shown in the following code:

```
sp_fulltext_database ['Enable']|['DISABLE']

sp_fulltext_database enable
```

Users must have the **db_owner** role to execute the **sp_fulltext_database** command. This one command activates the ability to perform a full-text search.

All other procedures regarding full-text search are useless unless this stored procedure is run first. If you want to verify whether a database has been enabled, you can use the following select query:

```
SELECT DATABASEPROPERTY ('database_name', 'IsFulltextEnabled')
```

When enabling a full-text search for a database, beware: If any previously existing full-text index catalogs exist in the file system, they will be dropped.

Also, when you enable full-text searches for a database, any previously created full-text indexing indicated by the system tables will be re-created.

> *Note: When performing a disable of full-text, all catalogs in the file system will be removed. The database system tables will also indicate that full-text indexing has been disabled.*

Finally, before a full-text query can be issued, SQL Server requires that full-text indexes exist. You can create full-text indexes, as described in the next section.

Creating A Full-Text Index

For a full-text search to be successful, it requires indexes to search through. These indexes will map significant words from registered columns in a database to the rows of the corresponding tables. Preparation of the indexes requires several tasks, including the following:

➤ Generating a full-text catalog

➤ Registering tables for full-text search

➤ Registering columns for full-text search

➤ Activating tables for a full-text index

➤ Starting the full-text index

The first step to creating a full-text index is to ensure that the database has been enabled for full-text indexing. Then, the next step is to create a full-text catalog for your indexes.

Generating A Full-Text Catalog

A full-text catalog is a file that stores the actual full-text index. Generating a full-text catalog produces an operating system file for the database and also produces the necessary metadata for the full-text catalog in the database system tables. The syntax for generating a full-text catalog is as follows:

```
sp_fulltext_catalog 'fulltext_catalog_name',
 ['create'|'drop'
  |'start_incremental'|'start_full'
  |'stop'|'rebuild']
 [, 'root_directory']
```

When generating a full-text catalog, the stored procedure must be provided with a unique catalog name for the database as well as an action. The available actions are:

➤ **CREATE** Generates the catalog file in the specified **root_directory**, and alters the table **sysfulltextcatalogs** to reflect the new catalog.

➤ **DROP** Removes an entry from **sysfulltextcatalogs**, and removes the file from the file system.

➤ **START_INCREMENTAL** Starts the population of the full-text index for changed rows. The indexed table must have a **timestamp** column.

➤ **START_FULL** Produces a full population for the full-text catalog based on every row of every table that has been registered to the specified catalog.

➤ **STOP** Halts population of a full-text index.

➤ **REBUILD** Regenerates a full-text index. The catalog file will be removed from the operating system and re-created.

The following code example will create a catalog called "PubsCatalog":

```
sp_fulltext_catalog 'PubsCatalog', 'create'
```

After the full-text catalog is set, the database's tables need to be registered for a full-text search.

Registering Tables For Full-Text Search

Registering the database tables marks them in the database as suitable for full-text search and starts the creation of metadata structures to store the indexes that will be developed later on. The stored procedure used to start this process is **sp_fulltext_table**, and it has the following syntax:

```
sp_fulltext_table ['table_name'],
['create'|'drop'|'activate'|'deactivate']
[,'catalog_name',
 'index_name']
```

As you can see in the syntax example, the **sp_fulltext_table** procedure uses the following options, which will allow you to make new tables eligible for full-text search or make other tables ineligible for full-text search:

➤ **CREATE** Generates the metadata for the table's full-text index. Before a table can have a full-text index created for it, the table must first have at least a unique index. The index name is required when using the create option.

➤ **DROP** Removes the metadata for the full-text index of a table. If a table is active, the full-text indexes will be deactivated before the metadata is removed.

➤ **ACTIVATE** Enables the full-text index data to be gathered. Before a table can be activated, it must have at least one column participating in the index.

➤ **DEACTIVATE** Halts the full-text index for the table. The index will no longer be populated. However, the full-text metadata will remain intact. The index can be reactivated by the **ACTIVATE** parameter.

This example creates a metadata for full-text search for the titles table in the PubsCatalog catalog based on the **index PK_titles**:

```
sp_fulltext_table 'titles', 'create', 'PubsCatalog', 'PK_titles'
```

After the tables have been registered for a full-text search, the next step toward creating a full-text index entails registering the columns that will participate in the full-text index.

Registering Columns For A Full-Text Search

Columns are registered via a stored procedure **sp_fulltext_column**. The syntax is as follows:

```
sp_fulltext_column 'table_name', 'column_name', {'ADD'|'DROP'}
```

In the preceding syntax example, **ADD** registers a column for full-text index participation, and **DROP** removes a column from full-text participation. The following examples will demonstrate the syntax registering and unregistering columns from full-text search. The first example registers the titles column from the titles table for full-text search. The second unregisters the title column:

```
sp_fulltext_column 'titles','title','ADD'
sp_fulltext_column 'titles','title','DROP'
```

After the necessary columns are registered, the full-text index must be activated.

Activating The Table For Full-Text Index

Activating a table for full-text means that all the columns that will participate in the full-text index have been registered and the table is now being set as ready for index population. A full-text index is activated by using the **sp_fulltext_table** stored procedure, as shown in the following code snippet:

```
sp_fulltext_table 'titles','activate'
```

After the index is activated, the catalog must be given a start command.

Starting The Index

A catalog must be given a command to begin the actual population of the index. This command is the stored procedure **sp_fulltext_catalog**. An example of a **fulltext_catalog** start is shown here:

```
sp_fulltext_catalog 'PubsCatalog', 'start_full'
```

This will start population of the **PubsCatalog** catalog with data from all the registered columns in all the registered tables assigned to the index catalog.

After the indexes are complete, queries can be performed that use the full-text search options.

Querying The Index

Finally, after all the other preliminary steps are taken care of, you can execute queries that make use of the index. This should not be done until the server has finished populating the index. This can be verified by using the following query:

```
select fulltextcatalogproperty ('catalog_name','PopulateStatus')
```

This query will return a binary value. A return value of **0** means that population of the index is complete. A return value of **1** means that the server is still in the process of populating the index.

To verify that specific columns have been full-text indexed, **ColumnProperty** can be queried, like this:

```
SELECT ColumnProperty ( Object_Id('table_name'),
                 'column_name', 'IsFullTextIndexed')
```

In the preceding example, a return value of **1** means that the column is part of the full-text index, and a value of **0** indicates that the column is not part of the full-text index. You can also verify which columns and tables are full-text indexed by using the following stored procedures:

➤ **sp_help_fulltext_catalogs** Provide the ID, name, rootdirectory, status, and the number of tables specified for the full-text catalog.

➤ **sp_help_fulltext_tables** Returns a list of tables that have been registered for full-text indexing.

➤ **sp_help_fulltext_columns** Returns a list of tables and columns that have been registered for full-text indexing.

Now that the catalogs have been created and populated, the next step is to make use of the full-text indexes by writing full-text queries that search for data in the full-text indexes.

Full-Text Query

The full-text query uses the indexes created for full-text search to locate the appropriate database records. The **SELECT** statement is used to perform full-text queries. SQL Server provides two predicates for implementing full-text queries: **CONTAINS** and **FREETEXT**.

CONTAINS

CONTAINS allows a full-text search to be performed on a word or a phrase for a given registered column. Keep in mind that, when you use the **CONTAINS** predicate, phrases must be enclosed in double quotation marks; if you perform a full-text search on a word, you do not need to enclose the word in double quotes. Further, the search condition can also be the first characters of a word followed by an asterisk (this is similar to using a wildcard). The syntax for using the **CONTAINS** predicate is as follows:

```
CONTAINS ({column_name|*}, 'search_condition')
```

An example of using **CONTAINS** to perform a full-text search for a word appears as follows:

```
SELECT Title, notes
FROM titles
WHERE CONTAINS (notes, 'Computer')
```

In the preceding example, the query asks to view all titles and notes columns in the title table, provided the notes column contains the word "Computer".

An example of using **CONTAINS** to perform a full-text search for a phrase looks like this:

```
SELECT title, notes
FROM titles
WHERE CONTAINS( notes, '"favorite recipes"')
```

In the preceding example, the query requests rows from the titles table provided that the notes column has the phrase "favorite recipes" embedded in it. And finally, using **CONTAINS** to perform a full-text search using the first characters of a word following by a wildcard looks like this:

```
SELECT title, notes
FROM titles
WHERE CONTAINS( notes, '"CO*"')
```

Note: This is one of the few places where the asterisk acts as a wildcard.

The preceding example will return rows from the titles table, provided the notes column contains a word that starts with the letters "CO".

Conducting Proximity Full-Text Searches

To provide more flexibility in searching, SQL Server also provides the ability to search for words that are used together in the same sentence or phrases. Full-text searches also allow you to search for words that are in close proximity to each other. To perform a proximity full-text search, you use the **NEAR()** function in the search clause. The **NEAR()** function takes no input parameters, but is flanked on either side by search phrases, as you can see in the following example:

```
SELECT title,notes
FROM titles
WHERE CONTAINS (notes, 'cooking near() computers')
```

The preceding example will return rows that have the words "cooking" and "computers" in close proximity to each other.

Searching For Singular And Plural Forms Of A Word

To search for words that have different variations, SQL Server provides the **FORMSOF()** function. The **FORMSOF()** function will search for both singular and plural forms of words (nouns and verbs). A single **FORMSOF()** function can work with nouns or verbs, but not both at the same time. The syntax for **FORMSOF()** is as follows:

```
FORMSOF(INFLECTIONAL, 'search phrase')
```

An example of using **FORMSOF()** looks like this:

```
SELECT title, notes
FROM titles
WHERE CONTAINS( notes, FORMSOF(INFLECTIONAL,'computer')
```

The preceding example will return rows that contain the word *computer* or forms of the word *computer* in the notes columns.

Weighting Search Clauses

You can assign certain words or phrases more importance in a query than others. SQL Server provides the **ISABOUT()** function in conjunction with the **WEIGHT()** function to grant some search clauses more weight than other clauses. The **ISABOUT()** function allows specification of the weighted keywords. The **WEIGHT()** function must also be provided with a decimal value from 0.0 through 1.0 as a weight factor. The syntax for using **ISABOUT()** and **WEIGHT()** is as follows:

```
ISABOUT ('search_phrase' weight(weight_factor,...)
```

An example of adding weight to a full-text search clause looks like this:

```
SELECT title
FROM titles
WHERE CONTAINS(title, 'ISABOUT ( cooking weight (.8),
computer weight (.4) )' )
```

The preceding example will return rows from the titles table that contain the word "cooking" or "computer". However, in this case, "cooking" is given more weight than "computer", so rows containing "cooking" will be ranked higher in value by the server.

Using Logical Operators

Search predicates , like **CONTAINS, FORMSOF()** and **ISABOUT()**, that are used for full-text search can be combined together via the use of the logical operators **AND, OR,** and **AND NOT.** The full-text predicates can also be used in conjuction with all other traditional predicates in the **SELECT** syntax. Following is an example of using logical operators in a full-text search. Rows will be returned, provided the titles mention "cooking", but not "computers" or "computer":

```
SELECT title_id, title, ytd_sales
FROM titles
WHERE CONTAINS( title,
' cooking AND NOT (computers OR computer)')
```

```
SELECT title_id, title, ytd_sales
FROM titles
WHERE CONTAINS( title, ' cooking AND NOT
FORMSOF(INFLECTIONAL, 'computer')')
```

FREETEXT

As an alternative to **CONTAINS**, you can use the **FREETEXT** predicate to conduct full-text searches. **FREETEXT** allows you to query a database based on a set of significant words found within the free-text string. SQL Server's full-text query engine will analyze the text and isolate all the significant words and noun phrases, and then it will generate the query based on those results. The syntax for the **FREETEXT** predicate is as follows:

```
FREETEXT ( 'column_name, 'search_text')
```

Following is an example showing the use of the **FREETEXT** predicate:

```
SELECT title FROM titles
WHERE FREETEXT (notes, 'The quick brown fox jumped over
the lazy dog ' )
```

In this example, titles will be returned from the titles table that contains words similar to those in the search_text phrase.

Practice Questions

Question 1

Which of the following statements are true about full-text queries? [Check all correct answers]

- ❏ a. Full-text queries can be performed with a FREETEXT clause.
- ❏ b. Full-text queries require a full-text index.
- ❏ c. Full-text queries can only be applied to registered columns.
- ❏ d. Full-text queries will only return exact matches.
- ❏ e. Full-text queries can be run by any user.

Answers a, b, c, and e are correct. Answer a is correct, because FREETEXT is a valid operator for full-text queries. Answer b is correct, because a full-text query will not function without a full-text index to search off of. Answer c is correct, because the only columns that can be searched via a full-text query can be registered columns. Answer e is correct, because there are no restrictions on the use of full-text queries. Answer d is incorrect, because options are available to generate less-specific results, such as use of the asterisk (*) as a wildcard in the text string and the **FORMSOF()** function.

Question 2

Which of the following statements are true about full-text indexes types? [Check all correct answers]

- ❏ a. Full-text indexes require at least a unique index on the respective tables.
- ❏ b. Full-text indexes can be implemented by any user.
- ❏ c. Full-text indexes are stored in the database.
- ❏ d. Full-text indexes are populated by **sp_fulltext_database**.
- ❏ e. Full-text indexes require a timestamp column.

Answer a is correct, because at least a unique index must exist on a table before it can be registered for full-text search. Answer b is incorrect, because a user must be at least a db_owner to implement full-text indexes. Answer c is incorrect, because the index is stored in the file system. Answer d is incorrect, because **sp_fulltext_catalog** is used to populate the index. Answer e is incorrect, because the index doesn't require a **timestamp** column unless the index is being populated incrementally.

Question 3

Consider the following statement:

```
Sp_fulltext_column 'authors','last_name','ADD'
```

What tasks must be completed first before this command can be run? [Check all correct answers]

❑ a. The full-text index must be started for population.

❑ b. The author's table must be registered for use with a full-text index.

❑ c. The full-text index option must be enabled for the database.

❑ d. A full-text catalog must be created for the index.

❑ e. The columns for the author's table must be registered for the full-text indexes.

The code example registers the last_name column from the authors table for use in a full-text index. Answer b is correct, because tables must be registered for full-text index before columns. Answer c is correct, because the full-text search option must be enabled before any command relating to full-text indexing is used. Answer d is correct, because before a column can be registered for full-text indexing, the catalog that stores the index must already exist. Answer a is incorrect, because before an index can start populating, it must first have all the necessary tables and columns registered to it. Answer e is incorrect because it does not answer the question—it merely states what the command will achieve.

Question 4

Examine the following query:

```
sp_fulltext_catalog 'author_catalog',
     'start_full'
```

Which of the following statements are true about full-text index types?

- ○ a. The full-text index will begin to populate for all rows that have changed.

- ○ b. The full-text index will begin to populate based on all the data in the registered columns.

- ○ c. The full-text index will be activated and ready for population.

- ○ d. The full-text index catalog author_catalog will be created.

- ○ e. The full-text index author_catalog table will be registered for the start_full index.

Answer b is correct, because the start_full option will start populating the index based on all the data in the registered columns. Answer a is incorrect, because index population based on changes is started with the start_incremental option. Answer c is incorrect, because the index should have been activated and ready for population before the code snippet was executed. Answer d is incorrect, because the author_catalog should have been created before population begins. Answer d is incorrect, because the code snippet has nothing to do with registration.

Need To Know More?

 Coffman, Gayle. *SQL Server 7: The Complete Reference*, Osborne/
McGraw-Hill, Berkley, CA, 1999. ISBN 0-07-882494-X. Chap-
ter 21 provides a complete T-SQL reference describing the
SELECT statement's full-text search options.

 MS SQL Server Books Online provides information about full
text search, look in the index for "select" or for "full-text search".

 Search the TechNet CD or its online version at **www.microsoft.com**.

 www.microsoft.com/sql
Find up-to-date information about using SQL Server here.

16

Monitoring

. . . .

Terms you'll need to understand:

✓ Showplan

✓ Optimizer

✓ Statistics

✓ Deadlock

✓ **dbcc showcontig**

Techniques you'll need to master:

✓ Using **SHOWPLAN**

✓ Updating statistics

✓ Diagnosing and resolving locking problems

✓ Using the SQL Server Profiler

After you develop a database application and have it implemented on the server, you should ensure that the application runs as efficiently as possible. Further, you should monitor and verify that SQL Server is also optimized for efficiency.

Microsoft provides several tools to help you look at the applications and queries that are being run by the server and the choices that SQL Server is using to run them, as well as tools to monitor the server to make sure the server is running at its best.

One way to optimize SQL Server is to make sure that queries are being performed as intended. When structures like indexes are created, they are used for increasing the performance of the application. The indexes are supposed to allow the SQL Server to locate data more efficiently. You can use SQL Server's Showplan statement to get a peek at what kind of choices the SQL Server is making. This can indicate whether or not an index is being used and why. These results can be helpful in improving query design and making queries as efficient as possible. This can also be used to help determine whether any new indexes need to be created.

Showplan

A Showplan statement can be used before an ad hoc query is executed to estimate the I/O cost of a query before it is run. This could prevent a badly developed query (such as one that produces a Cartesian product or returns too many rows) from being executed before the problem is corrected.

SQL Server provides two versions of the Showplan statement:

➤ **SET SHOWPLAN_TEXT**

➤ **SET SHOWPLAN_ALL**

Further, you can work with SQL Server's graphical version of Showplan in the SQL Query Analyzer.

> The new SHOWPLAN_TEXT and SHOWPLAN_ALL settings will display information about SQL Server's approach to resolving the query. Microsoft has added many new query processing plans to SQL Server 7—users should familiarize themselves with them.

SHOWPLAN_TEXT

This Showplan statement displays output as message text in most query editors like isql or the SQL Query Analyzer and provides information about how SQL Server will approach a query. Showplan will not display unless the option is set to **ON**, via a command used to toggle the option **ON** or **OFF** in isql, SQL Query Analyzer, or another script editor.

The syntax for using the **SHOWPLAN_TEXT** option is:

```
SET SHOWPLAN_TEXT [ON|OFF]
```

Listing 16.1 illustrates a run of a query when SHOWPLAN_TEXT has been turned on.

Listing 16.1   Set **SHOWPLAN_TEXT** query and results.

```
StmtText
-----------------------------------------------
select * from titles
where title_id = 'BU1111'


(1 row(s) affected)

StmtText
-----------------------------------------------
  |--Clustered Index Seek(pubs..titles.UPKCL_titleidind,
     SEEK:(titles.title_id=@1) ORDERED)
```

Listing 16.1 indicates that the query executed was **select * from titles where title_id = 'BU1111'**. It also indicates that the optimizer chose to use a clustered index seek to resolve the query. The index name is indicated by **UPKCL_titleidind**, which is the name of the clustered index on the titles table.

SHOWPLAN_ALL

Like **SHOWPLAN_TEXT**, the **SHOWPLAN_ALL** option provides users with detailed information about what SQL Server detects about a query and how the server intends to execute the query. However, **SHOWPLAN_ALL** should be used during runtime execution, while **SHOWPLAN_TEXT** is used when interpreting query plans on an ad hoc basis. When **SHOWPLAN_ALL** is turned on, you receive a table containing the query plan information. The tabular information will be easier to format and parse than the text-based output from **SHOWPLAN_TEXT**. As long as the **SHOWPLAN_ALL** option is turned on, queries will only be analyzed and not executed. To execute queries, you must ensure that **SHOWPLAN_ALL** is turned off.

The columns in the **SHOWPLAN_ALL** output table are:

➤ **StmtText** Contains the original SQL query analyzed by **SHOWPLAN**. This column will also contain **PLAN_ROWS**. The **PLAN_ROWS** option contains descriptions of the SQL Server's approach to a query.

This will indicate whether the Server decided to use a tablescan or chose to use an index.

➤ **StmtId** Indicates the number of the statement in the current batch. If the batch has multiple statements, the number will exceed **1**.

➤ **NodeId** Displays the node ID in the current query.

➤ **Parent** Displays the node ID or the parent step if the row is a child of a parent.

➤ **PhysicalOp** Describes the physical implementation used to execute the query. This is only used for **PLAN_ROWS**.

➤ **LogicalOp** Describes the Logical implementation used to execute the query. **LogicalOp** is only used for **PLAN_ROWS**.

➤ **Argument** Displays more detailed information about the query operation based on the search arguments in the query.

➤ **DefinedValues** Displays the list of values that will be used by the query. This includes columns specified in **SELECT** and **WHERE** clauses. **DefinedValues** is only used for **PLAN_ROWS**.

➤ **EstimateRows** Displays the number of output rows estimated by the SQL Server for the **PLAN_ROW**.

➤ **EstimateIO** Displays the estimated I/O to be performed on the query based on the **PLAN_ROW**.

➤ **EstimateCPU** Shows the estimated CPU cost for the **PLAN_ROW**.

➤ **AvgRowSize** Provides an estimated size of the return row.

➤ **TotalSubtreeCost** Supplies an estimated cost of the query. This is a cumulative value.

➤ **OutputList** Lists the columns to be output by the query.

➤ **Warnings** Lists the warning messages for the query.

➤ **Type** Specifies the node type for the query. This value can describe the type of query (such as **SELECT, INSERT, DELETE,** or **EXECUTE**), or, for **PLAN_ROWs**, it displays **PLAN_ROW**.

The syntax for **SHOWPLAN_ALL** is:

```
SET SHOWPLAN_ALL [ON|OFF]
```

Update Statistics

SQL Server uses an optimizer to develop the best, most I/O cost efficient way to execute queries. In order for **SHOWPLAN** and the optimizer to produce query estimates, some information must be handed to SQL Server that describes the data and the data's distribution. This information is stored in the statistics pages when an index is created. In an actively changing table, this information can become outdated. With outdated information in the statistics tables, the optimizer might make the wrong choices regarding query optimization, because the statistics produce inaccurate estimates.

To keep the optimizer running at its best, the table statistics should be optimized regularly. Although this was a scheduled task of the system administrator in earlier versions of SQL Server, the task has been automated in SQL Server 7. By default, the statistics are updated automatically by taking periodic random samples of the data from the table. The period is based on the size of the table and its rate of growth. If the sampled data does not seem to be producing the right query plans, then the defaults may be bypassed by running the **UPDATE STATISTICS** command manually. Listing 16.2 shows the SQL syntax used to update table statistics.

Listing 16.2   Syntax for **UPDATE STATISTICS**.

```
UPDATE STATISTICS {table_name}
[index_name | (index_or_column_list
[, ...n])
]
[WITH
[[FULLSCAN]| SAMPLE number {PERCENT | ROWS}]]
[[,] [ALL | COLUMNS | INDEX]
[[,] NORECOMPUTE]
]
```

With the **UPDATE STATISTICS** statement, the user is given many options on how the statistics can be updated. These choices range from2 choosing a table and all of its indexes or if it takes too long, an **UPDATE STATISTICS** command can be given for a specific index. The following elaborates on some of the options available in the **UPDATE STATISTICS** statement syntax shown in Listing 16.2:

➤ FULLSCAN The **FULLSCAN** option forces the SQL Server to perform a full scan of an index or table when gathering statistics. Performing a **FULLSCAN** on a table or index can be time intensive. An alternative to scanning an entire table or index is to choose a sample size.

➤ **SAMPLE** Rather than forcing SQL Server to base its statistics on a complete table, you can instruct SQL Server to build new statistics pages based on a sample of table data. The sample size can be entered as a percent or as a defined number of rows.

➤ **ALL|COLUMNS|INDEX** By default, the **UPDATE STATISTICS** command will affect only the statistics for indexes. The **UPDATE STATISTICS** command also allows you to update **COLUMNS**, **INDEX**, or both **INDEX** and **COLUMNS**, via the **ALL** keyword.

➤ **NORECOMPUTE** This option disables the ability to perform automatic updates for statistics via the **sp_autostats** stored procedure.

Sp_updatestats

In prior versions of SQL Server, each table required an individual **UPDATE STATISTICS** statement. The sp_updatestats stored procedure runs the **UPDATE STATISTICS** command for all user tables in the current database. Only users with the SA_ROLE and database owners can use this procedure.

Sp_autostats

In the past, updating statistics was a scheduled task for the system administrator. In SQL Server 7, the statistics are set to update automatically; this can be modified by using the **sp_autostats** stored procedure. The **sp_autostats** procedure can disable and re-enable automatic statistics updating on a table or a specific index for the table. The syntax for using **sp_autostats** to configure the automatic updating of statistics is:

```
sp_autostats 'table_name' [,'ON'|'OFF']['index_name']
```

 In the past, updating statistics was a very resource-intensive task. As such, it was normally performed when there were relatively few processes running on the server. This is still the case. The only way to reduce this load is to base the statistics on a sample of the data rather than the whole table. While this takes fewer resources to update the statistics and can potentially allow statistics to be updated during peak usage times, the statistics data will not be a truly complete representation of the data distribution. This could still affect the optimizer's ability to accurately judge query plans. In this case, the alternative is to schedule an update statistics command with the fullscan option during scheduled low usage periods.

Detecting And Resolving Locking Problems

By default, data accessed for reading or modification is locked by the server in 8K pages. This form of locking can produce contention problems in which many users are attempting to lock on to the same page of data and potential deadlock situations that will abort some users' transactions.

SQL Server uses many type of locks to hold onto data. Shared locks can be assigned for selecting data. Exclusive locks can be assigned when deleting data. To determine what kinds of locks are being used, run the **sp_lock** and **sp_who** stored procedures. The combined procedures can help to determine if any processes are being blocked, by whom, and why. Output of the **sp_lock** stored procedure includes the following columns:

➤ **Spid** System Process ID

➤ **Dbid** Database ID

➤ **ObjID** Object ID

➤ **IndID** Index ID

➤ **Type** Lock Type

➤ **Resource** Displays information about the lock resource that is stored in the syslockinfo.res text table.

➤ **Mode** Lock mode. Valid modes include:

   ➤ **S** Shared

   ➤ **U** Update

   ➤ **E** Exclusive

   ➤ **IS** Intent Shared

   ➤ **IX** Intent Exclusive

   ➤ **SIX** Shared with Intent Exclusive

➤ **Status** Lock request status, such as **GRANT WAIT** or **CONVERT**

Listing 16.3 displays a sample of output from an **sp_lock** execution.

Listing 16.3   Sample sp_lock output.

```
spid  dbid  ObjId       IndId  Type  Resource         Mode    Status
----  ----  ----------  -----  ----  --------------   ------  ------
1     1     0           0      DB                     S       GRANT
6     1     0           0      DB                     S       GRANT
7     1     0           0      DB                     S       GRANT
8     1     0           0      DB                     S       GRANT
9     1     0           0      DB                     S       GRANT
9     2     0           0      DB                     S       GRANT
9     5     0           0      DB                     S       GRANT
9     5     261575970   1      PAG   1:103            IS      GRANT
9     1     117575457   0      TAB                    IS      GRANT
9     5     261575970   0      TAB                    IS      GRANT
9     5     261575970   1      KEY   (42b753b5aa62)   IS-S    GRANT
9     5.    261575970   1      KEY   (45b852b7aa62)   IS-S    GRANT
10    5     0           0      DB                     S       GRANT
10    5     261575970   1      PAG   1:103            IS      GRANT
10    5     261575970   0      TAB                    IS      GRANT
10    5     261575970   1      KEY   (42b753b5aa62)   IS-S    GRANT
10    5     261575970   1      KEY   (45bc55b3aa64)   IS-S    GRANT
```

sp_lock output can be used in conjunction with the sp_who stored procedure to determine who has been granted locks and whether they are blocking the processes of other users.

The sp_who stored procedure outputs the following columns (see sample output in Listing 16.4):

➤ **spid** System Process ID

➤ **status** Process Status

➤ **loginame** Login of user running the process

➤ **hostname** Hostname or name of system calling the process

➤ **blk** Process ID that is preventing completion of the current process

➤ **dbname** Name of database used in the process

➤ **cmd** Type of SQL Server command executing the process

Listing 16.4   Sample sp_who output.

```
spid status     loginame             hostname blk dbname cmd
--  ---------   -----------------    -------- -- ------ ----------------
1   sleeping    sa                            0  master SIGNAL HANDLER
2   sleeping    sa                            0  pubs   LOCK MONITOR
3   sleeping    sa                            0  pubs   LAZY WRITER
4   sleeping    sa                            0  pubs   LOG WRITER
```

```
5  sleeping   sa                              0  pubs    CHECKPOINT SLEEP
6  background sa                              0  pubs    AWAITING COMMAND
7  sleeping   NT AUTHORITY\SYSTEM TENCHI 0  master  AWAITING COMMAND
8  sleeping   NT AUTHORITY\SYSTEM TENCHI 0  master  AWAITING COMMAND
9  sleeping   user1               KIYONE 10 pubs    UPDATE
10 runnable   user2               KIYONE 0  pubs    SELECT
```

In Listings 16.3 and 16.4, process 9 is being blocked by process 10. This means that user1 who is running process 9 must wait until the resources being held by process 10 are released.

Deadlocking

Deadlocking is a situation where two processes block each other. The two processes each have resources that the other wants, but can't receive them until the opposing process releases them, as displayed in Figure 16.1.

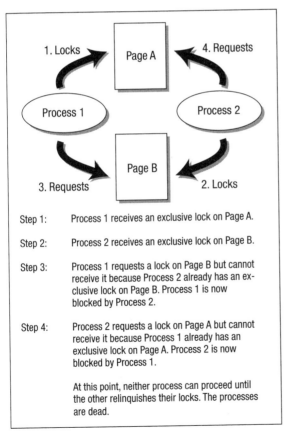

Figure 16.1   Deadlock diagram.

SQL Server detects deadlocks by looking for circular chains of lock requests. If a deadlock is discovered, one of the two locking processes will be declared a victim and be aborted. The other process will move to completion. The victim generates an Error 1205 and the server sends the victim a deadlock message stating that the transaction will have to be rerun. If this occurs in a stored procedure, the return code is **-3**. Applications developed for SQL Server should be designed to react to these error codes.

By default, SQL chooses the least-expensive transaction as the victim. However, a session can be configured to be a victim by using the **SET DEADLOCK_PRIORITY LOW** command. Setting **DEADLOCK_PRIORITY** to normal resets the default deadlock response. The syntax for using the **DEADLOCK_PRIORITY** option is:

```
SET DEADLOCK_PRIORITY {[LOW]|[NORMAL]}
```

dbcc showcontig

The **dbcc showcontig** is a command that will analyze the fragmentation of storage for the data and indexes. Fragmentation occurs when the SQL Server is forced to store data pages out of a contiguous sequence; this may happen when table pages are split when data is added to full existing pages. This can also happen to index pages as well. The output from **dbcc showcontig** can be used to find fragmentation and to correct it. Correction can be performed by dropping and recreating a clustered index for the table.

The syntax for **dbcc showcontig** is as follows:

```
dbcc showcontig [ ( table_id [, index_id] )]
```

The object id number for the table is **table_id**, and the object id number for the index is **index_id**.

Listing 16.5 presents an execution of **dbcc showcontig** for a table called rawdata with its associated output.

Listing 16.5   Sample dbcc showcontig output.

```
dbcc showcontig (197575742)
DBCC SHOWCONTIG scanning 'lookup' table...
Table: 'lookup' (309576141); index ID: 1, database ID: 8
TABLE level scan performed.
- Pages Scanned................................: 38
- Extents Scanned..............................: 5
- Extent Switches..............................: 4
- Avg. Pages per Extent........................: 7.6
```

```
- Scan Density [Best Count:Actual Count].......: 100.00% [5:5]
- Logical Scan Fragmentation ...................: 0.00%
- Extent Scan Fragmentation ....................: 20.00%
- Avg. Bytes Free per Page.....................: 199.3
- Avg. Page Density (full)....................: 97.54%
```

The output fields from **dbcc showcontig** are described as follows:

➤ **Pages Scanned**   Number of pages in the table or index.

➤ **Extents Scanned**   Number of extents in the table or index.

➤ **Extent Switches**   Number of times the **dbcc showcontig** statement moved from one extent to another while it traversed the pages of the table or index.

➤ **Avg. Pages per Extent**   Number of pages per extent in the page chain.

➤ **Scan Density**   [Best Count: Actual Count] The ideal number of extent changes if everything is contiguously linked.

➤ **Logical Scan Fragmentation**   Percentage of out-of-order pages returned when scanning the leaf pages of an index.

➤ **Extent Scan Fragmentation**   Percentage of out-of-order pages when scanning the leaf pages of an index.

➤ **Avg. Bytes Free per Page**   Average number of free bytes on the pages scanned.

➤ **Avg. Page Density (full)**   Indicates as a percentage how full the pages are.

The preceding listing shows that the table was 38 pages long and a total of 5 extents were scanned. The scan density report shows that the table rated at 100%, because the best estimate matched the actual count [5:5]. This table requires no additional modification.

SQL Server Profiler

SQL Server 7 comes packaged with a product called SQL Server Profiler. The Profiler is a monitoring tool that allows administrators to monitor predefined events, like login attempts, connections and disconnections to the server, the execution of T-SQL batches, and the monitoring of deadlocks.

SQL Server Profiler can create trace files or data-storage tables on the server. If the data is stored in tables on the SQL Server, then the Profiler can replay the stored queries to assist in analysis of problem queries. The Profiler is a tool supplied in the Enterprise Manager and can be located in the Tools menu. It can also be found in the SQL Server 7 group on the Start menu.

Practice Questions

Question 1

By default, how often are statistics updated?

○ a. Once a day

○ b. Once a week

○ c. Once a year

○ d. With each SQL statement

○ e. Never

Answer e is correct. By default, statistics pages are created at index-creation time. However, these pages are not updated until the **UPDATE STATISTICS** command is actually performed for a table or index. The default can be overridden by using the sp_autostats stored procedure. Answers a, b, c, and d are incorrect, because, by default, statistics pages are never automatically updated.

Question 2

By default, what statistics get updated with an **UPDATE STATISTICS** statement?

○ a. Indexes

○ b. Columns

○ c. Rows

○ d. Indexes and columns

○ e. Indexes, columns, and rows

Answer a is correct. By default, **UPDATE STATISTICS** only updates **INDEX** statistics. Answers b, c, d, and e are incorrect, because **UPDATE STATISTICS** does not update columns and rows by default.

Question 3

What kind of lock is described by the following sp_lock output?

```
spid  dbid  ObjId      IndId  Type Resource
      Mode   Status
----  ----  ---------- ------ ---- ---------- ---
      ---   ------
9     5     261575970  1      PAG  1:103
      IS    GRANT
```

○ a. An exclusive lock on the entire table

○ b. An exclusive lock on a page

○ c. A shared lock on a page

○ d. An intent shared lock on a page

○ e. An intent shared lock on a table

Answer d is correct, because the mode is IS for intent shared lock and the type is PAG for page. All other answers refer to the wrong types of lock.

Question 4

Which of the following takes place when a deadlock occurs? [Check all correct answers]

❑ a. Only one process is blocking another process

❑ b. Two processes are blocking each other

❑ c. One process will be declared a victim

❑ d. A 1205 error will be returned

❑ e. -1 will be returned by the stored procedure

The correct answers are b, c, and d. Answer b is correct, because a deadlock is caused when at least two processes block each other. Answer c is correct, because when a deadlock is discovered by the server, the process with the least amount of CPU time will be declared the victim and aborted. Answer d is correct, because when a deadlock is detected, an error code of 1205 is returned to the error handler. Answer a is incorrect, because two processes are required to block each other for a deadlock. Answer e is incorrect, because the appropriate value returned by a stored procedure is -3.

Question 5

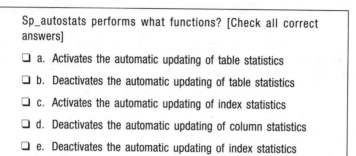

Sp_autostats performs what functions? [Check all correct answers]

❑ a. Activates the automatic updating of table statistics

❑ b. Deactivates the automatic updating of table statistics

❑ c. Activates the automatic updating of index statistics

❑ d. Deactivates the automatic updating of column statistics

❑ e. Deactivates the automatic updating of index statistics

Answers a, b, c, and e are correct; all are standard functions of the sp_autostats stored procedure. Answer d is incorrect, because the sp_autostats does not specifically address columns.

Need To Know More?

 Amo, William C. *Transact-SQL*, IDG Books Worldwide, Foster City, CA, 1998. ISBN 0-7645-8048-5. Chapter 17 describes the SQL Server Profiler.

 Coffman, Gayle. *SQL Server 7: The Complete Reference*, Osborne/McGraw-Hill, Berkley, CA, 1999. ISBN 0-07-882494-X. Chapter 17 describes SQL Profiler and SQL Server Performance Monitor. Chapter 21 provides a complete T-SQL reference.

 McGehee, Brad and Matthew Shepker. *Using Microsoft SQL Server 7.0*, QUE, Indianapolis, Indiana, 1998. ISBN 0-7897-1628-3. Chapter 10 describes what SQL Server items should be monitored.

 MS SQL Server Books Online contains information about monitoring, look in the index under "monitoring".

 Search the TechNet CD or its online version at **www.microsoft.com**.

 www.microsoft.com/sql
Find up-to-date information about using SQL Server here.

Remote Data Access

. . . .

Terms you'll need to understand:

✓ Remote procedure call (RPC)

✓ Distributed transaction

✓ Distributed query

✓ Linked server

✓ Fully qualified object name

✓ Rowset

✓ Friendly name

✓ Distributed Transaction Service

✓ Resource manager

✓ Transaction manager

✓ Two-phase commit

Techniques you'll need to master:

✓ Executing remote procedure calls

✓ Understanding the differences between an RPC and a distributed query

✓ Accessing remote data through linked servers

✓ Accessing remote data through ad hoc queries

✓ Understanding data conversions that take place in distributed queries

Most of the time, all the data a database application needs to access resides in one SQL Server. However, sometimes data is stored in multiple SQL Servers, or the data is stored in a medium other than in a SQL Server. Microsoft SQL Server provides two ways to access data that does not reside in a single SQL Server: remote procedure calls and distributed queries. Both ways of accessing remote data do so using a distributed query.

Remote Procedure Call

A remote procedure call, or RPC, is used to access data that resides on another SQL Server. RPCs are a legacy feature of SQL Server and cannot access data that is not stored in a SQL Server.

 SQL Server 7 can receive remote procedure calls from SQL Server 4.2a or higher. However, SQL Server 7 can only make remote procedure calls to SQL Server version 6 and higher.

To create a remote procedure call, the system administrator has to configure both servers to communicate with each other. After the servers have been configured, you can execute a remote stored procedure by using its fully qualified stored procedure name. Following is the syntax for a remote procedure call:

```
[exec[ute]]
    server_name.[database_name].[owner].stored_procedure
    [parameters[, parameter . . . ]]
```

A remote stored procedure can be used in SQL anywhere that a local stored procedure can be used. That is, a remote stored procedure can be:

➤ In a batch by itself

➤ Mixed with other queries in a batch

➤ Called inside of a stored procedure

➤ Added as an **EXECUTE** statement in an **INSERT** statement

The following example illustrates how to call a remote stored procedure:

```
exec MyOtherServer...sp_who
```

The previous example illustrates the simplest way to call a remote stored procedure. In this example, the system stored procedure, **sp_who**, is executed on the **MyOtherServer** server with no parameters. Here's another example:

```
insert Names execute
   MyOtherServer.pubs.joe.RetrieveAuthorNames
        @parm1 = 'A'
```

This example uses an RPC to retrieve data to insert into a table called Names. The **RetrieveAuthorNames** procedure, owned by **joe**, in the **pubs** database on **MyOtherServer**, is executed with the parameter **@parm1** being set to 'A'.

Any action that can be achieved in a local stored procedure can be achieved in a remote stored procedure. Therefore, you can use an RPC to execute any procedure on a remote server that you could execute if you logged directly onto the server. RPCs can return data using the standard three mechanisms that a local stored procedure can use:

➤ **Result sets** Records and individual values

➤ **Output parameters** One set of values for the procedure

➤ **Return status reports to the calling SQL Server** One integer value

Listing 17.1 shows a stored procedure that returns data with a result set, output parameters, a return status, and the SQL to execute it.

Listing 17.1   Remote procedure.

```
-- execute on the remote server in tempdb
CREATE PROC SysObjName
   @NumObj INT OUTPUT
as
SELECT name FROM sysobjects
   WHERE type = 'S'
SELECT @NumObj = @@ROWCOUNT
RETURN -30000
Go
--execute on the local server
declare @RetCnt int,
   @result int
exec @result = MyRemoteServer.tempdb..myp1 @RetCnt output
select ReturnStatus = @result, OutputParm =@RetCount
go


-- The following is the result set
name
----------
sysobjects
sysindexes
syscolumns
```

```
systypes
syscomments
sysfiles1
syspermissions
sysusers
sysdepends
sysreferences
sysfulltextcatalogs
sysindexkeys
sysforeignkeys
sysmembers
sysprotects
sysfiles
sysfilegroups
sysallocations

-- The following is the return status and the output parameter
ReturnStatus  OutputParm
------------  ----------
-30000        18
```

Distributed Queries

With distributed queries, SQL Server provides a method to access data in any data source using an OLE DB provider. This means that you can access data from any OLE DB data source. A distributed query allows you to access data in one or more remote data sources as if the data is a local table. Distributed queries differ from RPCs in a couple of key ways:

➤ Unlike an RPC, a distributed query can access data from multiple data sources in the same query.

➤ A distributed query performs a SQL statement on the local server that affects the data on the remote server.

Before using distributed queries, the connection must have the **ANSI_NULLS** and **ANSI_WARNINGS** options turned on, as in the following code snippet:

```
SET ANSI_NULLS ON
SET ANSI_WARNINGS ON
```

Although data sources queried through distributed queries are usually databases, OLE DB providers exist for a wide variety of files and file formats, including text files and spreadsheet data. If an OLE DB provider has not been created for your specific data source, you can probably use the OLE DB provider for ODBC to access your data source.

Linked Server

A *linked server* is a preconfigured OLE DB data source. The linked server can be referenced in SQL statements using the fully qualified object name. Before using a linked server, you must first configure the local SQL Server to access the remote OLE DB data source. The fully qualified object name is:

```
ServerName.DatabaseName.ObjectOwner.ObjectName
```

The following example illustrates a linked server being referenced in a **SELECT** statement:

```
SELECT * FROM OtherServer.SalesDB.dbo.Sale
```

Besides using the remote server name in a fully qualified object name, the linked server name can also be specified in an **OPENQUERY** function, which is covered later in this chapter. The **OPENQUERY** function can return a rowset that can be used in place of a table or view in SQL statements.

 A rowset is a set of rows that contains columns of data. Rowsets are central objects that OLE DB data providers use to return result set data in tabular form.

The main benefits of a link server include the following:

➤ A linked server provides remote data access.

➤ A linked server allows you to use distributed queries and transactions on heterogeneous data sources.

➤ A linked server allows you to access multiple heterogeneous data sources the same way.

OPENQUERY Function

The **OPENQUERY** function is used to execute a pass-through query at an OLE DB data source. The **OPENQUERY** function's syntax is as follows:

```
OPENQUERY(linked_server, 'query')
```

The parameters in the **OPENSERVER** function are the linked server's name and the query to execute. To use the **OPENSERVER** function, the local SQL Server must first be configured to access the linked server. The following example illustrates the use of the **OPENQUERY** function to perform a **SELECT** statement on a linked server:

```
SELECT *
FROM OPENQUERY(OtherSvr,
        'SELECT au_lname, au_fname FROM pubs..authors')
```

Ad Hoc Distributed Queries

If you have not predefined your remote data source, you can still access the remote data with an ad hoc distributed query using the **OPENROWSET** function. When using the **OPENROWSET** function, you specify the information needed to connect to the linked server. The rowset can then be referenced the same way as a table is referenced. The **OPENROWSET** syntax is as follows:

```
OPENROWSET('provider_name'
   {'datasource';'user_id';'password' | 'provider_string' },
   {[catalog.][schema.]object | 'query'})
```

As you can see in the preceding code syntax, the **OPENROWSET** function is passed all the information necessary to connect to a remote data source. The arguments are:

➤ **'provider_name'** Specifies a character string that represents the registered name of the OLE DB provider, as specified in the Registry. This is also called a "friendly" name.

➤ **'datasource'** Specifies a string that corresponds to a particular OLE DB data source. This string's format is specific to the OLE DB data source.

➤ **'user_id'** Specifies the username that is passed to the specified OLE DB provider.

➤ **'password'** Specifies the password that is associated with the 'user_id'.

➤ **'provider_string'** Specifies the provider-specific connection information needed to initialize the OLE DB datasource.

➤ **catalog** Specifies the name of the catalog or database that the ad hoc query will be accessing.

➤ **schema** Specifies the name of the schema or object owner.

➤ **object** Specifies the object name.

➤ **'query'** Identifies the query that is sent to and executed by the provider.

If the query returns multiple result sets, the **OPENROWSET** function will only return the first result set.

Data Conversion

When accessing remote data, the data will be converted to and from the local SQL Server's data type and code page. When retrieving data with a **SELECT, UPDATE, INSERT,** or **DELETE,** the remote data will be converted to the local SQL Server's data types and code page. When modifying data with an **INSERT** or **UPDATE,** the local SQL Server's data will be converted to the remote data source's data type and code page.

If the code page of the remote data is different than the local server's code page, the query results may be meaningless. For this discussion, let's look at the following query:

```
SELECT FirstName, LastName
    FROM OtherDataSource.DBName.ObjectOwner.PersonNames
    WHERE PersonKey = 'ABC'
    ORDER BY LastName, FirstName
```

If the remote data source has a different code page than the local SQL Server's code page, the comparison in the **WHERE** clause may not have the results you expect. If you run the preceding query on a remote server, it will return any row in which **PersonKey** is equal to 'ABC'. If you run the query on the local SQL Server, **PersonKey** will be converted to the local code page before the comparison takes place.

Distributed Query Limitations

SQL Server has a number of rules and limitations that come into effect when using distributed queries. The OLE DB provider can further limit the SQL that can be used by not supporting the complete OLE DB functionality. The following list contains SQL Server's distributed query rules and limitations:

➤ **SELECT** statements that only have **SELECT, FROM,** and **WHERE** clauses are allowed in a distributed query.

➤ The **INTO** clause is allowed as long as the table being created is on the local SQL Server.

➤ If the **select_list** contains a BLOB column from a remote table, the **SELECT** statement cannot contain an **ORDER BY** clause.

➤ The local SQL statement cannot reference remote BLOB columns with **IS NULL** and **IS NOT NULL.**

➤ All **INSERT, UPDATE,** and **DELETE** statements that modify data on the remote data server must meet the OLE DB data modification requirements.

➤ When accessing a remote table with a cursor, the **WHERE CURRENT OF** update and delete clause can only be used if the OLE DB provides the functionality.

➤ **READTEXT, WRITETEXT,** and **UPDATETEXT** are not supported against remote tables.

➤ **CREATE, ALTER,** and **DROP** statements cannot be used against remote servers.

➤ **STATIC** or **INSENSITIVE** cursors can reference remote tables.

➤ **KEYSET** cursors can reference remote tables only if the OLE DB provider meets the requirements documented in **KEYSET** cursor functionality.

➤ You cannot use **FORWARD-ONLY** cursor to reference a remote table.

 Although both remote procedure calls and distributed queries can access data in a remote SQL Server, Microsoft recommends that you use distributed queries when accessing remote data.

Distributed Transactions

When a transaction accesses data on two or more servers, the transaction is known as a *distributed transaction*. There are two main components in a distributed transaction: the resource manager and the transaction manager. A SQL Server (version 6.5 or greater) can participate in a distributed transaction with another SQL Server (version 6.5 or greater) or any data source that complies with the X/Open XA specification for distributed transaction processing.

 A transaction within a single SQL Server that spans two or more databases is actually a distributed transaction. In this case, SQL Server manages the distributed transaction.

Resource Manager

Resource managers are the servers that contain the data being accessed in the distributed query. A resource manager provides the resources to resolve part of a distributed transaction. SQL Server can operate as a resource manager in a distributed transaction that complies with the X/Open XA specification for distributed transaction processing.

Transaction Manager

The transaction manager coordinates a transaction across resource managers. Microsoft Distributed Transaction Coordinator (MS DTC), or any transaction manager that supports the X/Open XA specification for distributed transaction processing, can be a transaction manager in a distributed transaction. The transaction manager coordinates the transaction with the resource managers to ensure that the complete transaction is committed or rolled back together.

> *Note: If the transaction manager is not running, you cannot start a distributed transaction.*

Two-Phase Commit

A distributed transaction is treated similarly to a local transaction. When the transaction is complete, the application must issue a commit or a rollback transaction statement. The transaction manager then coordinates the commit or rollback transaction statement using a two-part process, called a *two-phase commit*. The two-phase commit consists of a prepare phase and a commit phase.

Prepare Phase

In the prepare phase, the transaction manager sends a prepare command to all the resource managers that are taking part in the distributed transaction. The resource managers then prepare the transaction so that it can be committed or rolled back. The resource managers then notify the transaction manager that they have completed the prepare phase. If any resource manager cannot complete the prepare request, the transaction is rolled back.

Commit Phase

After all the resource managers notify the transaction manager that the prepare phase is completed, the transaction manager notifies the resource managers to commit or roll back the transaction. If any resource manager cannot complete the transaction, the transaction is rolled back.

SQL Server In Distributed Transactions

There are several ways in which SQL Server can be included in a distributed transaction:

➤ If a local transaction is active and a distributed query is issued, the local transaction will be converted to a distributed transaction. The following code snippet illustrates a local transaction escalating to a distributed transaction:

```
BEGIN TRANSACTION
GO
UPDATE authors SET contract = 1
GO -- at this point it is a local transaction
UPDATE MyServer.Pubs.dbo.authos SET contract = 1
GO -- this transaction is now escalated
   -- to a distributed transaction
COMMIT TRANSACTION
GO
```

➤ A distributed transaction can be explicitly started with the **BEGIN DISTRIBUTED TRANSACTION** statement.

➤ Remote procedure calls can escalate a local transaction to a distributed transaction.

➤ ODBC or OLE-DB methods can be used to start a distributed transaction.

The SQL Server in which the distributed transaction is initiated is the transaction originator and controls the completion of the transaction. After the distributed transaction is initiated, when a **COMMIT TRANSACTION** or **ROLLBACK TRANSACTION** statement is issued for the connection, the controlling server requests the transaction manager to complete the distributed transaction across all resource managers involved.

BEGIN DISTRIBUTED TRANSACTION

The **BEGIN DISTRIBUTED TRANSACTION** statement is used to explicitly start a distributed transaction. The **BEGIN DISTRIBUTED TRANSACTION** syntax statement is as follows:

```
BEGIN DISTRIBUTED TRAN[SACTION]
        [transaction_name | @tran_name_variable]
```

RPCs Escalating Transaction

When executing an RPC inside of a local transaction, SQL Server can be configured so the local transaction escalates to a distributed transaction. The **sp_configure** stored procedure is used to configure SQL Server. The **sp_configure** syntax used to configure SQL Server's remote procedure escalation is as follows:

```
sp_configure "remote proc trans", [1 | 0]
```

If the **remote proc trans** option of **sp_configure** is set to **0**, then a remote procedure call inside of a local transaction does not escalate to a distributed transaction. If the **remote proc trans** option of **sp_configure** is set to **1**, then a remote procedure call inside of a local transaction will escalate to a distributed transaction.

 Remember to issue the **reconfigure** command after configuring SQL Server; otherwise, the configuration changes will not take effect.

Practice Questions

Question 1

In the following **SELECT** statement, what are the names of the tables being accessed? [Check all correct answers]

```
select * from sales..thisyear cross join
    old.othersales.joe.lastweek
```

❑ a. thisyear

❑ b. lastweek

❑ c. sales

❑ d. old

❑ e. joe

The correct answers are a and b. The **SELECT** statement accesses the **thisyear** and **lastweek** tables. Answer c is incorrect, because **sales** is the name of a database. Answer d is incorrect, because **old** is the name of the remote server. Answer e is incorrect, because **joe** is the owner of the **lastweek** table.

Question 2

Which of the following SQL batches will run a distributed transaction?
[Check all correct answers]

❏ a.
```
begin transaction
go
delete table1
go
update MyServer.dbo.Mytable set Column1 = 1234
go
commit transaction
go
```

❏ b.
```
sp_configure 'remote proc tran',1
reconfigure
go
exec Server2.mydb.myproc
go
```

❏ c.
```
begin distributed transaction
go
update server2.pubs..authors set contract = 1
go
commit transaction
go
```

❏ d.
```
begin transaction
go
delete mydb..table1
delete m2.mydb..table2
go
rollback transaction
go
```

The correct answers are c and d. Answer c explicitly starts a distributed transaction. Answer b implicitly starts a distributed transaction by accessing a remote data source while a transaction is in progress. Answer a is incorrect, because, in the **UPDATE** statement, **MyServer** is a database name, not a remote server name. Therefore, there is no distributed transaction. Answer b is incorrect, because, even though the server is configured to automatically escalate local transactions to a distributed transaction when an RPC is issued, a local transaction was not in effect when the RPC was issued.

Question 3

The **OPENQUERY** function is used to do which of the following?

- O a. The **OPENQUERY** function is used to modify data on a remote server.
- O b. The **OPENQUERY** function is used to execute an RPC.
- O c. The **OPENQUERY** function is used to make an ad hoc connection to an OLE DB data source.
- O d. The **OPENQUERY** function is used to access predefined remote data sources.
- O e. All of the above.

The correct answer is c. The **OPENQUERY** function is used for ad hoc queries against remote data sources. Answer a is incorrect, because the **OPENQUERY** function does not directly modify data. Answer b is incorrect, because the **OPENQUERY** function does not execute RPCs. Answer d is incorrect, because the **OPENQUERY** function is not used with predefined remote data sources. Answer e is incorrect, because only answer c provides the correct response.

Question 4

Which of the following SQL statements are valid in distributed queries? [Check all correct answers]

❑ a. select * into MyServer.tempdb..t1 from pubs..authors

❑ b. insert S2.pubs..jobs (job_desc,min_lvl,mxm_lvl) values (
       'My Job',1,2)

❑ c. select * from s3.pubs..authors

❑ d. drop table S2.tempdb..t3

The correct answers are b and c. Both answers b and c are accessing data on
another server. Answer a is incorrect, because you cannot use a remote table as
the table being created with a **SELECT INTO** statement. Answer d is incorrect, because you cannot drop a table in a distributed query.

Need To Know More?

Amo, William C. *Transact-SQL*, IDG Books Worldwide, Foster City, CA, 1998. ISBN 0-7645-8048-5. Chapter 16 contains information about distributed transactions.

Coffman, Gayle. *SQL Server 7: The Complete Reference*, Osborne/McGraw-Hill, Berkley, CA, 1999. ISBN 0-07-882494-X. Chapter 16 describes linked servers. Chapter 21 provides a complete T-SQL reference.

MS SQL Server Books Online contains information about distributed transactions, look in the index under "distributed transactions" or "Distributed Transaction Coordinator".

Search the TechNet CD or its online version at **www.microsoft.com**.

www.microsoft.com/sql
Find up-to-date information about using SQL Server here.

Sample Test

In this chapter, we provide pointers to help you develop a successful test-taking strategy, including how to choose proper answers, how to decode ambiguity, how to work within the Microsoft testing framework, how to decide what you need to memorize, and how to prepare for the test. At the end of the chapter, we include 40 questions on subject matter pertinent to Microsoft Exam 70-029: "Designing and Implementing Databases with Microsoft SQL Server 7."

Questions, Questions, Questions

There should be no doubt in your mind that you are facing a test full of specific and pointed questions. Currently, the SQL Server 7 exam may be a fixed-lenght test or an adaptive test. If it is a fixed-length test, the exam will consist of 49 questions that you must complete in 150 minutes. If it is an adaptive test (and the software should tell you this as you begin the exam), it will consist of somewhere between 25 and 75 questions (on average) and take somewhere between 30 and 90 minutes.

Whichever type of test you take, for this exam, questions belong to one of five basic types:

➤ Multiple-choice with a single answer

➤ Multiple-choice with one or more answers

➤ Multipart with a single answer

➤ Multipart with one or more answers

Always take the time to read a question at least twice before selecting an answer, and always look for an Exhibit button as you examine each question. Exhibits include graphics information related to a question. An exhibit is usually a screen capture of program output or GUI information that you must examine to analyze the question's contents and formulate an answer. The Exhibit button brings up graphics and charts used to help explain a question, provide additional data, or illustrate page layout or program behavior.

Not every question has only one answer; many questions require multiple answers. Therefore, it's important to read each question carefully, to determine how many answers are necessary or possible, and to look for additional hints or instructions when selecting answers. Such instructions often occur in brackets, immediately following the question itself (as they do for all multiple-choice questions in which one or more answers are possible).

Picking Proper Answers

Obviously, the only way to pass any exam is to select enough of the right answers to obtain a passing score. However, Microsoft's exams are not standardized like the SAT and GRE exams; they are far more diabolical and convoluted. In some cases, questions are strangely worded, and deciphering them can be a real challenge. In those cases, you may need to rely on answer-elimination skills. Almost always, at least one answer out of the possible choices for a question can be eliminated immediately because it matches one of these conditions:

➤ The answer does not apply to the situation.

➤ The answer describes a nonexistent issue, an invalid option, or an imaginary state.

➤ The answer may be eliminated because of the question itself.

After you eliminate all answers that are obviously wrong, you can apply your retained knowledge to eliminate further answers. Look for items that sound correct but refer to actions, commands, or features that are not present or not available in the situation that the question describes.

If you're still faced with a blind guess among two or more potentially correct answers, reread the question. Try to picture how each of the possible remaining answers would alter the situation. Be especially sensitive to terminology; sometimes the choice of words ("remove" instead of "disable") can make the difference between a right answer and a wrong one.

Only when you've exhausted your ability to eliminate answers, but remain unclear about which of the remaining possibilities is correct, should you guess at an answer. An unanswered question offers you no points, but guessing gives you at least some chance of getting a question right; just don't be too hasty when making a blind guess.

 If you're taking a fixed-length or a short-form test, you can wait until the last round of reviewing marked questions (just as you're about to run out of time, or out of unanswered questions) before you start making guesses. If you're taking an adaptive test, you'll have to guess to move on to the next question if you can't figure out an answer some other way. Either way, guessing should be your technique of last resort!

Decoding Ambiguity

Microsoft exams have a reputation for including questions that can be difficult to interpret, confusing, or ambiguous. In our experience with numerous exams, we consider this reputation to be completely justified. The Microsoft exams are tough, and deliberately made that way.

The only way to beat Microsoft at its own game is to be prepared. You'll discover that many exam questions test your knowledge of things that are not directly related to the issue raised by a question. This means that the answers you must choose from, even incorrect ones, are just as much a part of the skill assessment as the question itself. If you don't know something about most aspects of SQL Server 7, you may not be able to eliminate obviously wrong answers because they relate to a different area of SQL Server than the one that's addressed by the question at hand. In other words, the more you know about the software, the easier it will be for you to tell right from wrong.

Questions often give away their answers, but you have to be Sherlock Holmes to see the clues. Often, subtle hints appear in the question text in such a way that they seem almost irrelevant to the situation. You must realize that each question is a test unto itself and that you need to inspect and successfully navigate each question to pass the exam. Look for small clues, such as the mention of times, group permissions and names, and configuration settings. Little things like these can point at the right answer if properly understood; if missed, they can leave you facing a blind guess.

Another common difficulty with certification exams is vocabulary. Microsoft has an uncanny knack for naming some utilities and features entirely obviously in some cases, and completely inanely in other instances. Be sure to brush up on the key terms presented at the beginning of each chapter. You may also want to read through the Glossary at the end of this book the day before you take the test.

Working Within The Framework

The test questions appear in random order, and many elements or issues that receive mention in one question may also crop up in other questions. It's not uncommon to find that an incorrect answer to one question is the correct answer to another question, or vice-versa. Take the time to read every answer to each question, even if you recognize the correct answer to a question immediately. That extra reading may spark a memory or remind you about a SQL Server feature or function that helps you on another question elsewhere in the exam.

If you're taking a fixed-length test, you can revisit any question as many times as you like. If you're uncertain of the answer to a question, check the box that's provided to mark it for easy return later on. You should also mark questions you think may offer information that you can use to answer other questions. On fixed-length or short-form tests, we usually mark somewhere between 25 and 50 percent of the questions on exams we've taken. The testing software is designed to let you mark every question if you choose; use this framework to your advantage. Everything you will want to see again should be marked; the testing software can then help you return to marked questions quickly and easily.

For fixed-length or short-form tests, we strongly recommend that you first read through the entire test quickly, before getting caught up in answering individual questions. This will help to jog your memory as you review the potential answers and can help identify questions that you want to mark for easy access to their contents. It will also let you identify and mark the really tricky questions for easy return as well. The key is to make a quick pass over the territory to begin with, so that you know what you're up against; and then to survey that territory more thoroughly on a second pass, when you can begin to answer all questions systematically and consistently.

If you're taking an adaptive test, and you see something in a question or one of the answers that jogs your memory on a topic, or that you feel you should record if the topic appears in another question, write it down on your piece of paper. Just because you can't go back to a question in an adaptive test doesn't mean you can't take notes on what you see early in the test, in hopes that it might help you later in the test.

For adaptive tests, don't be afraid to take notes on what you see in various questions. Sometimes, what you record from one question, especially if it's not as familiar as it should be or reminds you of the name or use of some utility or interface details, can help you on other questions later on.

Finally, some Microsoft tests combine 15 to 25 adaptive questions with 10 fixed-length questions. In that case, use our recommended adaptive strategy for the adaptive part, and the recommended fixed-length or short-length strategy for the fixed-length part.

Deciding What To Memorize

The amount of memorization you must undertake for an exam depends on how well you remember what you've read, and how well you know the software. If you are a visual thinker and you see the drop-down menus and dialog boxes in your head, you won't need to memorize as much as someone who's less visually oriented. The tests will stretch your recollection of commands and functions of SQL Server. At a minimum, you'll want to memorize the following kinds of information:

➤ The differences between the different normal forms

➤ The T-SQL Data Manipulation Language

➤ The T-SQL Data Definition Language

➤ The T-SQL Transaction control statements and their behavior

If you work your way through this book while sitting at a machine with SQL Server installed, and try to manipulate this environment's features and functions as they're discussed throughout, you should have little or no difficulty mastering this material. Also, don't forget that The Cram Sheet at the front of the book is designed to capture the material that is most important to memorize; use this to guide your studies as well.

Preparing For The Test

The best way to prepare for the test—after you've studied—is to take at least one practice exam. We've included one here in this chapter for that reason; the test questions are located in the pages that follow (and unlike the preceding chapters in this book, the answers don't follow the questions immediately; you'll have to flip to Chapter 19 to review the answers separately).

Give yourself 105 minutes to take the exam, keep yourself on the honor system, and don't look at earlier text in the book or jump ahead to the answer key. When your time is up, or you've finished the questions, you can check your work in Chapter 19. Pay special attention to the explanations for the incorrect answers; these can also help to reinforce your knowledge of the material. Knowing how to recognize correct answers is good, but understanding why incorrect answers are wrong can be equally valuable.

Taking The Test

Relax. Once you're sitting in front of the testing computer, there's nothing more you can do to increase your knowledge or preparation. Take a deep breath, stretch, and start reading that first question.

There's no need to rush; you have plenty of time to complete each question and to return to those questions that you skip or mark for return (if you are taking a fixed-length or short-form test). If you read a question twice and remain clueless, you can mark it if you're taking a fixed-length or short-form test; if you're taking an adaptive test, you'll have to guess and move on. Both easy and difficult questions are intermixed throughout the test in random order. If you're taking a fixed-length or short-form test, don't cheat yourself by spending too much time on a hard question early on in the test, thereby depriving yourself of the time you need to answer the questions at the end of the test.

On a fixed-length or short-form test, you can read through the entire test, and before returning to marked questions for a second visit, figure out how much time you've got per question. As you answer each question, remove its mark. Continue to review the remaining marked questions until you run out of time, or you complete the test.

On an adaptive test, set a maximum time limit for questions (we recommend no more than five minutes if you're completely clueless), and watch your time on long or complex questions. If you hit your limit, it's time to guess and move on. Don't deprive yourself of the opportunity to see more questions by taking too long to puzzle over questions, unless you think you can figure out the answer. Otherwise, you're limiting your opportunities to pass.

That's it for pointers. Here are some questions for you to practice on.

Sample Test

Question 1

Which of the following SQL statements will place the dash in a nine-digit zipcode field from the address table? That is, what will convert 557460001 to 55746-0001? [Check all correct answers]

☐ a. select stuff (zipcode,6,1,'-') from address

☐ b. select substring(zipcode,0,4)+'-'+substring(zipcode,5,8) from address

☐ c. select stuff (zipcode,6 ,0,'-') from address

☐ d. select substring(zipcode,1,5)+'-'+substring(zipcode,6,4) from address

☐ e. select substring(zipcode,1,5)+'-'+substring(zipcode,6,9) from address

Question 2

What is a primary key constraint used for?

○ a. Identify a row in a database table

○ b. Improve the performance of database queries

○ c. Reduce contention when updating data

○ d. Enforce domain integrity

Question 3

> The following table will take up how much disk space for 100,000 rows?
>
> ```
> create table MyTable
>    ( a      int       not null,
>      b      char(400) not null,
>      c      datetime  not null
>    )
> ```
>
> ○ a. 800,000K
>
> ○ b. 50,000K
>
> ○ c. 40,000K
>
> ○ d. 44,480K
>
> ○ e. 42,112K

Question 4

> You have two tables—table Order is the parent table and OrderLine is the child table. How would you set up a delete trigger to cascade deletes?
>
> ○ a. The trigger should set up on OrderLine to remove Order rows when OrderLine is deleted.
>
> ○ b. The trigger should be set up on Order to remove OrderLine rows when the Order is deleted.
>
> ○ c. The trigger should be set up on Order to prevent the delete if OrderLine exists.
>
> ○ d. None of the above.

Question 5

Which normal form is the following table in?

```
create table Address
  ( AddressId      int not null,
    StreetAddress  varchar(120),
    City           varchar(120),
    State          varchar(120),
    ZipCode        char(9),
    PhoneNumber1   varchar(10),
    PhoneNumber2   varchar(10),
    PhoneNumber3   varchar(10),
    StateTaxRate   numeric(5,3),
    PriceOfTea     numeric(10,2),
    primary key ( AddressId)
  )
```

○ a. First normal form

○ b. Second normal form

○ c. Third normal form

○ d. It is not normalized

Question 6

Which normal form is the following table in?

```
create table Address
  ( AddressId      int not null,
    StreetAddress  varchar(120),
    City           varchar(120),
    State          varchar(120),
    ZipCode        char(9),
    StateTaxRate   numeric(5,3),
    PriceOfTea     numeric(10,2),
    primary key ( AddressId)
  )
```

○ a. First normal form

○ b. Second normal form

○ c. Third normal form

○ d. It is not normalized

Question 7

Which normal form is the following table in?

```
create table Address
  ( AddressId      int not null,
    StreetAddress  varchar(120),
    City           varchar(120),
    State          varchar(120),
    ZipCode        char(9),
    primary key ( AddressId)
  )
```

○ a. First normal form

○ b. Second normal form

○ c. Third normal form

○ d. It is not normalized

Question 8

What will happen with the following CREATE DATABASE command?

```
Create database MyDb on
    (name = dev1, filename='c:\mssql7\dev1',
     size=10)
```

○ a. An error will be generated, because a log file was not specified.

○ b. A database will be created that has data and log stored on dev1.

○ c. A database will be created that has data stored on dev1 and a log stored in a file called MyDB.ldf.

○ d. An error will be generated, because the extension .mdf was not specified for the file name.

Question 9

You want to create a Sales table that meets the following conditions:

➤ You plan on having remote servers set up in Denver, Tampa, and Minneapolis with a central site in Dallas.

➤ You want to be able to insert new customers in each remote server.

➤ You want to be able to report on the data from the central server in Dallas.

➤ You want unique IDs across all the servers.

➤ You will use replication to keep the data synchronized across all the databases.

How should you create the Sales table?

○ a. Create all the tables with the ID being an identity column.

○ b. Create the remote tables with an identity column, and, on the central table, make sure the ID column is not an identity.

○ c. Create the tables with the ID column being a uniqueidentifier data type.

○ d. Create the tables with the ID column being a uniqueidentifier data type with a default of GETID().

○ e. Create the tables with the ID column being a uniqueidentifier data type with a default of NEWID().

Question 10

Consider the following stored procedure:

```
create procedure MyP1 ( @a varchar(32))
as
begin tran
declare @b int
delete from a1 where au_lname like @a
select @b = @@rowcount
if ( @@error != 0) begin
rollback tran
return -200
end
delete from a2 where au_lname like @a
select @b = @b+ @@rowcount
if ( @@error != 0) begin
rollback tran
return -200
end
commit tran
return @b
```

Which of the following statements are true? [Check all correct answers]

❑ a. The procedure can only be run inside a transaction.

❑ b. If an error occurs in deleting from table a1, it will not delete from table a2.

❑ c. If an error occurs in deleting from table a2, the rows deleted from table a1 will be rolled back.

❑ d. The stored procedure is invalid and will not be created.

❑ e. None of the above.

Question 11

You currently have the following table:

```
Create table Sale
  ( SaleId     numeric(10) identity,
    CustomerId numeric(10),
    SaleNote   varchar(2000) default 'NONE',
    SaleDate   datetime)
```

You no longer want to store the SaleNote in this table. Which of the following is the best way to remove the SaleNote column from the table?

○ a. Bulk copy the Sale table out of the database, drop the Sale table, create a new Sale table, and bulk copy the data back into the new Sale table, ignoring the SaleNote column.

○ b. Alter the Sale table by dropping the SaleNote column.

○ c. Rename the Sale table. Use DTS to migrate the data creating a Sale table, skipping the SaleNote column. Then, drop the original Sale table.

○ d. Alter the Sale table by dropping the default on the SaleNote column and then dropping the SaleNote column.

Question 12

You have a blank table that contains identity columns, and you want to load a data file that currently contains values for the identity column into the table. Which of the following statements are true?

○ a. To load the data using bcp, you must use the –I parameter.

○ b. To load the data using bcp, you must use the –E parameter.

○ c. To load the data using bcp, you must first configure the database to allow identity inserts.

○ d. You cannot load the data with bcp.

Question 13

You want to enforce domain integrity on a table. Which of the following SQL Server features can you use? [Check all correct answers]

❑ a. Defaults

❑ b. Rules

❑ c. Triggers

❑ d. Foreign key

Question 14

What will happen when you execute the following SQL statement? [Check all correct answers]

```
select au_id, sum(royaltyper) from titleauthor
group by au_id, title_id
order by title_id, au_id
compute avg(sum(royaltyper)) by title_id
```

❑ a. The statement will fail.

❑ b. There will be a row for each author_id and title_id combination.

❑ c. There will be a row each time the title_id changes showing the average for each author that worked on that title_id.

❑ d. There will be a row each time the author_id changes showing the average for each author that worked on that title_id.

Question 15

Consider the following table definition:

```
Create table autos
(make varchar(20) not null,
model varchar(20) not null,
acquisition_cost money null,
acquisition_date datetime null)
```

What will happen when the following SQL is executed? [Check all correct answers]

```
Truncate table autos
Begin tran
  Insert autos (make,model) values ('Tucker',
    "Torpedo")
  If  exists (select * from autos)
    Rollback tran
  Else
    Commit tran
```

❑ a. The batch will fail, because the begin tran...commit tran pair are not properly nested.

❑ b. At the end of the batch, no rows will be in the table.

❑ c. At the end of the batch, one row will be in the table.

❑ d. All proper error handling will be performed.

❑ e. All proper error handling will not be performed.

Question 16

Consider the following table definition:

```
Create table autos
(make varchar(20) not null,
model varchar(20) not null,
acquisition_cost money null,
acquisition_date datetime null)
```

What will happen when the following SQL is executed? [Check all correct answers]

```
Truncate table autos
Begin tran
  Insert autos (make,model) values ('Tucker',
    "Torpedo")
  If  exists (select * from autos)
    Commit tran
  Else
    Print "Error: the row was not inserted into
    the table"
    Rollback tran
```

❑ a. This batch will fail, because the begin tran...commit tran pair are not properly nested.

❑ b. At the end of the batch, no rows will be in the table.

❑ c. At the end of the batch, one row will be in the table.

❑ d. All proper error handling will be performed.

❑ e. All proper error handling will not be performed.

Question 17

Consider the following table definition:

```
Create table autos
(make varchar(20) not null,
model varchar(20) not null,
acquisition_cost money null,
acquisition_date datetime null)
```

What will happen when the following SQL is executed? [Check all correct answers]

```
Truncate table autos
Insert autos (make,model) values ('Plymouth',
    "Prowler")
If @@error != 0
  return
Begin tran
  Insert autos (make,model) values ('Tucker',
    "Torpedo")
  If @@error != 0
    return
  If (select count(*) from autos) = 2
    Commit tran
  Else
    begin
      Print "Error: the row was not inserted
      into the table"
      Rollback tran
    end
```

❑ a. This batch will fail because the begin tran...commit tran pair are not properly nested.

❑ b. At the end of the batch, no rows will be in the table.

❑ c. At the end of the batch, two rows will be in the table.

❑ d. All proper error handling will be performed.

❑ e. All proper error handling will not be performed.

❑ f. The batch will fail, because of mismatched quotes in the insert statements.

Question 18

You are creating a database to contain member information for a social group. What is wrong with the following design? [Check all correct answers]

```
Create table member
  (last_name      char(20)      null,
   first_name     varchar(30)   not null,
   address_line1  varchar(30)   null,
   address_line2  varchar(30)   null,
   address2_line1 varchar(30)   not null,
   address2_line2 char(30)      null,
   spouse_name    char(30)      not null)
```

- ❏ a. This table is not normalized.
- ❏ b. Data types are chosen poorly.
- ❏ c. Column null properties are not chosen well.
- ❏ d. All fields are required.
- ❏ e. No fields are required.
- ❏ f. Some fields are required that probably should not be.
- ❏ g. Some fields are not required that probably should be.

Question 19

You are creating a database to contain member information for a social group. What could you change to make the design better? [Check all correct answers]

```
Create table member
        (last_name        char(20)        null,
        first_name        varchar(30)      not null,
        address_line1     varchar(30)      null,
        address_line2     varchar(30)      null,
        address2_line1    varchar(30)      not null,
        address2_line2    char(30)         null,
        spouse_name       char(30)         not null)
```

❑ a. Make last name not null.

❑ b. Create a candidate key for the table.

❑ c. Normalize the address fields into a different table.

❑ d. Make all character columns fixed length.

❑ e. Make all character columns variable length.

Question 20

The following table will take up how many pages for 100,000 rows?

```
create table MyTable
    ( a      int       not null,
      b      char(400) not null,
      c      datetime  not null
    )
```

○ a. 100,000

○ b. 50,000

○ c. 20,000

○ d. 10,000

○ e. 6,000

Question 21

The following table, with a clustered index on column a, will take up how many pages for 100,000 rows?

```
create table MyTable
  ( a     int       not null,
    b     char(400) not null,
    c     datetime  not null
  )
```

○ a. 100,000

○ b. 50,000

○ c. 20,000

○ d. 10,000

○ e. 6,000

Question 22

What do you need to do to place the following table in third normal form? [Check all correct answers]

```
create table Address
   ( AddressId      int not null,
     StreetAddress  varchar(120),
     City           varchar(120),
     State          varchar(120),
     ZipCode        char(9),
     PhoneNumber1   varchar(10),
     PhoneNumber2   varchar(10),
     PhoneNumber3   varchar(10),
     StateTaxRate   numeric(5,3),
     PriceOfTea     numeric(10,2),
     primary key ( AddressId)
   )
```

❑ a. Remove the phone repeating group.

❑ b. Turn the phone repeating group into an array.

❑ c. Remove the state tax rate.

❑ d. Remove the price of tea.

❑ e. This table is already in third normal form.

Question 23

Consider the following table definition:

```
Create table member
    (last_name       char(20)        null,
    first_name        varchar(30)     not null,
    address_line1     varchar(30)     null,
    address_line2     varchar(30)     null,
    address2_line1    varchar(30)     not null,
    address2_line2    char(30)        null,
    spouse_name       char(30)        not null)
```

Assuming this is the only query on the table, how would you in-dex for a name search (on last name, last name and first name, or partial string searches)?

○ a. Clustered on (first_name, last_name)

○ b. Nonclustered on (first_name, last_name)

○ c. Clustered on (last_name , first_name)

○ d. Nonclustered on (last_name , first_name)

○ e. No index is necessary

○ f. None of the above

Question 24

Which of the following can be accomplished with triggers? [Check all correct answers]

❑ a. Referential integrity enforcement

❑ b. Complex business rule checking based on before and after images of the data

❑ c. Rolling back the transaction that fired the trigger

❑ d. Additional table modifications of the base table or other tables

❑ e. Triggers are no longer available in version 7

Question 25

What is the value of @@trancount prior to entering a transaction?

○ a. null

○ b. 0

○ c. 1

○ d. 10

○ e. Insufficient information is provided

Question 26

What is the value of @@trancount after an unqualified rollback?

○ a. null

○ b. 0

○ c. 1

○ d. 10

○ e. Insufficient information is provided

Question 27

Consider the following stored procedure:

```
Create procedure lookup (@a int)
As
If @a is null
  Begin
    Print "You forgot to pass in a parameter"
    Return
  End
select * from sysobjects where id = @a
return
```

What will happen if this stored procedure is executed without a parameter?

○ a. The stored procedure will print "You forgot to pass in a parameter".

○ b. The stored procedure will do a lookup based on no parameter, returning all rows in the table.

○ c. The stored procedure will fail before it is run.

○ d. The server will print a message stating that you must provide a default value.

○ e. The server will print an error stating that you must provide a default value.

Question 28

The following statement was executed in osql:

```
create table MyTable

    ( a    int        null,
      b    char(400) null,
      c    datetime
    )
```

Which answers best describe the results of the statement? [Check all correct answers]

- ☐ a. MyTable is created in the database.
- ☐ b. All the columns in the table allow nulls.
- ☐ c. All the columns except column c allow nulls.
- ☐ d. MyTable is not created, because char cannot be 400 characters.
- ☐ e. Column a has been declared the primary key.

Question 29

Which of the following answers best describes the results of the following CREATE TABLE statement?

```
Create table MyTable
(id int not null,
price smallmoney not null,
markup numeric (5,2) not null,
msrp as price *(1+(markup/100)))
```

- ○ a. SQL Server stores a four-column table.
- ○ b. SQL Server stores a three-column table that acts like a four-column table.
- ○ c. A table is created that only allows null in the msrp column.
- ○ d. The markup column is seven digits wide.

Question 30

Which of the following statements are true about the REFERENCES CONSTRAINT? [Check all correct answers]

- ❑ a. Inserts into the referencing table that violate the reference constraint will not be completed.

- ❑ b. The referenced table must already exist when the referencing table is created.

- ❑ c. The referenced column must already exist when the referencing table is created.

- ❑ d. The referenced column must be the primary key or have a unique constraint.

- ❑ e. The referencing table can have only one reference constraint.

Question 31

Which of the following statements are true about the ALTER TABLE statement?

- ○ a. Columns can be dropped with the ALTER TABLE statement, even if they are referenced by a foreign key.

- ○ b. NOT NULL columns can be added to a table with the ALTER TABLE statement, provided the columns are declared with a default value.

- ○ c. Identity columns cannot be added to a table with the ALTER TABLE statement after it has been populated.

- ○ d. None of the above.

Question 32

Consider the following table:

```
Create table #atable
( a int null,
b varchar(25) null)
```

Which of the following statements are true? [Check all correct answers]

- ❑ a. #atable is a temporary table.
- ❑ b. #atable is accessible to all users.
- ❑ c. #atable is accessible only to its creator.
- ❑ d. #atable is deleted when the creator disconnects.
- ❑ e. #atable is created in the current database.

Question 33

Which of the following is true about full-text indexing?

- ○ a. Full-text indexes are stored in the file system.
- ○ b. Tables are allowed multiple full-text indexes.
- ○ c. Full-text indexes are created, managed, and dropped by Transact-SQL statements.
- ○ d. None of the above.

Question 34

Which stored procedure enables full-text indexing for a database?

- ○ a. sp_full_text_database
- ○ b. sp_fulltext_database
- ○ c. sp_fulltext_enable
- ○ d. None of the above

Question 35

What will happen with the following query?

```
SELECT Titles
FROM MyBooks
WHERE CONTAINS(Description, ' "Cajun Cooking" ')
```

○ a. A query will be performed on MyTable looking to find Descriptions containing the phrase "Cajun Cooking".

○ b. A full-text query will be performed on MyTable looking to find Descriptions containing the phrase "Cajun Cooking".

○ c. A query will be performed on MyTable looking to find Descriptions starting with the phrase "Cajun Cooking".

○ d. A full-text query will be performed on MyTable looking to find Descriptions containing the words "Cajun" and "Cooking".

Question 36

What will happen with the following query?

```
SELECT Titles, CategoryName
FROM MyBooks
WHERE CONTAINS (Description,
     'FORMSOF(INFLECTIONAL, "Spicy")')
```

○ a. A full-text query will be performed looking for Descriptions containing the word "Spicy".

○ b. A query will be performed looking for Descriptions containing the word "Spicy".

○ c. A full-text query will be performed looking for Descriptions starting with the word "Spicy".

○ d. A query will be performed looking for Descriptions starting with the word "Spicy".

○ e. A full-text query will be performed looking for Descriptions containing the word or any forms of the word "Spicy".

Question 37

Which of the following statements are true? [Check all correct answers]

```
SELECT Title
FROM MyBooks
WHERE CONTAINS(Description, 'ISABOUT (Cajun
    WEIGHT(0.9),
Cooking WEIGHT(0.5))' )
```

❏ a. The phrase "Cajun Cooking" is given more weight than just the word "Cooking" itself.

❏ b. The word "Cooking" should be near "Cajun".

❏ c. A full-text query will be done on MyTable looking to find Descriptions containing the words "Cajun" and "Cooking".

❏ d. A full-text query will be done on the phrase "Cajun Cooking".

❏ e. None of the above.

Question 38

What methods can be used to minimize deadlock occurrences? [Check all correct answers]

❏ a. Avoid the use of holdlock.

❏ b. Write transactions so that when different transactions modify the same tables, the tables are accessed in the same order.

❏ c. Do not allow user interaction with the database during a transaction.

❏ d. All of the above.

Question 39

Given the following query and SHOWPLAN_TEXT output, what is true about the query?

```
select * from titles
where title_id = 'BU1111'

StmtText
--------------------------------------------------
    -------
  |--Clustered Index
     Seek(pubs..titles.UPKCL_titleidind,
     SEEK:(titles.title_id=@1) ORDERED)
```

O a. The query would be executed using the clustered index.

O b. The query would be executed using the nonclustered index.

O c. The clustered index, UPKCL_titleidind, would be used to execute the query.

O d. A table scan is performed.

O e. The nonclustered index, UPKCL_titleidind, would be used to execute the query.

Question 40

What stored procedures would be used to help identify lock usage on a server?

O a. sp_help

O b. sp_who

O c. sp_help 'locks"

O d. sp_lock

Answer Key

1. c, e	11. d	21. e	31. b
2. a	12. b	22. a, c, d	32. a, c, d
3. e	13. a, b, c	23. d	33. a
4. b	14. b, c	24. a, b, c, d	34. b
5. d	15. b, e	25. e	35. b
6. a	16. c, e	26. b	36. e
7. c	17. c, d	27. c	37. a, b, c
8. c	18. a, b, c, f, g	28. a, b	38. d
9. e	19. a, b, c, e	29. b	39. c
10. e	20. e	30. a, b, c, d	40. d

Question 1

Answers c and e are correct; they both correctly display a hyphen as the sixth digit in a zipcode. Answer a is incorrect, because the third parameter in stuff indicates the number of characters to delete, so this answer will replace the sixth character with a dash (-). Answer b is incorrect, because the substring function's start position is one, not zero. Answer d is incorrect, because the third parameter is not the number of characters to extract, but is the end position.

Question 2

Answer a is correct. The primary key constraint can be used to ensure that all rows in a table can be uniquely identified through the primary key. Answer b is incorrect, because while a primary key constraint can improve the performance of a database, that is not the primary purpose of a primary key constraint. Answer c is incorrect, because while a primary key can reduce contention by having different users modifying different data pages, that is not the primary purpose. Answer d is incorrect, because a primary key constraint is used to enforce referential integrity, not domain integrity.

Question 3

Answer e is correct. The fixed row size is equal to 412 bytes long: 4 bytes for column a + 400 bytes for column b + 8 bytes for column c. The NULL bitmap is the integer part of 2 + ((3 columns +7)/8), or 3. Therefore, the total row size is 415 bytes. The number of rows per page is 8,096/(415+2) rounded down to the nearest integer, or 19 rows per page. The total number of pages is 100,000 rows/19 rows per page, or 5,264 pages, or 42,112K. Answers a, b, c, and d are incorrect, because they do not provide the amount of disk space required for the sample table.

Question 4

Answer b is correct. Answer a is incorrect, because it would cascade OrderLine to the parent table, but the Order table can have rows deleted, leaving stranded rows in the OrderLine table. Answer c is incorrect, because this trigger will prevent deleting rows. Answer d is incorrect, because the correct answer is provided.

Question 5

Answer d is correct. The table is not normalized. There is a repeating group for three phone number attributes. Answers a, b, and c are incorrect, because the table is not normalized.

Question 6

Answer a is correct. The table does not have repeating groups, so it is in at least first normal form. Answer b is incorrect, because **PriceOfTea** is not related to the **AddressId**. Answer c is incorrect, because the table is not in second normal form, so it cannot be in third normal form. Answer d is incorrect, because the table is normalized.

Question 7

Answer c is correct. The table is in third normal form. The table has been normalized so that there are no repeating groups of attributes. All redundant data and partial dependencies have been removed and all the existing attributes are dependent on the primary key. Answer b is incorrect, because although the table is in second normal form, it is not the best answer. Answer a is incorrect, because although the table is in first normal form, it is not the best answer. Answer d is incorrect, because the table is in third normal form.

Question 8

Answer c is correct. Answer c correctly describes the actions of the described statement. Because a log device is not specified, it will automatically create a log file based on the name of the database with an .ldf extension. Answer a is incorrect, because you do not have to specify files in a **CREATE DATABASE** statement. Answer b is incorrect, because with SQL Server 7, it is not possible to store log and data in the same file. Answer d is incorrect, because although it is recommended that you use the standard extensions for database files, it is not required.

Question 9

Answer e is correct. Answers a and b are incorrect, because an identity column does not apply across tables, let alone across servers. Answer c is incorrect, because creating the tables with the ID column being a uniqueidentifier data type will allow you to generate unique identifiers, but it's not as good as answer e, which generates uniqueidentifiers automatically. Answer d is incorrect, because there is no **GETID()** function.

Question 10

Answer e is correct. Answer a is incorrect, because the procedure can be run either inside or outside of a transaction. Answers b and c are incorrect, because **MyP1** is setting the variable **@b** before checking **@@error**. Therefore, **@@error** will be reset. Answer d is incorrect, because the stored procedure is valid SQL Syntax, and the tables do not have to be created before the procedure is created.

Question 11

Answer d is correct. Answer a is incorrect, because although it will make the changes that you want, there are more steps that take longer to run. Answer b is incorrect, because the altered table will fail. You cannot drop a column that has a default value. Answer c is incorrect, because although this will work, it takes more time and resources than answer d requires. Answer d will allow the dropping of a column without recreating the table and also accounts for the default constraint on the table.

Question 12

Answer b is correct. The –E parameter allows for identity values to be inserted via the bcp program. Answer a is incorrect, because the –I parameter is not a valid parameter for **bcp**. Answer c is incorrect, because you cannot configure a database to allow identity inserts. Answer d is incorrect, because you can load the data with the –E parameter.

Question 13

Answers a, b, and c are correct, because you can use defaults, rules, and triggers to enforce domain integrity. Answer d is incorrect, because a foreign key is used to enforce referential integrity, not domain integrity.

Question 14

Answers b and c are correct. Answer a is incorrect, because the statement is a valid SQL statement, and it will not fail. Answer d is incorrect, because the compute state will generate a row each time the title_id changes, not when the au_id changes.

Question 15

Answers b and e are correct. Answer a is incorrect, because **begin tran...commit tran** pairs do not need to be nested. Answer c is incorrect, because the row will be removed either by the **rollback tran** or by a database error. Answer d is incorrect, because all SQL statements do not have **@@error** checked after their execution. Answer b is correct, because the **If exists** statement checks to see if there are any rows in the table. If so, the inserts are rolled back. Since a truncate table was run before the transaction, there will be no rows left.

Question 16

Answers c and e are correct. Answer c is correct, because while the **rollback tran** is *always* executed, the rollback tran is no longer in a transaction. Answer a is incorrect, because **begin tran...commit tran** pairs do not need to be nested. Answer d is incorrect, because all SQL statements do not have **@@error** checked after their execution.

Question 17

Answers c and d are correct. Answer c is correct, because both rows should successfully be inserted. Answer a is incorrect, because **begin tran...commit tran** pairs do not need to be nested. Answer b is incorrect, because the **rollback tran** will not affect rows that are not in the transaction. Answer e is incorrect, because **@@error** is checked after execution. This makes answer d correct. Answer f is incorrect, because both single or double quotes are acceptable, as long as singles match with singles and doubles match with doubles.

Question 18

Answers a, b, c, f, and g are correct. The statement in answer a is false, because the two sets of addresses in the table imply that the table has not been completely normalized yet. Answer b is correct, because there is no consistency between what should be like datatypes. (For example, Address2_line2 should be similar to Address1_line2, as should first_name and spouse_name.) Answer c is incorrect, because it assumes any member will have a spouse and that all members have a second address but not necessarily a first address. This makes answer f and answer g correct. Answers d and e are incorrect, because **null** means not required, while **not null** means required.

Question 19

Answers a, b, c, and e are correct. Answer a is correct, because the more likely situation is that last_name will be a required field. Answer b is correct, because there is presently no key on the table and it is a better practice to have a primary key on every table. Answer c is correct, because the table is not normalized to first normal form. To do this, we could move the address information to a separate table. Answer d is incorrect, because **varchar** will take up less physical storage and improve performance.

Question 20

Answer e is correct. The fixed row size is 412 bytes long: 4 bytes for column a + 400 bytes for column b + 8 bytes for column c. The NULL bitmap is the integer part of 2 + ((3 columns +7)/8), or 3. The total row size is 415 bytes. The number of rows per page is 8,096/(415+2), rounded down to the nearest integer, or 19 rows per page. The total number of pages is 100,000 rows/19 rows per page, or 5,264. Answers a, b, c, and d are incorrect, because they each provide an incorrect number of required pages.

Question 21

Answer e is correct. The fixed row size is 412 bytes long: 4 bytes for column a + 400 bytes for column b + 8 bytes for column c. The NULL bitmap is the integer part of 2 + ((3 columns +7)/8), or 3. The total row size is 415 bytes. The number of rows per page is 8,096/(415+2), rounded down to the nearest integer, or 19 rows per page. The total number of pages is 100,000 rows/19 rows per page, or 5,264. A few indexes will not more than double the space requirement. Answers a, b, c, and d are incorrect, because they each provide an incorrect number of required pages.

Question 22

Answers a, c, and d are correct. Answer a is correct, because repeating groups violate first normal form. Answers c and d are correct, because the specified actions are not dependent on the primary key; thus, they violate third normal form. Answer b is incorrect, because there are no array structures in SQL. Answer e is incorrect, because answers a, c, and d are required before the table can be in third normal form.

Question 23

Answer d is correct, because nonclustered on (last_name, first_name) enables you to take advantage of index covering. Answers a and c are incorrect, because the query will not be covered. Answer b is incorrect, because nonclustered on (first_name, last_name) will not help a string search on last name. Answer e is incorrect, because an index is necessary. Answer f is incorrect, because the correct answer is provided.

Question 24

Answers a, b, c, and d are correct, because they all describe standard functionality of triggers. Answer e is incorrect, because triggers are available in SQL Server 7.

Question 25

Answer e is correct, because the question doesn't provide any information about whether the transaction is a nested transaction or the first transaction or a named transaction—we can't define what level of nesting we are at.

Question 26

Answer b is correct. An unqualified rollback always resets the **@@trancount** local variable to 0.

Question 27

Answer c is correct, because unless a stored procedure has a default value for its parameters, the stored procedure will fail to execute when called without parameters. Answers a and b are incorrect, because the procedure will not run. Answers d and e are incorrect, because the server doesn't provide messages or error statements that tell you how to code.

Question 28

Answers a and b are correct. Answer a is correct, because the syntax for the command is correct, and it will successfully execute and create MyTable. Answer b is correct, because in osql, the session is set to allow nulls by default when creating tables. Therefore, all the columns including column c will be created to allow nulls. This also makes answer c incorrect. Answer d is incorrect, because the maximum length of a char column is 8,000 characters. Answer e is incorrect, because there is no primary key constraint defined for the table.

Question 29

Answer b is correct, because the table is created with a computed column. This column is based on data stored in the other columns, so its data is not stored, only computed when used. For this reason, answer a is incorrect. Answer c is incorrect, because the price and markup columns used to calculate **msrp** are not null, so the column should never be null. Answer d is incorrect, because the **numeric (5,2)** means that the number is five characters wide with two digits following the decimal point.

Question 30

Answers a, b, c, and d are correct. Answer a is correct, because it correctly describes the performance of the references constraint when inserting into a referencing table. Answers b and c are correct, because a requirement of the references constraint is that the table and columns being referenced must exist when the constraint is created. Answer d is correct, because the referenced column is required to be unique or a primary key. Answer e is incorrect, because a table can have many reference constraints.

Question 31

Answer b is correct. SQL Server allows for Not Null columns to be added to a table provided a value may be assigned to all existing rows by default. Answer a is incorrect, because columns cannot be dropped if they are referenced in a primary key, unique, foreign key, or check constraint. Answer c is incorrect, because identity columns can be added after a table has been populated. SQL Server will populate the column. Answer d is incorrect, because the correct answer is provided.

Question 32

Answers a, c, and d are correct. Answer a is correct, because the # symbol makes the table a temporary table. Answer c is correct, because temporary tables are only accessible to their creators. Answer d is correct, because the table is automatically deleted when the user disconnects. Answer b is incorrect, because temporary tables are not accessible to all users—they are only accessible to their creators. Answer e is incorrect, because temporary data is stored in the tempdb.

Question 33

Answer a is correct, because full-text indexes are stored in the file system. Answer b is incorrect, because tables are only allowed one full-text index. Answer c is incorrect, because full-text indexes are maintained by stored procedures. Answer d is incorrect, because the correct answer is provided.

Question 34

Answer b is correct. The **sp_fulltext_database** is the stored procedure provided to enable full-text indexing for SQL Server databases. Answers a and c are incorrect, because the **sp_full_text_database** and **sp_fulltext_enable** stored procedures do not exist. Answer d is incorrect, because the correct answer is provided.

Question 35

Answer b is correct. The query is a full-text query that performs a search on the Description column for the phrase "Cajun Cooking". Answers a and c are incorrect, because they imply a regular query and **CONTAINS** is used only for full-text queries. Answer d is incorrect, because the phrase "Cajun Cooking" is in quotes and is searched as a phrase.

Question 36

Answer e is correct, because the **FORMSOF(INFLECTIONAL)** function allows SQL Server to look for related forms of the search word. Answer a is incorrect, because it restricts the search to just the word and not any of its other forms. Answers b and d are incorrect, because they refer to a regular query rather than a full-text query. Answer c is incorrect, because it claims the Description column must start with the word "Spicy".

Question 37

Answers a, b, and c are correct. Answers a, b, and c all correctly describe aspects of the full-text queries with weight functions. Answer d is incorrect, because it implies that the search is for a phrase. Answer e is incorrect, because correct answers are provided.

Question 38

Answer d is correct, because all the answers provide methods than can be used to minimize deadlocks. Using holdlock in stored procedures can generate deadlocks very easily. Transactions that access the same tables in the same orders can help to avoid deadlocks. Also, user interaction during a transaction leaves any exclusive or shared holdlocks open for a much longer than normal period of time, which can lead to deadlocks.

Question 39

Answer c is correct. The Showplan_Text output states that the index name is UPKCL_titleidind and that it is clustered. Technically, answer a is correct, but answer c is a better answer, because it is more specific. Answers b and e are incorrect, because the output indicates the selected index is a clustered index. Answer d is incorrect, because the table scan would not be performed if an index was chosen.

Question 40

Answer d is correct. The procedure **sp_lock** is used to identify the locks that are in use on a server. Answers a and c are incorrect, because **sp_help** will list or describe objects but not locks. Answer b is incorrect, because **sp_who** can be used to identify blocked processes resulting from locking contention but not the locks themselves.

Appendix A
Pubs Database

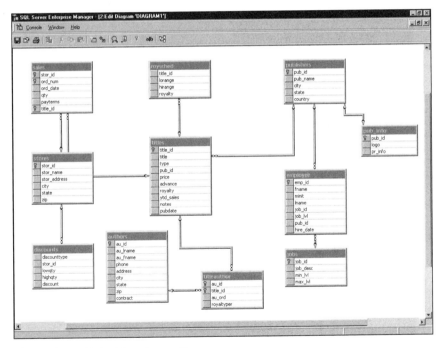

Figure A.1 Pubs Database diagram.

Pubs SQL

```
EXEC sp_addtype N'empid', N'char (9)', N'NOT NULL'
GO


EXEC sp_addtype N'id', N'varchar (11)', N'not null'
GO


EXEC sp_addtype N'tid', N'varchar (6)', N'not null'
GO
CREATE TABLE [dbo].[stores] (
        [stor_id] [char] (4) NOT NULL ,
        [stor_name] [varchar] (40) NULL ,
        [stor_address] [varchar] (40) NULL ,
        [city] [varchar] (20) NULL ,
        [state] [char] (2) NULL ,
        [zip] [char] (5) NULL ,
        CONSTRAINT [UPK_storeid] PRIMARY KEY  CLUSTERED
        ([stor_id])  ON [PRIMARY]
)
GO


CREATE TABLE [dbo].[publishers] (
        [pub_id] [char] (4) NOT NULL ,
        [pub_name] [varchar] (40) NULL ,
        [city] [varchar] (20) NULL ,
        [state] [char] (2) NULL ,
        [country] [varchar] (30) NULL CONSTRAINT
          [DF__publishers__country__0EA330E9] DEFAULT ('USA'),
        CONSTRAINT [UPKCL_pubind] PRIMARY KEY  CLUSTERED
        ([pub_id])  ON [PRIMARY] ,
          CHECK ([pub_id] = '1756' or [pub_id] = '1622'
                or [pub_id] = '0877' or [pub_id] = '0736'
                or [pub_id] = '1389'
                or ([pub_id] like '99[0-9][0-9]'))
)
GO


CREATE TABLE [dbo].[authors] (
        [au_id] [id] NOT NULL ,
        [au_lname] [varchar] (40) NOT NULL ,
        [au_fname] [varchar] (20) NOT NULL ,
        [phone] [char] (12) NOT NULL
                CONSTRAINT [DF__authors__phone__09DE7BCC]
                    DEFAULT ('UNKNOWN'),
        [address] [varchar] (40) NULL ,
        [city] [varchar] (20) NULL ,
```

```
        [state] [char] (2) NULL ,
        [zip] [char] (5) NULL ,
        [contract] [bit] NOT NULL ,
        CONSTRAINT [UPKCL_auidind] PRIMARY KEY  CLUSTERED
        ([au_id])  ON [PRIMARY] ,
         CHECK (([au_id] like
                '[0-9][0-9][0-9]-[0-9][0-9]-[0-9][0-9][0-9][0-9]')),
         CHECK (([zip] like '[0-9][0-9][0-9][0-9][0-9]'))
)
GO

CREATE  INDEX [aunmind] ON [dbo].[authors]([au_lname], [au_fname])
        ON [PRIMARY]
GO


CREATE TABLE [dbo].[titles] (
        [title_id] [tid] NOT NULL ,
        [title] [varchar] (80) NOT NULL ,
        [type] [char] (12) NOT NULL
                CONSTRAINT [DF__titles__type__117F9D94]
                DEFAULT ('UNDECIDED'),
        [pub_id] [char] (4) NULL ,
        [price] [money] NULL ,
        [advance] [money] NULL ,
        [royalty] [int] NULL ,
        [ytd_sales] [int] NULL ,
        [notes] [varchar] (200) NULL ,
        [pubdate] [datetime] NOT NULL
                CONSTRAINT [DF__titles__pubdate__1367E606]
                DEFAULT (getdate()),
        CONSTRAINT [UPKCL_titleidind] PRIMARY KEY  CLUSTERED
        ([title_id]        )  ON [PRIMARY] ,
         FOREIGN KEY
        ([pub_id]) REFERENCES [dbo].[publishers] ([pub_id])
)
GO

 CREATE  INDEX [titleind] ON [dbo].[titles]([title]) ON [PRIMARY]
GO


CREATE TABLE [dbo].[discounts] (
        [discounttype] [varchar] (40) NOT NULL ,
        [stor_id] [char] (4) NULL ,
        [lowqty] [smallint] NULL ,
        [highqty] [smallint] NULL ,
        [discount] [decimal](4, 2) NOT NULL ,
         FOREIGN KEY
```

```
                ([stor_id]) REFERENCES [dbo].[stores] ([stor_id])
) ON [PRIMARY]
GO
CREATE TABLE [dbo].[jobs] (
        [job_id] [smallint] IDENTITY (1, 1) NOT NULL ,
        [job_desc] [varchar] (50) NOT NULL
                CONSTRAINT [DF__jobs__job_desc__239E4DCF]
                DEFAULT ('New Position - title not formalized yet'),
        [min_lvl] [tinyint] NOT NULL ,
        [max_lvl] [tinyint] NOT NULL ,
         PRIMARY KEY  CLUSTERED
        ([job_id])  ON [PRIMARY] ,
        CHECK ([max_lvl] <= 250),
         CHECK ([min_lvl] >= 10)
)
GO


CREATE TABLE [dbo].[employee] (
        [emp_id] [empid] NOT NULL ,
        [fname] [varchar] (20) NOT NULL ,
        [minit] [char] (1) NULL ,
        [lname] [varchar] (30) NOT NULL ,
        [job_id] [smallint] NOT NULL
                CONSTRAINT [DF__employee__job_id__2C3393D0]
                DEFAULT (1),
        [job_lvl] [tinyint] NOT NULL
                CONSTRAINT [DF__employee__job_lvl__2E1BDC42]
                DEFAULT (10),
        [pub_id] [char] (4) NOT NULL
                CONSTRAINT [DF__employee__pub_id__2F10007B]
                DEFAULT ('9952'),
        [hire_date] [datetime] NOT NULL
                CONSTRAINT [DF__employee__hire_date__30F848ED]
                DEFAULT (getdate()),
        CONSTRAINT [PK_emp_id] PRIMARY KEY  NONCLUSTERED
        ([emp_id])  ON [PRIMARY] ,
        FOREIGN KEY ([job_id]) REFERENCES [dbo].[jobs] ([job_id]),
         FOREIGN KEY ([pub_id]) REFERENCES
                [dbo].[publishers] ([pub_id]),
        CONSTRAINT [CK_emp_id] CHECK (([emp_id] like
                '[A-Z][A-Z][A-Z][1-9][0-9][0-9][0-9][0-9][FM]') or
                ([emp_id] like
                '[A-Z]-[A-Z][1-9][0-9][0-9][0-9][0-9][FM]'))
)
GO
```

```
CREATE  CLUSTERED  INDEX [employee_ind] ON
     [dbo].[employee]([lname], [fname], [minit]) ON [PRIMARY]
GO

CREATE TABLE [dbo].[pub_info] (
     [pub_id] [char] (4) NOT NULL ,
     [logo] [image] NULL ,
     [pr_info] [text] NULL ,
     CONSTRAINT [UPKCL_pubinfo] PRIMARY KEY  CLUSTERED
     ([pub_id])  ON [PRIMARY] ,
      FOREIGN KEY ([pub_id]) REFERENCES
           [dbo].[publishers] ([pub_id])
)
GO

CREATE TABLE [dbo].[roysched] (
     [title_id] [tid] NOT NULL ,
     [lorange] [int] NULL ,
     [hirange] [int] NULL ,
     [royalty] [int] NULL ,
      FOREIGN KEY
     ([title_id]) REFERENCES [dbo].[titles] ([title_id])
) ON [PRIMARY]
GO

CREATE  INDEX [titleidind] ON [dbo].[roysched]([title_id])
     ON [PRIMARY]
GO

CREATE TABLE [dbo].[sales] (
     [stor_id] [char] (4) NOT NULL ,
     [ord_num] [varchar] (20) NOT NULL ,
     [ord_date] [datetime] NOT NULL ,
     [qty] [smallint] NOT NULL ,
     [payterms] [varchar] (12) NOT NULL ,
     [title_id] [tid] NOT NULL ,
     CONSTRAINT [UPKCL_sales] PRIMARY KEY  CLUSTERED
     ([stor_id],[ord_num],[title_id])  ON [PRIMARY] ,
      FOREIGN KEY
     ([stor_id]) REFERENCES [dbo].[stores] ([stor_id]),
      FOREIGN KEY
     ([title_id]) REFERENCES [dbo].[titles] ([title_id])
)
GO

  CREATE  INDEX [titleidind] ON [dbo].[sales]([title_id])
     ON [PRIMARY]
GO
```

```
CREATE TABLE [dbo].[titleauthor] (
      [au_id] [id] NOT NULL ,
      [title_id] [tid] NOT NULL ,
      [au_ord] [tinyint] NULL ,
      [royaltyper] [int] NULL ,
      CONSTRAINT [UPKCL_taind] PRIMARY KEY  CLUSTERED
      ([au_id],[title_id])  ON [PRIMARY] ,
       FOREIGN KEY
      ([au_id]) REFERENCES [dbo].[authors] ([au_id]),
       FOREIGN KEY
      ([title_id]) REFERENCES [dbo].[titles] ([title_id])
)
GO

CREATE  INDEX [auidind] ON [dbo].[titleauthor]([au_id])
      ON [PRIMARY]
GO

CREATE  INDEX [titleidind] ON [dbo].[titleauthor]([title_id])
      ON [PRIMARY]
GO

CREATE VIEW titleview
AS
select title, au_ord, au_lname, price, ytd_sales, pub_id
from authors, titles, titleauthor
where authors.au_id = titleauthor.au_id
   AND titles.title_id = titleauthor.title_id


GO
CREATE  PROCEDURE acur
  @auth_cur cursor varying output,
  @state char(2)  = "CA",
  @ctype int = 1
AS
if (@ctype = 1)
      set @auth_cur = cursor SCROLL for
            select au_lname
            from authors where state = @state
else
      set @auth_cur = cursor SCROLL for
            select au_lname, au_fname from authors

open @auth_cur
return 1

GO
```

```
CREATE PROCEDURE byroyalty @percentage int
AS
select au_id from titleauthor
where titleauthor.royaltyper = @percentage

GO

CREATE PROCEDURE reptq1 AS
select pub_id, title_id, price, pubdate
from titles
where price is NOT NULL
order by pub_id
COMPUTE avg(price) BY pub_id
COMPUTE avg(price)

GO

CREATE PROCEDURE reptq2 AS
select type, pub_id, titles.title_id, au_ord,
   Name = substring (au_lname, 1,15), ytd_sales
from titles, authors, titleauthor
where titles.title_id = titleauthor.title_id
   AND authors.au_id = titleauthor.au_id
   AND pub_id is NOT NULL
order by pub_id, type
COMPUTE avg(ytd_sales) BY pub_id, type
COMPUTE avg(ytd_sales) BY pub_id

GO

CREATE PROCEDURE reptq3 @lolimit money, @hilimit money,
@type char(12)
AS
select pub_id, type, title_id, price
from titles
where price >@lolimit AND price <@hilimit
  AND type = @type OR type LIKE '%cook%'
order by pub_id, type
COMPUTE count(title_id) BY pub_id, type

GO

CREATE TRIGGER employee_insupd
ON employee
FOR insert, UPDATE
AS
--Get the range of level for this job type from the jobs table.
```

```
declare @min_lvl tinyint,
   @max_lvl tinyint,
   @emp_lvl tinyint,
   @job_id smallint
select @min_lvl = min_lvl,
   @max_lvl = max_lvl,
   @emp_lvl = i.job_lvl,
   @job_id = i.job_id
from employee e, jobs j, inserted i
where e.emp_id = i.emp_id AND i.job_id = j.job_id
IF (@job_id = 1) and (@emp_lvl <> 10)
begin
   raiserror ('Job id 1 expects the default level of 10.',16,1)
   ROLLBACK TRANSACTION
end
ELSE
IF NOT (@emp_lvl BETWEEN @min_lvl AND @max_lvl)
begin
   raiserror ('The level for job_id:%d should be between %d and
      %d.', 16, 1, @job_id, @min_lvl, @max_lvl)
   ROLLBACK TRANSACTION
end

GO
```

Appendix B
Functions

. . . .

Table B.1	Scalar functions.	
Date Part	**Abbreviation**	**Description**
YEAR	YY	1753-9999
QUARTER	QQ	1-4
MONTH	MM	1-12
DAYOFYEAR	DY	1-366
DAY	DD	1-31
WEEK	WK	1-54
WEEKDAY	DW	1-7 (1=Sunday)
HOUR	HH	0-23
MINUTE	MI	0-59
SECOND	SS	0-59
MILLISECOND	MS	0-999

Table B.2 All of the functions available in SQL Server 7.

Function	Description
@@CONNECTIONS	Specifies the number of connects succeeded plus the number of failed connection attempts since SQL Server started.
@@CPU_BUSY	Specifies the time, in milliseconds, the CPU has been working since SQL Server started.
@@CURSOR_ROWS	Specifies the number of qualifying rows in the last cursor opened.
@@DATEFIRST	Specifies the value of the **SET DATEFIRST** parameter.
@@DBTS	Specifies the current **TIMESTAMP** in the current database.
@@ERROR	Specifies the error number for the last TSQL statement.
@@FETCH_STATUS	Specifies the status of the last cursor **FETCH** statement.
@@IDENTITY	Specifies the last inserted identity value.
@@IDLE	Specifies the number of milliseconds the SQL Server has been idle.
@@IO_BUSY	Specifies the number of milliseconds the SQL Server has spent doing input and output operations.
@@LANGID	Specifies the ID for the current language.
@@LANGUAGE	Specifies the name of the current language.
@@LOCK_TIMEOUT	Specifies the lock time-out setting in milliseconds for the current connection.
@@MAX_CONNECTIONS	Specifies the maximum number of simultaneous connections allowed by SQL Server.
@@MAX_PRECISION	Specifies the maximum precision for decimal and numeric types.
@@NESTLEVEL	Specifies the stored procedure nesting level.

@@OPTIONS	Specifies the current options set for the user.
@@PACK_RECEIVED	Specifies the number of input packets received.
@@PACK_SENT	Specifies the number of output packets sent.
@@PACKET_ERRORS	Specifies the number of packet errors.
@@PROCID	Specifies the object ID for the current stored procedure.
@@REMSERVER	Specifies the name of the remote SQL Server database.
@@ROWCOUNT	Specifies the number of rows affected by the last statement.
@@SERVERNAME	Specifies the name of the local server.
@@SERVICENAME	Specifies the Registry key for the SQL Server.
@@SPID	Specifies the server process ID of the current connection.
@@TEXTSIZE	Specifies the current **TEXTSIZE** option.
@@TIMETICKS	Specifies the number of microseconds per clock tick.
@@TOTAL_ERRORS	Specifies the total number of read/write errors.
@@TOTAL_READ	Specifies the total number of physical disk reads.
@@TOTAL_WRITE	Specifies the total number of disk writes.
@@TRANCOUNT	Specifies the number of active transactions.
@@VERSION	Specifies the date, version, and processor type.
ABS(*numeric_expr*)	Provides the absolute value of a specified value.
ACOS(*float_expr*)	Specifies the arc cosine in radians.

(continued)

Table B.2   All of the functions available in SQL Server 7 (continued).

Function	Description
APP_NAME()	Specifies the application name for the client process.
ASCII(char_expr)	Specifies the ASCII value of the first character in char_expr.
ASIN(float_expr)	Specifies the arcsine in radians.
ATAN(float_expr)	Specifies the arctangent in radians.
ATANS(float_expr,float_expr2)	Specifies the arc tangent, whose tangent is between the two given float expressions.
CASE	Evaluates a list of conditions, and returns a result.
CAST	Converts between data types.
CEILING(numeric_expr)	Returns the smallest integer greater than or equal to the specified value.
CHAR(int_expr)	Converts an integer to an ASCII character.
CHARINDEX(char_expr, expression,start)	Returns the starting position of the specified char_expr, else zero.
COALESCE(expr1, expr2,...)	Returns the first non-null expression.
COL_LENGTH(objname, colname)	Specifies the length of a column.
COL_NAME (obj_id,col_id)	Specifies the column name of an object.
COLUMNPROPERTY(id,column,property)	Returns information about the property for a column or procedure parameter.
CONVERT(datatype, expression[,style])	Converts between data types.
COS(float_expr)	Returns the cosine of the angle.
COT(float_expr)	Returns the cotangent of the angle.

CURRENT_TIMESTAMP	Serves as the equivalent to GETDATA().
CURRENT_USER	Serves as the equivalent to USER_NAME().
DATABASEPROPERTY (database,property)	Returns information about the database property.
DATALENGTH(char_expr)	Returns an integer number of characters in char_expr, ignoring trailing spaces.
DATEADD(datepart,number,date_expr)	Returns the date produced by adding specified number of date parts to date_expr.
DATEDIFF(datepart, date_expr1, date_expr2)	Returns date_expr2 - date_expr1, as measured by specified datepart.
DATENAME(datepart, date_expr)	Returns a specified part of a date_expr value as a string, converted to a name (for example, June) if appropriate.
DATEPART(datepart, date_expr)	Returns a specified part of date_expr value as an integer.
DAY(date)	Returns an integer for the day of a month.
DB_ID([db_name])	Specifies the database ID number.
DB_NAME([db_id])	Specifies the database name.
DEGREES(numeric_expr)	Converts radians to degrees.
DIFFERENCE(char_expr1,char_expr2)	Returns the difference between SOUNDEX values of expressions.
EXP(float_expr)	Returns the exponential value of the specified value.
FILE_ID(file_name)	Returns the identifier for a database logical file.
FILE_NAME(file_id)	Returns a name for the file ID.
FILEGROUP_ID(group_name)	Returns the identifier for the group_name.
FILEGROUP_NAME(group_id)	Returns the name for the identifier.
FILEGROUPPROPERTY(group_name,property)	Returns the property value for a group and property name.

(continued)

Table B.2   All of the functions available in SQL Server 7 (continued).

Function	Description
FILEPROPERTY(file_name,property)	Returns the property value for a file and property name.
FLOOR(numeric_expr)	Specifies the largest integer that is less than or equal to a specified value.
FORMATMESSAGE(msg_number,param_value[,...n])	Formats a message, similar to **RAISERROR** but only formats the message.
FULLTEXTCATALOGPROPERTY(catalog,property)	Returns information about a full-text catalog.
FULLTEXTSERVICEPROPERTY(property)	Returns information about a full-text service.
GETANSINULL([database])	Returns the default nullability for the database.
GETDATE()	Returns the current system date and time.
HOST_ID()	Specifies the current host process ID number of a client process.
HOST_NAME()	Specifies the current host computer name of a client process.
IDENT_INCR({tablename|viewname})	Returns the identity increment value.
IDENT_SEED({tablename|viewname})	Returns the identity seed value.
INDEX_COL(objname,index_id,key #)	Specifies the indexed column name.
INDEXPROPERTY(table_id,index,property)	Returns information about an index.
IS_MEMBER({group|role})	Returns **1** if the current user is a member of the NT group or SQL Server role, **0** if not a member, and **NULL** if the group/role is not valid.
IS_SRVROLEMEMBER(role [,login])	Returns **1** if the login is a member of the SQL Server role.
ISDATE(expression)	Returns **1** if the expression is a valid date.
ISNULL(expression, constant_value)	Specifies to replace NULL values with a specified constant.

Function	Description
ISNUMERIC(*expression*)	Returns **1** if the expression is a valid numeric.
LEFT(*char_expr,int_expr*)	Returns *int_expr* characters from the left of *char_expr*.
LEN(*char_expr*)	Returns the integer number of characters in *char_expr*, ignoring trailing spaces.
LOG(*float_expr*)	Specifies the natural logarithm.
LOG10(*float_expr*)	Specifies the logarithm base 10.
LOWER(*char_expr*)	Converts *char_expr* to lowercase.
LTRIM(*char_expr*)	Removes leading spaces.
MONTH(*date*)	Returns the integer for the month.
NCHAR(*int_expr*)	Converts an integer to a Unicode character.
NEWID()	Creates a new unique value of the data type **UNIQUEIDENTIFIER**.
NULLIF(*expression1, expression2*)	Returns a **NULL** value if expression1 equals expression2.
OBJECT_ID(*objname*)	Specifies the database object ID number.
OBJECT_NAME(*obj_id*)	Specifies the database object name.
OBJECTPROPERTY(*id,property*)	Returns information about objects.
PARSE_NAME(*object_name,object_piece*)	Returns the specific object name part from object_name, 1 object name, 2 owner name, 3 database name, and 4 server name.
PATINDEX(*%pattern%, expression*)	Returns the starting position of the specified pattern, else 0.
PERMISSIONS([*objectid[,column]*])	Returns a bitmap that indicates the permissions for the current user on the object.
PI()	Returns the constant value of 3.1415926....
POWER(*numeric_expr,power*)	Returns the value of *numeric_expr* to the power of *power*.

(continued)

Table B.2 All of the functions available in SQL Server 7 (continued).

Function	Description
QUOTENAME(char_expr[,quote_character])	Converts char_expr to a quoted unique valid identifier. quote_character can be a single quote, double quote, or left/right bracket.
RADIANS()	Converts degrees to radians.
RAND([int_expr])	Returns a random float number between zero and one, optionally using int_expr as a seed.
REPLACE(char_expr1,char_expr2,char_expr3)	Replaces all occurrences of char_expr2 in char_expr1 with char_expr3.
REPLICATE(char_expr,int_expr)	Repeats char_expr, int_expr times.
REVERSE(char_expr)	Reverses text in char_expr.
RIGHT(char_expr,int_expr)	Returns int_expr characters from the right of char_expr.
ROUND(numeric_expr,int_expr[,function])	Rounds off a numeric expression to the precision specified in int_expr. If the function is non zero, ROUND truncates.
RTRIM(char_expr)	Removes trailing spaces.
SIGN(int_expr)	Returns the positive (+1), zero (0), or negative (–1).
SIN(float_expr)	Returns the sine of the angle.
SOUNDEX(char_expr)	Returns a soundex value, a four-character value used to compare strings, of char_expr.
SPACE(int_expr)	Generates a string of int_expr spaces.
SQRT(float_expr)	Provides the square root of the specified value.
SQUARE(float_expr)	Returns the square of the expression.
STATS_DATE(table_id,index_id)	Specifies the date statistics were last updated for a specified index.

Function	Description
STR(*float_expr* [, *length* [, *decimal*]])	Converts numeric to character.
STUFF(*char_expr1, start, length, char_expr2*)	Replaces *length* characters from *expr1* at *start* with *expr2*.
SUBSTRING(*expression, start, length*)	Returns part of a string.
SUSER_ID([*login_name*])	Specifies a user's SQL Server ID number.
SUSER_NAME([*server_user_sid*])	Specifies a user's SQL Server login name.
SUSER_SID([*login_name*])	Specifies a user's SQL Server ID number.
SUSER_SNAME([*server_user_sid*])	Specifies a user's SQL Server login name.
SYSTEM_USER	Specifies the current user's SQL Server login name.
TAN(*float_expr*)	Returns the tangent of the angle.
TSEQUAL(*timestamp1, timestamp2*)	Compares **timestamp** values. Returns an error if **timestamp** values do not match.
TYPEPROPERTY(*type,property*)	Returns information about a data type.
UNICODE(*nchar_expr*)	Specifies the unicode integer for the first character of *nchar_expr*.
UPPER(*char_expr*)	Converts *char_expr* to uppercase.
USER()	Returns the current username.
USER_ID([*name_in_db*])	Specifies a user's ID number in database.
USER_NAME([*user_id*]) or SESSION_USER	Specifies a user's name in a database.
USERID([*user*])	Returns the user ID for the user.
VALID_NAME(*char_expr*)	Returns **0** if *char_expr* is not a valid identifier.
YEAR(*date expression*)	Returns the four-digit integer for the year.

Table B.3 Date parts.

No Century	With Century	Format Of The Converted String
N/A	0 or 100	mon dd yyyy hh:miAM (or PM)
1	101	mm/dd/yy
2	102	yy.mm.dd
3	103	dd/mm/yy
4	104	dd.mm.yy
5	105	dd-mm-yy
6	106	dd mon yy
7	107	mon dd, yy
8	108	hh:mm:ss
N/A	9 or 109	mon dd, yyyy hh:mi:ss:mmmAM (or PM)
10	110	mm-dd-yy
11	111	yy/mm/dd
12	112	yymmdd
13	113	dd mon yyyy hh:mi:ss:mmm (24 hr clock)
14	114	hh:mi:ss:mmm (24 hr clock)
20	120	yyyy-mm-dd hh:mi:ss (24h)
21	121	yyyy-mm-dd hh:mi:ss:mmm (24h)

Table B.4 Date conversion styles.

Value	Description	Example
0	Default conversion. Six digits, scientific notation when appropriate	1.23457e+006
1	Always 8-digit scientific notation	1.2345671e+006
2	Always 16-digit scientific notation	1.234567125000000e+006

Table B.5 Converting FLOAT or REAL Data Type to CHARACTER.

Value	Description	Example
0	Default conversion. No commas, 2 digits to the right of the decimal point	123456.12
1	Commas every 3 digits to the left of the decimal, 2 digits after the decimal point	123,234.12
2	No commas, 4 digits to the right of decimal point	1234.1234

Table B.6   Converting Money and smallmoney to character.

Function	Definition
avg([all | distinct]) *expression*)	Specifies the average of the (distinct) values in the numeric column.
count(*)	Specifies the number of selected rows. Only aggregate function that includes nulls.
count([all | distinct] *expression*)	Specifies the number of non-null values in the column.
max(*expression*)	Specifies the highest value in the expression.
min(*expression*)	Specifies the lowest value in the expression.
STDEV(*expression*)	Returns the standard deviation.
STDEVP(*expression*)	Returns the standard deviation for the population.
sum([all | distinct] *expression*)	Specifies the total of the values in the numeric column.
VAR(*expression*)	Returns the statistical variance.
VARP(*expression*)	Returns the statistical variance for the population.

Table B.7   Aggregate functions.

Function	Definition
CONTAINSTABLE(table, {, column | *}, <contains_search_ condition>)	Performs fuzzy logic searches in full-text queries.
FREETEXTTABLE(*table*, {, *column* | *}, *"free_text_string"*)	Matches meanings, not exact words in full-text queries.
OPENQUERY(*linked_server*."*query*")	Runs query against another data source.
OPENROWSET ("*provider_name*" {"*datasource*"'"user_id";"password"* | "provider_string"}, {[catalog.] [schema.]object | "query"})	Performs one-time ad hoc queries against a remote data source.

Appendix C
Transact-SQL
Syntax

Syntax Conventions

Table C.1	Syntax conventions.
Key	**Definition**
command	Command names, options, and other keywords
variable	Values you provide
{}	Indicates you must choose at least one of the enclosed options
[]	Means the value/keyword is optional
()	Parentheses are part of the command
|	Indicates you can select only one of the options shown (Like an or operator)
,	Means you can select as many of the options shown, separated by commas
...	Indicates the previous option can be repeated
expression	An expression that returns a single value can be restricted to one of the following types: char_expression constant_expression float_expression integer_expression numeric_expression binary_expression

Bulk Copy Programming
Listing C.1   The full syntax for BCP.

```
bcp [[database_name.][owner].]table_name
   {in | out | format} data_file
   [-m max_errors] [-f format_file] [-e err_file]
   [-F first_row] [-L last_row] [-b batch_size]
   [-n] [-c] [-w] [-N] [-6] [-q] [-C code_page]
   [-t field_term] [-r row_term]
   [-i input_file] [-o output_file] [-a packet_size]
   [-S server_name] [-U login_id] [-P password]
   [-T] [-v] [-k] [-E] [-h "hint [, ...n]"]
```

Table C.2   Table BCP optimizer hints.

Hint	Meaning
ORDER (column [ASC | DESC] [,n])	Sort order of the data in the data file.
ROWS_PER_BATCH = bb	Number of rows of data per batch. Do not used with the –b parameter.
KILOBYTES_PER_BATCH = cc	Number of kilobytes of data per batch.
TABLOCK	A table-level lock is acquired for the duration of the bulk copy operation.
CHECK CONSTRAINTS	Causes SQL Server to check table constraints during data loads.

Bulk Insert
Listing C.2   Full syntax for bulk insert.

```
BULK INSERT [['database_name'.]['owner'].]
   {'table_name' FROM data_file}
[WITH (
   [ BATCHSIZE  = batch_size]
   [[,] CHECK_CONSTRAINTS]
   [[,] CODEPAGE  = ACP | OEM | RAW | code_page]
   [[,] DATAFILETYPE  =
        {'char' | 'native'| 'widechar' | 'widenative'}]
   [[,] FIELDTERMINATOR  = 'field_terminator']
   [[,] FIRSTROW  = first_row]
   [[,] FORMATFILE  = 'format_file_path']
   [[,] KEEPIDENTITY]
   [[,] KEEPNULLS]
   [[,] LASTROW  = last_row]
   [[,] MAXERRORS  = max_errors]
   [[,] ORDER ({column [ASC | DESC]} [, ...n])]
   [[,] ROWTERMINATOR  = 'row_terminator']
```

```
    [[,] TABLOCK]
)
]
```

Comparison Operators

Table C.3   Comparison operators.

Operator	Meaning
=	Equal
<>	Not equal
!=	Not equal
>	Greater than
>=	Greater than or equal to
!>	Not greater than
<	Less than
<=	Less than or equal to
!<	Not less than

Select Statement
Listing C.3   Full syntax for a **SELECT** statement.

```
SELECT [ ALL | DISTINCT ] [ TOP n [PERCENT] [ WITH TIES] ] select_list
[ INTO table_name ]
[FROM {table_name | view_name}
    [ , {table_name | view_name} ... ]
[ WHERE search_conditions ]
[ GROUP BY aggregate_free_expression
    [ , aggregate_free_expression ... ]
    [WITH CUBE|ROLLUP] ]
[ HAVING search_conditions ]
[ ORDER BY { column_name | select_list_no } [ ASC | DESC ]
    [ , { column_name | select_list_no } [ ASC | DESC ] ... ] ]
[ COMPUTE row_aggregate(column_name)
    [ , row_aggregate(column_name) ] ...
    [ BY column_name [ , column_name ] ... ] ] ]
```

From Clause
Listing C.4   Full syntax for a **from clause**.

```
FROM
{ <table_or_view>| (select_statement)
    [AS] table_alias (column_alias ,. . . .]
```

```
| <table_or_view> CROSS JOIN <table_or_view>
{ { INNER | { FULL | LEFT | RIGHT } [OUTER]  JOIN } <table_or_view>
    ON <join_condition>}
}[, ...n]
```

Where Clause
Listing C.5   Full syntax for a where clause.

```
WHERE [ NOT ] <predicate> [ { AND | OR } [ NOT ] <predicate> ]
} [, ...n]

<predicate> ::=
{ expression { = | <> | != | > | >= | !> | < | <= | !< } expression
| string_expression [NOT] LIKE
                    string_expression[ESCAPE 'escape_character']
| expression [NOT] BETWEEN expression AND expression
| expression IS [NOT] NULL
| expression [NOT] IN (subquery | expression [,...n])
| expression { = | <> | != | > | >= | !> | < | <= | !< }
{ALL | SOME | ANY} (subquery)

| EXISTS (subquery)
}
```

Case Statement
Listing C.6   Full syntax for a case statement.

```
CASE expression
        WHEN expression THEN expresion [...]
        [ELSE expression]
    END
```

Listing C.7   Full syntax for a search case statement.

```
CASE
    WHEN column = expression THEN expression [...]
    [ELSE expression]
END
```

Cursors
Listing C.8   Syntax for declaring cursor statements.

```
defines a cursor
declare cursor_name [insensitive] [scroll] cursor
 for select_statment
 [for [read only | update [of column_list]}]
```

Listing C.9   Syntax for opening a declared cursor.

```
open cursor_name
```

Listing C.10   Syntax for retrieving a specific row from a cursor.

```
fetch [[next |prior | first | last | absolute n|
       relative n] from] cursor_name
[into @variable_name,...]
```

Listing C.11   Syntax for closing an open cursor.

```
close cursor_name
```

Listing C.12   Syntax for removing cursor data structures.

```
deallocate cursor_name
```

Data Manipulation

Listing C.13   Syntax for adding rows to a table.

```
insert [into] table_name [(column_list)]
  {values ({default | constant_expression}
    [, ...])
  | select_statement}
```

Listing C.14   Syntax for modifying rows in a table.

```
UPDATE {<table_or_view>}
 SET
   {column_name = {expression | DEFAULT}
   | @variable = expression } [, n]
  [FROM
    from_clause ]
  [WHERE
    <search_conditions>
    | CURRENT OF
       { { [GLOBAL] cursor_name } | cursor_variable_name} }
  ]
```

Listing C.15   Syntax for removing rows from a table.

```
delete [from] table_name
  [from {table_name | view_name} [, ...]]
    [where search conditions]
```

Listing C.16 Syntax for quickly removing all rows from a table.

```
truncate table table_name
```

Table Definitions
Listing C.17 The full syntax for creating a table.

```
CREATE TABLE table_name
( { ColumnName DataType
[ NULL | NOT NULL ] [ IDENTITY [(seed, increment )
[NOT FOR REPLICATION] ] ]
[ ROWGUIDCOL ]
[CONSTRAINT ConstraintName]
{ { PRIMARY KEY | UNIQUE } [CLUSTERED | NONCLUSTERED]
[WITH [FILLFACTOR = fillfactor_value]
[ON {filegroup | DEFAULT} ]
| [FOREIGN KEY] REFERENCES RefTable [ ( RefColumn ) ]
[NOT FOR REPLICATION]
| DEFAULT Constant_Expression
| CHECK [NOT FOR REPLICATION]
(LogicalExpression)
}] [ ...n]
| ColumnName AS computed_column_expression
| <table_constraint>
} [, ...n]
)
[ON {filegroup | DEFAULT} ]
[TEXTIMAGE_ON {filegroup | DEFAULT} ]
<column_definition> ::= { ColumnName DataType }
[ NULL | NOT NULL ]
[ IDENTITY [(seed, increment )
[NOT FOR REPLICATION] ] ]
[ ROWGUIDCOL ]
[ <column_constraint> ::=
[CONSTRAINT ConstraintName]
{ { PRIMARY KEY | UNIQUE }
[CLUSTERED | NONCLUSTERED]
[WITH [FILLFACTOR = fillfactor]
]
[ON {filegroup | DEFAULT} ]
| [FOREIGN KEY]
REFERENCES ref_table
[ ( ref_column ) ]
[NOT FOR REPLICATION]
| DEFAULT constant_expression
| CHECK [NOT FOR REPLICATION]
```

```
(logical_expression)
}
] [ ...n]

Ex:
CREATE TABLE authors_short
(author_id int not null,
 lastname varchar(40) not null,
 firstname varchar(20) null)
```

Listing C.18   The full syntax for altering a table.

```
ALTER TABLE Table_name
{
 [WITH CHECK | WITH NOCHECK]
  { [ALTER COLUMN ColumnName
      { [ NewDataType [ (precision[, scale] ) ]
            [ NULL | NOT NULL ] ]
        | [ {ADD | DROP} ROWGUIDCOL ]
      }
    ]
    | ADD
      { [{ ColumnName DataType }
          [ NULL | NOT NULL ]
          [ IDENTITY [(seed[, increment] )
          [NOT FOR REPLICATION] ] ]
          [ ROWGUIDCOL ]
        ]
        | ColumnName AS computed_column_expression
        | [[CONSTRAINT ConstraintName]
          { [ { PRIMARY KEY | UNIQUE }
            [ CLUSTERED | NONCLUSTERED]
              { ( column[,...n] ) }
                [ WITH [FILLFACTOR = fillfactor]
                ]
          [ON {filegroup | DEFAULT} ]]
          | FOREIGN KEY [(column[,...n])]
            REFERENCES ref_table [(ref_column[,...n])]
          [NOT FOR REPLICATION]
          | DEFAULT constant_expression [FOR column]
          | CHECK [NOT FOR REPLICATION]
            (logical_expression)
          }]
      }[,...n]
      | DROP
      { [CONSTRAINT] constraint
       | COLUMN column
      }[,...n]
```

```
    | {CHECK | NOCHECK} CONSTRAINT {ALL | constraint[,...n]}
  }
}
```

Indexes
Listing C.19   Syntax for creating an index.

```
create [unique] [clustered | nonclustered]
    index index_name
    on [[database,] owner.] table_name (column_name]...])
[with
    [fillfactor = x]
    [[,] ignore_dup_key]
    [[,] {sorted_data | sorted_data_reorg}]
    [[,] {ignore_dup_row | allow_dup_row}]]
[on segment_name]
```

Listing C.20   Syntax for dropping an index.

```
drop index [owner.]table_name.index_name
[,[owner.]table_name.index_name...]
```

Rules And Defaults
Listing C.21   Syntax for creating rules.

```
CREATE RULE RuleName
@variable operator expression
  [{and|or} ...]
```

Listing C.22   Syntax for dropping rules.

```
drop rule [owner.]rule_name[,
[owner.]rule_name...]
```

Listing C.23   Syntax for binding a rule to a column.

```
sp_bindrule rule_name,
    'table.column_name'
```

Listing C.24   Syntax for unbinding a rule from a column.

```
sp_unbindrule
    'table.column_name'
```

Listing C.25   Syntax for creating a default.

```
create default [owner]default_name
as constant_expression
```

Listing C.26 Syntax for dropping a default.

```
drop default [owner.]default_name[,
[owner.]default_name...]
```

Listing C.27 Syntax for binding a default to a column.

```
sp_bindefault default_name,
    'table.column_name'
```

Listing C.28 Syntax for unbinding a default from a column.

```
sp_unbindefault 'table.column_name'
```

Databases: Creating, Changing, And Dumping

Listing C.29 Syntax for creating a database.

```
CREATE DATABASE db_name
    [ ON [PRIMARY] ([ NAME = logical_file_name, ]
            FILENAME = 'os_file_name'
            [, SIZE = size]
            [, MAXSIZE = { max_size | UNLIMITED } ]
            [, FILEGROWTH = growth_increment] )
            | {FILEGROUP filegroup_name FILEDEFINITIONS}
            [,...n] ]
    [LOG ON {[ NAME = logical_file_name, ]
            FILENAME = 'os_file_name'
            [, SIZE = size]
            [, MAXSIZE = { max_size | UNLIMITED } ]
            [, FILEGROWTH = growth_increment]  } [,...n]
        [FOR LOAD | FOR ATTACH]
```

Listing C.30 Syntax for altering a database.

```
ALTER DATABASE database
    { ADD FILE <filespec> [,...n] [TO FILEGROUP filegroup_name]
    | ADD LOG FILE <filespec> [,...n]
    | REMOVE FILE logical_file_name
    | ADD FILEGROUP filegroup_name
    | REMOVE FILEGROUP filegroup_name
    | MODIFY FILE <filespec>
    | MODIFY FILEGROUP filegroup_name filegroup_property
    }
```

```
<filespec> ::=
  (NAME = 'logical_file_name'
  [, FILENAME = 'os_file_name' ]
  [, SIZE = size]
  [, MAXSIZE = { max_size | UNLIMITED } ]
  [, FILEGROWTH = growth_increment] )
```

Listing C.31   Syntax for loading databases.

```
load database {dbname | @dbname_var}
  from dump_device[, ...]
  [with options
    [[,] stats [ = percentage]]]
```

Listing C.32   Syntax for loading transactions.

```
load transaction {dbname |
 @dbname var)
   from dump_device [, ...]
   [with options]
```

Listing C.33   Syntax for dumping a database.

```
dump database {dbname |@dbname_var)
 to dump_device [, ...]]

  [with options
    [[,]stats [=percentage]]]
```

Listing C.34   The full syntax used to shrink
a database.

```
DBCC SHRINKDATABASE
( database_name [, target_percent]
[, {NOTRUNCATE | TRUNCATEONLY}]
)
```

Listing C.35   Syntax for dumping transaction logs.

```
dump transaction {dbname|
 @dbname_var}
 [to dump_device [, ...]]
 [with {truncate_only | no_log |
        no_truncate}
  {options}]
```

Listing C.36   Syntax to rename a database.

```
sp_renamedb "old_name","new_name"

use master
```

```
go
sp_dboption MyDB,'single','true'
go
sp_renamedb MyDB,'MyNewDB'
go
sp_dboption MyNewDB,'single','false'
go
```

Listing C.37   The full syntax to shrink a file.

```
DBCC SHRINKFILE
( {file_name | file_id }
{ [, target_size]
| [, {EMPTYFILE | NOTRUNCATE | TRUNCATEONLY}]
}
)
```

Listing C.38   Disk init.

```
NAME = 'logical_name',
    PHYSNAME = 'physical_name',
    VDEVNO = virtual_device_number,
    SIZE = number_of_2K_blocks
    [, VSTART = virtual_address]
```

Display Messages
Listing C.39   Print statement syntax.

```
print {"any ascii text"
  | @local_variable
  | @@global_variable
```

Listing C.40   Raise error syntax.

```
raiserror ({msg_id|msg_str},severity,state
  [, argument1[, ...]]])
  [with log]
7,0 Syntax to add to the new document
```

Full Text
Listing C.41   The syntax for generating a full
text catalog.

```
sp_fulltext_catalog 'fulltext_catalog_name',
 ['create'|'drop'
  |'start_incremental'|'start_full'
```

```
|'stop'|'rebuild']
[, 'root_directory']
```

Listing C.42   Registering tables for a full text search.

```
sp_fulltext_table ['table_name'],
['create'|'drop'|'activate'|'deactivate']
[,'catalog_name',
 'index_name']
```

Listing C.43   Registering columns for a full text search.

```
sp_fulltext_column 'table_name', 'column_name', {'ADD'|'DROP'}
```

Listing C.44   Activating a table for full-text index.

```
sp_fulltext_table 'titles','activate'
```

Listing C.45   Full syntax for a remote procedure call.

```
[exec[ute]]
   server_name.[database_name].[owner].stored_procedure
   [parameters[, parameter . . . ]]
```

Security

Listing C.46   Syntax for adding a login.

```
sp_addlogin login_name, password
  [, default_database [, default_language
     [, fullname ] ] ]]
```

Listing C.47   Syntax for removing a login.

```
sp_droplogin login_name
```

Listing C.48   Syntax for adding a user to a database.

```
sp_adduser login_name [, name_in_db
  [, group_name]]
```

Listing C.49   Syntax for removing a user.

```
sp_dropuser user_name
```

Listing C.50   Syntax for granting and revoking object permissions.

```
grant {all | permission_list}
   on [table_name [(column_list)] | view_name
```

```
[(column_list)]|
 stored_procedure_name |
 extended_stored_procedure_name}
 to {public | name_list}
revoke {all | permission_list}
 on {table_name [(column_list)] | view_name
 [(column_list)]|
  stored_procedure_name|
 extended_stored_procedure_name}
from {public | name_list}

deny {all | permission_list}
 on {table_name [(column_list)] | view_name
 [(column_list)]|
  stored_procedure_name|
 extended_stored_procedure_name}
from {public | name_list}
```

Listing C.51   Syntax for granting and revoking command permissions.

```
grant {all | statement_list}
  to {public or name_list}

revoke {all | statement_list}
  from {public | name_list}

deny {all | statement_list}
  from {public | name_list}
```

Listing C.52   Syntax for listing information about database users.

```
sp_helpuser [user_name]
```

Listing C.53   Syntax for listing security for objects and users.

```
sp_helprotect {object_name | user_name}
```

Listing C.54   Syntax to create a dynamic alias by the dbo to another user in the database.

```
setuser ["username" [with noreset]]
```

Set Statements

Table C.4 Set statements.	
Statement	**Description**
set datefirst number	Controls which day is the first day of the week
set dateformat {format | @format_var}	Specifies the format of date values in character strings used by SQL Server
set deadlock_priority { low | normal | @var}	Controls how SQL handles deadlocks
set lock_timeout milliseconds_to_wait	Changes the default and causes a timeout when resources have been locked
set concat_null_yields_null (on | off }	True yields a null when you concatenate a null with a string, otherwise it returns a string
set cursor_close_on_commit	Determines the behavior of a cursor when a commit is issued
set identity_insert	Allows you to specify a value for an identity column
set fips_flagger {entry | intermediate | full | off}	Used to check for SQL for compliance with the ANSI SQL -92 Standard
set language {language | var}	Allows you to specify a different language for a connection
set offsets	Used in conjunction with DB-Lib applications to find keywords in SQL
set procid	Used in conjunction with DB-Library to return stored procedures to the calling DB_Library applications
set quoted_identifier {on | off}	Instructs SQL Server to follow the ANSI SQL-92 standards
set arithabort {on | off}	Determines SQL Server Processing when either an arithmetic overflow or a division by zero occurs
set arithignore {on | off}	Determines which SQL Server error message is generated when an arithmetic overflow or a division by zero occurs ins select statements
set fmtonly {on | off}	Enables you to configure SQL Server to only return column information to the client

(continued)

Table C.4 Set statements *(continued)*.	
Statement	**Description**
set nocount {on | offf}	Used to stop SQL Server from sending the number of rows affected by a SQL statement back to the client after every SQL statement
set noexec {on | off}	Used to stop SQL statements from running
set numeric_roundabort {on | off}	Controls SQL Server behavior when arithmetic rounding of a values causes a query to lose precision
set parseonly {on | off}	Used to configure SQL Server to check the syntax of SQL statements
set query_governor_cost_limit int_value	Allows you to limit the queries that can run based on the amount of work SQL Server estimates the statement will take
set rowcount int_value	Allows you to limit the number of rows affected by a SQL Statement
set textsize {int_value | @int_var}	Specifies the number of bytes returned with a select statement
set ansi_defaults {on | off}	Used to turn on and off ANSI SQL behavior
set ansi_nulls {on | off}	Enables you to specify how SQL Server will behave when checking whether columns equal a null value
set ansi_padding {on | off}	Controls how SQL Server stores char, varchar, binary, and varbinary columns that either end in blanks or are shorter than the maximum column length
set ansi_warnings {on | off}	Specifies ANSI standard behavior for error conditions
set forceplan {on | off}	Determines the optimal order to perform a join
set showplan_all {on | off}	Instructs SQL Server to retrieve execution information about each SQL statement
set showplan_text {on | off}	Instructs SQL Server to retrieve execution information about each SQL statement

(continued)

Table C.4   Set statements (continued).

Statement	Description
set statistics io {on | off}	Instructs SQL Server to return information about the disk activity performed by a SQL statement
set statistics time {on | off}	Instructs SQL Server to return the number of milliseconds to parse, compile, and execute each SQL statement
set implicit_transactions {on | off}	Instructs SQL Server to implicitly begin transactions
set remote_proc_transactions {on | off}}	Affects SQL Servers behavior when a remote procedure call is made
set xact_abort {on | off}	Controls SQL Servers behavior when runtime errors occur
set no exec on	Stops any statement from executing except the set no exec
set transaction isolation level (read committed | read uncommitted | repeateable read | serializable}	Controls SQL Servers locking behavior

Stored Procedures

Listing C.55   Syntax for creating a stored procedure.

```
create procedure [owner.]procedure_name[;number]
  [(parameter1 [, parameter2]...[parameter255])]
[{for replication} | {with recompile}
  [{[with] | [,]} encryption]]
as sql_statements
```

Listing C.56   Syntax for executing a stored procedure.

```
[[execute]
{[@return_status = ]

{[[[server.]db.]owner.]procedure_name[;number]
  @procedure_name_var}
[[@parameter_name =] {value | @variable output
[,[...]]]
[with recompile]
```

Listing C.57   Syntax for displaying information about an object.

```
sp_help {type_name | procedure_name |
    table_name | view_name |
    rule_name | default_name}
```

Listing C.58   Syntax for listing indexes defined on a table.

```
sp_helpindex table_name
```

Listing C.59   Syntax for displaying creation text.

```
sp_helptext {rule_name | default_name
  | view_name | procedure_name
  | trigger_name}
```

Listing C.60   Syntax for renaming an object.

```
sp_rename {old_name |
  'table_name.old_col_name'}, new_name
```

Listing C.61   Syntax for displaying information on constraints.

```
sp_helpconstraint table_name [, detail]
```

Listing C.62   Syntax for listing all referenced objects.

```
sp_depends {trigger_name |
            procedure_name}
```

Listing C.63   Syntax for listing all triggers and stored procedures that reference a table or view.

```
sp_depends {table_name | view_name}
```

Listing C.64   Syntax for viewing current locks.

```
sp_lock [spid]
```

Listing C.65   Syntax for viewing current processes.

```
sp_who [spid]
```

Listing C.66   Syntax for listing database(s).

```
sp_helpdb [db_name]
```

**Listing C.67   Syntax for adding custom
error messages.**

```
exec sp_addmessage msg_id, msg_text,
  [,language [,{true | false} [,replace]]]
```

Listing C.68   Syntax for defining and displaying keys.

```
sp_primarykey table_name, col1 [, ...]
sp_foreignkey table_name, pk_table_name,
   col1 [, col2, ...]
sp_commonkey table1_name, table2_name,
   col1a, col2a [, col1b, col2b , ...]
sp_helpkey table_name
```

Table And View Commands
Listing C.69   The syntax to drop a table.

```
drop table [[database.]owner.]table_name
[,[[database.]owner.]table_name...]
```

Listing C.70   The syntax to create a view.

```
create view [owner.] view_name [(column_name [,column_name]...)]
 [with encryption]
as {select_statement} [with check option]0
```

Listing C.71   The syntax to drop a view.

```
drop view [owner.]view_name[,
[owner.]view_name...]
```

Listing C.72   The full syntax to alter a view.

```
ALTER VIEW view_name [(column [, ...n])]
 [WITH ENCRYPTION]
AS
select_statement
 [WITH CHECK OPTION]
```

Transactions And Locking
Listing C.73   Syntax for beginning a transaction.

```
begin transaction [transaction_name]
```

Listing C.74   Syntax for committing a transaction.

```
commit transaction [transaction_name]
```

Listing C.75   Syntax for rolling back a transaction.

```
rollback transaction
  [transaction_name | savepoint_name]
```

Listing C.76   Syntax for saving a transaction.

```
save transaction savepoint_name
```

Listing C.77   Syntax for setting a transaction level.

```
set transaction isolation level
  {read committed | read uncommitted
     serializable | repeatable read}
```

Triggers

Listing C.78   Syntax for creating a trigger.

```
create trigger trigger_name
  on table_name
  [WITH ENCRYPTION]
  for {insert | update | delete} [, ...]
  [WITH APPEND]
  [NOT FOR REPLICATION]
  as
[SQL_Statements]
[return]
This Syntax will drop a trigger
drop trigger trigger_name [,trigger_name [,. . . ] ]
This syntax will modify a trigger
alter trigger trigger_name
  on table_name
  [WITH ENCRYPTION]
  for {insert | update | delete} [, ...]
  [WITH APPEND]
  [NOT FOR REPLICATION]
  as
[SQL_Statements]
[return ]
```

Listing C.79   Syntax for checking if a column was updated or inserted.

```
if update (col_name)
  [ { and | or } update (col_name) ...]
```

Update Statistics
Listing C.80 Full syntax for update statistics.

```
UPDATE STATISTICS {table_name}
[index_name | (index_or_column_list
[, ...n])
]
[WITH
[[FULLSCAN]| SAMPLE number {PERCENT | ROWS}]]
[[,] [ALL | COLUMNS | INDEX]
[[,] NORECOMPUTE]
]
```

User-Defined Datatypes
Listing C.81 Syntax for creating a datatype.

```
sp_addtype typename, datatype,
        [{null | not null}]
```

Listing C.82 Syntax for dropping a datatype.

```
sp_droptype typename
```

Writetext And Updatetext Statements
Listing C.83 Full syntax for WRITETEXT and UPDATETEXT statements.

```
WRITETEXT {table.column text_ptr}
[WITH LOG] {data}

UPDATETEXT {table_name.dest_column_name dest_text_ptr}
{ NULL | insert_offset}
{ NULL | delete_length}
[WITH LOG]
[ inserted_data | [{table_name.src_column_name src_text_ptr}]
```

Glossary

ad hoc connector name—The **OpenRowset** function in the **FROM** clause of a query, which is used to make a one-time connection to an external data source.

aggregate functions—Functions that produce summary values. The aggregate functions are: **AVG, COUNT, COUNT(*), MAX, MIN, STDEV, STDEVP, SUM, VAR,** and **VARP**.

aggregate query—Any query using an aggregate function.

alert—A system-administrator-defined response to a SQL Server event.

alias—An alternative name for a table or column in expressions.

American National Standards Institute (ANSI)—The organization of American industry and business groups that develops trade and communication standards for the United States.

anonymous subscription—A pull subscription that enables a server that is known to the Publisher to receive a subscription to a publication, but only for the duration of the connection.

API server cursor—A server cursor built indirectly by calling an application programming interface (API), such as ODBC, OLE DB, ADO, and DB-Library. See also *cursor and server cursor.*

application log—A Windows NT file that records events. SQL Server can be configured to use the Windows NT application log.

application programming interface (API)—A set of routines that an application can call.

application role—A SQL Server database role in which the application takes control of security. This role is activated by a password.

article—The basic unit of replication. An article can be a table or a stored procedure.

authentication—The process of identifying users and verifying permissions while connecting to SQL Server.

authorization—The process of verifying permissions and access rights for a user after connecting to SQL Server.

automatic recovery—The automatic process of either rolling transactions forward or rolling transactions back when SQL Server is restarted. Automatic recovery is used to guarantee the consistency of databases.

automatic synchronization—An automatic replication process that synchronizes a Subscriber to a Publisher when a subscription is created.

back end—The processing performed by the database server.

backup—The process of making a copy of a database, transaction log, file, or filegroup stored on a tape, named pipe, or hard disk.

backup device—A tape, disk file, or named pipe that is used to either back up a database or restore a database.

backup file—A file that contains a backup.

backup media—Types of backup storage devices. You can use a file, a tape, or a named pipe to store the backup set.

backup set—The backup medium that is used for a single backup operation.

base table—An underlying table that makes up a view.

batch—One or more SQL statements that are executed by SQL Server.

bcp utility—A DOS-prompt utility that copies data between a SQL Server table and an operating system file in a format that the user specifies.

binary data type—A SQL Server data type used to store hexadecimal numbers. The binary data type can store between 0 and 8,000 bytes.

Binary Large Object (BLOB)—A SQL Server data type for binary data, such as graphics, sound, or compiled code. This data type can contain up to 2GB of data.

bit data type—A SQL Server data type that stores either 1 or 0.

blocks—One or more SQL statements between a **BEGIN** statement and an **END** statement.

Boolean expression—Any expression that returns a true, false, or null value.

candidate key—Any unique identifier for a row of data. A candidate key is also called a *surrogate key*.

Cartesian product—When two tables are joined together with no join arguments. A Cartesian product returns all the possible combinations of rows from the tables involved in a join operation.

cascading delete—Removes all of the related rows (or columns) in dependent tables.

cascading update—Updates all related dependent rows (or columns).

character set—The set of characters that SQL Server stores in **char, varchar,** and **text** data types. Every character set contains 256 letters, digits, and symbols specific to a country or language. The first 128 characters are the same for all character sets.

char(n) data type—A SQL Server data type that holds between 0 and 8,000 characters.

CHECK constraint—A constraint that verifies that the values being stored in a column match the domain.

checkpoint—A SQL Server system event that causes all changed data pages to be written to disk.

client—A process (a program or a task) that requests a service from a server application. Also, on a local area network, a computer that accesses shared network resources provided by a server.

client cursor—A cursor that is implemented on the client by an API.

client/server computing—A branch of computing in which processing is distributed between *clients* (programs typically optimized for user interaction) and *servers* (programs that provide centralized data management and network administration and security) on a local area network. Client/server architecture offers increased processing power and more efficient use of processing power than older architectures offer.

clustered index—An index in which the data is sorted in the order of the index values.

code page—See *character set*.

column—An individual piece of data in a row.

column-level constraint—A constraint that enforces column integrity.

commit—A process that saves changes to a database.

composite index—An index that consists of more than one column.

composite key—A key that consists of more than one column.

concatenation—Joining two or more character strings, expressions, or binary strings into one.

concurrency—The capability of multiple users accessing SQL Server at the same time.

connection—Any successful login to SQL Server.

connectivity—The capability of multiple processes to intercommunicate.

constant—Any static value that can be used in a query, not including functions, columns, or database objects.

constraint—A property of one or more columns in a table, limiting the values that can be stored in the column(s).

control-of-flow language—T-SQL statements that control execution flow of SQL statements.

correlated subquery—A subquery that uses values from the outer query to determine what rows are returned by the subquery.

cross join—A join that produces a Cartesian product as its result.

cursor—The act of processing a result set one row at a time. Cursors can be either client-side cursors or server-side cursors.

Data Control Language (DCL)—The SQL statements that control permissions on database objects.

Data Definition Language (DDL)—The SQL statements that create the tables and database structure.

data dictionary—The system tables that describe the database objects.

data file—A file that contains the data that makes up a database, as opposed to the files used to store the transaction log.

data integrity—The process of ensuring that data is accurate and reliable.

Data Manipulation Language (DML)—The SQL statements that insert, update, delete, or select data.

data migration—The movement of data from one data source to another. Also called *data transfer*.

data source—Any data that can be accessed through SQL Server.

data transformation—The process that changes a database's data structure or values when migrating data.

Data Transformation Services (DTS)—A SQL Server component that can import, export, and transform data.

data type—An attribute of a column describing what sort of information can be stored in the column.

database catalog—The system tables that contain the information describing the objects in the database.

Database Consistency Checker (DBCC)—A SQL Server statement used to check the logical and physical consistency of a database and to perform other system functions.

database diagram—A graphical representation of either the complete database schema or any part of a database schema.

database file—Either a data file or a transaction log file.

database management system (DBMS)—A program that controls access to data.

database name—A name that uniquely identifies a database on a SQL Server.

database object—Any one of the following database elements: table, index, trigger, view, key, constraint, default, rule, user-defined data type, or stored procedure.

database object owner—The database user that created the database object.

database owner (dbo)—The user that owns the database; he or she does not have to own the objects in the database.

datetime data type—A SQL Server data type that stores date and time information. A **datetime** data type consists of two 4-byte integers.

DB-Library—A series of high-level language application programming interfaces (APIs) for the client in a client/server system.

deadlock—A situation in which two or more users all have a resource locked and are waiting for the other users to release their locks.

decision support system—A database used to analyze data.

default database—The database that a login switches to when connecting to SQL Server.

default language—The language that a login will use to communicate with SQL Server.

denormalize—The process of adding redundant data into a database. This process will change the normal form of a table.

deny—To specifically say that a user or role does not have permissions to access an object or perform a task.

differential database backup—A database backup that dumps only the rows that have changed since the last full database backup.

dirty read—A read that retrieves data that has been changed, but not committed to the database.

distributed database—A database that is physically implemented on multiple database servers.

Distributor—In the Publish and Subscribe model of replication, the server that holds the distribution database.

domain—The set of valid values for an attribute.

domain integrity—The processes of ensuring that all attributes must be a valid member of their domain.

dump—A backup.

dynamic cursor—A cursor in which the result set is not static. That is, as you scroll through the result set, any data modifications made to the underlying data will show up in the result set.

dynamic locking—The SQL Server process that evaluates the most effective locking schema to use with every query.

entity integrity—A process that ensures that a table has a unique primary key.

equality join—A join based on a comparison of scalar values (=, > , >= , < , <= , < >, !<, and !>).

error log—An operating-system ASCII file in which SQL Server records messages.

event log—An NT system file that contains messages from any process that is on the computer.

exclusive lock—A lock that prevents any other process from obtaining a lock on rows of data currently being locked.

explicit transaction—A situation in which an application requests that a transaction not start until the application commits or rolls back the transaction.

expression—Any column, function, variable, subquery, or any combination of column names, constants, and functions connected by an operator that evaluates to a single value and used in place of a column in a SQL statement.

extended stored procedure—A function in an external DLL that is executed as if it is a SQL Server stored procedure.

extent—The unit that SQL Server uses to allocate space to a table or index. An extent is eight contiguous pages from one file, for a total of 64K of storage.

fetch—To retrieve a row or a set of rows during cursor processing.

field—A column in a database table.

file—An operating-system storage unit. A SQL Server database consists of two or more operating-system files.

filegroup—One or more data files in a database that are named to ease administration.

fill factor—A setting used to reserve free space in an index when the index is created. Fill factors reduce page splitting when a table grows.

fixed database role—A predefined role that controls access in a database.

fixed server role—A predefined role that controls access at the server level.

float data type—A data type used to hold floating-point numbers.

foreign key (FK)—One or more columns in a table that match the primary key of another table. In SQL Server, a foreign key can match any unique constraint of the other table.

forward-only cursor—A cursor in which rows can be read only in sequence from the first row to the last row.

front end—Any program that is used to access a database.

full outer join—An outer join that returns all the rows in both tables, even if the join conditions do not produce a matching row. See also *join* and *outer join*.

full-text catalog—The mechanism that stores a database's full-text index. A full-text catalog is stored external to SQL Server in an operating-system file.

full-text index—A special index on a table that, when enabled, allows a full-text search to be performed against the table. Unlike regular indexes, a full-text index does not automatically keep track of changes to the data.

full-text query—A **SELECT** statement that uses fuzzy logic and imprecise matches.

full-text service—The SQL Server component that is used in full-text queries.

grant—Allows a user or role to access a database object or perform an activity.

guest—A special SQL Server user account that allows any SQL Server login access to a database.

heterogeneous data—Data that comes from two or more data sources that are from different providers.

homogeneous data—Data that comes from one data source that is from one data provider.

horizontal partitioning—A physical design process that splits one table into multiple tables based on selected rows.

identifier—The name of a database object. An identifier must be unique within its scope.

identity column—A system-generated column that has the **identity** property. There can be only one identity column per table.

identity property—Identifies which column will be an identity column, and specifies that its values will be generated by SQL Server.

image data type—A SQL Server data type used to hold binary data. An **image** data type can hold up to 2GB of data.

implicit transaction—SQL Server's normal transaction processing, in which a SQL statement outside of a transaction is implicitly in a transaction by itself.

implied permission—The standard permissions that apply to a server-wide role and to a standard database role. The implied permissions can't be changed.

index—A database object that allows SQL Server to access data faster than scanning every row of data in a table for the results.

index page—A database page containing the data that makes up an index.

inner join—A join that combines two tables using join fields to determine the results.

insensitive cursor—A cursor with a result set that does not change as the underlying data changes.

int (integer) data type—A SQL Server data type that can be any integer from 2,147,483,647 through -2,147,483,648. Storage size is 4 bytes.

integrated security—Another name for Windows NT Authentication Mode.

intent lock—A lock that SQL Server places on data in an object to indicate that it wants to acquire a shared or exclusive lock.

isolation level—A setting used to control the locking behavior of SQL Server.

join—The process of combining data from two or more tables, views, or procedures.

join condition—Any clause that is used to control how tables are joined together.

kernel—The core SQL Server processing.

key—One or more columns that either uniquely identify a table or the relationships between two tables.

keyset-driven cursor—A cursor that does not show the effects of inserts and deletes to the underlying data, but does show any data modifications to the underlying data.

left outer join—An outer join in which all the rows for the first table are returned, even if there are not any related rows in the second table. See also *join* and *outer join*.

linked server—A remote OLE DB data source that has been identified to the local SQL Server.

local server—The SQL Server to which the user is currently connected.

local variable—A user-defined variable.

locale—Information that describes the language and country that a login will use when connecting to SQL Server.

lock—A restriction that affects another connection's capability to access resources.

lock escalation—The process in which multiple locks generated by a SQL statement can escalate to a higher locking level.

log file—A file or set of files that contains a record of the transactions that were run in a database.

Log Reader Agent—A process that replicates information from a database's transaction log to another database.

logical name—The internal name that SQL Server uses to identify a file.

logical operators—The **AND**, **OR**, and **NOT** operators.

login—Any operating-system user that can connect to SQL Server, or—if using SQL Server standard security—a login is an account that can connect to SQL Server. Login is also the process of connecting to SQL Server.

login identification—The account name that must be passed to SQL Server when standard SQL Server security is used.

login security mode—Identifies what type of security is allowed when connecting to SQL Server. You can either use Windows NT Authentication Mode or Mixed Mode.

many-to-many relationship—A relationship in which each row in the first entity has many related rows in the second entity, and each row in the second entity has many related rows in the first entity.

MAPI—An email application programming interface (API).

master database—The SQL Server system database that keeps track of server-wide resources.

Merge Replication—A replication type that allows data to be changed on multiple databases and merged back into a central database.

metadata—The data that describes the other database objects. See *system catalog*.

Mixed Mode—A security mode that allows users to connect using both Windows NT Authentication and SQL Server standard security.

model database—A system database that is used as a template for every new user-defined database.

money data type—A SQL Server data type used to store money values with an accuracy of four decimal places. A **money** data type can store values from 922,337,203,685,477.5807 through -922,337,203,685,477.5808.

named pipe—An interprocess communication (IPC) mechanism that permits access to shared network resources.

nchar data type—A SQL Server data type used to store up to 4,000 Unicode characters.

nested query—A query that contains one or more subqueries.

Net-Library—A library that controls the communication with SQL Server for a specific network protocol.

noise words—Words that do not take part in a full-text query.

nonclustered index—An index in which the physical order of the data isn't the same as the order of the index.

nonrepeatable read—A transaction isolation level in which a transaction can read the same table twice and get different results.

normalization rules—The rules that describe how to remove redundant data from an entity.

ntext data type—A SQL Server data type used to store Unicode data containing up to 1,073,741,823 characters.

NULL—An unknown value or a column in which there is no value.

nullability—Determines if a column must have a value or if it can allow nulls.

nvarchar data type—A SQL Server data type that can store up to 4,000 Unicode characters.

Object Linking and Embedding (OLE)—An application programming interface (API) for sharing objects among applications.

object owner—The user account that created the object.

object permissions—The permissions that have been granted or denied on a table or view.

ODBC driver—A DLL that allows an application to connect to an ODBC (Open Database Connectivity) data source.

OLE DB—A COM-based application programming interface (API) for accessing data. OLE DB can access data in any data-storage format—databases, spreadsheets, text files, and so on—for which an OLE DB provider is available.

OLE DB provider—The software that accesses the data source using the OLE DB API.

one-to-many relationship—A relationship in which every row in the first table can have many rows in the second table, but every row in the second table can have only one row in the first table.

one-to-one relationship—A relationship in which every row in the first table can have only one row in the second table, and every row in the second table can have only one row in the first table.

online analytical processing (OLAP)—An application and database designed to analyze data. An OLAP system will normally have a few users performing reporting queries.

online transaction processing (OLTP)—An application and database designed to perform a specific business function. An OLTP system will normally perform multiple well-defined queries.

Open Database Connectivity (ODBC)—An application programming interface for database material, which is aligned with the ANSI and the International Organization for Standardization (ISO) standards for a database Call Level Interface.

outer join—A join that returns rows even when the join conditions do not find a matching row in the other table.

package—A Data Transformation Services (DTS) object that defines the steps to perform while importing and exporting data.

page—SQL Server's internal storage mechanism. A SQL Server page is 8K.

page split—A situation in which inserting or updating data causes the rows on a page to grow to a size larger than a page. When a page split occurs, half of the rows will move to a new page.

parameter—In a stored procedure, a placeholder for a value that is going to be filled in when the procedure is executed. A parameter can be set to a constant or a variable.

Performance Monitor—A Windows NT application that provides status information about system performance and can be used to monitor SQL Server.

permissions—The authorizations that have been granted or denied on an object or statement.

permissions validation—The process that SQL Server uses to check whether a user has permissions to perform the SQL statement he or she is trying to execute.

positioned update—An update, insert, or delete that is performed on a row at the present cursor position. You can't perform a position update that inserts data when using server cursors.

primary key (PK)—The candidate key that was chosen to be the main identifier of a row of data in a table.

projection—The relational algebra function that allows you to retrieve a subset of the columns in a table.

proximity search—A full-text query that looks for words that are near each other in a column.

publication—One or more articles that are replicated as a unit.

Publication Access List—The logins that have access to a publication.

publication database—A database containing data that is being or can be replicated to other databases.

publish—To mark a set of data as being available for another database to subscribe to during the replication processes.

Publisher—In the Publish and Subscribe model of replication, the server that contains one or more publication databases.

pubs database—One of SQL Server's sample databases.

pull subscription—A type of replication in which the Subscriber requests the data changes from the Publisher.

push subscription—A type of replication in which the Publisher controls when the data changes are sent to a Subscriber.

range query—A query that looks for data rows in which a column is in a range of values.

ranking—In a full-text query, a value indicating the degree of matching of each word that is determined to match in a full text query. A value of 0 represents a low degree of matching; 1,000 represents the highest degree of matching.

read-only replication—When the replicated data is not allowed to be updated or changed by the Subscriber. This is also called a *read-only snapshot*.

real data type—A SQL Server data type used to store numbers with seven-digit precision.

record—Another name for a row.

recovery interval—The estimated time for a database to come back online when SQL Server is restarted after the system has abnormally shut down.

recursive relationship—A relationship in which a table is related to itself. This is also called a reflective relationship.

referential integrity (RI)—The rules that ensure that foreign keys have related primary keys.

relational data model—A data model based on set theory, relational algebra, and relational calculus.

relational database—A database based on the relational data model.

relational database management system (RDBMS)—A program that supports a relational database.

relationship—A situation in which one entity refers to the primary key of another entity.

remote data—Any data that is stored outside the SQL Server you are currently connected to.

remote procedure call (RPC)—An execution of a stored procedure that is not on the local server.

remote server—A SQL Server on the network that can be accessed through a user's local server.

remote stored procedure—A stored procedure on a remote SQL Server that can be executed through the local SQL Server.

remote table—A table that is external to the local SQL Server.

replication—The process of keeping data on one SQL Server in sync with the data on another SQL Server (through duplication).

result set—The rows returned from a **SELECT** statement.

return parameters—Parameters in a SQL Server that can return data to the caller.

revoke—To cancel a granted or denied permission.

right outer join—An outer join that returns all the rows in the second table, even when the join conditions do not find a matching row in the first table.

role—A SQL Server security unit that can be applied to users or logins to link together similar users.

roll back—To cancel a transaction and return the data modified in the transaction to its original state.

roll forward—A database recovery feature that causes committed transactions to be applied to the data, and causes uncommitted transactions to be rolled back when a SQL Server starts up.

row—A set of one or more columns. A row is equivalent to a record.

row aggregate—The results of a row aggregate function.

row aggregate function—An aggregate function that generates summary data in separate rows of the result set. A row aggregate function is used in a compute or compute by clause.

row lock—A row lock is when SQL Server locks one row in a table for a query.

rule—A database object used to specify the data that can be in a column.

savepoint—A user-defined marker that allows a transaction to be partially rolled back.

scalar aggregate—A function applied to all the rows in a table, generating an aggregate value as one of the columns returned.

scheduled backup—A backup that SQL Server Agent accomplishes automatically when the backup is defined and scheduled as a job.

schema—A description of a database using DDL.

scroll—A cursor that can move only forward.

search condition—A part of a **WHERE** or **HAVING** clause that limits the rows being returned.

Security Identifier (SID)—A unique value that identifies a user who is logged on to the SQL Server.

SELECT—A SQL statement that returns data from a SQL Server database.

select list—The elements that are being returned in a **SELECT** statement.

Select query—A query that uses the **SELECT** statement.

self-join—A table that is joined to itself.

sensitive cursor—Another name for a dynamic cursor.

server cursor—Any cursor that is performed using the SQL cursor statements.

server name—The name by which a SQL Server knows itself or other data sources. It can also be the name a client uses to identify a SQL Server.

shared lock—A lock that allows other users to read the data that is being locked.

smalldatetime data type—A SQL Server data type used to store date and time information to the minute.

smallint data type—An integer data type used to store whole numbers from 32,767 through -32,768.

smallmoney data type—A SQL Server data type that stores monetary values. These values range from 214,748.3647 through -214,748.3648, to four decimal places.

Snapshot Replication—A type of replication that takes periodic snapshots of the published data and applies them to the Subscriber database.

sort order—The order in which SQL Server evaluates character strings.

SQL—See *Structured Query Language*.

SQL-3—The latest version of the SQL standard; currently, it has not been approved.

SQL-92—The latest approved version of the standard for SQL, published in 1992; also referred to as SQL-2. It is sometimes referred to as ANSI SQL in the United States.

SQL Mail—SQL Servers interface to MAPI mail systems. It allows SQL Server to send and receive mail.

SQL Server Agent—A component of SQL Server that creates and manages local or multiserver jobs, alerts, and operators.

SQL Server Authentication—The process of verifying connections to SQL Server.

SQL Server login—See *login*.

SQL Server user— A database security account that allows SQL Server logins to use a database.

standard security—See *SQL Server Authentication*.

statement permission—The permission to execute T-SQL statements.

static cursor—A cursor that shows the data as it looked when the cursor was opened.

stored procedure—A collection of one or more T-SQL statements that are stored on SQL Server.

Structured Query Language (SQL)—A database query and programming language.

subquery—Any **SELECT** statement that is used to make up another query.

subscribe—To agree to receive a publication as part of replication.

Subscriber—In the Publish and Subscribe model of replication, the server that holds copies of published information.

surrogate key—In Microsoft terminology, a candidate key. In everyone else's terminology, an artificially generated key.

system administrator—Any user with the sysadmin role.

system catalog—The system tables in the master database that contain information about SQL Server. They do not contain information about tables in a database.

system databases—Four databases that are provided on a fresh SQL Server installation: master, tempdb, model, and msdb.

system stored procedures—A set of stored procedures provided by SQL Server that are used to access the system tables.

system tables—The tables that make up the system catalog and the database catalog.

table—A database object that stores data in a tablular (i.e., a collection of rows and columns) form.

table lock—A lock that will lock the compete table.

tabular data stream (TDS)—SQL Server's internal data-transfer protocol.

tempdb database—A system database used to store working objects.

temporary stored procedure—A stored procedure created in tempdb by pre-fixing the procedure's name with a number sign (#).

temporary table procedure—A table procedure created in tempdb by prefixing the procedure's name with a number sign (#).

text data type—A data type used to hold character data up to 2GB long.

timestamp data type—A datatype that generates a unique value for a database. Every new value generated will be one larger that the last value generated.

tinyint data type—An integer data type used to store whole numbers from 0 through 255.

Transact-SQL (T-SQL)—SQL Server's implementation of the ANSI SQL-2 standard and SQL Server's extensions to the standard.

Transact-SQL cursor—A server cursor that uses the T-SQL extensions to the declare cursor statement.

transaction—A logical unit of work.

transaction log—A specialized database file in which all changes to the database are recorded before the data changes are written.

trigger—Similar to a stored procedure, except that a trigger is automatically executed when data is modified.

tuple—The proper name for a row of data.

Unicode—A set of characters that are stored in the **nchar, nvarchar**, and **ntext** data types.

Unicode collation—The sort order for Unicode data.

union query—A query that merges results from two or more queries into one result set.

UNIQUE constraint—A constraint that enforces that the constrained column(s) are unique in a table.

unique index—An index that uniquely identifies a row in a table.

uniqueidentifier data type—A SQL Server data type containing a globally unique identifier (GUID) number, stored as a 16-byte binary string.

update—To modify data by adding new data, removing existing data, or modifying existing data.

user databases—Any SQL Server database other than the four system databases.

user-defined data type—A data type that was created by a user. This data type must be based on one of the SQL Server standard data types.

username—The name that a login uses when it is using a database.

varbinary data type—A data type used to store binary data up to 8,000 bytes long.

varchar data type—A data type used to store character data up to 8,000 bytes long.

variables—An object used to temporarily store values. A variable name starts with an at symbol (@).

vertical partitioning—A physical design practice that splits a table into multiple tables for different sets of columns. Every row in the original table has a row in each of the new partitioned tables.

view—A logical table made from a **SELECT** statement that retrieves data from one or more tables.

wildcard characters—The characters used in pattern matching with the **LIKE** keyword in the **WHERE** clause.

Windows NT Authentication—A process that enables a user with an NT user account to connect to SQL Server.

Windows NT Event Viewer—A Windows NT application that views events.

Windows NT Performance Monitor—A Windows NT utility that can help system administrators monitor the activity of Windows NT and processes, including SQL Server that run on NT.

write-ahead log—The transaction logging method used by most RDBMSes. In this method, the data changes are written to the log before the changes are made to the data.

Index

Bold page numbers indicate sample
exam questions.

" (double quotation mark), 89, 199
' (single quotation mark), 89, 199
@@CURSOR_ROWS function, 104
@@ERROR function, 104, 219, **364**, **367**,
   369, **386**, **387**
@@FETCH_STATUS function, 104, 219
@@IDENTITY function, 104, 219
@@NESTLEVEL function, 104, 219, 262
@@OPTIONS function, 175-176
@@parm, 236
@@ROWCOUNT function, 104, 136,
   252, 255
@@SERVERNAME function, 105, 219
@@SPID function, 105, 219
@@trancount global variable, 275, 276,
   284, **375**, **389**
@@VERSION function, 105, 219

A

ABS function, 105
ABSOLUTE, cursor, 232
Access. *See* Remote data access.
ACTIVATE statement, full-text index, 311
Adaptive test, 5-8, 10-11, 357, 358
ADD statement, full-text index, 311
Ad hoc distributed queries, 342
AgeRule rule, 196
Aggregate functions, 103, 111-113, **129**
ALL|COLUMNS|INDEX option,
   UPDATE STATISTICS option, 326
ALL keyword
   GROUP BY clause, 96
   select list, 88
ALTER DATABASE command, 55-57
Alternate keys, 19, 20

ALTER statement, 38
   distributed queries, 344
   stored procedure, modifying, 238, 239
ALTER TABLE ADD command, 78
ALTER TABLE command, 76-77, **378**, **390**
   with added columns and constraints,
      77-78
   column alteration, 78-79
ALTER TABLE DROP command, 78
ALTER TRIGGER statement, 250
ALTER VIEW statement, 206-207
ANSI-92 SQL standard, isolation levels,
   279-280
ANSI_DEFAULTS option, 167-168
ANSI joins, 116-117, **123**, **124**
ANSI NULL DEFAULT option, 58, 175
ANSI_NULL_DFLT_OFF option,
   168, 176
ANSI_NULL_DFLT_ON option,
   168, 176
ANSI NULLS option, 58, 176
ANSI_NULLS option, 169, 176, 340
ANSI_PADDING option, 136,
   169-170, 176
ANSI standard, quotation marks, 89
ANSI WARNINGS option, 58
ANSI_WARNINGS option, 170, 176,
   178, 340
API cursors, 228
ARITHABORT option, 164, 176
ARITHIGNORE option, 164, 176
ASCII function, 105
Associative entity, 23, 24
Attribute optionality, 19
Attributes, 16, 18-19
AUTOCLOSE option, 58
Autogrow, 39
AUTOSHRINK option, 58

B

Back-end cursors, 228
Batches, 216, **240**
BATCHSIZE parameter, BULK INSERT statement, 142-143
BCNF (Boyce Codd Normal Form), 27
BCP (Bulk Copy Program), 263, 290-294, **302, 303, 365, 386**
BEGIN DISTRIBUTED TRANSACTION statement, 277, 346
BEGIN...END construct, 223
BEGIN TRAN statement, 259, 260, 274, 276, 278, **367-369, 387**
BETWEEN clause, 95
BINARY, 120, **153**
Binary data type, 71, 110
Binary tree. *See* b-tree.
Bit data type, 19, 71, 109
BLOB columns, distributed query, 343
Boyce Codd Normal Form. *See* BCNF.
BREAK statement, 225
b-tree, 184, 186
Bulk Copy Program. *See* BCP.
BULK INSERT statement, 141-145
Business rules, 29, 246

C

Calling process, 260
Candidate keys, 19, 20
Cardinality, relationship, 21, 22
Cartesian Product, 114
Cascading delete trigger, 251-255, **360, 384**
CASE clause, 106-108
CASE function, 105, 106
CASE statements, 223-224
CAST function, 105, 110
Catalog procedures, 44
Certification exam. *See* SQL Server 7 certification exam.
Char data type, 71, **81**, 110, 136
CHAR function, 105
CHAR parameter, BULK INSERT statement, 143
Check constraints, 74-75
CHECK_CONSTRAINTS parameter, BULK INSERT statement, 143
Check option, views, 205-206
Checkpoints, 278-279
Clustered indexes, 184-186, 187, 188, **191-193, 382, 392**

CODEPAGE parameter, BULK INSERT statement, 143
Column, data types, 70, 71, **81, 82**
Column aliases, 90, **122**
Column list, 134-135
COLUMN_LIST, cursors, 231
Column mappings, DTS, 297-298
Columns, 68, 70
    altering, 78-79
    binding rule to, 197
    column aliases, 90, **122**
    computed columns, 76, **390**
    constraints, 72-76, **83, 378, 390**
    defaults, 196, 198-201, **211, 212**, 246, **366, 386**
    identity columns, 70, 72, **82**, 135, **363, 365, 385, 386**
    keys, 19-21, **34**
    name, 70, 87, 91
    permissions, 207
    registering for full-text search, 311, **318**
    ROWGUIDCOL property, 72
    select list, 87-89
    views, 201
Combination exam, 6-8
Comments, programming, 217
Commit phase, distributed transaction, 345
COMMIT TRANSACTION statement, 346
COMMIT TRAN statement, 274, 277, 278, **367-369, 387**
COMMIT WORK statement, 274
Common keys, 19, 20, 114
Comparison operators, 93
Composite key, 19, 20
COMPUTE BY extensions, 102-103
COMPUTE clause, with SELECT statement, 119
Computed columns, 76, **390**
COMPUTE extension, 102-103
CONCAT_NULL_YIELDS_NULL option, 58, 161
Conditional execution statements, 221-224
Conditional insert trigger, 257-258
Configuration
    database, 58-60
    default settings, 174-175
    session configuration, 157-176, **177-180**
    viewing settings, 174-175
Constraints, 72-76, **83, 378, 390**
CONTAINS predicate, full-text query, 313-316

CONTAINSTABLE function, 113
Controlling server, 277
CONVERT function, 105, 110
Coordinating server, 277
CREATE DATABASE command, 39,
  52-53, **363, 385**
CREATE INDEX statement, 278
CREATE statement, 38
  catalog file, 310
  distributed queries, 344
  full-text index, 311
CREATE TABLE command, 68-69,
  377, 390
  check constraint, 75
  computed column, 76
  foreign key reference constraint, 73
  primary key declaration, 73
  reference constraint, 73
CREATE TRIGGER statement, 249
Cross joins, 114, 115, 116
CUBE keyword, GROUP BY clause, 97-100
Current database, 61
CURSOR_CLOSE_ON_COMMIT
  option, 162, 176
CURSOR CLOSEONCOMMIT
  option, 58
Cursor procedures, 44
Cursors, 227-235, **241**
  closing, 234-235
  de-allocating, 235
  declaring, 229-231
  fetching rows, 231-234
  modifying rows with, 234
  triggers and, 262

D

Data
  access. *See* Remote data access.
  constraints, 72-76, **83, 378, 390**
  data types, 70, 71, **81, 82**, 290, **370, 387**
  importing and exporting, 290-297, **302,
    303, 365, 386**
  modifying table data, 133-140, **151-154**
  retrieving. *See* Data retrieval.
  rules, 196-198, 209-210, **212**, 366, **386**
  tables. *See* Tables.
  transforming, 190, 197-301, **303, 304**
  views, 201-208, **212, 213**
Database, **370, 371, 387, 388**. *See also*
  Relational database.
  altering, 54-58, **64**
  changing owner, 54
  configuring, 58-60

creating, 52-53, **63**
defined, 50, 68
design. *See* Database design.
file groups, 51
files, 50, 51
indexes, 184-190, **191-193**
maximum number of file groups, 51
maximum number of files, 50
reducing size, 57-58
removing, 54
renaming, 55
shrinking, 57-58
types, 16-17
using, 61
viewing information, 60, **63**
views, 201-208
Database design
  basic steps, 16, 68
  file groups, 51
  first step, 68
  logical phase, 16, 17-29
  maintainability, 31
  modeling for, 17-18
  performance, 31
  physical phase, 16, 29-32
Data conversion, remote data, 343
Data conversion precedence, 109-110
Data Definition Language (DDL), 276
Data dictionary, 38
Data integrity. *See* Integrity.
DATALENGTH function, 105
Data modeling. *See* Modeling.
Data retrieval, 85-121, **122-133**
  COMPUTE BY extensions, 102-103
  COMPUTE extension, 102-103
  FROM clause, 89-92
  full-text search, 307-316, **317-319**
  functions, 103-113
  GROUP BY clause, 96-101
  HAVING clause, 101-102
  image data, 120-121
  index covering, 187
  indexes, 184-190, **191-193**
  joining tables, 113-119
  ORDER BY clause, 102
  remote data, 343
  SELECT statement, 86-121, **122-133**
  subqueries, 118
  text data, 120-121
  TOP clause, 119-120
  UNION statement, 118-119
  WHERE clause, 92-96
Data Transformation Package. *See* DTP.

Data type conversion, 109-111, 112
Data types, 70, 71, **81, 82**, 290, **370, 387**
Date
  parts, 108-109
  SET statements, 158-160
DATEADD function, 105
Date conversion styles, 110-111
DATEDEIFF function, 105
DATEFILETYPE parameter, **BULK INSERT** statement, 143
DATEFIRST option, 158-159
DATEFORMAT option, 159-160
Date function, 104, 108
DATENAME function, 105
DATEPART function, 105, 159
Datetime data type, 71, 109
DBCC SHOWCONTIG command, 330-331
DBCC SHRINKDATABASE command, 57
DBCC SHRINKFILE command, 57-58, **62**
DBCC USEROPTIONS command, 174-175, **179**, 280
DB_NAME function, 105
DBO USE ONLY option, 58
db_owner role, 308, **318**
DDL. *See* Data Definition Language.
DEACTIVATE statement, full-text index, 311
Deadlocking, 329-330, **333, 381, 392**
DEADLOCK_PRIORITY option, 160, 330
Decimal data type, 71, 109
DECLARE statement
  cursors, 230
  local variables, 217
Default definitions, 75-76
Default isolation level, 280
DEFAULT property, 56
Defaults, 196, 198-201, **211, 212**, 246, **366, 386**
DEFAULT TO LOCAL CURSOR option, 59
DEFAULT VALUES option, 137
DELETE statement
  distributed query, 343
  views, 204-205
Denormalization, 30
Dependent entities, 18
Dependent relationship, 23, 24

Derived tables, 90
Devices, 51-52
Dirty data pages, 278
Dirty reads, 173, 279, 282
DISK INIT command, 51-52
DISTINCT keyword
  select list, 88
  TOP clause, 119-120
Distributed queries, 44, 340-344, **351**
Distributed Transaction Coordinator, 277
Distributed transactions, 277, 344-347, **349-350**
Domain enforcement, triggers, 246
Domain integrity, 29, 30, **33, 366, 386**
Domain restrictions, rules, 196-198
Double quotation mark, 89, 199
DROP DATABASE command, 54
DROP DEFAULT statement, 199
DROP PROC statement, 238
DROP RULE statement, 196-197
DROP statement, 80, **83**, 202
  catalog file, 310
  distributed queries, 344
  full-text index, 311
DROP TABLE command, 80
DROP TRIGGER statement, 249
DSS (Decision Support System), 16-17
DTP (Data Transformation Package), 295
DTS (Data Transformation Service), 44, 294-300, **302, 304**
DTS Column Mapping screen, 297
DTS COM Programming Interfaces, 297
DTS Create Table SQL Statement screen, 298
DTS Export Wizard, 296, **302**
DTS Import Wizard, 295-296
DTS package, 296
DTS Package Designer, 296-297
DTS Transformation screen, 298, 299
dtswiz utlity, 300-301, **303**
Dynamic cursors, 228, 230

E

EIS. *See* Executive information system.
"Elephant ear" relationship, 23
ELSE statement, 107
EMPTYFILE option, 58
ENCRYPTION option, 236
Encrypt option, 201
Entities, 16, 18

Entity integrity, 28, 30, **33, 34**
Entity relationship models
  (E/R diagrams), 17
E/R diagrams. *See* Entity
  relationship models.
Error codes, deadlocking, 330
ESCAPE clause, 123
Event handler, **242**
Exam. *See* SQL Server 7 certification
  exam.
Exclusive lock, 281, 327
Executive information system (EIS),
  indexes, 190, **192**

F

Fallback value, 75
FETCH command, cursors, 231-234
FETCH NEXT statement, cursors,
  232-233
Field terminate, formal file, 291
FIELDTERMINATOR parameter,
  BULK INSERT statement, 143
Fifth normal form, 24, 28
File. *See* Files.
File format, SQL Server, 290
File groups, 51, 56
FILEGROWTH parameter, 53
File name extensions, 50
FILENAME parameter, 53
Files
  ALTER DATABASE command, 56
  default size, 52-53
  moving to new file group, 56
  names, 50
  removing, 62
  removing empty files, 56
  shrinking, 57-58
  target size, 58
FIPS_FLAGGER option, 162
FIRST, cursor, 232
First normal form, 24, 25, 26, **34, 362, 385**
FIRSTROW parameter, **BULK INSERT**
  statement, 143
Fixed-length test, 5, 7-10, 355, 356, 358
Float data type, 71, 109, 111
FMTONLY option, 164-165
FOR ATTACH parameter, 53
FORCEPLAN option, 170
Foreign key constraints, 73-74, **83**
Foreign keys, 19, 20, 21, **34, 366, 386**
FOR LOAD parameter, 53
Format file, 290

FORMATFILE parameter, **BULK**
  INSERT statement, 143
FORMAT option, BCP utility, 291
FORMSOF() function, 314-315
FOR READ ONLY, cursors, 231
FOR UPDATE, cursors, 231
Forward-only cursor, 230, 344
Fourth normal form, 24, 27-28
FREETEXT predicate, full-text query,
  313, 316, **317**
FREETEXTTABLE function, 113
FROM clause, 89-92, 145
Full outer join, 115, 117
FULLSCAN option, **UPDATE**
  STATISTICS option, 325
Full-text catalog, 309-310
Full-text index, 309-313, **317, 379, 391**
Full-text query, 313-316, **317, 380, 381,**
  391
Full-text search, 307-316, **317-319**
  full-text index, 309-313, **317, 379, 391**
  logical operators, 315-316
  preparing for, 308-309
  proximity full-text searches, 314
  singular and plural forms, 314-315
  weighting, 315
Functions, 103-113
  aggregate functions, 103, 111-113, **129**
  rowset functions, 103, 113
  scalar functions, 103-111

G

General Extended procedures, 44
GETDATE function, 105
GLOBAL, cursor, 230, 231
Global temporary tables, 79-80, **82**
Global variables, 104, 218, 219, 233
GOTO statement, 225
GROUP BY clause, 96-101
  aggregate functions, 111, 113
  ALL keyword, 96
  CUBE keyword, 97-100
  ROLLUP keyword, 97, 98, 100
  with **SELECT** statement, 119

H

HAVING clause, 101-102, **130**
  aggregate functions, 111
  with **SELECT** statement, 119
  subqueries, 118
HOLDLOCK, 280
Host field file order, formal file, 290

Host file data field type, formal file, 290
Host file data length, formal file, 291

I

Identity, 34
Identity columns, 70, 72, **82**, 135, **363**,
    365, **385**, **386**
IDENTITY_INSERT option, 135, 162-163
IF...ELSE construct, 222
IF EXISTS construct, 222-223
IF UPDATE test, 255-256
IMAGE column, retrieving text, 120-121
Image data type, 71, 109
IMPLICIT_TRANSACTIONS option,
    172-173, 176, **178**
IN clause, 94
Independent entities, 18
Independent relationship, 23
Index covering, 187
Indexes, 184-190, **191-193**
    clustered, 184-186, 187, 188, **191-193**,
        382, 392
    creating, 187-188
    full-text index, 309-313, **317, 379, 391**
    management, 189
    name, 188
    nonclustered, 186-187, 188, **191-193**,
        382, 392
    unique indexes, **34**
    uniqueness check, 189
Inner join, 114, 115, 116
Insensitive cursors, 229, 344
INSERT statement, 134-140, **151**
    distributed query, 343
    views, 204-205
Int data type, 70, 71, 109
Integrity, 28-29, 30, **33, 34**
Intent Shared lock, 281, **333**
Intent To Write lock, 281
INTO clause, distributed query, 343
ISABOUT() function, 315
ISDATE function, 105
ISNULL function, 105
ISNUMERIC function, 106
Isolation levels, 279-280, **285**
isql, 322

J

JOIN clause, 113
Joins, 113-119
    ANSI joins, 116-117, **123, 124**
    cross joins, 114, 115, 116
    inner join, 114, 115, 116
    outer join, 114-115, 116
    three-way join, 204
    views, 201

K

KEEPIDENTITY parameter, BULK
    INSERT statement, 144
KEEPNULLS parameter, BULK
    INSERT statement, 144
Keys, 19-21, **34**
Keyset cursors, 228, 230, 344

L

LANGUAGE option, 163
LAST, cursor, 232
LASTROW parameter, **BULK INSERT**
    statement, 143, 144
.ldf files, 50
LEFT function, 106
Left outer join, 114-115
LEN function, 106
LIKE clause, 94-95, **123**
Linked server, 341
LOCAL, cursor, 230
Local temporary tables, 79, **82**
Local transaction, 345, 346
Local variables, 217-218
Locking, 160-162, 173, 279-283, **285-286**,
    333, 382, 392
    deadlocking, 329-330, **333, 381, 392**
    escalation, 281
    granularity, 280
    isolation levels, 279-280, **285**
    overrides, 282
    setting levels, 283
    troubleshooting, 327-331
    types of locks, 281
LOCK_TIMEOUT option, 161
Log files, 50, 51
Logical file name, 50
Logical model
    converting to physical model, 29-30
    database design, 16, 17-29
Logical operators, 315-316
LOWER function, 106
LTRIM function, 106

M

Maintenance tasks, 31
Mandatory optionality, 22, 23
Many to many cardinality, 22

MASTER database, 38-39, 40, **46**
    creating system procedures, 45
    devices, 52
    options, 60
Master logfile, 40
master.mdf, 40
Master primary datafile, 40
mastlog.ldf, 40
Math function, 104
MAXERRORS parameter, **BULK**
    INSERT statement, 143, 144
MAXSIZE parameter, 53
.mdf files, 50
MERGE PUBLISH option, 59
Message handler, 218-219
Metadata, 38, 40
Metadata function, 104
Microsoft certification exam. *See also* SQL
    Server 7 certification exam.
    testing formats, 4-6, 7
    Web resources for, 12-14
Microsoft Distributed Transaction
    Coordinator (MS DTC), 345
MODEL database, 38, 39-40, **46**
    creating new database, 53
    devices, 52
Modeling, 17
Model logfile, 40
modellog.ldf, 40
model.mdf, 40
Model primary datafile, 40
Money data type, 71, 109, 111
Monitoring, 322-331, **332-334**
    SHOWPLAN_ALL statement, 170-
        171, 323
    SHOWPLAN_TEXT statement, 171,
        322-323, **382, 392**
MONTH function, 106
MSDB database, 38, 40, **46**
msdbdata.mdf, 40
msdb logfile, 40
msdblog.ldf, 40
msdb primary datafile, 40
MS DTC (Microsoft Distributed
    Transaction Coordinator), 345

N

Name
    columns, 70, 87, 91
    database, changing, 55
    file names, 50
    indexes, 188
    qualifying object names, 91-92
    relationship, 21, 22
    stored procedures, 236
    tables, 69, **81,** 87, 89-90, 91
    temporary tables, 79
    triggers, 248
NAME parameter, 53
NATIVE parameter, **BULK INSERT**
    statement, 143
Nchar data type, 71
.ndf files, 50
NEAR() function, 314
Nested triggers, 262-263
NEXT, cursor, 232
NOCOUNT option, 165, 176, **178**
NOEXEC option, 165
NOLOCK statement, 279, 282
Nonclustered indexes, 186-187, 188,
    191-193, 382, 392
No nulls, 19
NORECOMPUTE option, **UPDATE**
    STATISTICS option, 326
Normalization, 16, 21, 24-28, **33, 361, 362,**
    370, 385, 387
NOT FOR REPLICATION, triggers,
    248
NOT keyword, 95-96
Not null, 70
NOTRUNCATE option, 57, 58
NTEXT column, retrieving text, 120-121
Ntext data type, 71, 109
Null, 68, 70, 75
NULLIF function, 106
NULL option, **WHERE** clause, 96
Numeric data type, 71
NUMERIC_ROUNDABORT option,
    165-166
Nvarchar data type, 71, 109

O

OFFLINE option, 59
OFFSETS option, 163
OLE Automation Procedures, 44
OLE DB providers, 340
OLTP database. *See* Online Transaction
    Processing database.
One to many cardinality, 22
One to one cardinality, 22
Online Transaction Processing database
    (OLTP database), 16, 17, 190, **192**
OPENQUERY function, 113, 341-342, **350**

OPENROWSET function, 113, 342
OPTIMISTIC, cursors, 230
Optimization, 322, 325
Optionality, 19, 22-23
Optional relationship, 22, 23
ORDER BY clause, 102
  distributed query, 343
  with SELECT statement, 119
ORDER parameter, BULK INSERT
  statement, 143, 144
osql, **377, 389-390**
Outer join, 114-115, 116

P

PAGLOCK, 282, **333**
PARSEONLY option, 166
Pattern matching characters, 94, 95
PERCENT option, TOP clause, 119
Performance, 31
  file groups, 51
  locking problems, 327-331
Permissions
  columns, 207
  triggers and, 262
Phantom rows, 173
Physical database, indexes, 184-190,
  191-193
Physical file
  location, 52
  name, 50
Physical model
  converting logical model to, 29-30
  database design, 16, 29-32
Prefix length, formal file, 291
Prepare phase, distributed transaction, 345
prepare to commit command, 277
Primary file group
  removing, 56
  viewing information, 71
Primary files, 50
Primary key constraints, 72-73, **359, 384**
Primary keys, 19, 20, **34**
PRIMARY parameter, 53
PRINT statement, 218-219
PRIOR, cursor, 232
Procedures, **240**
PROCID option, 163
PUBLISHER option, 59

Q

Query-execution statements, 164-167
QUERY_GOVERNOR_COST_LIMIT
  option, 166
Querying, **380, 381, 391**
  CONTAINS predicate, 313-316
  distributed queries, 44, 340-344, **351**
  FREETEXT predicate, 313, 316, **317**
  full-text index, 312-313, **317, 379, 391**
  full-text query, 313-316, **317, 380, 381,**
    391
  SHOWPLAN_ALL statement, 170-
    171, 323
  SHOWPLAN_TEXT statement, 171,
    322-323, **382, 392**
Quotation marks, ANSI standard, 89, 199
QUOTED_IDENTIFIER option, 59,
  163,
  176, **178**

R

RAISERROR statement, 219-221
READ COMMITTED, 173, 279
READ_ONLY, cursors, 230
READ ONLY option, 56, 59
READTEXT command, 120-121, 344
READ UNCOMMITTED, 173, 279
READWRITE property, 56
Real data type, 71, 109, 111
REBUILD statement, catalog file, 310
RECOMPILE, 236
RECONFIGURE command, 347
Recovery, 278, **284**
RECURSIVE TRIGGERS option, 59
Redundant attribute, 25
Reference constraint, 74, **378, 390**
Referential integrity (RI), 29, 30, **33**
  determining, 255
  triggers, 246, 257
Relational database, 21
  components, 16, 18
  defined, 68
  denormalization, 30
  design. *See* Database design.
  integrity, 28-29, 30, **33, 34**
  maintainability, 31
  normalization, 16, 21, 24-28, **33, 361,**
    362, 370, 385, 387
  performance, 31
  security, 32

unique identifiers, 70, 72
Relationship
  cardinality, 21, 22
  name, 21, 22
  optionality, 22-23
Relationships, 21-24
RELATIVE, cursor, 232
Remote data access, 337-347, **348-351**
  distributed queries, 44, 340-344, **351**
  distributed transactions, 277, 344-347,
    349-350
  remote procedure call, 276, 338-340, 344
Remote procedure call. *See* RPC.
REMOTE_PROC_TRANSACTIONS
  option, 173
remote proc trans option, **sp_configure**
  stored procedure, 346
REPEATABLE READ, 173, 280
Replication procedures, 44
Reporting database, 17
Resource manager, 344
Result set, 87
Retrieving data. *See* Data retrieval.
RETURN statement, 226
RI. *See* Referential integrity.
RIGHT function, 106
Right outer join, 115
ROLLBACK TRANSACTION
  statement, 346
ROLLBACK TRAN statement, 259-260,
  274, 275, 345, **367-369**, **387**
ROLLBACK WORK statement, 274
Rolling back, transactions, 274, 275, 278,
  345, **375**, **389**
ROLLUP keyword, **GROUP BY** clause,
  97, 98, 100
ROWCOUNT option, 166, 219
ROWGUIDCOL property, 72
ROWLOCK, 282
Rows, **366**, **371**, **372**, **386**, **388**
  cascading delete trigger, 251-255, **360**, **384**
  conditional insert trigger, 257-258
  cursors, 231-234
  inserting multiple rows, 138-140
  inserting single row, 136-138
  insert trigger, 256-257, 260-261, 263
  phantom rows, 173
  update trigger, 251, 253, 254-255, 258-259
  views, 201
Rowset, 341
Rowset functions, 103, 113
ROWTERMINATOR parameter, **BULK
  INSERT** statement, 143, 144

RPC (remote procedure calls), 276,
  338-340, 344, 346
RTRIM function, 106
Rules, 196-198, **209-210**, **212**, **366**, **386**

S

SAMPLE option, **UPDATE
  STATISTICS** option, 326
SAVEPOINT command, 260-261
Savepoints, 260-261
SAVE TRAN statement, 274, 276
Scalar functions, 103-111
Schema lock, 281
SCROLL_LOCKS, cursors, 230
SCROLL option, cursors, 229, 232
Search clauses, weighting, 315
Searching, 308
  full-text query, 313-316, **317**
  full-text search, 308-313
  logical operators, 315-316
  proximity full-text searches, 314
  singular and plural forms, 314-315
  weighting, 315
Secondary files, 50
Second normal form, 24, 25-26, **362**, **385**
Security, 32, 44, 104, 201, 203-204
SELECT INTO_BULKCOPY option, 59
SELECT INTO statement, 140-141,
  154, **351**
Select list, 87-89
SELECT statement, 86-121, **122-133**, **348**
  CASE statement, 223
  COMPUTE BY extensions, 102-103
  COMPUTE extension, 102-103
  CONTAINS predicate, 313-316
  distributed query, 343
  FREETEXT predicate, 313, 316, **317**
  FROM clause, 89-92
  full-text search, 313-316
  GROUP BY clause, 96-101, 119
  HAVING clause, 101-102, 119
  IF EXISTS construct, 222-223
  inserting multiple rows, 138-140
  isolation levels, 279-280
  ORDER BY clause, 102
  select list, 87-89
  subqueries, 118
  trigger, 263
  UNION statement, 118-119
  variables, 217-218
  views, 201-208
  WHERE clause, 92-96
Self-recursive relationship, 23, 24

SERIALIZABLE, 173, 280
Server column name, formal file, 291
Server column order, formal file, 291
Servers
    controlling server, 277
    coordinating server, 277
    linked server, 341
Session configuration, 157-176, **177-180**
SESSION_USER function, 106
SET ANSI_DEFAULTS statement, 167-168
SET ANSI_NULL_DFLT_OFF
    statement, 168
SET ANSI_NULL_DFLT_ON
    statement, 168
SET ANSI_NULLS statement, 169
SET ANSI_PADDING statement, 169-170
SET ANSI_WARNINGS statement, 170
SET ARITHABORT statement, 164
SET ARITHIGNORE statement, 164
SET
    CONCAT_NULL_YIELDS_NULL
    statement, 161
SET
    CURSOR_CLOSE_ON_COMMIT
    statement, 162
SET DATEFIRST statement, 158-159
SET DATEFORMAT statement, 159-160
SET DEADLOCK_PRIORITY
    statement, 160, 330
SET FIPS_FLAGGER statement, 162
SET FMTONLY statement, 164-165
SET FORCEPLAN statement, 170
SET IDENTITY_INSERT statement,
    162-163
SET IMPLICIT_TRANSACTIONS
    statement, 172-173
SET LANGUAGE statement, 163
SET LOCKIMPLEMENTS
    statement, 279
SET LOCK_TIMEOUT statement,
    161, **179**
SET NOCOUNT statement, 165
SET NOEXEC statement, 165, **177**
SET NUMERIC_ROUNDABORT
    statement, 165-166
SET OFFSETS statement, 163
SET options, 227
SET PARSEONLY statement, 166, **177**
SET PROCID statement, 163
SET
    QUERY_GOVERNOR_COST_LIMIT
    statement, 166, **177**

SET QUOTED_IDENTIFIER
    statement, 163
SET
    REMOTE_PROC_TRANSACTIONS
    statement, 173
SET ROWCOUNT statement, 166, **177**
SET SHOWPLAN_ALL statement,
    170-171, **177**, 322
SET SHOWPLAN_TEXT statement,
    171, 322-324, **382, 392**
SET statement, 158-174
    date and time statements, 158-160
    isolation levels, 279-280
    locking statements, 160-161
    miscellaneous, 161-163
    query-execution statements, 163-167
    SQL-92 settings statements, 167-170
    statistics statements, 170-172
    transaction statements, 172-174
    variables, 217-218
SET STATISTICS IO statement, 171
SET STATISTICS TIME statement, 172
SET TEXTSIZE statement, 166
SET TRANSACTION ISOLATION
    LEVEL statement, 173
SET XACT_ABORT statement, 174
Shared lock, 281, 327
Shared With Intent Exclusive lock, 281
Short-form test, 5-10
SHOWPLAN_ALL statement,
    170-171, 323
SHOWPLAN_TEXT statement, 171,
    322-323, **382, 392**
SHRINKDATABASE command, 57
Simulation exam, 5
Single quotation mark, 89, 199
Singleton key, 19, 20
SINGLE USER option, 59
SIZE parameter, 53
Smalldatetime data type, 71, 109
Smallint data type, 71, 109
Smallmoney data type, 71, 109
sp_autostats stored procedure, 326, **334**
sp_bindefault stored procedure, 199-200
sp_bindrule stored procedure, 197
sp_changedbowner stored procedure, 54
SP_CONFIGURE command, 176
sp_configure stored procedure, **remote
    proc trans** option, 346
sp_dboption stored procedure, 58
sp_fulltext_catalog stored procedure, **318**

sp_fulltext_database command, 308, **379, 391**

sp_fulltext_table stored procedure, 310-311, 312

sp_helpdb stored procedure, 60, **63**

sp_helpfile group stored procedure, 60, **63**

sp_helpfile stored procedure, 60, **63**

sp_help_fulltext_catalogs stored procedure, 313

sp_help_fulltext_columns stored procedure, 313

sp_help_fulltext_tables stored procedure, 313

sp_help stored procedure, 239, **382, 392**

sp_indexoption stored procedure, 283

sp_lock stored procedure, 326-328, **333, 382, 392**

sp_renamedb stored procedure, 55

sp_unbindefault stored procedure, 200

sp_unbindrule stored procedure, 197

sp_updatestats stored procedure, 326

sp_who stored procedure, 326-328, **382, 392**

SQL-92 settings statements, 167-170

SQL. *See* Structured Query Language.

SQL Mail Extended Procedures, 44

SQL Query Analyzer, 322

SQL Server Agent procedures, 44

SQL Server 7 certification exam, 354
adaptive test, 5-8, 10-11, 357, 358
ambiguous questions, 355-356
combination exam, 6-8
exam readiness, 2
fixed-length test, 5, 7-10, 355, 356, 358
guessing, 355
layout and design, 4-5
Microsoft resources for, 12-14
Microsoft testing formats, 4-6, 7
preparation, 11, 357-358
questions, 3, 4-5, 9, 354-356
sample test, 11-12, **359-382, 383-393**
self-assessment, 2, 12
setting, 3
short-form test, 5-10
simulation exam format, 5
test strategy, 7-9, 354-357, 358
time allotted, 3, 9, 354, 358

SQL Server Enterprise Manager, 5, 18, 32, 61

SQL Server Profiler, 331

SQL Server Profiler Extended Procedures, 44

SQL statements
comparison operators, 93
quotation marks, 89, 199
table aliases, 89-90, 91, 92

START_FULL statement, catalog file, 310

START_INCREMENTAL statement, catalog file, 310

STATIC, cursor, 230

Static cursors, 228, 344

Statistics, updating, 325-326, **332**

STATISTICS IO option, 171

Statistics statements, 170-172

STATISTICS TIME option, 172

STOP statement, catalog file, 310

Stored procedures, **240, 241, 364, 376, 379, 386, 389, 391**
distributed transactions, 277
inserting multiple rows, 139-140
name, 236
remote procedure calls, 276
triggers, 246-264, **265-267**
T-SQL, 235-239

STR function, 106

String function, 104

Structured Query Language (SQL), 86

STUFF function, 106

Subqueries, 118

SUBSCRIBED option, 59

SUBSTRING function, 106

Surrogate key, 20

SUSER_SNAME function, 106

sysallocations table, 41

sysaltfiles table, 41

syscharsets table, 41

syscolumns table, 43

syscomments table, 43

sysconfigures table, 41

sysconstraints table, 43

syscurconfigs table, 41

sysdatabases table, 41

sysdepends table, 43

sysdevices table, 41

SYSDEVICES table, 52

sysfilegroups table, 43

sysfiles table, 43

sysforeignkeys table, 43

sysfulltextcatalogs table, 43, 310

Sysindexes, 186

sysindexes table, 43

sysindexkeys table, 43

syslanguages table, 41
syslockinfo table, 41
syslogins table, 41, **47**
syslogs table, 40
sysmembers table, 43
sysmessages table, 41
Sysname data type, 71
sysobjects table, 43
sysoledbusers table, 41
sysperfinfo table, 41
syspermissions table, 43
sysprocesses table, 41
sysprotects table, 43
sysreferences table, 43
sysremotelogins table, 41
sysservers table, 41
System databases, 36-40
System files, 40
System function, 104
System procedures, 44
System tables, 38, 41-43, **46-47**
systypes table, 43
sysusers table, 43, **47**

T

Table aliases, 89-90, 91, 92
Table data, modifying, 133-140, **151-154**
Tables, 360-363, 365, 367-369, 371, 372, 379-380, 384-388, 390
    adding data, 133-140, **151-154**
    adding to, 77-78
    altering, 76-79, 365, 386
    cascading delete trigger, 251-255, 360, 384
    columns. *See* Columns.
    constraints, 72-76, **83**
    creating, 68-70, **363**, 377, **385**, **390**
    deleted and inserted tables, 251-259, **266-267**
    derived tables, 90
    disk space required, **360**, **384**
    dropping, 80, **83**
    dropping from, 78, **365**, **386**
    file groups, 51
    IF UPDATE test, 255-256
    joining, 113-119
    keys, 19-21
    maximum number of columns, 70
    name, 69, **81**, 87, 89-90, 91
    number of pages, **371**, **372**, **388**
    registering for full-text search, 310-311, **317**
    removing, 80, **83**

    rows. *See* Rows.
    table aliases, 89-90, 91, 92
    temporary tables, 39, 79-80, **82**, **379-380**, **390**
    triggers, 248
    update trigger, 251, 253, 254-255, 258-259
TABLOCK, 282
TABLOCK parameter, **BULK INSERT** statement, 143, 144
TABLOCKX, 282
Target size, files, 58
TEMPDB database, 38, 39, 40, **46**, 52
tempdb logfile, 40
tempdb.mdf, 40
tempdb primary datafile, 40
templog.ldf, 40
Temporary tables, 39, 79-80, **82**, 262, 379-380, **390**
TEXT column, retrieving text, 120-121
Text data type, 71
Text and Image function, 104
Text pointer, 120, **131**
TEXTPTR function, 120
TEXTSIZE option, 166
Third normal form, 24, 26-27, **35**, 362, 373, 385, 388
Time, **SET** statements, 158-160
Time data, data types, 71
Timeout period, **179**
Timestamp data type, 71, 109
Tinyint data type, 70, 71, 109
TOP clause, 119-120
TORNPAGE DETECTION option, 59
Transaction control statements, 273-275
TRANSACTION ISOLATION LEVEL option, 173
Transaction log, 40, 278-279
Transaction manager, 344, 345
Transactions, 272-283, **284-286**, 375, 389
    batches, 216, **240**
    control statements, 273-275
    distributed transactions, 277, 344-347, 349-350
    flow in, 275-276
    limitations, 276-277
    locking in, 279-283
    management, 273, 344, 345
    rolling back, 274, 275, 278, **375**, **389**
    savepoints, 260-261
    triggers during, 259-262
Transaction statements, 172-174

Transact-SQL. *See* T-SQL.
Triggers, **4-5**, 246-264, **265-267**, 366, 374, 386, 389
   conditional insert trigger, 257-258, 260-261, 263
   creating, 248-250
   cursors and, 262
   deleted and inserted tables, 251-259, **266-267**
   during transactions, 259-262
   examining, 263-264
   firing, **4**, 246-247, **265**
   IF UPDATE test, 255-256
   modifying, 250-251
   name, 248
   nested triggers, 262-263
   permissions and, 262
   removing, 250
   savepoints, 260-261
   temporary tables and, 262
   update trigger, 251, 253, 254-255, 258-259
   uses, 246, **265**
   views and, 262
Troubleshooting
   deadlocks, 329-330, **333**, **381**, **392**
   locking problems, 327-331, **332**, **333**
TRUNCATEONLY option, 57
TRUNCATE TABLE statement, triggers, 249, 263
TRUNC.LOG ON CHKPT option, 59, 60
T-SQL
   batches, 216, **240**
   comments, 217
   conditional execution statements, 221-224
   cursors, 227-235, **241**
   GOTO statement, 225
   PRINT statement, 218-219
   RAISERROR statement, 219-221
   RETURN statement, 226
   SET options, 227
   stored procedures, 235-239
   WAITFOR statement, 226
   WHILE loops, 224-225
TSQL join extensions, 116, 146
TSQL joins, 115-116, **130**
Tuples, 16
Two-phase commit, 277, 345

U

Unicode data, data types, 71
UNION statement, 118-119
Unique constraint, 73
Uniqueidentifier data type, 71, 72, 110, 135-136, **363**, **385**

Unique identifiers, 70, 72
Unique indexes, **34**
UNLIMITED parameter, 53
Update lock, 281
UPDATE statement, 145-147, **153**, 200, 272
   distributed query, 343
   triggers, 251-259
   views, 204-205
UPDATE STATISTICS command, 325, **332**
UPDATETEXT statement, 147-149, 344
Updating statistics, 325-326, **332**
UPDLOCK, 282
UPPER function, 106
USE command, 61
User-configuration options, 174-176
User-defined integrity, 29, 30
USER_NAME function, 106

V

Varbinary data type, 71, 110, 120, 136, **153**
Varchar data type, 71, **81**, 110, 136, **371**, 388
Variables, 217-218, 219
Views, 201-208, **212**, **213**
   ALTER VIEW statement, 206-207
   check option, 205-206
   column limit, 208
   defined, 196
   DELETE statement, 204-205
   INSERT statement, 204-205
   modifying data with, 150
   triggers and, 262
   UPDATE statement, 204-205

W

WAITFOR statement, 226, **242**
Web Assistant procedures, 44
WEIGHT() function, 315
WHERE clause, 92-96, 102, **130**
   aggregate functions, 129
   BETWEEN clause, 95
   IN clause, 94
   LIKE clause, 94-95
   NOT keyword, 95-96
   NULL option, 96
   subqueries, 118
   syntax, 92-93
   UPDATE statement, 146
WHERE CURRENT OF statement, distributed query, 344

WHILE loop, 224-225, 233
WIDENATIVE parameter, BULK
   INSERT statement, 143
Wildcard characters, 94, 95
WITH APPEND, triggers, 248
With Check Option, 201
WITH TIES option, TOP clause, 119
WRITETEXT statement, 147-149

distributed query, 344
triggers, 249

X

XACT_ABORT option, 174

Y

YEAR function, 106